Private Sector Involvement in the Euro

Private Sector Involvement in the Euro traces the activities of two non-governmental organizations: the Association for the Monetary Union of Europe (AMUE) and its parent organization, the Committee for the Monetary Union of Europe. These groups have helped to pave the way to the euro both by working on its realization and for its general acceptance. This book investigates the role the private sector played in the creation of the euro and discusses key issues such as whether there was an alternative to the single currency and if Europe's citizens had a voice in the construction of the EMU.

This fresh look at how the EMU came about challenges a number of well-established integration theories. It shows that European integration is not only the work of governments and supranational institutions but the result of more subtle processes involving the emerging European civil society. The model on the power of ideas suggested in this book is applied to the work and impact of the two NGOs but has explanatory power for the process of European integration which goes well beyond the limits of this empirical study.

This book will interest students, researchers, and policy makers with an interest in Europe and its monetary union.

Stefan Collignon is Professor of European Political Economy at the London School of Economics and Political Science. He was previously Director of Research and Communication at the Association for the Monetary Union of Europe. **Daniela Schwarzer** is a Journalist at the *Financial Times Deutschland* and a part-time lecturer at the Freie Universität Berlin.

Routledge advances in European politics

1 **Russian Messianism**
Third Rome, revolution, communism and after
Peter J.S. Duncan

2 **European Integration and the Postmodern Condition**
Governance, democracy, identity
Peter van Ham

3 **Nationalism in Italian Politics**
The stories of the Northern League, 1980–2000
Damian Tambini

4 **Uncertain Europe**
Building a new European security order
Edited by Graham Timmins and Martin Smith

5 **Widening the European Union**
The politics of institutional change and reform
Edited by Bernard Steunenberg

6 **Institutional Challenges in the European Union**
Edited by Madeleine Hosli, Adrian van Deemen and Mika Widgrén

7 **Europe Unbound**
Enlarging and reshaping the boundaries of the European Union
Edited by Jan Zielonka

8 **Ethnic Cleansing in the Balkans**
Nationalism and the destruction of tradition
Cathie Carmichael

9 **Democracy and Enlargement in Post-Communist Europe**
The democratisation of the general public in fifteen Central and Eastern European countries, 1991–1998
Christian W. Haerpfer

10 **Private Sector Involvement in the Euro**
The power of ideas
Stefan Collignon and Daniela Schwarzer

Private Sector Involvement in the Euro

The power of ideas

Stefan Collignon and Daniela Schwarzer

Routledge
Taylor & Francis Group
LONDON AND NEW YORK

First published 2003
by Routledge
11 New Fetter Lane, London EC4P 4EE

Simultaneously published in the USA and Canada
by Routledge
29 West 35th Street, New York, NY 10001

Routledge is an imprint of the Taylor & Francis Group

Typeset in Baskerville MT by
Newgen Imaging Systems (P) Ltd, Chennai, India
Printed and bound in Great Britain by
St Edmundsbury Press, Bury St Edmunds, Suffolk

British Library Cataloguing in Publication Data
A catalogue record for this book is available from the British Library

Library of Congress Cataloging in Publication Data
Collignon, Stefan, 1951–
Private sector involvement in the euro: the power of ideas / Stefan Collignon and Daniela Schwarzer.
p. cm.
Includes bibliographical references and index.
1. Economic and Monetary Union. 2. Euro. 3. Monetary unions–European Union countries. 4. Monetary policy–European Union countries. 5. Non-governmental organizations. I. Schwarzer, Daniela. II. Title.

HG925 .C6563 2002
332.4′94–dc21 2002068225

ISBN 0-415-30175-0

Money has not been generated by law. In its origin it is a social, and not a state-institution. Sanction by the authority of the state is a notion alien to it. On the other hand, however, by state recognition and state regulation, this social institution of money has been perfected and adjusted to the manifold and varying needs of an evolving commerce, just as customary rights have been perfected and adjusted by statute law.

Karl Menger[1]

La force des idées simples exprimées tout uniment et répétées de la même façon invariable. Cela désarme au moins la méfiance, qui est la source principale des malentendus.

Jean Monnet[2]

1 Karl Menger, On the origin of money. *Economic Journal* 2, June 1892.
2 Jean Monnet. *Mémoires*. Paris: Fayard, 1976.

Contents

Illustrations

Figures

Tables

Charts

Acknowledgements

This book is based on a research project conducted at the European Institute of the London School of Economics and Political Science in 2001. Part of it has been funded by the Association for the Monetary Union of Europe (AMUE), a group of major companies and banks. This organization contributed to the creation of monetary union in Europe for fifteen years. As it was the only organization of this kind, a large part of our empirical account on private sector involvement in EMU is concerned with the AMUE and its sister organization the Committee for the Monetary Union of Europe (CMUE). Part of the account draws on the personal experience and direct observations of the authors who both used to work for the AMUE; Stefan Collignon as Director for Research and Communication from 1989 to 1998, and Daniela Schwarzer from 1996 to 1999, last as Head of the Information Department. As previous active involvement may raise methodological questions, we wish to point out that we have employed a large variety of other empirical sources other than our memories and private documentation. We have exploited the archives of the AMUE, of the CMUE, the Helmut Schmidt archive in Hamburg as well as the personal documentation that some of the actors involved have made accessible. We conducted in-depth interviews with decision-makers in the political, administrative, and corporate sector, who have closely observed or even participated in the work of the Association over the years, including the time when the authors were not yet involved. Our referees have confirmed that our account offers insights into the complex process leading to the introduction of Europe's single currency that so far have not been available. We warmly thank all those who have helped us reconstruct the private sector's way to EMU by sharing their memories and ideas in interviews or by giving us access to archives and private documentation. Our academic interest, however, is also a theoretical one. The introduction and the epilogue develop a framework, which guided our analysis and interpretation in the remaining four chapters. In fact, the Lehrer and Wagner model of consensus building is not only an analytical tool but has also consciously inspired our practical work while we were active in the AMUE.

We also wish to thank all the others who have contributed to our work with advice and additional information. Especially Bertrand de Maigret has given us his continued support throughout our study. Birgit Wohlgemuth, David Brown, and Emma Weekes have shown expertise and patience when typing and editing our manuscript, and Christopher Johnson and Emma Weekes have corrected our English. Academic colleagues who commented on the theoretical framework include Paul Taylor, Kevin Featherstone, Bob Leonardi, Charles Goodhart, Bob Hancké, Ben Friedman, and Keith Lehrer. We wish to thank all of them, including our three anonymous referees.

Paris, April 2002

Abbreviations

AMUE	Association for the Monetary Union of Europe
AUME	Association pour l'Union Monétaire de l'Europe
BAT	British American Tobacco
BDA	Bund der Deutschen Arbeitgeber (German Employers' Federation)
BDI	Bund der Deutschen Industrie (Federation of the German Industry)
BIS	Bank of International Settlement
CEO	Chief Executive Officer
CDU	Christlich Demokratische Union (Christian Democratic Union)
CISL	Confederazione Italiana Sindacati Lavoratori (Italian Trade Union Federation)
CMUE	Giscard–Schmidt Committee for the Monetary Union of Europe
CNPF	Comité National du Patronat Français (French Employers Confederation until 1998)
CRC	Composite Reserve Currency
CSU	Christlich Soziale Union (Christian Social Union, Bavarian branch of CDU)
DEM	Deutschmark
DG	Directorate General
DVU	Deutsche Volksunion (German rightwing extremists)
EBA	European Banking Association
EC	European Community
ECB	European Central Bank
ECU	European Currency Unit
EIB	European Investment Bank
EMS	European Monetary System
EMU	European Monetary Union
EP	European Parliament
ERM	Exchange Rate Mechanism
ESCB	European System of Central Banks
ETU	European Trade Union
EU	European Union
EUR	Euro
FEE	Federation of European Accountants

FES	Friedrich-Ebert-Stiftung
GDP	Gross Domestic Product
HEC	Ecole des Hautes Etudes Commerciales
IGC	Intergovernmental Conference
IPPR	Institute for Public Policy Research
MEDEF	Mouvement des Entreprises de France (French Employers Federation from 1998)
MEP	Member of European Parliament
MIT	Massachusetts Institute of Technology
MP	Member of Parliament
NGO	Non-Governmental Organization
NLG	Dutch Guilder
PDS	Partei Demokratischer Sozialisten (German Democratic Socialists, successors of Eastern German Communist Party)
RPR	Rassemblement pour la République (French neo-gaullist party)
SEA	Single European Act
SME	Small- and Medium-Sized Enterprise
SPD	Sozial demokratische Partei Deutschlands (German Social Democratic Party)
TEU	Treaty of the European Union
TUC	Trade Union Confederation
UDF	Union pour la Démocratie Française (French Christian Democrats)
UK	United Kingdom
UNICE	Union des Conféderations de l'Industrie et des Employeurs d'Europe (Union of Industrial and Employers' Confederations of Europe)

1 Introduction

Public consensus and EMU

What an idea! The same currency circulating from the Algarve to Lapland, from Shannon to Vienna. With the introduction of notes and coins in 2002, the process of European monetary integration has come to its conclusion in twelve countries. At the end of the bloodiest of all centuries, Western Europe has come to peace. It has agreed upon new institutions to manage its affairs jointly, and opened its market of 350 million people. The creation of a European currency is an impressive symbol of this achievement. The path to the euro has been a long and tortuous one. More than thirty years ago, the Werner Plan, for the first time, set out a strategy for European monetary integration – and failed. However, the quest for monetary stability continued. It led to the creation of the European Monetary System (EMS) in 1979, without which European Monetary Union (EMU) would not have been possible. Many factors – political, economic, institutional, historic, normative, and personal – have contributed to the Maastricht Treaty of 1991. This pinned down the objective of an EMU. The factors that made governments stick to their commitments up to the start of EMU on 1 January 1999, and after, are manifold. Through all those years, an important convergence of economic ideas and reasoning has taken place in Europe. But despite this deepening policy consensus no one could be sure until spring 1998 whether EMU would really start as scheduled.

An ever-increasing literature is now explaining how EMU came about (see for example Gros and Thygesen 1992; McNamara 1998; Dyson and Featherstone 1999; Heisenberg 1999; Klau and Quatremer 1999; Moravcsik 1999; Szasz 1999; Verdun 2000; Howarth 2001).[1] Few studies, however, have looked at the role of the private sector, especially the business and banking community, which were not only most directly affected by the costs and the benefits of the single currency, but which also took an active role in the run-up to EMU.[2] Likewise, the role of non-governmental organizations (NGOs) is only briefly touched upon. The role of the Giscard–Schmidt Committee for the Monetary Union of Europe (CMUE) and of the Association for the Monetary Union of Europe (AMUE) has been mentioned in some of the literature.[3] Yet, the two groups are not analysed precisely, neither in their nature and function, nor in their impact. All too often, their assessment is subject to speculation and not based on the available empirical material.[4]

These inaccuracies reflect a broader trend in European integration literature; studies on the major steps of integration focus on governmental and supranational actors, but leave little room for non-state actors. The theoretical models explaining the treaty revisions all accord a minor or no importance to the non-governmental sector. Is this because actors beyond the state had no impact and no role to play – or is it due to the methodological difficulty of grasping them and modelling their influence?

The overwhelming influence of governmental actors on policy outcomes in intergovernmental negotiations cannot be contested. National governments in co-operation with supranational institutions have been the crucial actors in establishing the institutions of the European Union (EU). Yet, to understand this process, it is necessary to understand where governmental preferences come from and which ideas they seek to institutionalize whilst discarding others. Here, organized interests have a role to play and the literature on two-level games (Putnam 1988) as well as that on preference formation (e.g. Moravcsik 1999) has advanced our comprehension of how the process works.[5] But it is also necessary to explain where the ideas for the institutions came from, and how the public accepted these institutions. These processes involve more actors than governmental and administrative elites, reflecting domestic interests. It implies broader developments than intergovernmental negotiations. European integration studies may not have progressed in this domain for two reasons. Working on non-state actors, and especially the private sector, involves the difficulty of accessing data and reliable sources in order to grasp their organizational complexity, their channels of communication and influence.[6] In contrast, the intergovernmental bargaining process is a fairly transparent domain of government negotiations. Although access may be restricted, documents with a track record of governmental positions are usually available. Concentrating on governments and a few supranational actors also has advantages for theorizing integration. Models only need to account for a limited number of more or less unitary actors who negotiate in order to maximize their objectives. In addition to these practical issues of research efficiency, there is also the theoretical issue of research methodology of how to gauge the extent of transborder convergence other than by the impacts on government negotiators.[7] This problem is equivalent to economists' difficulties in disentangling preferences from choice.[8] Our book focuses on the process of producing policy options, that is, developing ideas and concepts that are then the object of political choice by governments. We identify a network of experts that has not only suggested solutions to open questions, but has also identified questions that had to be solved and thus influenced the agenda setting process. The process of identifying problems and suggesting solutions was a very open one, involving both, European and national officials, sometimes elected politicians, but also the private sector, and very often including communication efforts that were usually well received by the national press. Thus, the deliberative processes of problem identification and solution development influenced the knowledge, identities, and normative frames of decision-makers and societal groups involved, and therefore their preferences.[9] Looking only at the process of political choice alone means only looking at the tip of the iceberg. This view discards the complex and subtle social processes of preference formation and neglects the vast infrastructure of institutional change and its subsequent sustainability. Unless more attention is paid to social processes beyond governments, the analysis of integration misses the deeper structures of the social acceptance of the euro and the underlying societal consensus. This was a necessary condition for governments to proceed and for institutions to be accepted.[10]

Part of this process was the activity of private actors, who promoted the EMU objective and were committed to unparalleled trans-European co-operation. At the core of this movement were two transnational, non-governmental groups and their networks: the CMUE and the AMUE. Their functioning, their agenda, and their impact on other actors and public opinion are at the centre of our analysis. The Giscard–Schmidt Committee was created in 1986 to push for EMU, assembling 21 former ministers, active bank presidents, and major business leaders. It stopped its activities soon after the agreement on the Maastricht Treaty. The AMUE was founded in 1987, partly involving the same people. Representing over 400 large European companies and banks, it worked for European monetary integration for one and a half decades. It was dissolved in April 2002. It interacted closely with European and national politics, the broader private sector, and the academic sphere as it followed a double objective: pushing for integration and finding out what had to be done to establish EMU and make a success of it.

Our first objective is to provide empirical evidence about the relevance of the private and non-governmental sector as a strategic partner for governmental and supranational decision-makers in the run up to EMU. Case studies on lobbying in the EU often content themselves to show that interest groups or individual companies gained access to decision-makers (e.g. Bouwen 2001). We do not agree with the simplification that access to decision-makers can be taken as a proxy for impact in the study of lobbying. However, only a detailed empirical account[11] of episodes in which the AMUE and the CMUE interfered, drawing on as many sources as possible, can show if and *how* both NGOs 'made a difference'. Our second objective is to derive a theoretical framework for interpreting the role of certain non-governmental actors in the process of European integration. The AMUE and CMUE functioned as meeting points and fora for the development and exchange of ideas and established a transnational dialogue on EMU. They brought together national and European political and economic elites, whilst the AMUE members engaged heavily in broad public campaigns. Research activities lead the organizations to establish a network of experts, which they used both for the generation and the spreading of new ideas related to EMU. They linked national business and political communities to each other, and transported the ideas and interests emerging from the network to national and European political elites and the broad public. Some ideas were accepted by other agents in the private and public sector and became part of the dominant policy consensus, others were rejected and forgotten. Its communicative action enabled the CMUE and AMUE to contribute to the construction of the consensus, upon which EMU is based.

We argue that the CMUE and AMUE and their networks have had an impact on the national formation and the European convergence of policy preferences in four regards:

1 They defined and modified the ideas about monetary integration and actively 'converted' other major European corporates to support the single-currency project. These companies have then, in internal and external communication, publicly and in private exchange with government officials, taken a strong position in favour of the euro.
2 They have also helped to mobilize support for the governments' objectives and contributed to the societal consensus that was needed to make the new institutions of EMU and the euro work in practice. Given the high respect its members enjoyed in their domestic communities, the AMUE was able to participate actively in the public debate on the euro. As national preferences are formed with regard to national constituencies, the AMUE has – among other factors – contributed to the *convergence* of national preferences by accrediting pan-European, border-transcending ideas and perspectives. Through this convergence, national preferences were converted into a European policy consensus.
3 They have provided administrations and governments with information, evidence, ideas, and arguments related to the single currency. Especially, the European Commission used this connection frequently. This input was very well received as political and administrative actors were confronted with a high degree of uncertainty and, in part, a conceptual void as the creation of a European currency of this scope in a modern and open economy had no historical example.
4 The AMUE has produced evidence and guidelines for the private sector on how to manage the changeover to the single currency and how to prepare European companies and banks for the euro in practical terms. This helped to prepare the grounds for the euro to work in theory and practice and facilitated the selection of efficient policies.

Before we start our empirical account, which provides examples for these functions, this chapter introduces the theoretical background of our analysis. Given their nature and ways of operating, we argue that the CMUE, AMUE, and their network can best be grasped as an *epistemic community*. We then discuss how far existing integration theories are able to integrate our historical–factual account into their explanatory model. While constructivist works on the role of ideas offer some useful clues, we find that the main integration theories do not sufficiently account for the phenomenon, because the objects of research and the epistemological foundations of their social theories differ. The chapter concludes with our own model on the impact of ideas and the nature of consensus building in the integration process. This is then applied to the CMUE and AMUE in subsequent chapters.

Grasping actors beyond the state

Lobbies and civil society in the EU

Economic or societal initiatives beyond the state have been dealt with in the literature on civil society and in the burgeoning studies on lobbying. Indeed, the private sector is becoming increasingly well organized in influencing domestic and European policy choices and regulation.[12] Also, policy makers seek close contact with private decision-makers as the complexity of regulative needs in the high-technology era is growing, and capital mobility increases the pressure to act in the interests of domestic business.[13] Studies on European lobbying show that the relatively weak EC bureaucracy also needs to develop a manageable and stable set of relationships with interest groups (Mazey and Richardson 1993: 4). The creation of EMU is an example for the rising interdependence among politics and business, although this is rarely pointed out. EMU, like the Single European Market, was motivated politically and economically and affected the short- and long-term economic interest of many European businesses. Governments and national and European administrations depended on the private sector's input to prepare and practically implement the euro. Political leaders actively referred to business support in their argument that EMU would enhance the continent's welfare.

While analyses of policy making in the EU usually include the lobbying activities of special interest groups, little evidence has been presented on whether and how lobby groups influence the process of intergovernmental treaty negotiations, and thus the constitution of institutions. This reflects the empirics; lobbying focuses more on legislation than on treaty negotiations.[14] There are at least two reasons for this. First, EU legislation and the implementation of programmes impact private actor's performance more directly and perceivably[15] than the results of intergovernmental bargaining. These *regulative rules* and functional policy decisions, for example, EU laws for the single market, create different externalities than constitutive rules.[16] Private-sector lobbying has significantly increased with the single-market process in the late 1980s and 1990s, and is strongest in segments where the material stake in cross-border transactions is greatest and most obvious. Companies with special interests in these sectors will press for a reduction of national barriers and for the establishment of regulative rules and standards (Stone Sweet and Sandholtz 1998: 15). Second, treaty negotiations remain shielded from non-governmental actors. Legislative actors are more easily accessible than governmental delegations involved in treaty revisions or other major strategic decisions. Also, negotiators have little demand for the information goods and know-how pressure groups can offer as technical details usually remain subject to the later regulation.[17]

The practical work of the AMUE and CMUE before and during treaty negotiations on EMU, and in the process of subsequent regulation and national implementation, partly resembles that of traditional lobbying activities. However, the objective was rather different. Most activities were directed towards *establishing* and not regulating EMU, that is, towards setting up *constitutive rules*, which made the institutional fact of a single currency possible. These rules created something from nothing, while lobbying for regulations seeks to redistribute something that already exists. It was also concerned with *creating the collective acceptance of the rules*, which set up a new institution.[18] This form of activity is fundamentally different from the rent-seeking activities of special interest groups usually analysed in the lobbying literature.

A further, and at first sight purely formal, feature distinguished the AMUE from other European business lobbies. Banks and companies were direct AMUE members, and not members of national interest groups existing only under a European umbrella. This had more than operational implications. Companies and banks opted for membership voluntarily, as they strongly supported the AMUE's goal. They were open to discussions with partners from other European countries to bring forward the common goal, which mostly allowed a rapid convergence of positions and the identification of European solutions. In other interest organizations, for example, the industrial federations assembled in Unice, interests are usually first formed at national levels, and then 'confronted' on the EU level. They often mirror those of national delegations exchanged in intergovernmental bargains.[19] Here, bargaining among different special interests is dominant, while the AMUE work was based on deliberation with the objective of consensus building. Once this was achieved, business leaders could play an active and pro-European role in their national debates. Also, the AMUE explicitly directed its communication not only towards decision-makers as lobby groups would tend to do, but targeted multipliers and the public in general. It did not only defend positions, which it derived directly from its members' objectives, but had a wider approach. The AMUE fulfilled think-tank functions in that it developed knowledge and evidence on how EMU would be feasible and successful for many other sectors than only the large multinational companies and banks that were active in the Association. These features illustrate similarities to non-governmental organizations working for public goods.

Private-sector agency

It may seem daring to describe an association, which represents large companies and banks, as an NGO working for a public good. Does this not contradict the notion of economic actors as utility maximizers? Discussions about the willingness and motivation of the corporate and financial sector to support EMU usually assume that companies aim to maximize material or pecuniary gain and, therefore, seek distributive arrangements that favour their bottom line. For example, Jeffrey Frieden identified 'Europe's leading financial and multinational firms have been the stronghold of support for breaking down remaining barriers to EC financial and monetary integration' (Frieden 1991: 441). He argues that monetary arrangements affect sectoral income distribution, which is why the profit maximization motive determines preferences for particular regimes. He thus identifies the AMUE as a group of companies belonging to sectors, which benefited from European monetary union. McNamara, in contrast, points out that there were no clearly differentiated sectoral demands for macroeconomic and exchange rate policies as Frieden's specific-factors theory predicts (McNamara 1998: 40). She even questions the role of multinationals in general; 'there is little evidence to indicate that they have been proactive in pushing for specific policies' (McNamara 1998: 37).

Our first answer to this dispute is our empirical account which proves that the business and banking sectors have indeed proactively pushed for EMU. Our second answer is that the concepts of sectoral demands and sectoral interest group lobbying in itself may be misleading, as they assume that successful lobbying brings about externalities, which can be internalized by the activists to a large degree. This may be true in the case of lobbying for regulation and redistribution – but not in respect to lobbying for a public good. At the heart of the debate between Frieden and McNamara lies a confusion between regulative and constitutive rules.[20] The CMUE and AMUE sought exchange rate and monetary stability, which they perceived as material benefit in the short and long run – there is no reason to assume altruism. Most member companies did have an interest in cross-national sales and investment, and a stable monetary framework did help them realize commercial interests. But this was a constitutional issue. Europe's multi-currency standard was seen as a disadvantage in international competition, especially when compared with US and Japanese firms. Many of them even went beyond the pure economic assessment of creating a monetary union. They shared the strategic view that the reduction of tensions among national states and economies was crucial for ensuring the continent's stability.[21]

With their subjectively motivated engagement for the creation of EMU, the companies and banks contributed to the achievement of a public good: exchange rate stability and a common stability-orientated monetary policy. The objective of their lobbying could not be fully internalized and it thus had different consequences than the redistributive rent seeking of other lobbying activities. The result is an economic constitution providing a stable background for their commercial activities, which all other actors can share.[22] Material gains were a necessary condition for the AMUE and its members to contribute to the achievement of EMU, but not a sufficient one. Chapters 2–5 illustrate that pro-European attitudes and a deep conviction about the strategic necessity of European integration can be found in many statements from the AMUE, from individual board members to member companies. Deep interest in European integration led business leaders reflect on the state and nature of integration. Over the years, they came to understand EMU creation was not only a matter of governmental bargaining towards a new community treaty, but necessitated broad acceptance of the currency amongst individuals. This explains why the AMUE completely reframed its approach from an elitist network with direct access to decision-makers, to increasingly acting as a broad public communicator about the basic sense of European integration.

Non-state actors working for common goods such as a clean environment or peace are often defined as part of the 'civil society'. As transnational activities increased, this concept, which was initially developed for the nation-state, found its way into the analysis of international relations.[23] Early enlightenment philosophers contrasted civil society with public authority as a sphere that is private in its entirety (Habermas 1992: 433). Nowadays, civil society is mostly discussed as an alternative arena outside or between the state and the market (Deakin 2001; also Cohen 1995). The distinction among NGOs and corporate actors is often drawn between lines of motivation. While NGOs are the 'good guys' pursuing common goods (such as human rights or environmental protection) through voluntary and charitable action, corporate interest representations are profit seeking, private utility-maximizers. The Giscard–Schmidt Committee and the AMUE obviously comprised of individual utility-maximizers, that is, companies and banks. However, their members acted collectively and individually in support of a public good – often out of a private commitment, which was compatible with the wider strategic interests of their companies. The lobbying group concept thus has limitations for understanding the specificity of the AMUE and CMUE, not only in terms of objectives, but also in terms of strategies and impact.

An epistemic community for EMU

In pursuing the objective of monetary and exchange rate stability and EMU, the AMUE developed stable relationships and a wide network with people who agreed with the Association's objective, but were not necessarily AMUE members.[24] Some of these people contributed to the development of know-how and policy suggestions through their participation in AMUE activities, others used the information provided and had an important role in distributing the ideas developed by the AMUE. Hence, rather than defining strict organizational limits (such as AMUE = Secretariat + Board + Sherpas + 400 members) it makes sense to understand the AMUE and CMUE as networks (see Chart 1.1).

The binding element amongst the members of the network was the objective of a successful realization of EMU. Their interaction within the network was mainly targeted at identifying problems, finding suitable solutions and developing joint strategies to implement these. A characteristic of the network were thus the efforts to enable structured, mutual learning processes, consensus building around contentious or new questions and the spreading of these ideas. A common policy enterprise with individuals who shared cognitive frameworks and causal beliefs intended as input into the policy-making process before the final decision-taking, has been called epistemic community. Other concepts have also been developed to grasp the role of experts in the policy-making process. These, however, are less applicable to our case study. For example, the concept of policy networks is less clearly defined and does not put particular emphasis on the generation and spreading of knowledge and ideas. The advocacy coalition approach likewise deals with groups sharing a common belief system, but is more appropriate to explain policy outcomes when there are rivalling coalitions. Also, the advocacy coalition concept according to Sabatier (1993: 25) focuses on shared belief systems, that is, basic values, causal assumptions, and problem perceptions, but less on (the generation of) knowledge. Thus, for our case, the epistemic community concept, which also includes shared normative, principled, and causal beliefs is more appropriate. This concept emphasizes the 'intellectual' work and input first of all identifying broad objectives and derived intermediate goals. Secondly, it is

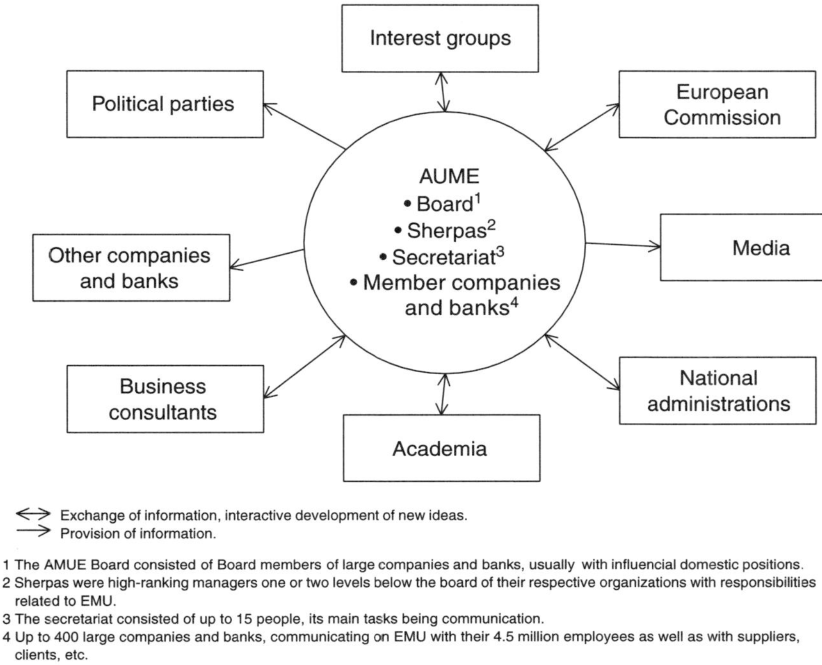

Chart 1.1 Exchange of information in the AMUE network of multipliers.

very open to include different kinds of actors. See Verdun (1998: 10). Peter Haas has defined epistemic communities by four characteristics:

> An epistemic community is a network of professionals from a variety of backgrounds, they have: (1) a shared set of normative and principled beliefs, which provide a value-based rationale for the social action of community members; (2) shared causal beliefs, which are derived from their analysis of practices leading or contributing to a central set of problems in their domain and which then serve as the basis for elucidating the multiple linkages between possible policy actions and desired outcomes; (3) shared notions of validity – that is, intersubjective, internally defined criteria for weighing and validating knowledge in the domain of their expertize; and (4) a common policy enterprise – that is, a set of common practices associated with a set of problems to which their professional competence is directed, presumably out of the conviction that human welfare will be enhanced as a consequence.
>
> (Haas 1992: 3)

The epistemic community concept has been used in various case studies related to EMU,[25] but has never been applied to the CMUE or AMUE. Researchers emphasize that epistemic communities do not have a particular interest in the public good they defend by rather act as 'altruistic scientifics' who provide their knowledge in a transnational preference formation process.[26] We do not wish to imply that the CMUE and AMUE members did not defend their interests when engaging for EMU. Applying the epistemic community concept to the two NGOs and their network is helpful to understand the generation and spreading of knowledge and ideas within the network and beyond its limits which impacted other actors in shaping their preferences. More fundamentally, we cannot agree to the idea that any politically involved person is interest free – they act within a normative framework and against a knowledge background which determines their positions. This is precisely what the definition by Haas emphasizes. Regardless whether actors in the policy process have a vested interest or not, for our analysis we deem it more important to understand how they influence policy making. Applying the four characteristics set out by Haas to the network, allows clarification of its nature and gives some hints how its influence can be modelled. (1) All activists shared the normative understanding that the continent's stability, peace, and economic well-being were achievements, which should be safeguarded and strengthened. (2) They were convinced that closer European integration and especially exchange rate stability should be assured in order to prevent economic and political disequilibria. (3) Over the years and through thorough exchange of experts from the business, academic, administrative, and political sphere, the AMUE network shared an intersubjective understanding of the economic and strategic reasons why EMU was needed and how it could be achieved. This common cognitive framework became the background for assessing and validating political developments in the EU. (4) Promoting the EMU and influencing its future shape by suggesting ideas and providing knowledge was their shared policy enterprise, once a member of the network had reached a consensus on the conditions and sub-goals of the creation of a monetary union.

The role of epistemic communities can best be grasped by highlighting three specificities of policy processes – especially when the 'discovery' of new realms or the creation of institutions in the process of EU integration is concerned: uncertainty, interpretation, and the institutionalization of ideas. Haas argues that actors have difficulties defining their interests when uncertainty reigns. Epistemic communities can highlight dimensions of issues, provide data, knowledge, and arguments, which help actors define their interests. In this view, interests are not seen as an independent variable, but as a dependent variable[27] influenced by the knowledge, ideas, and interpretation offered, for example, by epistemic communities. Indeed, the concept of epistemic communities has been praised as 'a vehicle for the development of insightful theoretical premises about the creation of collective interpretation and choice' (Adler and Haas 1992: 368).

However, the concept alone tells us little about how ideas actually have an impact. It has been criticized for neglecting 'the ideational qualities that enable ideas themselves to affect policies. Instead, the causal effects of ideas on policies are displaced onto the political effects of experts' (Yee 1996: 86). This gap can be filled. First, by showing how ideas were actually developed in the AMUE network and spread into the broad public and the political sphere – usually in the form of 'reports'.[28] Second, a theoretical framework needs to model how ideas can actually gain political relevancy and become consensual in the society. If we claim that the epistemic community we describe made a difference, we need to show the mechanism through which this influence was exerted.

Before we do this, we recapitulate in how far existing theoretical works on European integration have prepared the ground for our study. We consider three strands of research work: multi-level governance studies, integration theory explaining major treaty amendments, and constructivism. Earlier, we have said that analysis of multi-level governance or of policy making in the EU pays some attention to lobbies as actors on the political scene, although these studies are not concerned with treaty and institutional dynamics in the EU. This is the realm of integration theory. Integration theory explains major treaty amendments; however, it only pays limited attention to non-governmental actors. Yet, as the CMUE's and AMUE's domains were precisely pushing for constitutional change leading to EMU, it is worthwhile placing our analysis in the context of existing integration theories. There is a third analytical approach we should take into account before we present our own model of the impact of an epistemic community for EMU: social constructivism, which is concerned with social processes and ideational aspects of integration. Chart 1.2 gives an overview of the theoretical approaches and why they cannot fully account for the impact of a transnational epistemic community for EMU.[29]

In order to explain the impact of the actors we analyse we first need a model, which leaves room for non-state actors in an integration process formally based on intergovernmental decisions for treaty amendments. The model should,

Chart 1.2 Table of integration theory approaches

Approach	*Governance studies: analysis of EU policy-making*	*European integration theory*	*Constructivism*
Aspects useful for our analysis	Actors: pays attention to lobby groups as actors on the EU political scene	Formal creation of institutions: explains major treaty amendments which set up formal institutions	Construction of institutions: acknowledges the importance of social processes in the construction of reality and in the formation of preferences
Limitations for our empirical case	No concern about treaty amendments and institutional dynamics. Corporate lobbies modeled as rent-seekers attempting to influence decision-makers	Little attention paid to non-state actors and social processes underlying the construction of institutions. Restricted understanding of preference formation	No model provided to grasp multi-level consensus building processes

secondly, explain the role of ideas in the integration process. And thirdly, given the AMUE's orientation to mediate across national borders and among different spheres (economic–administrative–political–broad public–academic) with the objective of creating mutual understanding around a certain set of ideas, this model has to account for its consensus-building capacity.

Research on EMU: state of the art

Explanations of European integration have, for a long time, been dominated by two competing strands of integration theory: (neo-)functionalist and intergovernmentalist works.[30] While both approaches have undergone many refinements and their boundaries have become increasingly blurred, we can still distinguish how they model the influence of non-governmental actors and the private sector. In the subsequent sections, we first review the role and influence accorded to these actors by the two mainstream integration theories. We find that both theories leave little room for our observations. The reasons are not just the choice of focus on other actors, but lies in fundamental differences in the way preference formation is understood. We then turn to more recent approaches to the analysis of the EU, which offer some links explaining the function of the AMUE in the integration process. Against this background, we suggest our model of the influence of an epistemic community in the course of European monetary integration.

Liberal intergovernmentalism

In his analysis of the five decisive treaty agreements in *The Choice for Europe*, Moravcsik (1999)[31] argues that integration occurs through intergovernmental bargains, while supranational actors, such as the European Commission, only play a minor role. He follows the realist (also Putnam 1988; Wolf and Zangl 1996) argument that integration strengthens the state, as it removes constraints on its actions. Domestic politics is internationalized in the sense that national executive officials bring domestic issues to the bargaining table where they compromise with little additional domestic input. Integration only proceeds as long as self-interested states can use it to safeguard national interests. Moravcsik assumes that states are *unitary* and *rational*. But, in contrast to structural international relation theories such as realism, liberal intergovernmentalism[32] argues that bargaining positions of member states are determined by domestic conditions and not only by their relative position of power in the international system. 'Each theory [...] should highlight the purposive choices of states and social actors within constraints rather than the unintended dynamics of broad structural processes' (Moravcsik 1999: 15). They pursue a coherent national strategy vis-à-vis other states in an effort to realize their particular objectives, which arise out of domestic political competition. State elites are constrained by their individual, autonomous domestic arena given their re-election objective. The private sector is assigned a strong role in domestic preference formation. While scholars of European integration have long argued whether geopolitics or economic interest is the stronger force driving integration, Moravcsik accords a clear primacy to economic interest: interest groups impose tighter constraints on policy than security concerns or ideological visions of politicians and the public could (Moravcsik 1999: 7). His central claim is that economic interest has advanced integration; 'primarily the commercial interest of powerful economic producers and secondarily the macroeconomic preferences of ruling governmental coalitions' (Moravcsik 1999: 3).

As Moravcsik identifies economic interest as driving integration, we expect to be able to link our account to his work on EMU. For him, interest groups in the domestic arena act in line with expectations of material gains or losses and influence national preference formation accordingly,[33] which is then reflected in government positions.[34] In return the private sector supplies political legitimacy to national governments.[35] In this 'bottom-up' view of politics, 'demands of individuals and societal groups are treated as analytically prior to politics' (Moravcsik 1997: 517). The state is 'not an actor, but a representative institution constantly subject to capture and recapture, construction and reconstruction by coalitions of social actors' (Moravcsik 1997: 518). Property, risk, information, or organizational capacities are understood to influence the relative position of domestic social groups competing for influence in national preference formation. The nature of representative institutions determines which social coalitions are represented in foreign policy. Moravcsik's liberal intergovernmentalism has the benefit of being a theory of preferences over outcomes. It acknowledges the societal foundation of governmental preferences, thus linking European politics and institution building to domestic political processes and emphasizes that the realization of commercial interest is the driving force of integration. Yet, our account of an NGO representing companies and banks does not seem to fit in fully. This is due to his understanding of the nature of the integration process. Moravcsik sees integration 'as a process in which they [governments] define a series of underlying objectives or preferences, bargain substantive agreements concerning co-operation, and finally select appropriate international institutions in which to embed them' (Moravcsik 1999: 5). If, however, integration is understood to go beyond formal institution building as a result of an intergovernmental bargain, the liberal intergovernmentalist focus has shortcomings. It leaves no room for the analysis of social processes, which allow to the building on trust and mutual respect leading to shared norms and policy consensus. However, as we argue in more detail below, this is precisely how the network for EMU contributed to the integration process. Moravcsik assigns little importance to two key components of our account: transnational non-governmental activity and the genesis, the spreading, and the impact of ideas. He concedes that *state* preferences may *reflect* patterns of transnational societal interaction:

> [S]ocial demands are derived not simply from 'domestic' economic assets and endowments, but from the relative position of those assets and endowments in global markets. Similarly, the position of particular values in a transnational cultural discourse may help define their meaning in each society. In this regard, liberalism does not draw a strict line between domestic and transnational levels of analysis.
>
> (Moravcsik 1997: 523)

Yet, Moravcsik rejects explanations emphasizing the consensus building power of the transnational activities such as the Delors Committee. His discussion is conducted through the 'power lens'; he claims that no evidence is available about the transnational Central Bankers' Committee exercising any power during the negotiations. The little attention paid to the more subtle effects of the central bankers' activities is a logical consequence of the theoretical model of European policy outcomes being determined by domestically founded preferences based on commercial interest. The purely rationalist model neglects the impact of the ideational content on the dynamics of preference formation, and thus does not account for ideational preference changes as a result of societal cross-border interaction. Where transnational activities do not lead to the exertion of power they are discarded – and with them all possible effects of these social activities. Once national preferences are formed, they are taken to the European level in order to be 'confronted' with other national preferences in intergovernmental bargains, which are characterized by the strategic behaviour of the parties. Each negotiator arrives at the bargaining table with pre-fixed preferences. In the subsequent interaction negotiators aim to maximize their objectives.

This notion of strategic bargaining has been contrasted with the notion of arguing, or communicative action, as Habermas has called it. While the objective of negotiating is to maximize instrumental utility, the purpose of arguing and deliberation is mutual understanding. This implies that actors can learn and change their preferences through social interaction. In bargaining, 'the other' is a constraint, an obstacle to self-fulfillment; in communicative action the other is a partner that enlarges the potential and range of self-realization. Hence, the two approaches lead to very different views of European integration. Chart 1.3 visualizes on the first level the liberal intergovernmentalist model of preference formation and strategic negotiation leading to European integration. The arrows from and to the second level show where our argument about the impact of the transnational epistemic community needs to be hooked in to complete the picture.

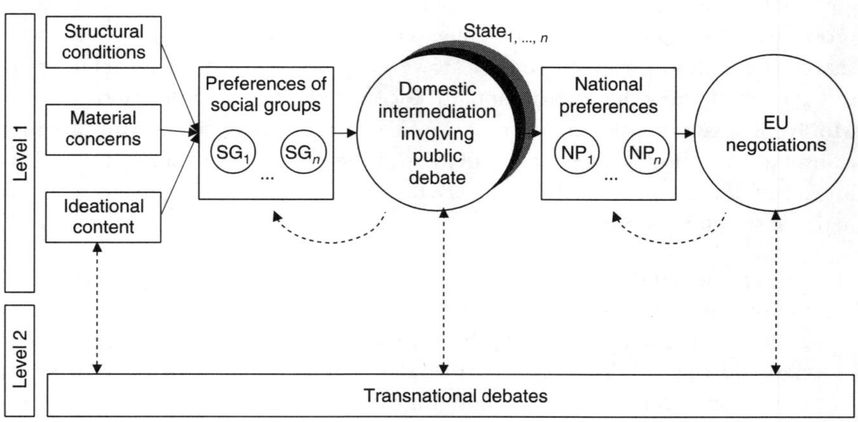

Chart 1.3 Transnational debates and European preferences.

We argue that (transnational) social interaction can modify the weighting of variables that feed into preference formation and it can determine the intermediation of preferences in the domestic political system. It can influence the way national preferences are represented by governmental officials in international encounters as well as the course and outcome of international negotiations. Before we analyse this view in more detail, we turn to the other major theory of European integration and the way it models the activity of transnational actors.

Neo-functionalism

Early *functionalists* pictured integration as a linear process, caused by spillovers. These were understood to result from functional interdependence or linkages of tasks, mostly in economic terms, forcing political actors to redefine their agenda.[36] Thus, progressive integration was seen as the result of governmental behaviour oriented towards systemic requirements. Neo-functionalists later acknowledged that the process was not automatic. Functional spillovers describe a contingency; but political pressure is a prerequisite for integration to advance. This pressure can be fostered by supranational actors who are understood to mobilize other actors, for example, domestic politicians or officials, interest groups, or public opinion in favour of specific policies by disseminating ideas and information. They can also 'push' governments towards integration by initiating negotiations in advancing proposals and suggesting potential solutions, and mediate among governments to develop compromises. However, the neo-functionalist model only describes how national barriers are overcome within a particular functional category *after* the integration process has been launched. It says nothing about the circumstances that set the process in motion. In neo-functionalist theory, the private sector seems to press for regulation of an already existing process of integration, rather than being genuine motors of this process.[37]

The role assigned to interest groups is, therefore, differs from the view of liberal intergovernmentalism. For neo-functionalists, they are allies of supranational authorities, rather than a feedback mechanism in the principal–agency relationship. Institutions such as the European Commission establish close ties with these groups along similar lines as those cultivated by technocrats in the national civil services with local associations.[38] Neo-functionalists argue that supranational institutions even foster transnational activities of interest groups. Due to its power of initiative, the Commission has an incentive to build working alliances with pressure groups behind the scene in order to prepare the proposals submitted to the Council. If technical, legal, or political information is scarce and asymmetrically distributed among national governments, supranational actors can benefit from their centrality in transnational networks. This provides them with evidence, expertise, and support, and allows them to act as policy entrepreneurs. These hypotheses concur with the description in Chapter 4 of the close working relationships between the AMUE and the Commission in the mid-1990s. The Commission tried to re-launch the process of EMU after the EMS crisis using the issue of technical preparations for the changeover to the single currency to provide a new impulse for the agenda. While national debates on EMU were strongly politicized and even questioned the whole project, the Commission put forward its Green Book, which was adopted at the Madrid European Council in December 1995. By preparing a changeover scenario and timetable for the introduction of the single currency based on input from the AMUE, the Commission gained technical insights that were not yet shared by national governments, and it added a technical dimension to the highly politicized debate on EMU. It was able to maintain and strengthen mutual respect among actors and individuals that could otherwise have been lost in the conflict of highly 'political' interests. This reinforced the policy consensus at a time when it was threatened by other events. The Commission arguably triggered progress in this domain, yet its initiatives only succeeded because governments renewed their commitment to the final goal of the single currency. Hence, the questions remain: What made governments accept their own preference for EMU? What role, if any, did the private sector play in this?

Models of preference formation

We have shown that the role assigned by the two dominant integration theories to non-governmental and corporate actors does not fully seize the essence of what we observed empirically: that the transnational epistemic community for EMU produced ideas (know-how and derived policy suggestions based on theoretical and empirical evidence) and contributed to transnational consensus building around these issues. The reasons are not that intergovernmentalism and neofunctionalism fail to define relevant decision-makers. Rather, their model of preference formation does not grasp complex realities of social interaction in the integration process. Both theories leave no or little room for one of our central propositions: preference formation is more than an individual or autistic process, taking place in the inner world of consciousness. Rational behaviour is social behaviour and, therefore, based on communication where actors refer to themselves and others, and make claims that need justification (Habermas 1996).

The liberal tradition Moravcsik follows sees governments as the *agents* of the 'people' (the *principal*). The two are linked by a social contract (the constitution),[39] establishing rules by which governments are able to act in accordance with collective (or majority) preferences of the principal. The fundamental idea says legitimacy of social rules and institutions depends on free and public acceptance by all individuals they bind (Freeman 1990: 122–57), although problems with the autonomy of the agent may exist (*agency slippage problem*). What distinguishes different economic and political theories is how they model the justification for this acceptance. Collective choice is a result of competing single rational agents' preferences acting strategically in non-co-operative games.[40] Social contract agreement is interpreted via instrumental rationality.[41] This approach has often been identified with 'methodological individualism'. Single actors deliberate 'about their given desires and interests in fixed circumstances in which they face a range of options from which they must choose' (Freeman 1990: 126).

Research in this tradition usually simply *assumes* actors' preferences. When these exogenous preferences are deduced from their material and strategic situation, that is, the *background* of preference formation, and when this background is treated as exogenously given and static, we speak of a *naturalistic model of preference formation.*[42] This approach dominates realist theories of social choice and, usually, intergovernmentalist explanations of European integration. Just like social processes, normative considerations only play a role in preference formation if part of the background. Reasons and arguments for the justification of public choices take an instrumental role with respect to each actor's particular concerns. They explain which option maximizes the (given) individual utility function, with the objects of desire defined by reference to the actor alone (also Gauthier 1986: 311). Due to this isolationist view of individualism, preferences are naturally heterogeneous between different individuals who live in different contexts. As peoples' backgrounds differ in different countries, conflicting preferences are also reflected on the government level. This approach focuses on conflict, or on co-operation based on strategic bargaining, instead of consensus building and trust. The 'other' is not included into the actor's own world as someone who makes a contribution, but is seen as a constraint, or worse, as an enemy. Thus, co-operation is modelled as an instrumental acceptance of a Pareto-improvement in individual actors' positions, although this gain may be unobtainable due to informational obstacles described by the prisoners' dilemma. Collective preferences only change when structural changes in the environment alter the pay-off in strategic interactions.

Like liberal intergovermentalism, neo-functionalism is based on a utilitarian concept of politics and instrumental rationality. While early functionalism associated pro-integrative attitudes and the unselfish pursuit of a common good (i.e. the ideology of European federalism), neo-functionalism postulates that supra-, sub-, and national actors all follow their self-interest. However, neo-functionalism has a more dynamic view of the context, that is, the systemic requirements, which determine preferences. The background is transformed by structural developments, which open new opportunities of strategic intervention. If structural change has destabilized an institutional equilibrium, one can either attempt to mend the original structure or advance to new institutional arrangements. This introduces ambivalence into policy preferences allowing room for persuasion, loyalty, and expectation, and hence for social norms and non-governmental action. From this point of view, neo-functionalism opens the door beyond naturalistic preferences, although the theory itself does not do so.

An alternative to the Hobbsian approach sees collective choice taking place in the context of norms and institutions based on agreements and consensus.[43] It includes 'the idea of social co-operation [as] an independent moral component' (Freeman 1990: 124) in addition to a conception of each individual's rational good. The Hobbesian idea of 'isolated individuals, abstracted from social relationships' is rejected, because it 'amounts to a refusal to acknowledge others as having claims of their own which warrant recognition' (Freeman 1990: 132).[44] We will not discuss the implications of morals for the justification and acceptance of social contracts. What matters here is that preferences may not only reflect natural desires and self-reflected preferences by isolated individuals, they can also explicitly refer to another person's preferences. Thus, the one-dimensionality of preference formation is replaced by two-dimensionality.[45] We believe that multi-dimensionality in preference formation is crucial for understanding European integration and goes beyond intergovernmentalism. Despite its utilitarian foundations, two-dimensionality in determining preferences is implicit in neo-functionalist explanations of European integration. Haas has formulated this in his famous definition:

> Political integration is the process whereby political actors in several distinct national settings are persuaded to shift their loyalties, expectations and political activities toward a new centre whose institutions possess or demand jurisdiction over the pre-existing national states.
>
> (Haas 1958: 16)

Such shift of loyalties comes about through *persuasion*, that is, through listening and learning, and not through strategic bargaining. There is a *softness* in this model of preference formation, which realists and intergovernmentalists would reject by asking the question why anyone should act against his own interests. Yet, preference shifts, which are based on persuasion and do not reflect a change in the material or strategic situation, are not necessarily irrational. Normative considerations resulting from a process of evaluation and deliberation are not incompatible with the pursuit of self-interest.

Constructivism

Social constructivists' analysis of European integration focuses on the processes of social interaction, normative diffusion, and identity shaping in the building of formal and informal institutions. Constructivists are concerned with the nature, origins, and functioning of social facts, that is, 'intersubjective[46] understandings', which groups take for granted. Thus, they investigate the construction and the communication of norms through discursive practices (Aspinwall and Schneider 2001: 13). They have introduced the analysis of ideas, the impact of shared beliefs, and processes of communicative action into the research agenda of EU studies.[47] In contrast to naturalistic preference models, social constructivism does not push the role of social institutions, such as shared norms, into a background whereupon preferences are formed, but 'they would like to understand how social beliefs influence the way people perceive, talk and act' (Marcussen 2000: 5). Constructivists have thus substantially re-evaluated the state- and interest-centred concepts based on the assumption of a unified actor. Interests and preferences are treated as endogenous to interaction, and cannot be derived just from material positions. Constructivists rather assume that generally accepted ideas, that is, norms and causal understandings, influence preference formation.[48] At the heart of constructivist theory the individual is perceived as a social creature, which gathers knowledge and develops an identity via constant social interaction. Understandings of 'reality' emerge and are continuously reconstructed in a process of interaction. Hence, individual and collective preferences are influenced by social interaction. The study of a European reality therefore requires analysing European social interactions.

Traditional theories do not ask how preferences are shaped in discursive settings and pay little attention to the function of arguments in deliberative processes.[49] However, 'processes of argumentation, deliberation, and persuasion constitute a distinct mode of social interaction to be differentiated from both strategic bargaining – the realm of rational choice – and rule-guided behaviour – the realm of sociological institutionalism' (Risse 2000: 1). Arguing and deliberating with the aim of reaching mutual understanding are a third mode of social action distinct from instrumental rationality in utility-maximizing action and regulated rule-guided behaviour. The understanding that arguing and bargaining processes are complementary casts a fresh look on the otherwise often-blocked rationalist–constructivist debate. Arguing is a prerequisite for negotiations, as it helps actors 'to develop a common knowledge concerning both a definition of the situation and an agreement about the underlying rules of the game' (Risse 2000: 2). It also helps finding optimal solutions for commonly perceived problems and for agreeing on common norms. The traditional integration theories are silent on the role of common understandings and the sense of collective identity and intentionality. Eriksen and Fossum (2000) have pointed out that communication and deliberation leading to identity building and legitimacy is necessary to achieve and sustain stable institutions and co-operative patterns of behaviour. Hence, the exchange of arguments, which under certain conditions discussed later, yields consensus, is a necessary condition for setting up effective social institutions – such as money.

Constructivists have also relaxed the one-dimensional preference model of rationalist approaches. For instance, Risse points out that actors who engage in arguments do so only because they are prepared to change their views of the world, their interests, and even their identities. Our empirical analysis shows that the epistemic network for EMU engaged in arguing processes in public discourse helping to reframe certain perceptions related to European monetary integration. Although we cannot prove this formally without counter-factuals, we can reasonably assume that this had some impact on the negotiating elites' opinions, perceptions, and approaches. We can show how the perceptions and positions of members of the AMUE network changed in the course of interaction within the network. We give examples of how they engaged directly in argumentative exchanges with decision-makers and administrative elites. This process of approaching both the broad public and the elites is brought together in our consensus model outlined later and formalized in Annexe 1.

While constructivist work has enlarged the field of European integration theory by raising interest in the generation, spreading, and implementation of certain ideas, most empirical studies limit their analysis to technocratic and political elites and thus only deal with the shared causal beliefs of leaders (see McNamara 1998; Gargarella, 2000; Marcussen 2000; Aspinwall and Schneider 2001). Little work has been done on the transformation of the general public's preferences.[50] Martin Marcussen's book on the *Social Construction of EMU*[51] examines the evolution of the elite consensus favouring a narrow set of macro-economic governance principles, which became firmly established legitimate reference points. He shows how, when, and why new ideas, such as the neo-liberal policy consensus, were adopted and models of an ideational life-cycle. Similarly, Kathleen McNamara's *The Currency of Ideas* explores about the emergence of a 'neo-liberal policy consensus which redefined state interests in co-operation, underpinned stability in the EMS and induced political leaders to accept the domestic policy adjustments' (McNamara 1998: 3). Thus, while their methodology distinguishes Marcussen and McNamara from the established theories, their choice of relevant actors stays in line with mainstream integration theory. In this respect, they remain behind Peter Hall's book on the spread on Keynesian doctrines across nations (Hall 1989), which identified three approaches explaining how economic ideas gain influence: the economist-, the state-, and the coalition-centred approach. The AMUE partially followed the coalition-centred approach by mobilizing 'support among broad coalitions of economic groups on whose votes and goodwill elected politicians ultimately depend' (Hall 1989: 12).[52] In addition, it also privileged 'the role of professional economists and stressed the impact of expert advice on policy' (Hall 1989: 8).[53] It also became a genuine generator of ideas whose contribution supported the construction of EMU. We study various ideas developed within the CMUE and AMUE network over the years, for example, the notion of a single, rather than a common currency, suggestions for the changeover scenario, but also very fundamental conceptions about peace and stability on the European continent. Our interest is, first, to present the ideas developed by the two organizations (CMUE and AMUE) and their members. This allows us to get a clearer picture of the companies' and banks' motives to engage in an organization such as the AMUE. Second, we show how these ideas spread within the network and beyond its limits into the public sphere, contributing to the consensus on EMU – with the exception of Denmark, the United Kingdom, and Sweden.

The impact of the CMUE and the AMUE, and their main achievement, was the provision of knowledge and arguments and the creation of trust. In order to explain how ideas could become so powerful, we need a theory of consensus building for Europe as a whole. Ideas are necessary for setting up institutions, which are based on public consensus. We share the constructivist understanding that institutional structures are social rather than naturalistic. European integration must be understood as a socially constructed institutional fact. It is a cumulative process, where prior decisions form a basis upon which new decisions are made (Aspinwall and Schneider 2001: 12). Peter Hall has given the well-known definition of institutions as 'the formal rules, compliance procedures, and standard operating practices that structure the relationship *between individuals* in various units of the polity and economy' (Hall 1986: 19).[54] The constructivist approach is attractive for our purposes, as it opens the analysis for the role of *individuals* in the integration process. We will show that the CMUE and AMUE were a network of individuals. At the same time, the constructivist approach requires a theory on how individual preferences can be transformed into collective consensus, which is the basis of informal institutions such as norms, cognitive patterns, and cultural practices. This is precisely where the AMUE made its genuine contribution to the creation of the euro; it helped to create an environment of mutual respect and trust across borders and cultures from where the euro-consensus emerged.

Consensus and the construction of social reality

Explaining the integration process: epistemological foundations

As we have seen, established integration theories offer some links connecting transnational actors such as the CMUE and AMUE to the integration process. Neo-functionalism would interpret the CMUE or the AMUE as self-interested groups being both promoters and the result of the integration process, though probably fostered by supranational actors such as the European Commission. Liberal intergovernmentalism would attribute importance to both organizations if proven that respective material interests in EMU gained enough political weight to influence national preferences. This understanding cannot be sufficient for two reasons. First, we have a different object of explanation; we wish to not only model the role of NGOs in relation to nation states, but to investigate the process of transborder preference convergence around a set of ideas. We are less interested in the lotus flower than in the mud that feeds its growth. The second point is, we take a different view of modelling collective preferences. Our approach demands some fundamental reflections on the epistemological foundations of preferences and the role of ideas.[55] We can then explain the role of CMUE/AMUE as an epistemic community, allowing new ideas and evidence for the creation of EMU, and also as a forum for deliberation and as a point of crystallisation for consensus on policy preferences.

To start, we will make the following analytical distinctions;[56] *beliefs* are the subjective ideas that arise in individual's minds in a given context (background). Some beliefs influence cognition about how the world is, others are normative, that is, are ideas how the world ought to be. *Desires* are unmitigated normative beliefs. Not all beliefs are worthy of our trust. What makes them trustworthy is our capacity to evaluate them. A positive evaluation of belief is called *acceptance*. Acceptance of a cognitive belief as true may yield knowledge. Similarly, acceptance of desires after positive evaluation is called preferences. Hence, preferences (and knowledge) are dependent on evaluation systems. We may say that a desire is the *prior* and preferences the *posterior* state of mind. The two are related to each other through an individual's evaluation system, which – apart from individual dispositions – contains social norms reflecting the aggregated consensus in a group or society and the weight of evidence accumulated overtime. From this perspective, the concept of preferences in realist, liberal intergovernmentalist and neo-functionalist theories, but also in the rational choice approach to institutionalism is *naturalist*, because these theories assimilate preferences to desires.[57] By making the evaluation system part of the background, they do not allow any degree of autonomy for norms and values that may render them inconsistent with desires. Consequently, they have no room for deliberation, argumentation, and justification processes to overcome this inconsistency.

Most researchers in the naturalistic tradition assume actors' preferences as given.[58] They argue that preferences reflect actors' interests, for example, power maximization. Once these preferences are identified, researchers derive the rest of the theory from them.[59] However, the theories do not tell us why actors should accept these beliefs and desires at all – there is an 'epistemic surd' (Lehrer 1997: 61). This 'surd' hides the fact that the validity of propositions depends on the context in which they are used; the justified acceptance of a desire or belief always requires additional *independent* information (Searle 1979; Lehrer 1990: 64).[60] Thus, for a simple belief like 'the Deutschmark was the best currency in Europe' to be rationally acceptable, actors need to have independent information on what a good currency is (freely convertible, a good store of value, widely used, etc.), but also how it performs under various circumstances, such as recessions, inflation, political shocks. Even if we only consider its performance under standard conditions, we still need to know if standard conditions apply to the present, the future, etc. Consequently, beliefs are dependent on their relationship to other beliefs – they cannot be 'basic' in that all other theoretical propositions are derived from them.

There is an alternative theory to basic beliefs; the evaluation of a proposition and the acceptance of a desire as justified depends on a reciprocal relation of *coherence* among assumptions belonging to a system (Lehrer 1990: 87).[61] A proposition, idea, or desire is acceptable if it coheres with a system of assumptions, that is, does not contradict the system and explains something better than alternative assumptions (Lehrer 1990: 95), or is consistent with the normative rules of evaluation such as conventions, ethics, etc. Hence, there is competition between ideas. Acceptable ideas 'fit' better into a given evaluative system than others. Different evaluative systems will not necessarily accept the same ideas, or lead to the same preferences.[62] However, ideas are 'politically salient only when embedded within some set of existing cognitive and political structures' (Goldstein 1993: 256). Ideas thus only matter if they change the context. Most obviously, ideas that become institutionalized, for example, as binding rules, impact actor's preferences and behaviour. On a cognitive level, accepted ideas, or desires that become preferences, enter the cognitive background of the evaluating individual and contribute to the accumulated stock of knowledge.[63] This includes 'the possibility that actors can learn new patterns of reasoning and may consequently begin to pursue new State interests' (Haas 1992: 2).[64] Judgements about preferences, objectives, interests will be accepted as appropriate or true if it is more reasonable for a person to accept one preference rather than another on the basis of a given evaluation system (Lehrer 1997: 63). Once they are accepted, their innovative content will marginally transform the evaluation system itself.[65] In this model, preferences are not dependent on exogenously given naturalistic properties, but they are the output of a cognitive system of evaluation, which is the background for all judgements.[66]

Desires and preferences

Our distinction has two implications. First, beliefs, desires, and ideas are only acceptable (on an individual and collective level) if they cohere with an already accepted, and therefore independent, evaluation system. The verification of coherence is called the process of deliberation. In such a process, there is competition between propositions, beliefs, desires, or ideas, and also between evaluative systems. What is an acceptable preference depends on whether it is reasonable to accept it. That reasonableness does not only depend on individual (utility-) considerations. It is pre-structured by shared common values, that is, a general acceptance or consensus. This consensus is partly 'always already there' (Habermas 1987: 119), and will partly emerge from the exchange of arguments and debate relating to their justification. Second, the evaluative system is not invariant. As a result of new information, exchange of arguments and communicative action, the system itself may change. Consequently, the preferences and judgements derived from it also change. This analysis is highly relevant for integration theory. Without communication and deliberation, separate 'national cultures' would inevitably lead to different, and often incompatible, collective preferences. The only way to deal with such *conflict of interests* is then strategic bargaining. This solution does not eliminate conflict – it only overshadows it by focusing on benefits. In our view, the essence of European integration after the Second World War was to *overcome conflict* by creating trust-enhancing institutional structures between not only governments, but also between people, that is, individuals.[67] Our study of private sector involvement in the creation of the euro is framed by this broader concept of European integration.

Before we turn to the mechanisms of social interaction that lead to preference and evaluative system changes of societies, we have to deal with one theoretical objection to this approach. Coherence theories of knowledge may appear as an infinite regress, because the truth of one proposition is justified by reference to a system of other propositions. Critics argue that there are no *basic* or self-explanatory beliefs, which are justified in themselves and constitute the foundation of everything else. Hence, coherence theory lacks an anchor in objective reality to justify its own acceptance. Our answer is this: there exists a context in which beliefs guarantee their own truth. This context is social reality and the beliefs are those that *create institutional facts*. Searle has distinguished between 'brute facts' and 'institutional facts'. The former exist independently of human observation, behaviour, or thoughts. It is a brute fact that the sun is 93 million miles away from the earth or that a 10 euro banknote is a piece of paper 12.5-cm long. Institutional facts, in contrast, depend on human agreement and only exist within human institutions; there have to be the human institution of 'money' for a specific type of piece of paper to be a 10 euro banknote (Searle 1995: 2, 27). While paper can exist independently of any observer (it is ontologically objective), money as an institution only exists relative to the attitudes of observers (its mode of existence, the ontology, is subjective). For something to be a valid euro note it is not enough to say; 'this piece of paper is a 10 euro bill because I think so'. There are exact rules that need to be followed and objective conditions to be met that will make certain tokens 'money'. In fact, an individual will only think a piece of paper is money because it has been created as money by certain constitutive rules that he or she knows everyone follows. However, even if social facts only exist subjectively in people's minds and are thus 'observer-relative', they are *epistemologically objective*. They do not go away because I subjectively reject them.[68] Collectively agreed beliefs guarantee their own truth, without them institutional facts would not exist.[69] This implies that through institutions the normative content, on which institutional facts are founded, is part of the evaluation system. This in turn transforms individual desires into rational preferences on an ongoing basis. There is nothing 'natural' about individual or collective preferences.

Institutions as social facts

Searle uses the example of money to explain the idea that institutional facts only exist because people *collectively accept* or agree that they exist:

> Being thought to be money is a necessary but not a sufficient condition [for money to be money]. For something to be money there has to be more than just a set of attitudes, even though the attitudes are partly constitutive, and essentially constitutive, of a type of phenomenon being money. I have to say 'type' because particular token instances might be counterfeit. A particular bill might be thought to be money, when in fact it is counterfeit. The general point remains: a type of thing is money over the long haul only if it is accepted as money. And what goes for money, goes for social and institutional reality generally. So, money, language, property, marriage, government, universities, cocktail parties, lawyers, presidents of the United States are all partly – but not entirely – constituted under these descriptions by the fact that we regard them as such. An object fits one of these descriptions in part because we think that it does, or we accept or recognize it as such.
>
> (Searle 1998: 112)

With respect to the theory of European integration, Searle's analysis of social reality allows us to progress by shifting our focus from agreements among policy makers to societal consensus and general acceptance.[70] Explaining how European consensus as a foundation for single European currency came about requires first a description of the content of the belief, which was to ensure that the euro counted as money and would replace other currency denominations.[71] Second, we must show how individual and national policy preferences were revalued in the process of deliberation in order for convergence of collective European preferences to a European policy consensus becoming a reality. Our study shows how this process worked in a small sector – in the network created by the CMUE and the AMUE – and how it was linked to society and politics. This narrow analysis can be no more than a starting point, a paradigm. Yet, hopefully our theoretical model would inspire researchers to consider broader societal and political processes required for the successful establishment of common institutions.

Setting up a new institution – European rather than national money – requires the definition and application of a system of constitutive rules.[72] This statement implies more than negotiating a new constitution (the Maastricht Treaty). It is insufficient to assume European authorities imposed the euro on a more, or rather less, willing populace, and that all that matters is the analysis of governments maximizing power in decreeing a new institution. As Searle has shown, three conditions are required for the construction of institutional facts. First, the new set of rules has to reflect what he calls *collective intentionality*, that is, a consensus that 'we' intend to do this.[73] Chapters 2–5 show how the AMUE contributed to the creation of this policy consensus. Second, specific *functions had to be assigned* to the means of using and managing one currency, such as setting up a European central bank, determining the legal tender, defining the stability, and growth pact. In this respect, we analyse how the AMUE fulfilled a useful role as an intermediary between political authorities and society at large assuring coherence between the new rules and the economic context in which they had to operate. Third, the *constitutive rules* of the institution of European money had to be *codified* before they could become part of the new EMU background.[74] The Maastricht Treaty was a first step towards codification. Here, the AMUE's input was marginal, although it helped pre-structure the content of a single currency and the setting of a date. The second step was the formulation of a legal framework for the currency changeover, where the AMUE played a leading role.

Explaining the integration process: preference formation and consensus

According to Peter Haas, epistemic communities influence policies 'by articulating cause-and-effect relationships of complex problems, framing the issues for collective debate, helping actors to identify their interests, proposing specific policies and identifying salient points for negotiation' (Haas 1992: 2). Yet, just how these activities affect policies remains open for dispute. If epistemic communities make a difference, the link between ideas and policies has to be shown. We would argue that ideas and beliefs cause changes in policy *preferences*, while decision-makers *choose and implement* policies that maximize collective preferences. The two need to be kept separate.[75] This distinction assigns a clear function to epistemic communities; they generate and promulgate ideas that affect collective preferences.

If this claim is valid, we need to show how collective preferences are formed. We have so far defined individual preferences as the posterior state of mind after desires have been evaluated. The next step is to explain how rational individual preferences become collective. The aggregation of collective preferences has been a major riddle since Arrow formulated his 'impossibility theorem' (Arrow 1963). The theorem states that there is no constitutional rule, which will simultaneously satisfy five 'reasonable' conditions guaranteeing consistency with a rational evaluation system.[76] One paradoxical conclusion from this theorem is that social welfare functions, that is, the determination of collective preferences, are necessarily dictatorial, which is incompatible with modern liberalism. An immense body of work has been written attempting to solve this dilemma, mostly focusing on the reasonableness or desirability of Arrow's criteria. Keith Lehrer and Carl Wagner have proposed a different route. In their view, Arrow's result is due to 'limiting the input of individuals to a simple report of their preferences' (Lehrer and Wagner 1981: 114–21), that is, what we called desires. They prove axiomatically that by extending the information base to the preferences of other individuals in the group, a dictatorial social welfare function can be avoided. In essence, they claim that the information individuals possess may rationally commit them to consensus (Lehrer and Wagner 1981: 13).

Based on previous work by French (1956), deGroot (1974), and others, Lehrer and Wagner (1981) present a model for aggregating preferences, or rather intensities of preferences, with the purpose of obtaining the most reasonable summary of information contained in a group at a specific time. The basic idea[77] is that individuals do not only consider their own preferences, but also those of others because they may be uncertain about the reasonability of their own desires and they may discover validity in normative claims by others.[78] Other people may know more or their beliefs may be relevant in other ways, which affect the individual's evaluation. As a consequence, they may feel committed to a (weighted) aggregate of preferences, which are not necessarily the same as their own prior individual preferences. The adjustment happens through a deliberative process where each individual re-evaluates his 'personal beliefs' by assigning weights (including possibly weight zero) to other members of the group. These weights, valued between zero and one, can also be interpreted as degrees of preference for accepting some belief (Lehrer 1997: 130). Hence, an individual's adjusted preference would reflect the weighted average of all group members' preference intensities for a given option. The reason for aggregating in this way is that it reflects the optimal degree of knowledge about preferences, given the distribution of trust among the members of the group.[79] Of course, if there is no trust, an individual would assign weight one to himself, and zero to all others. We are then back to Hobbes' world of conflict.

However, by one individual adjusting his own preferences in this way, the preferences of all others will change as well, as these members of the group will now take into account this individual's new preference. Hence, a dynamic process of evaluation and preference adjustment is put into motion that will, under certain rather simple conditions, converge towards an equilibrium representing unanimous collective consensus. The minimal conditions are: (1) *Mutual respect* (i.e. no dictatorship), meaning that each person pays some respect (positive weight) to his own beliefs and preferences and at least to one other person in the group. (2) *Connectedness* condition, that is, the matrix of weight assignments can be arranged in such a way that there exists a chain of respect from each member of the group to some other. This keeps them indirectly connected (and implicitly respecting each other), even if they are at first ignorant about each other (i.e. giving zero weight to each other). *These two conditions are sufficient to yield consensus.* In equilibrium, each individual assigns exactly the same weight to the beliefs and preferences of every member of the group and consequently they rationally share the same ranking of preference intensities for different policy options. Hence, consensus reflects unanimity on a given issue. At this point, the process of deliberation and communication will come to a halt, and it is rational for every individual to be committed to the chosen option because the consensually chosen policy reflects all available information optimally.[80] However, the two minimal conditions say nothing about the *speed at which the system converges to consensus.*

As long as the process of deliberation and communication is ongoing, there is *dissensus*. Dissensus means that individual preferences do not (yet) reflect the aggregated consensual weights. The variance of individual preferences from the equilibrium is a measure of dissensus, but it is not the same as *conflict*; for conflict implies the absence of equilibrium.[81] Hence, the speed of adjustment determines the degree of dissensus in a community. A thicker matrix of reciprocal weights across society accelerates convergence and, therefore, reduces dissent. In general, it is true that the more balanced the relative weight distribution is, that is, the greater the trust among members of the group, the faster will be the convergence to equilibrium and therefore the more consensual will this society appear.

Note that this does not imply that everyone needs to know everything. All that is required for consensus to emerge is that the two minimal conditions are fulfilled. In other words, if there is no dictator (unit weight for himself), and a chain of respect connects the group, the system will ultimately converge to consensus.[82] If, however, the chain of respect is broken, convergence is impossible and the system disintegrates into conflicting groups. The reason is that if individuals in a group receive no respect (zero weight) from others, they may regard themselves as excluded from membership in the community and they are uncommitted to the consensus that emerges between the 'in'-group (Lehrer and Wagner 1981: 83). Thus, *when mutual respect breaks down, conflict is inevitable*. This logic can also be turned around and used for the integration of groups and hence for European integration: by assigning positive weight to each other, individuals create the epistemic foundations for consensus on their collective intentionality and ultimately for their collective identity. This avoids conflict.

How epistemic communities create consensus

For the study of European integration, this theory of consensus has far-reaching consequences. European history over the last 200, if not 400, years has been marred by repeated bouts of excessive nationalism when mutual respect for members of different countries and cultures was interrupted and the connectedness condition broke down. Drawing lessons from this experience, the fathers of European unification sought to create structures whereby exchange across borders and practical interaction between people (especially via the economy) would create trust and mutual respect. There had to be more than intergovernmental co-operation, as an increasingly denser matrix of mutual respect was needed in order to avoid conflict. If citizens only trusted their elected leaders and the leaders did not trust each other, conflict would be unavoidable. If a chain of respect existed across borders, but was rather thin, the speed of convergence to equilibrium consensus would be slow and dissensus would be the salient feature in Europe. The reason is that the few trusted intermediaries between the cultures would have a difficult task producing all the evidence and arguments required to shift the consensus within the dissenting groups. Hard conflict would probably be avoided, but proper European consensus would be dominated by mistrust. So if European integration is to develop dynamically and constructively, it has to create conditions for the emergence of European consensus through mutual respect and trust, and not just the consent of the governed to the (supposedly) welfare-enhancing actions of governments.

Epistemic communities, like the AMUE and CMUE studied here, have a particular role in creating mutual respect and societal consensus across borders. They contribute to the convergence of policy preferences though content and form. Content means they produce new ideas and empirical evidence, through think-tank functions, leading to a revaluation of prior beliefs and desires, derived from given backgrounds. As new evidence became common knowledge, these backgrounds changed.

As epistemic communities are networks, they also have a structure, which contributes to the creation of policy consensus. First, within the network they fulfil the function of a *discussion forum* where the process of deliberation and information exchange among members who trust each other facilitates the rapid emergence of an internal policy consensus. This has been true for the Giscard–Schmidt CMUE, but even more so for the business network of the AMUE. The CMUE launched the market-led approach to EMU that subsequently brought together a large number of companies and banks. Amongst these business partners, discussions about ideas for a single currency, or on the technical requirements for the changeover scenario, created a business consensus, which policy makers learned to respect. But their convergence on policy preferences was even larger than on narrow business concerns, as, for example, the early discussions on price stability reveal. In this respect, the main advantage of the epistemic community consisted in the high degree of trust between the members active in the CMUE and AMUE; it helped to create consensus among participants more rapidly than other professional organization could achieve.[83] It is important that strategic considerations with respect to other partners of deliberation were absent at this stage. Second, the consensus among the members of the epistemic community became a powerful idea in itself because the members of the network were able to inspire a high degree of trust in the European population at large. When Fiat in Italy, Deutsche Bank in Germany, Générale de Belgique or Solvay in Belgium, and Philips in the Netherlands explained why a single currency was required in a single market, their arguments often carried more weight than the declarations of policy makers. The member companies of the AMUE employed in total more than eight million employees, that is, over 6 per cent of Europe's working population, and it is not unreasonable to assume that these employers deserved privileged respect from those who worked for them. Hence, this structure 'thickened' the matrix of European respect and trust across borders and cultures. As a consequence, our model predicts that dissensus on policy issues between countries has narrowed. This enabled policy makers to conclude agreements that would have otherwise not been feasible.

The plan of the book

Chapter 2 looks at the foundation of the Giscard–Schmidt Committee. It explains the logic of the EMS' founding fathers when they attempted to re-launch monetary union in Europe. The chapter returns to the story of the EMS and the long-term perspectives the two statesmen had in mind with its foundation and theorizes on various concepts of institutional powers that were dominant in the late 1970s and 1980s. We show how the initiative by the Giscard–Schmidt Committee pushing for a European currency contributed to make other policy makers, in particular, Chancellor Helmut Kohl and Commission President Jaques Delors, adjust their policy priorities. As a consequence, the European Council in Hannover in 1988 set up the Delors Committee, which produced the blueprint for the Maastricht Treaty.

Chapter 3 describes how the political initiative of the two elder statesmen led to organized transnational corporate action in the EU through the foundation of AMUE. It pictures the first years of AMUE activities. One major debate about EMU is carved out: should Europe have a single currency, or would it suffice to introduce a European currency in addition to the existing national ones? Chapter 3 tells the story on how the AMUE clarified the concept of a single European currency versus a common currency and provided evidence on the benefits of the former. These ideas were then taken on board by the Commission who incorporated them into the study 'One market, one money', and by the European Council in Madrid, 1989, which endorsed the concept of a single currency.

Chapter 4 investigates with AMUE activities in the first half of the 1990s. These include, first, attempts to influence the final date for starting EMU in Maastricht. It then turns to the post-Maastricht depression in the EU after the negative Danish referendum, as well as the EMS crisis and the declining support for EMU among the European public, which nearly derailed the process. The chapter gives details how the Commission tried to re-ignite the debate in the mid-1990s with its Green book and other activities, in which the AMUE became a strategic partner. In Chapter 4, we also show some ideas put forward by the AMUE, but not taken up by policy makers: the creation of an Ecu-zone for Central and Eastern Europe, broadening the anchor in the EMS, reinforcing exchange rate stability between Europe, the United States, and Japan. Timing and insufficient weight of the Association's partners may explain these failures.

Chapter 5 analyses the wave of anti-euro-populism, which dominated public opinion up to May 1998 and hampered a timely preparation for the changeover by companies. It then describes the AMUE's attempts to strengthen Maastricht consensus on sustainable economic policies often in close co-operation with European and national institutions, such as the EU Commission, the European and national Parliaments, and professional associations. The converging policy consensus finally produced results in the form of reaching the Maastricht criteria. After the start of EMU, the AMUE reoriented its activities on the practical issues of introducing notes and coins. With the issue of the new currency in 2002, it had fulfilled its function and the Association was dissolved. The short epilogue summarizes our ideas and draws conclusions for research and policy making.

2 Foundations

The consensus about exchange rate stability, which forms the core of all arguments for EMU, has roots far back in history. The experiences of the two world wars made political decision-makers and many others sensitive to the downsides of exchange rate flexibility. These insights led to the different attempts at monetary stabilization of the Bretton Woods System, the Snake, and the EMS. This chapter outlines the global strategic view shared by Helmut Schmidt and Giscard d'Estaing, the two men who founded the EMS, and subsequently sought to develop it into EMU. Seeing a window of opportunity in 1986, Giscard and Schmidt founded two NGOs, assembling prominent members of the European business and political elite, the CMUE and one year later the AMUE. Although, given the different background of historic experience, different actors reached different conclusions about the 'right' monetary order, a consensus around some ideas started to emerge.

In the late 1980s the idea was still dominant that the Ecu basket at the heart of the EMS could be developed into a European currency, which would then bring about exchange-rate stabilization and monetary integration almost automatically. However, this could only work if the Ecu was widely used. Hence, private-sector engagement was deemed crucial. The need for political commitment to the objective of exchange-rate stability, the creation of a monetary union, and the need for an institutional back-up was only recognized later.

The origins of the Giscard–Schmidt Committee (CMUE)

On a bright spring day in 1986, Valéry Giscard d'Estaing, the former French President,[1] went to visit his friend and former colleague, Helmut Schmidt, in Bonn.[2] He travelled with Paul Mentré, his confident, intellectual powerhouse and at the time President of the French investment bank Crédit National. The purpose was to convince the former German chancellor to join him in launching an initiative to revive European integration. Giscard had been a convinced European for all of his life. He had personally experienced 'the absurdity of war'[3] and was convinced that France alone was too small to play a role in preserving peace. A few months earlier, the Single European Act (SEA), a new Community treaty, had been signed, mentioning EMU as a goal for the community. However, both elder statesmen doubted that the new treaty would create a sufficient dynamic environment. They were dissatisfied with the long period of Eurosclerosis since they had left office. Over the last three years, Valéry Giscard d'Estaing had grown impatient. He considered that Helmut Schmidt and himself had the obligation, and the capacity, to re-ignite the dynamics of monetary integration that they had started seven years ago with the creation of the EMS. 'Nothing is happening, we have to act' was his message to a somewhat hesitating Schmidt.[4]

Their discussion in Bonn concentrated on two subjects: European security during 'the new Cold War and new arms race' (Schmidt 1985: 15–16) between Reagan's America and the Soviet Union, and the need to strengthen the role of the EMS and the Ecu. European defence was certainly not an issue, which Schmidt and Giscard could easily agree upon, and after the failure to create a European Defence Community in 1954, a political opportunity for advancing European integration in this field had not emerged. Hence, they focused on monetary integration.

Eight years earlier, Giscard and Schmidt had invented the EMS. They had done so single-handedly, meeting first conspiratorially at their homes[5] because they knew that new ideas got crushed easily when talked about before they are ripe (see also Heisenberg 1999: 54–6). Schmidt remembered how they had spread papers all over his kitchen table, the largest table in his house in Hamburg. The EMS was supposed to be the first step to full monetary union, which should follow two years later. They wanted to turn Europe into a zone of monetary stability when they established the EMS in 1978, only five years after the demise of the Bretton Woods monetary system.[6]

Both men were disappointed how their successors as President of France and Chancellor of the Federal Republic of Germany had neglected their heritage[7]. In 1986, inflation differentials between France and Germany were still unacceptably high and in eight years the French franc had lost more than a quarter of its value against the Deutschmark. Monetary integration had not advanced in Europe.

Schmidt's and Giscard's idea that reinforced monetary co-operation in the EMS should lead to a European currency went back to Jean Monnet.[8] In 1957, Monnet and Yale professor Robert Triffin had proposed a European Reserve Fund, the free movement of capital, and a common fiscal policy. 'Via money, Europe could become political in five years', Monnet said (Duchêne 1994: 312). Giscard had first demanded a common currency in 1964 when he was Charles de Gaulle's finance minister (Howarth 2001: 23).[9] But de Gaulle's interest, intellectually supported by Jaques Rueff, was primarily to re-balance the power of the United States in the international system. The time was not yet ripe for a European currency. This idea only became salient with the generalized floating of currencies after the breakdown of the Bretton Woods System in 1971.[10] After the Werner Plan in 1970, Giscard had supported the idea of a single currency, but the plan failed under the impact of the two oil shocks.

In order to remedy the 'monetary chaos' and to move beyond fixed exchange rates, Giscard and Schmidt not only invented the exchange rate mechanism in the EMS, but also the Ecu as an 'embryo' of a European currency as Giscard called it. This unit of account was based on a basket of currencies and placed at the centre of the EMS. Giscard was particularly proud of the name 'Ecu' which simultaneously reflected an old French currency and the Anglo-Saxon acronym for European Currency Unit (see Giscard d'Estaing 1988: 151–2; 2000: 97–100). In a second stage, the Ecu was supposed to become a proper European currency, managed by a EMF. Giscard's idea was simple: by gradually reducing the fluctuation margins between currencies in the system, the exchange rates between national monies and the Ecu would become increasingly fixed. Monetary union would be achieved when all exchange rates were permanently locked and the Ecu became a perfect substitute for national currencies. This system was meant to oblige governments to co-operate in monetary matters and the symmetry in the adjustment mechanism was to ensure the political acceptability of this discipline in France, where *monetarism* and *Etatism* were closely linked.[11] Several technical instruments were supposed to push this development: 20 per cent of national foreign exchange reserves were deposited with the EMF against Ecu; a divergence indicator was to show when a national currency would err too far away from the average, and narrowly defined intervention margins around central parities stipulated when central banks had to intervene in order to stabilize exchange rates. The system also provided ample credit facilities to counter market speculation, while it simultaneously put pressure on governments to converge with their economic policies. At the same time, the Ecu was to be used by central banks as a settlement currency for official debt and for payments by the European Community (EC). Subsequently, European businesses and banks started to use the Ecu in their private transactions.

However, these plans were never fully realized (Ludlow 1982; Dyson and Featherstone 1999; Heisenberg 1999). In particular, the German Bundesbank rejected the idea of the Ecu becoming a currency in a proper sense.[12] It opposed a symmetric system centred around the Ecu, in which a divergence indicator would trigger automatic central bank interventions. The German monetary authorities feared that this would undermine their control of domestic monetary aggregates. In reality, the exchange rate mechanism of the EMS was managed after 1979 as a parity grid in which the Deutschmark effectively became the anchor. Exchange interventions still took place in US dollars, not in Ecu. Not surprisingly, many observers outside Germany increasingly had the impression that the Bundesbank had a rather lopsided understanding of monetary co-operation. It meant that the rest of Europe had to follow German interest rates, set to maintain domestic price stability, and adjust their respective policies accordingly.[13] For Giscard, the only truly positive surprise in recent years had been the rapid development of Ecu financial products by private markets.

A window of opportunity

Helmut Schmidt hesitated when Valéry Giscard d'Estaing explained how he wanted to re-activate the drive for monetary integration in Europe. He did not want to be seen as 'spitting into the soup' of their successors, but saw the need and opportunity for action. In the mid-1980s, international currency upheavals, domestic public opinion, and geostrategic changes created circumstances in which monetary integration could be put back on the agenda. First of all, exchange rate volatility in the 1980s had become more than a nuisance and created some of the most dramatic currency upheavals in the history of mankind. While the price of the US dollar was close to 4 Deutschmarks during most of the 1960s, it fell to 1.86 Deutschmarks by early 1979 after the demise of the Bretton Woods System. In February 1985, it was back to 3.17 Deutschmarks, seriously undermining the competitiveness of the US economy and threatening a major collapse of the world economy (Funabashi 1988; Henning 1994). This development made the Reagan administration more inclined to monetary co-operation (Dominguez and Frankel 1993). With the so-called Plaza agreement of September 1985, the G7 countries agreed to a controlled devaluation of the US dollar, which thereafter continuously depreciated until it reached the price of 1.58 Deutschmarks in 1987. This yo-yo-economy, as Helmut Schmidt called it, put extraordinary pressure on German and European export industry. It also damaged economic growth worldwide and hindered economic integration in Europe. The continued dollar depreciation between 1985 and 1987 also became a major cause for increased speculation and massive capital flows into the Deutschmark as international investors re-adjusted their portfolios. Concerned about their impact on money supply, the Bundesbank kept interest rates high in order to discourage domestic credit expansion. Yet, this sustained the attractiveness of the Deutschmark for foreign investors, while putting other currencies in the EMS under pressure. A Brussels official described: 'During that time we spent nearly all our days and many nights in the Monetary Committee dealing with speculative attacks and realignments'.[14] A reform of the existing EMS was in the air. As its founders, Schmidt and Giscard felt the need to contribute.

Second, public opinion became more favourable towards European integration. After nearly a decade of economic crisis, two oil price shocks, high inflation, low growth, and rising unemployment, the international economic outlook had improved. By the end of 1986, the oil price had come down by some 40 per cent compared to the 1979 peak. Growth in Europe started to resume and unemployment was falling. In parallel, the feeling of political Eurosclerosis seemed to disappear. Three events had contributed to this renaissance of Europe: France's renewed commitment to European construction, the creation of a single market, and the liberalization of capital controls.

After two years of disastrous economic policy experiments, during which expansionary economic policy supposed to foster private consumption and growth, Mitterrand undertook an economic policy U-turn in 1983. With increasing inflation and external trade deficits he argued that inflation had to be brought down to make the French economy more competitive in Europe and the world. Despite serious pressure from party colleagues, Mitterrand decided – out of commitment to Europe – not to leave the EMS (Aeschimann and Riché 1996: 29). Economic convergence was no longer a mere hope. The man who led the first Western European government comprising communist ministers achieved what his predecessors had failed to do: he converted France to economic rigour and a market economy.[15] The *exception française* was finished (Uterwedde 1988; Favier and Martin-Roland, tome 1 1999: 602). One sign of France's new emphasis towards Europe was the appointment of Jacques Delors as President of the European Commission in 1985. As Finance Minister, he had convinced Mitterrand to stay in the EMS. Now he was to become the architect of Europe's new house. Delors managed to align the French, British, and German governments in the creation of the European internal market. The SEA, signed in February 1986, changed the decision-making procedures in European policy making. It opened the way for a radical programme of deregulation and supply-side reform and set the objective of abolishing all non-tariff barriers in the European single market by 1992. For the first time a treaty set out EMU as a goal. This gave Giscard and Schmidt a formidable justification to renew their efforts for EMU in 1986.

There was an inherent logic to link EMU to the internal market. The single market was to allow for enormous improvements in the allocation of resources. This required the complete liberalization of capital movements, but also exchange-rate stability in order to prevent the incentives for investment from being distorted by inappropriate government policies or speculative market bubbles. However, the three objectives of free markets, unrestricted movements of capital and stable exchange rates were inconsistent with national monetary policy autonomy. Padoa-Schioppa coined the notion of an *inconsistent quartet* (Padoa-Schioppa *et al.* 1987, 1992, 2000b)[16] as national monetary autonomy could lead to volatile exchange rates, distorting relative prices in a single market for goods and services. Stability could only be achieved by pooling monetary sovereignty and fixing exchange rates. Furthermore, under the Socialist government France had become converted to the idea of financial liberalization. This was partly because the control of inflation and the need to re-establish macroeconomic equilibria required a more market-oriented approach to the financing of domestic and external deficits instead of the traditional 'overdraft economy' (Hicks 1974; Howarth 2001). In addition, French banks perceived the opportunities to reap benefits if they were the leaders of a single market for financial products on the European continent. They put pressure on the government to allow Paris to become the second financial centre in Europe after London (Dyson and Featherstone 1999: 150). Their ambition was supported by a financial innovation: markets had discovered the Ecu. As Giscard kept repeating with pride, the Ecu had become the world's third largest currency in the bond market after the dollar and Deutschmark. In June 1984, the French government had permitted the introduction of the Ecu on the foreign-exchange market of the Paris Bourse and the French Treasury had started to issue a substantial amount of government bonds in Ecu. The rapid development of the Ecu in private markets had been a surprise. By March 1986, European banks held Ecu assets worth 61 billion and Ecu bonds of 7 billion. Private banks also had established a clearing system and made Ecu payments as if it was a normal currency. Thus, despite the official reluctance in the early 1980s to move from the EMS to monetary union, the private sector was already expressing its desire for a European currency.

Third, in addition to economic conditions and the European political situation, the foreign-policy environment was changing. When Mikhail Gorbachev became President of the Soviet Union, hope rose that the Cold War tensions could relax. However, both Giscard and Schmidt remained concerned about Europe's incapacity to speak with one voice in international affairs. The countries could not agree on a common position regarding the US bombing of Libya, they were ignored at the failed summit between US President Ronald Reagan and Gorbachov in Reykjavik, they were absent in the strategic debate about arms control, and gave divergent responses to Reagan's strategic defence initiative. While Schmidt spoke of the 'abdication of Europe' (Schmidt 1985: 21), Giscard said: 'In political terms, Europe is a black hole in the galaxy of international relations'.[17] Both were convinced that a monetary identity would help Europe affirm itself on the international scene.

When Giscard came to see Schmidt in Bonn in 1986, he was in a privileged position to put the EMU back on the political agenda. In March, the socialist President Mitterrand had lost his left-wing majority in parliament and the first period of cohabitation between a left-wing President and a right-wing government had started under the premiership of the Gaullist Jacques Chirac. Edouard Balladur had become Finance Minister. Giscard remained outside the government, but as founder of the centrist Union Pour la Démocratie Française (UDF) party and member of Parliament he was a leading figure in the centre–right alliance supporting the government. Within a month after coming into office, the Chirac–Balladur government requested the devaluation of the French franc within the EMS, in order to restore competitiveness. They argued that a *stable franc* should reflect economic fundamentals, but should not become an objective in its own right. The negotiations between the European finance ministers about the devaluation turned out to be very difficult and Giscard noticed that France got isolated, which he thought was contrary to strategic French interests. He disapproved of the way the government handled the situation and saw a need to reaffirm France's long-term strategic interests by strengthening the EMS and moving towards EMU.

Learning from Jean Monnet

The key to the construction of Europe had been co-operation between France and Germany. The very special alchemy between the two peoples and their partly contradictory, partly complementary cultures and value sets marked by romanticism and classicism, pragmatism and rationalism, centralism and federalism, Étatism and social market economy, ensured that any orientation defined or accepted between France and Germany was situated at the confluence of different tendencies that existed across Europe.[18] Against this background, the personal relationship between Schmidt and Giscard was a particular *Glücksfall*.[19] They shared common views not only about economic analysis, but also about the historic experiences of their respective nations (Schmidt 1996: 259). The mutual respect and trust between the two men was 'self-evident' ('selbstverständlich', Schmidt 1996: 261) and extended to delicate personal confessions about family matters (Giscard d'Estaing 1988: 730; Schmidt 1996: 262). They first met in the late 1950s when they were invited to Monnet's Action Committee for the United States of Europe as newcomers to the political scene.[20] Both were fascinated by Monnet, one of the founding fathers of the EU, who, in the words of John F. Kennedy 'had done more to unite Europe in twenty years than all the conquerors in a thousand' (quoted in Duchêne 1994: 345).[21] Although he was never elected to any office, had no party as political 'base', and assumed international administrative jobs only for short periods, Europe's history was intertwined with Monnet's life for over thirty years (for a complete biography see Duchêne, see also Giscard d'Estaing 1989: 27; Schmidt 1996: 252–5; 2000: 125). He masterminded the Schuman plan that set up the European Coal and Steel Community in 1951 whose first High Commissioner he became. In 1955, he founded the Action Committee in order to re-launch European integration after the rejection of the European Defence Union by the French parliament. The Committee supported Paul Henri Spaak, the chief of Belgian diplomacy, who chaired the intergovernmental conference in Messina that led to the Treaty of Rome and the creation of the European Common Market.

From Monnet, Giscard and Schmidt learned a new vision of European politics: not balance of power, but co-operation.[22] Helmut Schmidt put it succinctly: 'The less the international weight of a country, the greater is the need to work with others' (Schmidt 1985: 4). Giscard d'Estaing recalls his last meeting with Monnet in 1977, two years before Monnet died. Moments after taking leave from the French President, Monnet returned saying: 'I have come back [...] because I wanted to tell you: I have seen by your way of acting, that you have understood the essential! You have understood that France has become too small to solve her problems on her own' (Giscard d'Estaing 1988: 122).

Monnet's vision went beyond governments. His fundamental message consisted in one phrase: 'We are not forming a coalition of states, we are uniting men' (Jean Monnet's speech in Washington, 30 April 1952). This meant that a truly peaceful Europe required the support and everyday consensus by people to give legitimacy to such a project. Without consensual legitimacy no political or international order is sustainable. His intention was to forge direct links between people by economic integration. As a former businessman, Monnet intuitively felt that doing business together would bring about mutual respect across borders. Given the national constraints, Monnet's method consisted in 'changing the 'context' by transforming the way in which people experience closely related kinds of behaviour. Monnet believed that 'men are changed by what they do' (Duchêne 1994: 375–6). Like for a man climbing a mountain, step by step, the perspective changes minimally, but inexorably all the time. It was important not to look at the entire complexity of problems, but to act pragmatically on a small number of leverages in order to create a movement.[23] However, co-operation and integration could not be based on goodwill alone. Rules and institutions had to make it sustainable. Monnet had sought institutions that would make people work together across borders in concrete ways, for example, the common management of coal and steel industries[24] and later a Customs Union. His functionalist approach to integration was an enormous success. What people 'did' changed, and with it their perspective on the world. Between the late 1950s and the early 1990s, the share of intra-European community trade nearly doubled from 37 to 61 per cent. But this achievement was threatened by monetary instability after the Bretton Woods System broke down in the early 1970s. Hence, Giscard and Schmidt identified the need for adding the EMS as a monetary dimension to the economic integration of Europe.

Finally, Monnet also inspired Schmidt and Giscard when they created the CMUE in 1986. As members of Monnet's Action Committee, they had witnessed and experienced the power of a group of convinced and engaging individuals who shared fundamental beliefs and ideas. In Bonn, they quickly agreed that they needed a vehicle to re-launch monetary integration. Bearing in mind the achievements of the Monnet's Action Committee for the United States of Europe, they decided to set up the CMUE.[25] The purpose was to determine the key decisions necessary for the progress to monetary union and empress them on important political decision-makers. The Committee would also distribute documents to clarify what was at stake and educate public opinion about EMU. Following the spirit of Jean Monnet, it would reflect a balance between different nationalities, political circles, the world of banking, industry, and universities.[26]

A joint Grand Strategy

Giscard was familiar with the technical implications of monetary integration. By profession he was an *inspecteur des finances* who had been educated at the elite universities École Polytechnique and the École Nationale d'Administration. He shared Schmidt's far-reaching and historic vision of strategic interests. In addition, he had a profound scientific training, which he applied to economics and financial management. Giscard has acknowledged Schmidt's superior expertise in matters of defence (Giscard d'Estaing 1988: 126),[27] but there is little doubt that he had a more complex understanding of economic and financial theory and technicalities. He enjoyed theoretical problems to a degree that as a young Finance Minister he would sometimes distract himself by solving differential equations during the long hours of Ecofin-Councils while the civil servants were negotiating the wording of common texts.

When Giscard d'Estaing explained his idea of re-launching the EMU in Bonn, the former German chancellor listened carefully. He agreed with Giscard, as he had done so often in the past. He was also worried about the world economy, but in addition to Giscard's economic interpretation he also saw the foreign policy dimension of currency issues (Schmidt 1967: 196). In the Stimson lectures he delivered at Yale University in 1985, Schmidt had spoken of a 'Grand Strategy' that conceptually unified foreign policy, economic policy, and military strategy: 'All three must operate within one and the same framework. [...] The goals that any nation, or group of nations, sets for itself must be consistent over all the three fields' (Schmidt 1985: 5–6). While responsible exchange-rate management was aimed at international *economic equilibrium*, foreign policy had to maintain a *strategic balance* between powerful states in order to preserve peace. Intellectually, this preoccupied him all his life. Schmidt had returned from war as a young soldier to his hometown Hamburg where he started to study economics in the winter of 1945. His first professor in monetary economics was Karl Schiller, whom he later followed as Economics and Finance Minister. In his master's thesis, Schmidt compared German and Japanese monetary reform after the war. In 1957, as a member of the German parliament, he was involved in the legislation of the Deutsche Bundesbank Act where he was keen to avoid repeating the mistakes of the deflationist policies of the Reichsbank before 1933 (Schmidt 1996: 414).[28] Schmidt had a profound knowledge of German history and the economic and social distortions, which led to the rise of Hitler. This distinguished him from strict ordo-liberal theorists, who were preoccupied by fundamental principles of a liberal economic 'order' (see Tietmeyer 1999) and the historical experience of hyperinflation.[29]

Schmidt was one of the first Social Democrats who accepted NATO membership and thought about military strategy. In an article of January 1962, he criticized the lack of strategic studies in German universities and linked military strategy to economics: 'Strategy as a social science is similar and comparable to economics, not only because both disciplines are based on the economic principle, but also because they share epistemological foundations. In both disciplines we work with theoretical models, which then get adapted, step-by-step, to the complex data of real situations' (Schmidt 1967: 483). This view on shared epistemological foundations of strategic security and economic analysis partially explains Schmidt's commitment to the EMU. Schmidt did not see Germany's interests and preferences in terms of a simple dichotomy of security externalities versus economic motivations as modern integrationist theories often assume (e.g. Moravcsik 1998). For Schmidt, 'securing peace required also international economic balance' (Schmidt 1990: 147). Economic welfare and military security were complementary aspects of a Grand Strategy. He considered Keynes's contribution to the creation of the Bretton Woods System as the 'master piece' of a Grand Strategy to preserve peace. Schmidt's views of both economic and strategic problems, as outlined in the Yale lecture, can be modelled as a general equilibrium, while the focus on either military or economic motives for European integration uses partial equilibrium analysis. In order to understand Schmidt's and Giscard's preferences for EMU, it is useful to clarify some of the fundamental concepts that influenced their views.

An equilibrium model for European integration

Schmidt's comprehensive strategy, of course, took into account the substantial benefit from co-operation; for example, higher economic growth or increased security. However, he was also concerned about what we may call 'procedural gains'.[30] These concern the impact of institutions on actors' ability to solve conflicts or adapt co-operation to changing environments, or in other words: to bring co-operation back into equilibrium. In the language of game theory, an equilibrium is reached when interdependent actors have no reason to change their plans of action, because the results or pay-offs of their actions do not conflict.[31] An equilibrium in this sense is more than a military balance of power where opposing factors neutralize each other. It implies that overall costs and benefits of a range of policies balance each other. However, such equilibrium is not static. The environment may change, structures are transformed, preferences shift, and actors are replaced. These events, sometimes called shocks, make actors re-adjust their behaviour. This may lead to conflict with the actions of others. If conflict arises, the question is if, and how actors can return to an equilibrium. Institutions, that is, a set of rules, compliance procedures, and moral and ethical norms designed to constrain the behaviour of individuals (North 1981: 201) can help to solve conflicts and find a new equilibrium in which actors are committed to peaceful co-operation. Modern economic and political theories explain that 'institutions matter' (cf. Drazen 2000; Schneider and Aspinwall 2001) by modifying the distribution of information or inhibiting free-rider problems, actors' preferences may change, and their behaviour becomes more predictable and rule compliant. Institutional rules can, therefore, enhance stability. If institutions constrain behaviour in such a way that conflict after some external shock is minimized, this represents a 'procedural gain' in addition to the 'material gain' resulting from the realization of maximizing utility in the equilibrium situation. These procedural gains contribute to the stability of general equilibria.

A dominant motive in Schmidt's personal and strategic thinking has always been *reliability* (Verlässlichkeit), that is, the consistency of other actors' behaviour, which gained importance as interdependencies grew.[32] He was convinced that institutions could not only help solve political and economic conflicts but – along with rising interdependence – could also increase the reliability of national action. This is why he and Giscard first invented the EMS and subsequently created the European Council as a regular institution for policy co-ordination. After the Second World War, it seemed insufficient to base a European strategy only on co-operation between sovereign powers as in the nineteenth century (Schmidt 2000: 122). Stable co-operation seemed to require at least a partial delegation of decision-making power to common bodies (Duchêne 1994: 19–20; Schmidt 2000: 121–6). International anarchy characterized by national power politics had to be replaced by a civil order in which laws and institutions allowed co-operative solutions and increased the legitimacy of joint agreements.

Germany's history and geopolitical position was the key for Schmidt's understanding of the country's interests and strategic policy orientations. Over centuries, Germany had been the focus for centripetal advances from neighbouring peoples such as the Romans, Vikings, Genghis Khan, Turks, Swedes, French, and Russians. And it had been at the core of centrifugal attacks against other people in Europe such as Italy, Turkey, the Middle East, Baltic States, Poland, France, and most violently under Hitler against nearly all of Europe. Schmidt drew a far-reaching conclusion: it was in Germany's (and Europe's) interest to avoid coalitions that could turn against Germany and the only way to do so was by tying her into a large EU (Schmidt 1990: 260). Schmidt was convinced that in the long run the Germans would only remain closely bound to the West, if the French helped them. This required a joint 'Grand Strategy' for Europe (Schmidt 1985: 56).

The idea that institutions such as rules for co-operative decision-making could help contain self-interested conflicts between sovereign states became consensual in continental Western Europe after the Second World War. The purpose of European co-operation was to prevent another war.[33] The 'realism' of a Hobbesian-type anarchic world had been replaced by Humeian-type whiggish[34] liberalism. By delegating at least some powers of decision to common bodies, the European ground rules were changed. Instead of aggressive competition between States, the norms of democracy and peaceful interaction could prevail. Joint governing bodies flattened frontiers as barriers to the rule of law, so that relations between states reflected domestic standards instead of threatening them (Duchêne 1994: 20).

The balance of power strategy

Schmidt's concept of integration as a strategic equilibrium based on institutions differed from the British view or that of other, more peripheral countries. British policy towards Europe throughout the nineteenth century and into the early twentieth century promoted a balance of power in the continent. If there was a threat that one state could reach a dominant position, the British counter-weight was thrown into the other pan of the scale. It did so against Napoleonic France, and against Germany in both 1914 and 1939 (George 1999: 12). This concept favours *discretionary* policies, while the continental approach seeks *rule-based behaviour* (Kissinger 1957: 5–6).[35] The balance of power strategy was appropriate for a world power, which was by definition unconstrained. After the war, Britain had difficulties to adapt to small power status (Turner 2000: 7) and to accept the idea that one could reap higher benefits from pooling sovereignty. The procedural gains of co-operative behaviour remained hidden behind emotionally laden terms like patriotism, nationalism, and sovereignty (Turner 2000: 78–9). As Amery put it, 'the ideal of a United Europe does not evoke the same response in Britain as it does in most countries on the continent' (Amery 1952: 9). Turner has explained this by 'the legacy of greatness' (commonwealth and Empire) and the different circumstances in not having been occupied by a foreign power and not having suffered the extensive physical damage of other countries in Europe.[36] Thus, in his famous speech in Zurich in 1946, Winston Churchill wanted to see the recreation of 'the European family [...] and provide it with a structure under which it can dwell in peace, in safety and in freedom. We must build a kind of United States of Europe'. Yet he saw Britain's role outside the closest family – more as a distant cousin (see Turner 2000: 42–3).[37]

The only British Prime Minister who was ever fully committed to the modern idea of Europe was Edward Heath, previously a member of Monnet's Action Committee.[38] With Margaret Thatcher, Britain returned to its nineteenth century view of sovereignty. In her famous Bruges speech in 1988, she described her European vision as 'preserving the different traditions, parliamentary powers and a sense of national pride [that have] been the source of Europe's vitality through the centuries.' She also believed that Britain had unusual influence due to 'historical distinction, skilled diplomacy and versatile military force.' From this perspective it was only logical if she proclaimed on British sovereignty: 'We have surrendered enough' (Moravcsik 1999: 149). The power balancing game kept the United Kingdom mentally, and for a long time politically, outside Europe. The choice of binding itself as little as possible by institutional obligations in Europe resulted in Britain *free riding* on the Continent's stability.[39] It also inhibited the deepening of mutual respect across borders. As a consequence, Eurosceptic British media can still exploit and re-enforce xenophobic attitudes and even today, nearly forty years after the Elysée Treaty for German–French partnership, British diplomacy is still tempted to exploit cracks in the Franco-German axis, rather than contributing to the creation of common institutions.

Institutions for monetary stability

Helmut Schmidt and Valéry Giscard d'Estaing had both experienced the break-up of the Bretton Woods international monetary system in 1973 as Finance ministers. Without rules constraining the United States to search a co-operative solution, the institution was not sustainable. At the time, Europe had no alternative framework. The mainly discretionary monetary co-operation in the 'Snake' (1972–79) also failed and it became clear that only a much more solid institutional structure could ensure long-term economic and monetary stability in Europe (McNamara 1998). The creation of the EMS in 1979 was a first step in this direction. It was founded on the idea that stronger (critics would say more rigid) rules were required to stabilize fundamental economic equilibria.[40]

In the early 1980s, many continental countries understood that stronger institutionalization in monetary co-operation was required, although British authorities rejected it. Schmidt and Giscard had always seen a European currency as their ultimate objective. In 1986, they saw the opportunity to make a new advance. They intended to strengthen the EMS, in order to bring about greater correspondence between the monetary policies of central banks as part of a broader convergence of the economic policy mixes of individual governments. They thought this had now become a political imperative because Europe was embarking on the creation of the single interior market. In his Yale lectures Schmidt said, 'We are way behind the true common markets that exist within the United States and inside Japan. The Japanese have one currency for a market of 120 million people, the Americans one currency for 235 million. But we in Europe have ten currencies for 275 million people!' (Schmidt 1985: 48). Hence, he lent his full support to Valéry Giscard d'Estaing.

The Committee's ideas and activities

Giscard and Schmidt formally launched the CMUE in Heidelberg on 13 November 1986, announcing twenty-one ex-Ministers, bank presidents, and active business leaders of major international enterprises as members.[41] Credibility, standing and influence were important selection criteria. Some obvious candidates of impeccable European commitment were discarded because their names would have caused antagonisms in their respective capitals. Paul Mentré and Uwe Plachetka became Executive Secretaries reporting to the Co-Presidents Schmidt and Giscard. The Committee's message was simple: 'Let us build on the success of the EMS and turn the Ecu into a true European currency'. This required macroeconomic convergence, a European Central Bank (ECB) and wider use of the Ecu. The need for economic and budgetary discipline in order to stabilize exchange rates was a message dear to Giscard although he did not necessarily favour the Bundesbank's deflationary policies. He considered inflation as economically and socially destructive and intellectually favoured monetary stability as it had prevailed under the Gold Standard. As Finance Minister, he had consolidated public budgets in the 1960s, against pressures from his Prime Minister Georges Pompidou.[42] In the 1970s he had to compromise with the dominant dirigiste and Etatist forces in the French establishment, but he now saw the opportunity to return to monetary stability in a European context. Schmidt also wanted to promote the Ecu, and the Yen, as international reserve currencies. Schmidt would point out that at least two US Presidents had accumulated a significant mountain of debt at home and abroad and thereby created a source of instability for macroeconomic policies. Without saying so publicly, he was concerned that the looming problem of the American foreign debt could cause a financial crash with far-reaching consequences, which made the issue of a second and third reserve currency salient.[43]

After the launch of the Committee, Giscard and Schmidt frequently met with the other members and senior policy makers in Europe. The first full working session took place on 18 December 1986 in Brussels, followed by three sessions per annum in the following years.[44] The first task was to formulate an Action Programme for European Monetary Union. The Co-Presidents set up working groups, for example, on the mission and status of an ECB, the link between the official and private Ecu, or ways to develop private operations in Ecu.

The Action Programme of January 1988 recognized that the EMS had contributed to greater exchange rate stability between European currencies. Exchange-rate volatility among currencies participating in the EMS had been reduced by one-third, thereby increasing the security of investment and trade in the internal market. It had imposed discipline and convergence of economic and monetary policies, gradually reducing inflation differentials amongst these countries. However, the Committee considered this convergence as insufficient. Exchange rates still had to be adjusted too often in order to compensate for the loss of competitiveness resulting from different inflationary performances. Although the Action Programme was only completed in January 1988, the Committee's deliberations influenced policy debates well before. The CMUE's work anticipated the French Finance Minister Balladur's Memorandum on European Construction of 8 January 1988 and the German Foreign Minister Genscher's answer, the Memorandum for the Creation of a European Currency Area and a European Central Bank of 26 February 1988 (see Dyson and Featherstone 1999: 325–32).[45]

The Committee made six propositions: creation of an ECB, general convergence of economic policies, participation of all European currencies in the ERM at narrow margins, full liberation of capital movements, unification of the financial circuits of public and private Ecus, and finally development of private operations in a European currency. The Committee thought that the next step towards EMU required institutional reforms to accelerate the convergence of economic and monetary policies. Hence, the Action Programme favoured a revision of the Treaty of Rome: 'Only a ratified treaty that affirms the European objective of monetary stability and organizes the explicit transfer of competencies is fully compatible with the missions by which central banks have presently been charged by national laws.' In this respect, the Action Programme reflected an evolution of Schmidt and Giscard's earlier thinking. The Committee had established *institutional change* as an objective. But the method to get there was to complement the institutional approach by a *market-led* approach. The underlying idea was that market pressure would force institutional change. The development of the Ecu in private markets would ultimately require an ECB as an issuing bank: 'The Ecu will then not only fulfil the function of central bank money, but also circulate as a parallel currency' (CMUE 1988). At the Brussels meeting in December 1986, in the presence of the Commission President Jacques Delors, Giscard d'Estaing gave an unambiguous definition of what this meant: he wished to develop 'the parallel use of national and European currencies, not the substitution of national currencies by a European currency.'[46] This reflected a long-standing idea in his thinking. He had first proposed the creation of a parallel European currency in 1964. It was then called Composite Reserve Currency (CRC), the value of which he suggested should be determined by member states' gold reserves. Its objective was to ensure the survival of the common agricultural policy in the context of international monetary instability, as well as to challenge the position of the dollar as the dominant international reserve currency. In January 1965, he lent his support to a Commission proposal for the rapid introduction of a parallel currency, circulating in addition to national currencies (Howarth 2001: 23–4). While he had talked of a single currency after the Werner Report in the early 1970s, Giscard had now, in the mid-1980s, been convinced that the time was not yet ripe for getting rid of Europe's inherited currencies. For him, the 'construction of Europe implied a dialectical movement between the political will of governments and the spontaneity of citizens, between economic policy action and market phenomena.'[47] If markets and citizens used the European currency, this provided the legitimacy to progress with European integration. This was particularly important as it was perfectly clear that national central banks, and in particular the Bundesbank, were opposed to change their status.[48] Thus, developing the Ecu seemed an alternative route to the distant goal of a unified currency: not an artificial concept imposed on a reticent public, but an idea adopted by Europe's private sector. If markets revealed a preference for a European currency, political authorities and monetary authorities would have to take this fact into account. Giscard's approach overlapped with the thinking of Helmut Schmidt who had circulated a private paper in August 1986, mapping a pragmatic path for the Ecu where no amendment to the Treaty of Rome had yet been thought necessary.

Promoting the Ecu

The idea of a parallel currency had gained prominence in 1975 when a group of economists[49] proposed the introduction of a parallel currency of constant purchasing power, which would compete with national currencies in all monetary functions. They assumed that a stable parallel currency would slowly crowd out more inflationary currencies and thereby become dominant (Gros and Thygesen 1992), an idea developed by Nobel Prize winner Friedrich Hayek. The All Saints Day Manifesto was a radical proposal out of despair at a time when inflation was at 20 per cent in Italy.[50] Max Corden, Professor at John Hopkins University, later called the proposal 'brilliant – except that it seems to me regrettably a "non-starter"' (Corden, 1992). The Giscard–Schmidt market-led approach to EMU differed in one important point from traditional parallel currency theories. While these believed in a natural crowding-out of national currencies, the CMUE saw markets as an instrument to encourage institutional change. They had an important ally in Brussels. The European Commission had developed the idea that the Ecu, which was initially only a unit of account in the EMS, could actually be turned into 'true' money.

The brain behind these thoughts was Tommaso Padoa-Schioppa, a central banker and from 1979 to 1983 Director General of the Commission's DG II under the Commissioner François-Xavier Ortoli. Born in Italy in 1940, Padoa-Schioppa was a brilliant intellectual and a passionate European. He was influenced from early age by his brother who frequented federalist circles in Pavia and introduced him to the writings of Altiero Spinelli and Mario Albertini, two outstanding European federalists. Padoa-Schioppa also studied Luigi Einaudi, the distinguished liberal economist who after the war became central bank governor and then the first President of the Italian Republic. Einaudi had urged in 1918 the creation of a European federal state as the only way to establish a lasting and peaceful order in Europe. In 1943, he argued that the time had come to deprive nation-states of the power to print money, and to attribute it to a supranational authority (Padoa-Schioppa 2001a). Padoa-Schioppa was too young to have been a member of the Monnet Action Committee, but was greatly inspired by Monnet's memoirs. Later, he became a close confidant of Jacques Delors and was one of the most influential founding fathers of EMU.[51] In 1983, he laid out a three-step process by which the Ecu could become 'true' money – the most coherent strategy promoting the Ecu:

> The first stage is 'definition'. The Ecu does not exist in any form or for any function. Only its definition exists. 'Someone' declares that the Ecu is worth DM 0.828, plus Fl. 0.286, etc. Such a declaration has no practical market effect. We have had this stage already. The 'someone' was the EC Council in its decision of 18 December 1978.

The second stage is 'free-floating'. On the basis of the declared definition, some operators begin to bundle Ecus and to deal in them. This adds a new line and a new column to the exchange rate matrix. If exchange rate arbitrage produces consistent values, the figures in the Ecu line and column will probably, at least initially, be a mere reflection of the movement of the other currencies. The Ecu will be influenced, but will exert no influence of its own. Behind the other lines and columns of the matrix, there lie whole systems of production, trade, income, and prices expressed in those currencies; and behind them, states, armies, and central banks. In contrast, the Ecu is backed by little more than the EC agricultural prices denominated in Ecus, but in fact administered in national currencies and controlled by a 'green rate' system. Neither an army nor a central bank, merely an EC Council decision and the idea, once expressed even by de Gaulle, that 'cette Europe, un jour il faudra bien la faire'. However, the fact that exchange rate impulses run only one way, from national currencies to the Ecu, is not a logical necessity, it is only a practical probability. Rather than the consequence of the will of legislators and official authorities, it is only the result of behavioural choices made by operators. Indeed, nothing prevents a businessman from quoting the price of a newspaper or a service or a bond in Ecus and then actually dealing in them in another currency.

If Ecu trading were to outstrip trading in other currencies, it could well happen that the Ecu would become something different from a mere sum of other currencies: it would become a currency on its own, with an identified supply and demand. It is even conceivable that impulses in the exchange rates would also flow from the Ecu rather than only towards it. Obviously arbitrage would continue to make sure that currency rates in the matrix were consistent, but there is nothing that forces the Ecu market rate to be always identical to the one declared. In a sense, the definition of the Ecu as a basket would become a relic of the past in the same way as the gold definition of paper currencies. The Ecu would be a free-floating currency. This would bring us to the height of the second stage. In a different scenario, Hayek has explored this process in his essay on *The Denationalisation of Money* (Hayek 1990).

The third stage is 'governed exchange'. 'Somebody' buys or sells Ecus in order to regulate the price. To do so efficiently, he has to be able to create Ecus or, if he wants to buy them, to offer something attractive in return, such as another currency, financial assets or gold. If his objective is not profit but stabilisation or, more generally, to offer the public a high quality monetary standard, he will in fact be acting like a 'government'.

The process described here is only partly a chronological sequence. Each of the three stages may exist in part, or coexist with parts of the other two. Today we find elements of the first stage together with seeds of the second and third. Some of these seeds have grown and multiplied at impressive speed. There is no certitude that we will ever see the complete picture. But no reason to assert that we never shall.

(*Ecu Newsletter* 1983. Reprinted in Padoa-Schioppa 2000b: 65–6)

When President Giscard d'Estaing and Chancellor Helmut Schmidt created the Ecu in 1979 as part of the EMS, they had set the first stage. Private operators then initiated the second stage with the creation of 'private' Ecus. The founders of the EMS believed that by promoting a wider use of the Ecu by the private sector and by central banks, pressure to move to stage three would rise. The development of the Ecu, therefore, became a major focus of the Committee for the Monetary Union. There was a simple reason for this: with the ink hardly dry on the SEA,[52] the prospect for a further amendment of the Treaty seemed remote. Meanwhile, the private sector had expressed its interest in the Ecu to exploit the full potential of the internal market. Significant weight was, therefore, given to the development of private-sector operations in a European currency. While the European Monetary Co-operation Fund, set up by the EMS, had never become more than a formality, and the official ECU had not really become the core of the system, the private Ecu had developed more rapidly than the founders of the EMS had expected. Partly, this reflected financial markets' need to hedge against exchange risk in Europe. Partly, it was the consequence of active involvement by public authorities. The French, Italian, and some other governments, and also the Commission and the European Investment Bank (EIB) had denominated large bond issues in Ecu. France, Italy, and Belgium allowed financial operations in Ecu, which were impossible in national currency, because of exchange controls. Even more important was probably the European Commission's decision to set up the Ecu Banking Association (EBA). The Commission had to make frequent payments in Ecu for which it required a clearing system as transfers in component currencies of the Ecu basket were cumbersome. There was a need to multilateralize the settlement of transactions and achieve cost savings. In 1981, Tommaso Padoa-Schioppa, as Director General of the DG II, invited five bankers from JP Morgan, Crédit Lyonnais, San Paolo di Torino, Kredietbanken, and Lloyds to set up a clearing system. The private banks turned to the Bank for International Settlements (BIS) in Basle for logistical support. A few months later, joined by fifteen other private banks and the EIB in Luxembourg, they set up the EBA in Paris whose primary objective was the clearing of Ecu payments. Dominique Rambure, first at Crédit Lyonnais, later San Paolo di Torino, became President and Gilbert Lichter General Secretary. The creation of this private Ecu payment system greatly facilitated the use and development of Ecu in the private sector.

Giscard and Schmidt thought that the private use of the Ecu could create a dynamic environment in support of EMU. A more widespread use of the Ecu by central banks and private actors could be a vehicle for financial integration. If the Ecu was widely used by companies, politicians would follow the market lead. Hence, a campaign should explain how companies could use it in their daily operations. But, in addition, political authorities had to get involved in the development of the Ecu, especially in order to remove administrative obstacles. Widespread use of the Ecu was proof that the European interior market required a European currency. The benefits that companies expected from the single market in terms of cost reductions, efficiency, and dynamism in international competition would not materialize unless they operated in a domestic space, similar to their American and Japanese competitors, that would express simultaneously economic and monetary union (CMUE 1988: 5).

These efforts were supported by the European Commission, who introduced modifications for the Ecu rise in the 1985 and 1987 reforms of the EMS. It tried several times to push member states to modify legislation to make the Ecu a recognized currency. In this they were successful in France, Belgium and Haly. But, the Bundesbank did not particularly welcome these proposals, having been hostile to the Ecu from the beginning. Germany was the only country in Europe where the private use of the Ecu was prohibited. The Central Bank argued that Ecu contracts were in fact indexed Deutschmark contracts and German law did not allow indexation. On a more profound level, the Bundesbank feared that a private mechanism for currency creation would reduce national monetary authorities' control of monetary aggregates. The Bundesbank was one of the two last major central banks in the world that framed monetary policy decision in terms of controlling money supply through aggregates like M3.[53] If an increasing number of residents held Ecu deposits, these aggregates would become meaningless. The increased use of the Ecu could undermine price stability and weaken public trust in the Deutschmark (Tietmeyer 1993). Recognizing this danger, the Giscard–Schmidt Committee suggested that the control of the Ecu supply should be ensured by an ECB: institutional progress should support the Ecu. In contrast to the later suggestions by the Delors Group, for the Giscard–Schmidt Committee setting up an ECB did not imply 'the realisation of all final objectives of economic and monetary union' (CMUE 1988: 13). Its functions resembled more what later became the European Monetary Institute (EMI): to guard price stability in the member states, and to contribute to the development of the Ecu. Thus, in addition to the wider use of the Ecu by national central banks, through a pooling of reserves, a narrowing of margins and interventions conducted in Ecu, the proposed ECB would have had some immediate functions (a common monetary discipline through reserve requirements) and some preparatory tasks for future developments, as later granted to the EMI. However, the CMUE insisted that such an ECB needed 'unquestionable characteristics of autonomy and independence with respect to governments and community authorities' (CMUE 1988: 13).

Yet, the Committee also found that the experience of the past ten years 'has taught us that it is difficult to reach political agreements of an ambitious scope and that international co-operation is not always perceived by all as a benefit in and of itself' (CMUE 1988: 13). As governments and central banks resisted giving up their power, market forces had to contribute to European unification. Companies should make broader use of the Ecu in financial reporting, finance, and commercial operations, if the Ecu was not to remain relegated to the interbank market as a mere financial innovation. A working group of the Committee developed the topic of European financial market integration, analysed the advantages in terms of efficiency and stability for markets and the intermediation process, and verified that the usefulness of a more extended use of Ecu in the markets would lead to the integration of financial structures in Europe. Finally, it called for instruments and institutional procedures for achieving the widespread use of the Ecu.

These proposals challenged German ordo-liberal convictions, as they transgressed the strict dividing line between the public and private sectors (Tietmeyer 1999: 22). Helmut Schmidt did not object to Giscard's agenda. While he put more weight on the need for policy co-operation and institutional changes in the functioning of the EMS, he pragmatically agreed with a market-led approach to EMU. He did not feel particularly constrained by the German consensus: after all, he was just a private citizen.[54] Even Bundesbank President Karl Otto Pöhl ducked the issue when he was invited to a Committee meeting in Bonn in March 1987. He simply emphasized that a new institutional framework was necessary in order to make significant progress with respect to the official Ecu. He saw a need for these reforms because of the 'over-determination' of a single market, which would work with free capital flows under the requirements of stable exchange rates and autonomous national monetary policies.[55] The German Finance Minister Gerhard Stoltenberg, who attended the meeting, insisted on the need to improve the convergence of economic policies when capital markets were liberalized. Only Wilfried Guth, Chairman of the Supervisory Board of Deutsche Bank, who supported Stoltenberg on capital liberalisation, warned the Committee not to focus too much on the development of the Ecu as this could lead to a rejection of monetary union within leading German business circles. Pierre Bérégovoy, the former French Socialist finance minister, turned the issue of public acceptance into a different direction: the main aim of a European currency needed to be stability of employment. This topic was not only to be a French pre-occupation even after EMU was formally established, but also remained on the Committee's and later the AMUE's agenda up to the start of EMU. Bérégovoy was later asked to investigate how the social partners could be involved in the CMUE dialogue. The Association produced studies and position papers, well before this topic had entered national debates.

At the press conference following this meeting, the Committee's Co-Presidents emphasized the need for action on three levels: political authorities had to press for European integration; central banks should develop the EMS; and the private sector should develop the European currency for the single market. While Stoltenberg called these actions 'long-term objectives', Schmidt was interested in what could be done *now*. During the deliberations of the Committee he had pencilled on his documents that pragmatic action was needed. He added a list of To dos: the United Kingdom would have to join the ERM or leave the Ecu basket; the lira had to narrow its intervention margin within the EMS from the 6 per cent band to 2.5 per cent; international capital flows must be fully liberalized, implying that the Bundesbank had to lift its prohibition on using the Ecu as a currency in Germany. Finally, financial transactions of the common agricultural policy should be switched to Ecu.

The lack of drama at the meeting of the Giscard–Schmidt Committee in Bonn is in many ways remarkable. Maybe Pöhl and Stoltenberg did not insist on German positions hostile to the Ecu and a parallel currency out of politeness.[56] After all, Schmidt and Giscard were respected elder statesmen. Or they thought this to be a private meeting without consequences. However, a consensus shared by the CMUE and German authorities emerged: stable exchange rates were necessary in a single market which required giving up national policy autonomy.

Padoa-Schioppa's inconsistent quartet was a shared cognitive foundation of the debate. The dissent was only about the methods to reach this objective.

Political authorities in Germany must have considered the promotion of the Ecu as something close to an aggression. In his book *The Road to European Monetary Union*, André Szász, a former influential official of the Dutch Central Bank, claims that France ('the Ecu's spiritual parent') had one central objective in promoting the Ecu: to shift the burden of economic adjustment from weak currency countries to the main creditor country, Germany (Szász 1999: chapter 9). Similar assessments can be found in other academic publications (e.g. Dyson and Featherstone 1999: 142; Howarth 2001) and indirectly in Bundesbank statements. It is a generally accepted proposition in Germany that French authorities sought wider public and private use of the Ecu as a parallel currency in order to decrease the dominance of the Deutschmark (also Ohr 1993). If that were true, or if it were the whole story, why would Helmut Schmidt lend support to this 'French' initiative by Giscard? Looking at their public statements and their archives, and confirmed by our interviews, a different picture emerges: Giscard and Schmidt pursued long-term strategic aims that relativized the short-termed considerations of monetary and financial experts. Their intention was to set France, Germany, and Europe on a convergence path to European unification, because they expected integration to yield substantial and procedural gains to all participants. By contrast, Central bankers and Treasury officials were concerned with their narrow policy responsibilities, which they judged in terms of competence and power and not of strategic interests. In order to fully understand this context, it is useful to recall how Germany had become the dominant monetary power in Europe.

Historic flashback: France, Germany, and the demise of Bretton Woods

When Europe emerged from the rubble of Second World War, a new economic consensus emerged. In 1944, the architects of the international monetary system of Bretton Woods were convinced that the 'free and flexible exchange rates' of the inter-war period were among the main culprits for the economic and political turmoil that ultimately led to Hitler and war. Jean Denizet recalls the Bretton Woods conference: 'All the delegates may not have been great economists, but they had all been in leadership positions in the 30's, they had all sifted through their memories during five years of war trying to understand: "Where did we go wrong? What were our biggest mistakes?" They had all reached the same conclusion: there had been a great many mistakes, starting with the 1919 Versailles treaty itself, but the central error had been the inability to restore a stable exchange rate system after the first world war. At the bottom of the whole economic disorder that brought Hitler to power, and thwarted any attempt at resistance, was an exchange rate problem' (Denizet 1989). The economic consequences of excessive nationalism and insufficient policy co-ordination were competitive devaluations in the 1920s and 1930s. By contrast, in the Golden Age of Bretton Woods (1944–73), exchange rates between the main industrial countries were 'fixed but adjustable' with respect to the US dollar, which was pegged against gold. National authorities declared a central rate against which they would buy and sell dollars, although they accepted fluctuation margins of ±1 per cent around the central parity. At these points, central banks had to intervene in the market and buy or sell in case of any excess demand for currency. The central rates could be changed only in case of a 'fundamental disequilibrium'. Since the ±1 per cent band around the dollar implied a maximum fluctuation of 4 per cent between any other two currencies, European countries limited their bands to ±0.75 against the dollar. As a consequence, companies doing business in Europe had a maximum currency risk of 3 per cent. Over the next quarter of the century, world trade expanded vigorously, inflation remained moderate, and the participating countries experienced economic growth and prosperity of unknown proportions (Bordo and Eichengreen 1993). The triptych of high investment, high exports, and considerable wage moderation can explain the exceptionally high economic growth in Europe (Crafts and Toniolo 1996). Low exchange-rate volatility in Europe, thanks to the Bretton Woods System, created security and, therefore, a greater willingness to invest in productive resources. Also, most European currencies were undervalued against the dollar, which increased the return on European investment (Collignon 2002: 9–16).

The Bretton Woods System came under pressure in the mid-1960s. The US expansionist monetary and budgetary policies during the Vietnam War were inconsistent with the dollar's role as the world's anchor currency. Given the relative inflexibility of the Bretton Woods System, these policies led to its destruction when the perceived incompatibility of different national policy stances gave rise to large speculative capital flows (James 1996: chapter 8). Not surprisingly, American economists lead by Milton Friedmann increasingly agreed that 'a greater degree of flexibility in exchange rates would be a desirable innovation' (Okun 1970: 15).[57] Practical men in Europe were confronted with high costs due to monetary volatility. Given the growing degree of European market integration they favoured exchange rate stability.[58]

From the mid-1960s onwards, inflationary pressures started to spread from the United States to Europe. The German Bundesbank raised interest rates, thereby attracting massive capital inflows. The under-valuation of the Deutschmark, coupled with insufficient domestic demand led to a fast expanding current account surplus which became quasi-endemic as German prices increased less than in most major trading partners. Thus, there were good arguments that the Deutschmark needed to be revalued and massive waves of speculative capital flooded the German capital market. In France, de Gaulle had defined monetary stability as a priority for the Fifth Republic when he came to power in 1957. However, in May 1968 he was forced to concede major wage increases at the *accords de Grenelle*, and the credibility of French financial solidity was shattered. The franc came under speculative attacks and was devalued by 11 per cent in August 1969 after de Gaulle had resigned. Meanwhile, capital inflows to Germany continued unabatedly. In September 1969, one day after Willy Brandt's Social Democrats had won the election, Germany first floated the Deutschmark and then fixed it against the dollar at DEM 3.66, an appreciation of 9.3 per cent.

Thus, within a few months, relative prices between Europe's two main trading partners had changed by over 20 per cent (James 1996: 193–7).

Among Europeans, a consensus emerged that monetary co-ordination was necessary to stabilize exchange rates. In February 1969, Raymond Barre, then Vice-President of the European Commission, presented a plan which was taken up by the Hague summit in December, where Brandt and Pompidou called for the creation of an economic and monetary union. The Luxembourg Prime Minister Pierre Werner was charged with presenting a report, in which he gave the blueprint for a single European currency. The Werner Report of 1970 had many similarities with the Delors Report two decades later, such as the idea of progressing in three stages and achieving a high degree of economic convergence. However, it was more ambitious postulating a 'single currency' and stressing the centralization of fiscal policy competencies (Dyson and Featherstone 1999: 290). These supranational ideas went far beyond what traditional Gaullists would accept (Howarth 2001: 46–50). They were born in a climate of crisis, but widespread consensus around the need for monetary union had not yet developed. Therefore, the political commitment was weak when the oil shock hit. Quite the opposite occurred after the EMS crisis in 1994, when the consensus about the need for monetary stability had strengthened.

Between 1968 and 1969, US banks had borrowed heavily from abroad. Short-term capital inflows amounted to US$ 11.8 billion. When US monetary conditions eased, the flow reversed. Between January and May 1970, US$ 9.6 billion were re-directed to Germany, but the German financial market was by far too small to absorb such expansion of liquidity. Otmar Emminger, at the time Vice-President of the Bundesbank, later said the 'Deutsche Mark was the epi-centre of the American currency quake' (quoted in James 1996: 214–5). The Bundesbank lowered interest rates in order to discourage speculative capital flows – again a remarkable difference to events in the 1990s, when Germany pursued high interest rate policies, causing significant problems for many European neighbours (Heisenberg 1999: 30).[59]

The cleanest solution to the currency problems would have been a devaluation of the dollar. Yet the Americans refused. 'The dollar is our currency and your problem' was the famous dictum by US Treasury Secretary John Connally. The German establishment was divided over how to deal with these capital inflows. Bundesbank President Karl Klasen was against floating the Deutschmark, saying that the 'Community needs fixed mutual exchange-rate relationships and would do so even if there were no common agricultural market' (quoted by Heisenberg 1999: 30). He recommended the imposition of capital controls. Klasen was supported by then Defence Minister Helmut Schmidt, one of the few trained economists in the government. The Bundesbank Vice-President Otmar Emminger led the second faction. He believed that floating the Deutschmark would give the German monetary authorities the autonomy to concentrate on domestic stability. Yet, in 1971, this 'Germany first' group did not yet have a majority in the Bundesbank central council. The Economics Minister Karl Schiller tried to find a middle way. Given that the dollar was the main problem and not the European currencies, why not have all EU currencies float jointly against the dollar? At an Ecofin meeting on 8 May 1971, under the chairmanship of Giscard d'Estaing, Schiller's request was rejected by France and Italy who were afraid that, by being linked to the strong Deutschmark, they would be pulled up into a large appreciation against the dollar.[60] Thus, two days later the Deutschmark was led to float alone. For the first time, Germany had asserted its priority of domestic stability over international regime arrangements. It was a major policy co-ordination failure from which Helmut Schmidt learned that monetary co-operation with France was central.[61]

Only three months later, President Richard Nixon suspended the convertibility of dollars into gold. The demise of the Bretton Woods System created new urgency for European monetary policy concentration. When even France became a target for speculative capital inflows from the United States, Paris was finally willing to join Germany in a floating currency bloc that consisted of the six original EC founders, soon joined by the British pound, Irish punt, the Danish, and even the Norwegian Krona. The European currency bloc was called 'the snake in the tunnel', after the Americans agreed in December 1971 to stabilize exchange-rate variations within a wider band of ±2.25 per cent. However, gold convertibility was not restored. US capital outflows did not stop. Bundesbank President Klasen sought to impose further capital controls against the opposition of Karl Schiller. When Chancellor Willy Brandt sided with the Bundesbank, Schiller resigned and Schmidt became his successor. He immediately checked with Giscard d'Estaing whether there was any willingness on the French side to have the snake float freely against the dollar. This was not the case. However, only nine months later renewed speculation and an unwillingness on the American side to honour their commitments led to the suspension of the tunnel in March 1973. The 'snake' was now 'in the lake' (Heisenberg 1999: 39) and a new international monetary regime began: bloc floating. Countries pegged to regional anchor currencies, which floated with flexible exchange rates (Collignon 1999a, 2002). Germany had become the dominant monetary power in Europe. Although financial markets pushed it into this position, the prime architect of the Deutschmark-bloc was Otmar Emminger, who succeeded twice in realising his own design against Helmut Schmidt's preferred options (Heisenberg 1999).[62]

The weaknesses of bloc floating

The original arrangements under the snake had several technical weaknesses, which made the system brittle, and led France and Italy to leave and rejoin the bloc several times.[63] First, the system worked *ad hoc*, without formal sanctions for non-intervention, or even consultations among members when parities were crossed. Second, weaker currency countries were disadvantaged because they had to use their own currency reserves, which were scarce and easily depleted. Third, the system worked asymmetrically. The weaker currencies had to intervene, even if the snake was pulled up by a strong currency. This was of particular chagrin to Giscard (Giscard d'Estaing 1988: 138). The search of greater *symmetry of obligations* in the system was at the core of French, but also Italian objectives in monetary co-operation. Giscard wanted Germany to shoulder some of the adjustment burden, and that should be perceived as a sign of European solidarity. He therefore wished to put the Ecu at the core of a new system as a reference unit, and as a symbol of mutual responsibility in economic management.[64]

The Germans, especially the Bundesbank, responded that economic discipline would reduce inflation and stabilize exchange rates. Although this became the dominant discourse in Europe until the start of EMU in 1999, not all partners agreed. Recent years had shown that currency crises were not only caused by 'fundamental disequilibria', such as inflation differentials, but were increasingly dependent on capital mobility and speculation by international investors. In the second half of the 1970s and early 1980s, capital flows exploded world-wide, as a consequence of the need to recycle petrodollars from the two oil shocks in 1973 and 1979 (Padoa-Schioppa and Saccomanni 1994). Second, although the objective of creating currency blocs was reducing risk and maximizing productive investment and growth (Collignon 1999a), a currency bloc predominantly benefited the anchor currency, here Germany. The periphery has to live with a deflationary bias.[65]

Furthermore, the larger the inflation differentials are within the bloc, the greater is the anchor currency's required appreciation against the floating world currencies. For example, in a rigid asymmetric EMS Italian inflation would cause a balance of payment surplus in Germany, requiring an appreciation of the Deutschmark with respect to the dollar. Greater symmetry in the functioning of the floating bloc would have mitigated these pressures. Such symmetry is what Giscard and Schmidt sought when they secretly planned the EMS. In the end, however, Emminger and the Bundesbank prevailed and the new EMS worked as a strengthened bloc-floating regime (Heisenberg 1999: 51).[66] It reinforced the deflationary pressures in the periphery that either required exit (a strategy refused by France in 1983, but unavoidable for Italy and the United Kingdom in 1992) or 'competitive deflation', as chosen by the Netherlands and France in the late 1980s and 1990s. Ultimately, only monetary union could overcome the dilemma of asymmetry. When Giscard and Schmidt met in 1986, they were aware that the present monetary system was not sustainable for long in a single market.

The Association for the Monetary Union of Europe (AMUE)

The need for dialogue with the private sector

By early 1987, the CMUE had chosen to complement the objective of institutional reform to create an EMU by a market driven path with the Ecu as a parallel currency. Consequently, it intended to foster operations in Ecu by European companies. It thus set up a CMUE working group on private Ecu development chaired by Etienne Davignon, a convinced European since he had met Paul Henri Spaak at the age of 13. After a diplomatic career, he had become European

Commissioner in charge of the single market, industrial policy, and trade in 1977 under Commission President Roy Jenkins. The Commission then was a rather isolated administration limiting its contact to the private sector, to industrial, and professional associations. Davignon considered these as hired officials, so he sought contact with the company bosses to learn what was needed in the creation of a single market.[67] In 1981, he brought together large European information technology firms to develop proposals for the technology programme and European technical norms. This was unusual, since business leaders usually talked to their governments but not to European Commissioners. François-Xavier Ortoli, who later succeeded Jenkins as President of the Commission, supported him in his innovative approach. In 1983, they helped to create the European Round Table of Industrialists[68] with Peer Gyllenhammar, Chief Executive Officer (CEO) of Volvo. Davignon's work for the single market was also supported by Wisse Dekker, chairman of Philips, who significantly contributed to the Commission white paper agenda of June 1985 that prepared the SEA (Moravcsik 1999: 355–8). Davignon left the Commission in 1985 and joined Société Générale de Belgique whose Chairman he became in 1988. His rich experience made Davignon the ideal choice to bridge policy and business interests in the Giscard–Schmidt Committee.

At a CMUE meeting in March 1987, Davignon reported the first findings of his working group, which had discovered close synergies between the private and official Ecu. In his own company, greater private use of Ecu could add up to 2.5 per cent to the profit margin through reductions in the cost of monetary management. However, private companies needed to be convinced of the political will to make the Ecu the European currency. Without a fixed timetable, businesses would not change their methods and practices. Davignon thus argued for explicit political commitments and an institutional backing for the Ecu. He anticipated the fundamental idea developed by the AMUE in its 1990 study *A Strategy for the Ecu*,[69] and even more importantly the core of the Maastricht scenario for achieving EMU.[70] However, time did not seem ripe for a political commitment, only a few months after the most recent European Union Treaty had been signed. Giscard pursued his idea of the tenaciously voluntaristic use of the Ecu in European companies, although he was aware of the difficulties.

Gathering support

To this end, Giscard had met with several European business leaders, such as Giovanni Agnelli, Chairman of Fiat, Cornelis van der Klugt, Chairman of Philips, Jacques Solvay, and Fejo Sickinghe to whom he was related, and also with François-Xavier Ortoli, who meanwhile had become Chairman of the French oil company Total. They were willing to give him support in assuring the Ecu's development. This led Giscard to suggest the foundation of an association to support the market-driven approach of the Giscard–Schmidt Committee. It should bring together important personalities from major companies and banks from throughout Europe. Giscard had prepared this idea well in advance and at the CMUE meeting in March 1987 he even suggested organizational details. In order to balance nationalities, he suggested the President should be Dutch and the Vice-President could be Italian, thinking of Cornelis van der Klugt, Chairman of Philips, and Giovanni Agnelli.

Van der Klugt himself had preferred Agnelli to become President, but the Fiat chairman did not feel comfortable in this role, although he had been a fervent European all his life. This was not only due to Fiat's important economic interests in the European market. The *Avvocato*, as he was widely called, was profoundly committed to the values and the cultural and political foundations, which provided the basis of European integration. In 1996, he re-edited a book written in 1918 by his own grandfather Giovanni Agnelli and Attilio Cabiati, one of Italy's foremost economist's at the time. In this book Agnelli and Cabiati had written: 'We unhesitatingly believe that there is only one way of ensuring that war will never break out in Europe again, a way which requires very careful consideration: the federation of the European states under a single ruling and governing body'. In 1996, the grandson reiterated the bold commitment: 'Eighty years on the topic of political union still remains the great unresolved issue for Europe, which has not yet been able to reach the same stage which it has achieved (despite all difficulties) on the question of economic union. Similarly, the strong and necessary connection and interdependence between European ideals, democracy and well-being continues to remain at the heart of the whole European project' (Agnelli and Cabiati 1996: xiii). Yet, despite these profound convictions, *l'avvocato* did not wish to be seen as the leader of the new Association. He felt that this role would carry greater credibility if the Association's president came from one of the smaller Northern European countries. He, therefore, suggested Cornelis van der Klugt as President. Van der Klugt finally accepted, partly because he thought that the new Association was in the interest of Philips. His company was suffering from the fragmented European market, and van der Klugt envied his Japanese competitors who operated in a large unified market. For him it was obvious that Europe needed a single currency in order to regain its industrial strength and dynamism.[71]

Giscard had also already identified a future general secretary of the Association: Bertrand de Maigret. They knew each other well.[72] De Maigret had the profile of a political entrepreneur. He had worked in technical co-operation and development first in the Caribbean, and later with Christiane Scrivener at a governmental association in Paris. In 1968, he joined Chase Manhattan Bank in Paris but became gradually more involved in politics. He was elected to the Paris City Council in 1970, serving as one of four Vice-Presidents of Paris in the mid-1970s. When Giscard ran for President in 1974, de Maigret organized the National Support Committee for his campaign. After the election, de Maigret continued to support him as President of the National Committee in Support of the President of the Republic until he was himself elected a member of the Assemblée Nationale for La Sarthe in 1977. He had run a hotly contested campaign using the commercial marketing techniques he had learned at the business school HEC. In Parliament he served as a member of the foreign policy commission and the finance commission, but in 1981, when Mitterrand's *vague rose* swept to power, de Maigret lost his seat by 200 votes. He returned to the private sector as financial director working successively for two large French companies. When Giscard asked him in 1987 to build up a club of European businessmen to support the CMUE, de Maigret was ready for a new challenge. He liked the idea of working for Europe's unification with major business leaders. His father and two of his uncles had been killed during the war and he felt strongly that European integration was the foundation of peace. So he said 'yes'.

At the end of April 1987, de Maigret discussed the brief of what was to become the Association for the Monetary Union of Europe[73] with François-Xavier Ortoli. Ortoli was a convinced European, who had graduated from the Ecole Nationale d'Administration as *inspecteur de finances* three years before Giscard d'Estaing. Ortoli then worked closely with Bernard Clappier during the creation of the common market and the Treaty of Rome. He attended the first meeting of the European Commission on 7 January 1958 under the Presidency of Walter Hallstein and became Director-General of the internal market in Brussels at the age of 33. Later he worked as *Directeur de cabinet* for Georges Pompidou and became French Finance Minister (1968–69). In the 1970s, he returned to Brussels first as President of the European Commission (1973–77) and then as Vice-President until 1984. All his life he worked closely with the private sector in Europe and abroad. In 1984, he became Chairman of Total Compagnie Française des Pétroles and President of the French employers' federation CNPF International in 1989. Although not a formal member of the Giscard–Schmidt Committee, Ortoli was in contact with Giscard d'Estaing and Davignon. Ortoli's motivation to get involved in a business group to support European monetary union was his life-long commitment to European unification. Total, his company, was much more dollar-oriented, given its oil interests, but Ortoli was convinced that the single market needed a single currency. He agreed to serve as Treasurer of the Association. He insisted that the Association had to represent business leaders from each country of the EC in order to carry weight with public opinion and policy makers. The mission was clear: to find an industrial equivalent to the political weight of the Giscard–Schmidt Committee. This meant developing contacts with large European companies and arguments that fitted into their business strategy. They turned to their friends all over Europe to enlist support.

By the end of May, a few weeks before the next CMUE meeting in Brussels, Valéry Giscard d'Estaing received Giovanni Agnelli, the President of Fiat, Cornelis van der Klugt, President of Philips, Jean-Réné Fourtou, the new President of Rhône-Poulenc, François-Xavier Ortoli and Paul Mentré together with Bertrand de Maigret for a lunch at his private home at 11, rue de Benouville in Paris's prestigious sixteenth arrondissement. In the aristocratic environment covered by paintings and historic memorabilia and with a beautiful view onto the garden, Giscard explained to his guests the idea of building up a group of influential European entrepreneurs who could push political leaders towards completing Monetary Union. He and Schmidt had created the EMS to provide monetary stability for Europe. But with the single market arriving in 1992, it was important to go a decisive step further. The Ecu had already become a European currency in financial markets and they as business leaders with pan-European interests could develop its use within their own companies. This would help politicians to push for institutional changes.

Giscard's guests felt honoured by the invitation. They agreed with the founders of the EMS that they had to do something in order to overcome 'Eurosclerosis'.[74] But they did not see clearly what to do with his idea, so they asked de Maigret to set up a programme and check the legalities of setting up an association. While de Maigret was working along these lines, Cornelis van der Klugt met separately with Agnelli and two other business leaders in Eindhoven in August without informing de Maigret. The Philips Chairman was still hesitating to commit to the new project. He was careful to keep his autonomy with respect to Europe's two elder statesmen and did not want to be seen as the financial supporter of any political movement or party. After he received de Maigret's initial projects in the summer, it took him two or three months until he finally responded favourably. On 6 October 1987, the formal founding meeting of the Association for the Monetary Union of Europe (AMUE) took place in Agnelli's office in the via Marconi in Turin.

Giscard d'Estaing announced the idea of a new Association to the CMUE meeting on 15 June 1987.[75] Agnelli promised to enlist the support of European employers' associations and to look for initiatives to support the link between monetary integration and the single market. However, van der Klugt was still careful to keep some autonomy. He declared that it was not the task of companies to assume the role of governments when supporting the realization of the European idea. Giscard welcomed the commitment by these leading European businessmen in view of the intensifying competition between American, Japanese, and European companies and said he hoped the Association would contribute to increased awareness in economic and financial quarters of the activities of the CMUE. Governments would much more readily act when they heard from the leaders of large European enterprises that a European currency was a necessity. Thus, the Committee accepted the AMUE as an integral support to its own program for action.

Structures and objectives

The Association was organized according to a simple principle. Bertrand de Maigret was Secretary-General, with a small secretariat in Paris. The essential decision-making power would remain with the Board of Directors, consisting of leading industrialists from each country of the EU. A personal Sherpa, a member of their company with direct access to the CEO, would liase between the Paris office and the Directors. Former President Giscard d'Estaing and Chancellor Helmut Schmidt were invited as members of the Board *ex officio*, but would send their representatives Paul Mentré and Uwe Plachetka, respectively, to represent them.

The first objective of the newly founded Association was to find European companies as active members for the Association. Initially, the Board consisted of Cornelis van der Klugt as President, Giovanni Agnelli as Vice-President, and François-Xavier Ortoli as Treasurer. Hans Merkle of Robert Bosch AG had joined at the request of Helmut Schmidt, just like Wilfried Guth, the chairman of the supervisory board of Deutsche Bank. Jacques Solvay agreed to represent Belgium.[76] Later, the AMUE had at least one, for larger countries often two, Board members for each member state of the EU.[77] At its first meeting, the Board established a general guideline to keep the industrial companies as the leading authority in the Association. It was thought that the single market required the active involvement of companies, while banks would be more inclined to benefit from the monetary disorder of flexible exchange rates. The new Board members were hands on: Van der Klugt and Agnelli agreed to write the manifesto of the Association and Ortoli a letter to potential new members, while de Maigret would create a brochure explaining the purpose of the Association.

De Maigret set himself three tasks. First, he looked at means to promote the use of the Ecu as an expression of companies' interest in the development of the European currency. Documents on the use of the Ecu were prepared, reinforced by arguments on the necessity of monetary stability in Europe and its impact on the overall stability of companies. A brochure, 'The Ecu for enterprises', was developed by the accountancy firm Touche Ross. An opinion survey, co-financed by the Commission and the Ecu Banking Association, found out what companies thought about the Ecu. Direct marketing actions were envisaged with mailings signed by CEOs of major companies. Members of the Association should participate in public meetings, TV, and radio programmes. It was envisaged to sponsor high-visibility events such as European football championships, student associations, or seminars for the business community. Even advertising gadgets were considered to be useful for the promotion of the Ecu.

Second, membership was developed in different countries and links were established with national and European decision-makers. In the first year after its foundation, the Association had gained 16 members in Belgium, 26 in France, 20 in Greece, 31 in Italy, 33 in the Netherlands, 15 in Spain but only 1 member each in Luxembourg, the United Kingdom and Germany (see Figure 2.1). This uneven distribution reflected both the personal credibility of the individual entrepreneurs and the general receptiveness to the idea of EMU in their country. When Giovanni Agnelli in Italy or Carlos March in Spain and later Belmiro de Azevedo in Portugal asked colleagues to join the Association, no one dared to stay on the fence. In Germany and the United Kingdom, the political environment was more complicated. In early 1989, Hans Merkle won over Daimler Benz and the three large German private banks Deutsche, Dresdner, and Commerzbank. However, his efforts with Bertelsmann and Siemens were at first not successful. Membership only started to take off in summer 1992, after Hans Merkle invited a distinguished group of German industrialists to a dinner at Schloss Kronberg, outside Frankfurt. It was attended by Giscard d'Estaing, Hermann J. Abs, the legendary old man of Deutsche Bank, and Chancellor Helmut Kohl as the main speaker. The majority of the German entrepreneurs present received Kohl's pro-European creed with barely disguised hostility. However, Hans Merkle with the help of Hilmar Kopper, the chairman of Deutsche Bank, subsequently recruited a critical mass of German companies for AMUE.

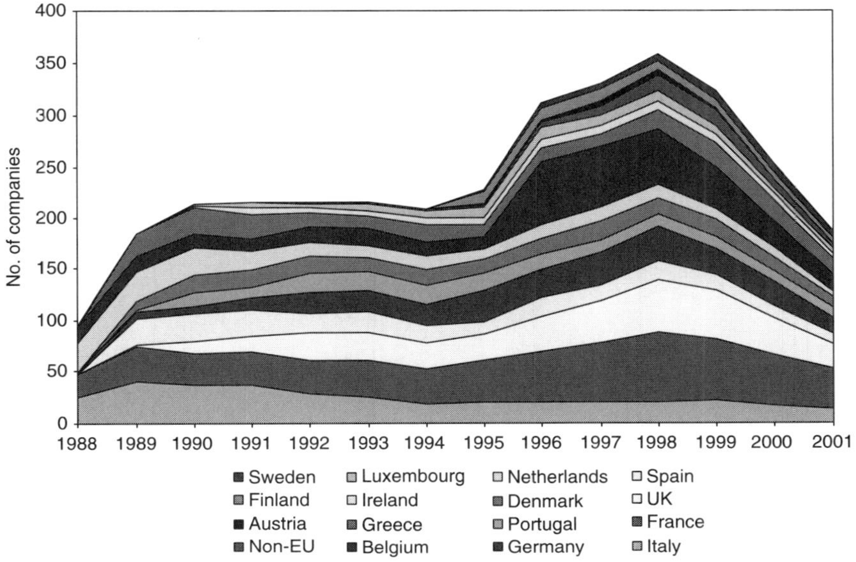

Figure 2.1 Membership in the AMUE.

In the United Kingdom, Patrick Sheehy, Chairman of British American Tobacco (BAT) Industries, was enthusiastic about the Association, yet he was compelled to act with supreme caution. Sheehy had been active in the European Round Table of Industrialists. During those years, BAT was commercially engaged in retailing, cosmetics, paper and packaging, tobacco, and financial services. Hence, the completion of the single market was of crucial strategic interest. Sheehy was well aware of the need for monetary stability in the single market and, therefore, asked his Deputy, Sir Brian Garraway, to represent him on the Board of AMUE. But given the Thatcher government's increasing opposition towards monetary integration, he found it difficult to motivate other British companies to join the Association. High respect for the prime minister seemed to preclude high respect for European integration beyond the creation of the single market. Nevertheless, with de Maigret's help the Association was able to organize a seminar on the Ecu with the Confederation of British Industry (CBI). Progress with membership only came after the United Kingdom had joined the ERM and the idea of EMU started to become credible in 1990. The increased membership seemed not only to reflect a commitment to EMU, but at least for some, simply the need to be aware what was going on in Europe.[78] The British members were unique in that they organized as a club that met once a month to discuss EMU-related issues.

The third line was to deepen the understanding and knowledge on the Ecu and to work out a general philosophy for companies' attitude towards monetary integration. In the beginning, the intellectual work of the Association was to a large degree dependent on the work of the Giscard–Schmidt Committee. It fully accepted the market-led approach to EMU. By promoting the use of the Ecu in European companies, they thought they would pave the way for a European currency. Yet things proved to be more complex. By asking companies to support their project, Giscard and Schmidt had uncorked the bottle. Once the genies were out, they soon had their own agenda.

3 A common or a single currency?

The market-driven approach to EMU had seemed a neat strategy to bring Europe closer to monetary union without needing a prior top-level political commitment. However, the promotion of the Ecu reached its limit – and the strategy developed by the Giscard–Schmidt Committee turned out to have less impact than hoped for. As soon as monetary stabilisation spread, the Ecu's main advantage of risk reduction diminished. It became clear that companies needed a single, not a supplementary currency to fully profit from the single market.

Despite its limits the market-driven approach to EMU had triggered a political process, which led to the Delors Report on EMU. In close co-operation with European central bankers, the Commission President suggested an institutional approach to EMU, including the creation of a European Central Bank. But the report hesitated on linking it explicitly to a single currency. The input and support of the private sector remained crucial in putting the single currency on the Maastricht agenda.

Hopes and doubts about the Ecu

Bertrand de Maigret was furious. He was trying to win over a leading French consultancy firm, Bossard Consultant, as a partner to set up training seminars on the use of the Ecu for the middle management of large companies. At the meeting in May 1989 with Bossard, his new colleague, Stefan Collignon, asked critical questions about the purpose of the Ecu-promotion programme that implicitly put the whole project into question. 'If you do this again', he fumed afterwards, 'there is no point in your working for this Association'.

Business and the Ecu

De Maigret was convinced that the use of the Ecu should be promoted as strongly as possible. Market research had shown that a vast majority of business leaders desired a common currency as a complement to the single market.[1] Eighty-six per cent of all respondents, 60 per cent in Germany, 79 per cent in the United Kingdom and 98 per cent in Italy favoured stable exchange rates, leading to lower cost and risk in currency management and supported the idea of using money as a vehicle to Europe's unification. The credibility of a big internal market seemed to be in question, as long as no common currency ensured its coherence and irreversibility. However, the Ecu was insufficiently known: Ten years after its creation, only 5 per cent of all business leaders responded that they knew the Ecu very well and 30 per cent rather well. While 47 per cent of businesses had already used it in Italy, only 5 per cent in the Netherlands and the United Kingdom had done so. For many, the Deutschmark seemed more competitive, especially for treasury operations in foreign currency. The poll revealed the reasons: the weight of old habits, the absence of an ECB, and insecurity about the future institutional environment. In view of the enormous public relation activities that followed ten years later for the introduction of the euro, it is interesting that 84 per cent of business leaders requested better information about the use of the Ecu and 75 per cent thought that their bank was in the best position to provide it. The Gallup study concluded that 'a vast information effort and clear public support would lead to a vigorous development of the private use of the Ecu'.

This seemed to confirm the market-led approach to EMU developed by the Giscard–Schmidt Committee.[2] If companies used the Ecu to save money, it would send a clear message not only to policy makers, but also to the public in general. The AMUE shared the consensus that the Ecu should be pushed. Despite significant reluctance in Germany and the Netherlands, they believed in the power of practical activities to demonstrate the private sector's commitment to a European currency. They cared little about the bitter political conflicts between central banks and finance ministries over the Ecu issue.

De Maigret knew that some Germans hoped the Deutschmark would become the European currency. Even outside Germany, some journalists and academics argued that the most direct way to get to a European currency was to Europeanize an existing national currency. For example, Richard Cooper, Professor at Harvard University and a former chairman of the Federal Reserve Bank of Boston, had first nominated the British pound sterling for this role because of the highly developed financial market in London. He later switched allegiance to the Deutschmark for reasons of credibility (Cooper 1994). However, this would not have been politically acceptable within the European Community. A European currency had to be politically neutral and the Ecu as a currency basket was exactly that.

Thus, the Association chose the Ecu as its battlefield. It started to report successful experiences by companies in its newsletter *Ecu for European Business*. In its first issue in 1989, Alcatel N.V. reported that the Ecu was its 'European weapon'. As allowed by Dutch law, the company published and reported all its results and pre-tax annual result in Ecu, without having to convert it back into guilders. Alcatel also made short-term investments by buying Ecu-denominated commercial paper from banks and was the only firm of such a size, which used the Ecu for all management purposes. A few months later, Saint-Gobain's 'attitude of bold confidence vis-à-vis the Ecu' was described. Club Méditerranée considered 'the Ecu as an "ordinary currency" which may present some opportunities on occasion'. And when three leading European food distributors concluded a 'European Retail Alliance', they chose the Ecu as the unit of account for the deal.

It was also possible to denominate payments by VISA, American Express, and Diners in Ecu even in retailing (see *Ecu for European Business*, No. 3, January 1990).

Educating the private sector

However, these were examples of avant garde innovators. The majority of the companies remained ignorant about how the Ecu could be used profitably. In 1989, the Association had published *A Guide to the Ecu* together with the consulting firm Touche Ross, which was translated into six languages and distributed to more than 400,000 businesses within a year. It sought to clarify what the Ecu was and how it could be applied usefully in the different functions of European companies. The European Commission services supported this project. Especially the head of the Ecu unit, Thierry Vissol, was an eager advocate of Ecu promotion as he considered its market success a key for its political success.[3] The guide book was the first of many projects[4] where the Association functioned as an intermediary between the Commission and public opinion, or more precisely the business sector in Europe.[5]

The next step was to train business people in seminars and put together a training manual. The consulting firm Bossard Consultants decided to support the AMUE, which was working with a staff of only five people. Bossard had a commercial interest in access to leading European companies. The European single market was to be completed in 1992 and Bossard's partners saw the opportunity to establish themselves as a European consulting firm. Smaller and larger companies had very different information needs. Large groups had gained experience with the Ecu and were interested in practical and technical details. General issues, such as 'the Ecu as a price stabilizing factor', 'development prospects of the Ecu', or 'the advantages of a common currency for business', found greatest interest among smaller companies. As these activities were at first centered on France, de Maigret looked for someone to promote the Ecu in Germany and the United Kingdom. As a former businessman, Collignon had the right profile.[6] In addition, he could complement de Maigret's own political affiliation with Giscard d'Estaing, as he was a Social Democrat close to Helmut Schmidt.

First scepticism towards the Ecu

While the Association sped up its efforts to promote the Ecu as strongly as possible in co-operation with various business partners, first signals arose that the strategy was reaching its limits. Dialogue with the AMUE member companies gradually showed that simply promoting the Ecu was not enough, as it did not fully solve their practical problems.

In financial markets, the Ecu had proved to be a simple and efficient hedging tool against exchange rate volatility between European currencies, which created uncertainty for investors. Also, the returns for Ecu bonds were significantly more stable than for Deutschmark, French franc, or Sterling bonds. As interest rates in the twelve EU member states did not move in tandem – in fact sometimes they were moving in opposite directions – interest rates on Ecu instruments, reflecting the average of the currency basket, were less volatile.[7]

A similar argument could be made for commercial transactions. If companies operating in the European market denominated their sales contracts in Ecu, they could reduce their average exchange risk, could save costs of hedging and multi-currency management and stabilize income. However, the risk-reducing impact of the Ecu basket disappeared in the second half of the 1980s. Inflation had come down everywhere in Europe and with it exchange rate volatility. By aligning monetary policy to the Bundesbank, interest rate movements started to converge. The potential savings in hedging costs from using the Ecu became less important, while the *transaction cost* argument gained weight. As most large European companies had a strong production base in their home state, they needed to convert their net Ecu receipts into national currencies in order to pay suppliers, wages, and taxes. Club Méditerranée would have liked a common currency for all European operations as this would have facilitated the financial management of the different holiday clubs all over Europe. For them, the Ecu as a thirteenth currency did not simplify anything. To use it in the holiday villages, clients would have had to change their national currency into the Ecu, while the Club then had to change them back into the national currency for local purchases at the camp locations. This would have caused a duplication of transaction costs and made the Ecu more costly than simply going from one national currency to another. Only a single currency would bring real benefit.[8] When using the Ecu as a common currency, the savings gained from reducing exchange rate volatility therefore had to outweigh the transaction costs in order to make the Ecu commercially attractive (see also Lomax 1991).

Hans Merkle's Sherpa Adolf Ahnefeld found out in an in-house workshop in July 1989 that the demand for Ecu in Robert Bosch AG's commercial transactions had decreased since the mid-1980s as a result of greater currency stability in Europe. Bosch encountered no difficulties invoicing in Deutschmarks. Although Bosch's share of foreign markets in total sales was more than 50 per cent, up to 80 per cent of production originated within Germany and three thirds of their sub-contractors and suppliers resided in the Federal Republic. The need for greater use of Ecu would only have arisen if Bosch had diversified significantly into European production sites outside Germany. Although Robert Bosch AG had recently made a major investment in the United Kingdom, the overall impact on the company was still relatively small. The Ecu so far was only one *additional* currency and not a substitute currency. Ahnefeld, therefore, wrote to the Association in Paris: 'A eurogesture of introducing Ecu would lead to greater costs, and is hardly justified'.

Deutsche Bank was pessimistic about promoting the Ecu for different reasons. What mattered in achieving EMU was the irrevocable fixing of exchange rates and the free and unrestricted flow of capital within the single monetary area. An economic and cultural revolution as the prerequisite for a stable monetary union was required, not a parallel currency. Germans would only assent to giving up the

Deutschmark if the new European currency would be at least as stable in terms of inflation as its predecessor. Therefore, the Association should focus on the promotion of price stability and the creation of an independent European central bank rather than promoting the Ecu. From a German point of view, the AMUE's role was to foster a European stability consensus.

There were exceptions, but they remained limited niches. If there was a need for settlement in a common currency between large companies, which operated a clearing-house arrangement, the Ecu was suitable. For example Fiat, the Italian car company, settled all its intra-group accounts in Ecu. As a rule, the Ecu was most widely used by companies in countries with weak currencies who wanted to protect the value of their short-term financial assets. Sometimes, it also was possible to take the Ecu as a compromise currency for contracts between companies in strong and weak currency countries. In these cases the risk was equally shared between appreciating and depreciating currencies. Despite this interest in the Ecu as a store of value, the currency basket had very little use as a means of transaction.

The need for a political approach

The fact that the 'risk reducing' argument was disappearing, while the 'transaction cost' argument gained prominence had important consequences for the Ecu strategy in the transition to full EMU. If transaction cost obstacles persisted even in a monetary union with permanently locked exchange rates, common market-forces would not replace national currencies by the thirteenth currency spontaneously. Transaction costs would maintain a barrier to the perfect flow of goods and capital within the single market. The real breakthrough consequently required two things: a political decision to create a *single* currency and an institution to manage it. Therefore, the Association needed to support the political approach to EMU that the Delors Report had traced out. The market-led approach proposed by the Giscard–Schmidt Committee was suited to expressing the private sector's interest in exchange rate stability and in a European currency. It assigned a transitional role to the Ecu: the 'basket Ecu' had to serve as the precursor of the 'Ecu single currency'. Promoting the Ecu as a forerunner to the single currency made sense. Developing it into a parallel currency did not. When Collignon attended the meeting with de Maigret and Bossard Consultants, he shared the insights gained from his discussions with AMUE member companies and expressed doubts about the attractiveness of a promotional programme on the commercial aspects of the Ecu. Would companies really send middle management for training on Ecu-issues and pay a fee for seminars? His view, however, conflicted with the marketing study, which documented private sector interest. Bossard was committing a significant amount of money to the programme. Most importantly, the perspective of a political approach to EMU seeming so far away, the AMUE at least wanted to do something practical to push for monetary integration. So it stuck to the project and in summer 1989, they all worked feverishly on a training manual for a series of seminars.

Delors' ambivalence

New stability in the EMS

Since the Giscard–Schmidt CMUE had started its work in 1986, significant progress to EMU had been achieved at the political level. The last realignment in the EMS had taken place in January 1987, expressing a new logic resulting from increased capital mobility. While previous adjustments in exchange rates used to correct fundamental distortions caused by inflation differentials, the 1987 crisis was prompted by speculative unrest in currency markets linked to the dollar's weakness (Collignon 1994: 35). In this respect, the crisis resembled the difficulties experienced in the early 1970s, but in the meantime international capital markets had grown to stupefying proportions. The stock of international loans to non-banks rose from US$ 175 billion at the end of 1973 [5 per cent of industrial countries' Gross National Product (GNP)] to US$ 2,365 billion in 1987 and to US$ 3,660 billion by 1992, representing 25 per cent of the industrial countries' GNP. The volume of international equity transactions grew by 18 per cent per annum between 1979 and 1988, reaching US$ 1,200 billion in 1988 (Collignon 1994a: 106).

In January 1987, the Bundesbank had to spend up to US$ 10 billion to support the French franc, although there was no fundamental disequilibrium. It became clear that better co-ordination of monetary policies, in particular with regard to interest rates, was required. This led to the so-called Basle–Nyborg agreement in September 1987, which strengthened the exchange-rate mechanism in the system and laid the foundation for a five-year period of stability.

Economic reasons for monetary integration

The EMS crisis of January 1987 coincided with the deliberations of a small group of economists, led by Tommaso Padoa-Schioppa, who had been asked by Commission President Jacques Delors to investigate the economic consequences of the Community enlargement to Spain and Portugal and the creation of a single market. Padoa-Schioppa was influenced by Richard Musgrave's works on public finance, which had become standard economic theory in the 1960s. It distinguished between the allocative function (efficiency), the stabilization function and the distributive function (equity) of government action. The efficiency issue was now tackled by the single market, the equity dimension by the debate (and final resolution in 1988) on the European Community's structural funds. The stability issue related to exchange rate management and hence the EMS. Padoa-Schioppa's Report was published in April 1987 under the title *Efficiency, Stability and Equity. A Strategy for the Evolution of the Economic System of the European Community*. As regards monetary stability, the report coined the notion of an 'inconsistent quartet'[9] which required further progress in monetary integration. It started unambiguously: 'The elimination of capital controls, coupled to the requirement of exchange rate stability, [...] will require moving closer to unification of monetary policy. In a quite fundamental way, capital mobility and exchange rate fixity together leave no room for independent monetary policies. In these conditions, it is pertinent to consider afresh the case for a strengthened organization of monetary co-ordination or institutional advances in this field' (Padoa-Schioppa *et al.* 1987: 5). Originally, Padoa-Schioppa's intentions went further. He had wished to put the objective of the EMU prominently into the centre of the report, but he was opposed by Mervyn King, at the time professor at the London School of Economics. However, the report was crucial in convincing Delors in 1988 that he had to tackle monetary issues during his presidency.[10] The report also did not go unnoticed by Giscard and Schmidt who invited Padoa-Schioppa to present his findings at a CMUE meeting at Val Duchesse.[11]

Balladur's and Genscher's memorandum

A political impulse came from the Balladur memorandum in December 1987, where the French finance minister raised the question of creating 'a zone with a single currency'. The German foreign minister Hans-Dietrich Genscher, who issued his own memorandum on 8 January 1988, favourably received this proposition. Both men had important domestic reasons for their initiatives to re-ignite EMU, but the work of the CMUE was an important catalyst. Dyson and Featherstone report that at the time Giscard was lobbying Balladur and saw Delors regularly. The CMUE had a direct influence via the *Tresor* and indirect impact via political rivalry between Giscard's centrist UDF and Balladur's Gaullist Rassemblement pour la République (RPR) on the Balladur Memorandum. It echoed most of the issues discussed by the group. Chancellor Kohl was initially reluctant to follow Genscher, but had been alerted by the fact that leading German bankers, Walter Seipp, chairman of Commerzbank, and Alfred Herrhausen of Deutsche Bank had called for the creation of an ECB 'as soon as possible' (Dyson and Featherstone 1999: 711). In addition, Genscher drew Kohl's attention to the positive climate being generated by the work of the new Giscard–Schmidt CMUE. By playing up Schmidt's public profile on the EMU, he was in effect inviting Kohl to outflank his predecessor with whose strong leadership qualities he was often disparagingly compared.

Balladur's and Genscher's initiatives were all the more powerful as Germany assumed the EC presidency in the first semester of 1988 and Kohl needed a success. It came at the Hannover European Council in June 1988, which was one of the most decisive events in the long march to European monetary union. Commission President Jaques Delors was given the mandate to convene a committee and prepare a report on how to reach monetary union. The idea to appoint Delors as chairman of this Committee had originally come from Giscard d'Estaing and Schmidt,[12] to the great surprise of Bundesbank President Karl Otto Pöhl, who feared this to be an intrigue to undermine German monetary policy.[13] The secret architects behind the scenes were Pascal Lamy, Delors' chef de cabinet and Joachim Bitterlich, Kohl's chief advisor.[14] The Delors Committee put monetary union back on the agenda – for the first time since the Werner

Report in 1970. It consisted mainly of central bankers, but also of two members of the Giscard–Schmidt Committee, Miguel Boyer, and Niels Thygesen. After some tractations, Padoa-Schioppa became rapporteur with Gunter Baer from the Bundesbank as his *Aufpasser*.[15]

The Delors Report

Delors submitted his report to the Council of Economic and Finance Ministers in April 1989. It was a milestone on the way to EMU and laid the foundations for the Maastricht Treaty. Delors had been able to avoid the pitfalls of discussing *whether* EMU was desirable – an approach that had already proved successful when Paul-Henri Spaak chaired the Messina Conference leading to the Treaty of Rome and the Common Market in the 1950s. The Committee focused on *how* EMU could be achieved and proposed a blueprint for an *institutional route* to EMU. It was based on four ideas: insistence on price stability, independence of the ECB, convergence of the economies before merging the currencies, and a transition period in three stages. The impact of the Delors Report, however, cannot exclusively be explained by the foresight in the content. What also mattered was the societal and political role of the Committees members. Central bankers usually have a high degree of credibility – especially in countries like Germany and the Netherlands where the institution had a technical-expert-renomme rather than a politicized nature. In the terms of our consensus model this means that they commanded high respect in their national constituencies and could thus play an influential role in the consensus building process. As Marcussen (2000: 98) points out, this role even strengthened in periods in which policy makers were searching for ways to conceptualize economic reality. These periods constitute a window of opportunity to promote views on widely believed macroeconomic cause–effect relationships – such as the idea of a stability-oriented monetary policy. Marcussen also emphasizes, that the central bankers had already prepared the way for their ideas to be accepted as they had been pushing central bank ideas at the end of the 1970s and during the 1980s.

The report picked up on Padoa-Schioppa's idea of an 'inconsistent quartet' as the fundamental rationale for EMU: with full freedom of capital movements and integrated financial markets, incompatible national policies resulting in different inflation rates would quickly translate into exchange rate tensions and put an increasing and undue burden on monetary policy. Particular emphasis was given to the fact that the single market would increase economic interdependence which would reduce the room for independent policy manoeuvre and amplify the cross-border effects of developments originating in each member country.

A large part of the report focused on the need for economic convergence and on institutional arrangements. On convergence it said: 'Despite a marked downward trend in the average rate of price and wage inflation, considerable national differences remain. There are also still notable divergences in budgetary positions and external imbalances have become markedly greater in the recent past. […] there are areas where economic performances will have to be made more convergent'.[16] Institutionally, the Delors Committee realized that economic and monetary union implied 'far more than the single market programme' which had basically been implemented through directives that harmonized standards, and established 'mutual recognition'. The EMU required an ECB, as the need for much more binding procedures was particularly far-reaching in the field of monetary policy. The German insistence on a strong institutional commitment was in line with the general European consensus on rule-based integration, discussed in Chapter 1. Amongst other reasons this helps to explain why EMU was in the end accepted by most member states, but not by the Tory government in the United Kingdom.

An independent European Central Bank

Delors had accomplished a major achievement by creating a unanimous consensus behind the principle of an *independent* ECB with the aim of maintaining price stability. For years, the Bundesbank had insisted on the *need for a single monetary policy* once exchange rates had been permanently locked (Padoa-Schioppa 2000b: 170). It has often been affirmed that Delors and the Committee 'accommodated' the demands of the Bundesbank in order to obtain agreement. Yet, Bundesbank President Karl Otto Pöhl was concerned about the relatively high degree of dissent in the Committee that was reflected in papers on parallel currencies, the role of the Ecu and the institutional arrangements for the transition.[17] Nevertheless, according to one member all central bankers were convinced that a European monetary union would only work if there was a centralized monetary policy and an independent central bank to run it.[18] Most of them indeed seemed to agree professionally that one had to centralize decisions on the supply of money and credit as well as on other instruments of monetary policy, including interest rates, in order to maintain price stability, and these decisions had to be taken free from external pressures. However, institutional dynamics had kept many of them from saying so, as – in EMU – this would mean reducing their own power. In the Delors Committee they acted in a personal capacity and that allowed them to express an unmitigated preference for central bank independence.[19] However, political authorities outside of Germany and the Netherlands had not yet overtly accepted this view. Marcussen (2000), however, points out that the consensus among central bankers was already rather stable when they entered the Committee. He even goes as far as saying that the governments who sent the bankers to the Committee were aware of this fact, and thus, had clear expectations about the recommendations in the report. In Italy, Banca d'Italia became de facto increasingly more independent under Carlo Azeglio Ciampi, while the credibility of government was seriously undermined by *partitocrazia*. In France, the acceptance of central bank independence was more ambiguous. While Mitterrand gave tacit support to Banque de France Governor Jacques de Larosière's ideas of an independent ECB in the Delors Committee, the *Tresor* and Finance minister Pierre Bérégovoy were less inclined to such developments.[20] At the political right, and especially amongst Gaullists, the *Etatiste* attitudes of French elites dominated, who wanted to keep control over money as an instrument for their policy objectives. The Prime Ministers Edouard Balladur and Alain Juppé resisted central bank 'independence' and favoured 'autonomy' until the very end when the statutes of the Banque de France were changed under the pressure of the EMS-crisis.[21] This political environment largely explains why Giscard d'Estaing emphasized softer forms of monetary integration in the 1980s, such as the EMF suggested by the CMUE, or the pooling of reserves, previously proposed by Jean Monnet and Robert Triffin.

By accommodating the demands of the central bankers, Delors managed to tie Germany into the political consensus for building EMU. There has been speculation whether the Bundesbank took a particularly uncompromising stance in order to deter others from EMU. In its annual report for 1989, the German central bank had set the mark: 'Stringent demands in terms of stabilisation policy must be met by any European central banking system. It is only on this condition that it would be acceptable for EC member states with stable currencies to relinquish their national monetary policy sovereignty. One major requirement would be that the guidelines on monetary policy are unequivocally geared, at Community level, with binding effect for the entire currency area, to the priority of the target of price stability'. Heisenberg (1999: 110–11) claims that Bundesbank President Karl Otto Pöhl revealed his intention to prevent EMU when he said: 'No West German government would accept the Delors Report's proposal for a new European central banking system unless it was given safeguards at least equivalent to those enjoyed by the statutorily independent Bundesbank... [and I doubt] whether other European governments are prepared to accept those conditions. The economies of the member states were too divergent to make a European central bank more than a distant prospect.' The truth is that Pöhl was ambivalent.[22] Pöhl's personality was entirely cosmopolitan, at ease with the beauties of life and enjoying the company of intelligent people. This distinguished him from most of his colleagues in the Central Bank Council, which was stuffed by a large number of provincial ex-politicians, some of an outright nationalist and reactionary brand. Given that the Bundesbank President's role was more that of a chairman than that of a CEO, Pöhl always had to tread a careful balance in his public statements. However, even if Pöhl was pro-European by instinct, he also had serious doubts about the policy commitments in weak currency countries. He probably felt intellectually more at ease in the Anglo-Saxon than the Latin world and was, therefore, not convinced that France and Italy were about to change economic philosophy in a radical way. In this respect, his doubts may simply have reflected the uncertainties of the time. Nobody knew in 1989 whether the EC member states were willing to abandon monetary sovereignty. In an article in the *Corriere della Sera*[23] Padoa-Schioppa recorded a conversation with Pöhl in February 1982 after the Bundesbank had prevented the move to stage two of the EMS: 'If you propose a European Central Bank based on a treaty, I can be with you. But strings to the Bundesbank without a clear juridical base are unacceptable'. Padoa-Schioppa pointed out, that the Bundesbank Presidents Pöhl, Schlesinger, and Tietmeyer always honoured 'not only the negative, but also the positive part of the phrase'.

Frequent contacts in the Bundesbank, including Pöhl's office, gave the AMUE the impression that full monetary union with an independent central bank was Pöhl's first choice. He was aware that the Deutschmark was too small to play the role of the world's second currency. Status quo was only second best. However, Bundesbankers seemed to be driven by fears about the transition. As one member of the Bundesbank said in 1990: 'Our draft for the statute of the future ECB is paradise. The way to it is purgatory. But if we get stuck in it, it will be hell'.[24] Not surprisingly, during most of the Maastricht negotiations Germany sought to keep the transition period as light and unconstraining as possible.[25] The shift from national monetary policies to a single monetary policy was an inescapable consequence of permanently locking exchange rates and therefore constituted one of the principal institutional changes.

The Delors Committee did not formulate the statutes of a future ECB. The committee of EC Central Bank Governors did that after the European Council in Madrid had accepted the Delors Report in 1989. Pöhl had not expected this endorsement, but when he was elected a few month later chairman of Central Bank Governor's Committee for a period of three years, he immediately ceased the opportunity to suggest a blueprint for the statutes of the future ECB. The central bank concept proposed by the Bundesbank was the most coherent and therefore also the least crisis-prone monetary arrangement. Without major alterations, these ideas were incorporated into the Maastricht Treaty – again to Pöhl's utter amazement.[26]

The Delors Committee pointed out that the Treaty of Rome would have to be changed as part of the transition strategy in three stages. During stage one all member states would join the ERM and strengthen economic and monetary convergence. Actions would be taken to complete the internal market and reduce the existing disparities in economic performance. All obstacles to financial integration were to be lifted and co-ordination of monetary policy strengthened. It was explicitly mentioned that 'all impediments to the private use of the Ecu would be removed' (Committee for the Study of Economic and Monetary Union 1989). Stage two was to start after the new Treaty had come into force as a period of transition to the final stage. It would be a training process leading to collective decision-making, while the ultimate responsibility for policy decisions would remain at this stage with national authorities. How this transition would take place in practice remained open, although the report echoed ideas from the Giscard–Schmidt Committee whereby the fluctuation margins in the EMS should be narrowed. The third and *final stage* would commence with the move to irrevocably locked exchange rates and the transfer of full monetary competences to the European System of Central Banks.

Probably the greatest strength of the report resulted from the consensus among the central bankers of the Delors group on what the final stage of EMU should look like. This was a professional decision, not politics. Neither Leigh-Pemberton, the Governor of the Bank of England, could refrain from making a contribution, nor could Pöhl, whom Marcussen quotes as having said: 'It was 'a mistake to take part in the Delors Committee, I couldn't defend German interests. If I had boycotted it I could not have stopped the process, but I could have slowed it down. I would have been freer to criticize the Delors report' (Marcussen 2000: 113). Margaret Thatcher did not understand this epistemic dynamic, when she hoped 'that paragraphs would be inserted which would make it clear that EMU was in no way necessary to the completion of the single market' (Thatcher 1993: 708).[27] Her diplomatic advisor Charles Powell recorded: 'we thought the Delors Committee was a good way of sidelining the idea. We expected the governors to be sceptical and to keep the wide-eyed commission officials out. They disappointed. Kohl told us it was just a committee. We underestimated the other side' (Marcussen 2000: 113).

Although the Delors Report was a clear blueprint for European economic and monetary union, it remained unclear how to get there. It had two inter-related weaknesses. One was the failure to set a timetable for the stages and give a clear definition of their nature; the other was an uncertainty about the status of the European currency. Stage one was to start on 1 July 1990, but no dates were set for the beginning of stage two and three. Its progress over the ill-fated Werner Report of 1970 was to view the three stages as a single process. A decision to start on the first stage implied the decision to embark on the entire process, an automaticity Margaret Thatcher always tried to prevent.[28] However, the nature of the second stage was not defined. Without clear political objectives the members of the Delors Committee could not agree on the institutional arrangement for the transition. Some members advocated the creation of an EMF, but Pöhl was opposed. He feared that the EMF would have to provide resources for intervention purposes without any conditions attached and, therefore, could not impose sufficient convergence constraints in the direction of non-inflationary growth. Moreover, mixing central bank functions with governmental responsibility was not compatible with central bank independence.

Rejecting a parallel currency

This institutional dissensus had consequences for the role given to the Ecu during the transition. As we saw in the last chapter, some followed the idea that the promotion of the Ecu could lead to the emergence of a parallel currency. German and Dutch central bankers rejected this. Wim Duisenberg,[29] then President of the Dutch Central Bank, argued in a paper presented to the Delors group:

> The development of the Ecu as a parallel currency would by itself not diminish the exchange rate risks, neither outside nor inside the EMS. There is no inherent disciplinary capacity of the private Ecu, which would bring about price and exchange rate stability. This can be brought about only by firm national policies directed towards domestic price stability.[30]

For Duisenberg, a parallel currency was the opposite of a monetary union, which he defined 'as an area with either a single currency or with national currencies where fluctuation margins were eliminated, full convertibility guaranteed and central rates irreversibly locked'.[31] Bundesbank President Karl Otto Pöhl linked the idea of a parallel currency directly to the Ecu. He objected to the promotion of the Ecu on the basis that a parallel currency involved:

> The risk that national monetary policy would no longer be able to fulfil its mandate to ensure stability owing to larger-scale central bank interventions.[32]

During the deliberations of the Delors Committee, Pöhl also pointed out 'that for day-to-day payment operations (cash transactions, settlement operations by machine, cashless payment transactions) a parallel currency would be entirely impractical'. This led him to the conclusion that 'little would be gained politically by introducing a parallel currency but that much would be placed at risk in terms of stability policy'. This view was accepted unanimously in the Delors Report, and the parallel currency was rejected. The Report did, however, indicate that the impact of financial innovation, the degree of financial integration and 'the development of the private, and in particular banking, use of the Ecu *would have to be taken into account*' when the detailed blueprint for the transition from the second to the third stage of EMU was to be designed. This was a backdoor for the Giscard–Schmidt market-led strategy to reach EMU. At the first Annual Conference of the AMUE held at the European Parliament in Strasbourg in early 1989, Delors encouraged the assembled industrialists to develop the use of Ecu: 'If you show by your behaviour that you need a European currency, politicians will have to take this into account'. Nevertheless, the report remained careful on pushing the idea of a single currency and vague on the transition scenario:

> *Economic and monetary union* in Europe would imply complete freedom of movement for persons, goods, services and capital, as well as irrevocably fixed exchange rates between national currencies and, finally, a single currency. [...] The three above mentioned requirements define a single currency area, but their fulfilment would not necessarily mark the end of the process of monetary unification in the Community. The adoption of *a single currency*, while not strictly necessary for the creation of a monetary union, might be seen – for economic as well as psychological and political reasons – as a natural and desirable further development of the monetary union. A single currency would clearly demonstrate the irreversibility of the move to monetary union, considerably facilitate the monetary management of the Community and avoid the transaction costs of converting currencies. A single currency, provided that its stability is ensured, would also have a much greater weight relative to other major currencies than any individual Community currency. The replacement of national currencies by a single currency should therefore take place as soon as possible after the locking of parities.

The argumentation on the advantages of a single currency reflects the caution that was appropriate, given the political state of mind in Europe. The idea of one single currency was still far from being accepted in many European capitals.

The Delors Report was consequently ambiguous and often controversially interpreted. On the Ecu, the Report stated:

> The Ecu has the potential to be developed into such a *common currency*. This would imply that the Ecu would be transformed from a basket of currencies into a genuine currency. The irrevocable fixing of exchange rates would imply that there would be no discontinuity between the Ecu and the single currency of the union and that Ecu obligations would be payable at face value in Ecus if the transition to the single currency had been made by the time the contract matured.[33]

The Delors Report saw the basket-Ecu as a common currency that would become increasingly stable with respect to component currencies as monetary and economic policies converged. In stage three they would be perfect substitutes and, therefore, one day the Ecu could replace other denominations. But the report's formulation left the question open, whether the change from the common to the single currency would be an institutional act or the result of a gradual crowding out.

The private sector and the Delors Report

The Delors Report had traced out an institutional approach to EMU, which the governments followed closely in subsequent years. For the private sector it became the reference for all strategic work. The AMUE Board, chaired by Cornelis van der Klugt, the president of Philips, noted that the report reflected to a large extent the proposals submitted by the AMUE to the European Parliament and the Commission in January 1989. Yet, they felt a need to proceed. The increased exchange rate stability in the EMS had not yet translated into lower volatility in interest rates and the British pound sterling was still not a member of the exchange rate mechanism. Hence, the Board members exhorted governments to pursue the path to EMU: 'In view of growing economic integration and the interdependence of Community members a passive "wait-and-see" attitude towards monetary union might jeopardise the benefits of economic convergence already set in train. If all member states agree with the objective, why not make progress and negotiate as swiftly as possible?'[34] They also called for the AMUE to intensify its activities to promote the Ecu, especially as ignorance remained high.

As there were no firm dates in the Delors Report for stages two and three, the AMUE still saw the need for a market dynamic making the process of monetary integration irreversible. However, the AMUE became increasingly aware of the weaknesses of the Ecu development: It could not create an irreversible momentum. Conversations with staff members at the Bundesbank and meetings with the German business community through chambers of commerce and the industrialists' association (BDI) had alerted the AMUE to the intensity of German resistance to giving up the Deutschmark. Attachment to the Deutschmark was not simply a matter of power play by the administrative infrastructures of government and central bank. More importantly, it reflected a widely shared popular consensus. Collignon had been shocked by the overtly nationalistic overtones he had heard at a BDI meeting. Political progress to monetary union thus also required a shift in public opinion and greater mutual respect for each others' arguments. German officials and public opinion were largely ignorant of the changing economic cultures in neighbouring countries. Greater use of the Ecu in Germany could be a vehicle to further a European viewpoint. At the same time, the Association understood that it had to address German concerns about price stability and institutional arrangements regarding central bank independence. This would lend support to the pro-EMU forces in Germany. Simply promoting the Ecu did not suffice to achieve this objective.

In addition, the role sketched out for the Ecu in the Delors Report would not remove the high transaction costs from using a common currency side by side with national currencies. And these costs would prevent greater use of the Ecu not only during the transition phase, but also subsequently when exchange rates were irrevocably locked. The work with the AMUE member companies made clear: a common currency was not the answer to Europe's monetary problems.[35] A political decision to create a single currency, replacing all others was needed. The market-led strategy to EMU was a start. However, it could only complement the institutional approach.

One market, one money

Delors was aware that he had not fully solved the issue of creating a monetary union. He was worried that his Report would be filed with historic documents like its precursor, the Werner Report. Soon after he had transmitted his report to the Ecofin, Delors asked his staff, especially Joly Dixon in his cabinet, Michael Emerson, Director for the Economic Evaluation of Community Policies, and Pierre Mingasson, previously Director of Monetary Affairs, to think about ways to convince the general public in Europe of the benefits of a monetary union. He had thought of a major study like the famous Cecchini Report, which had established the benefits resulting from the single market programme. However, Emerson quickly pointed out that the new project was more complicated: there were not only benefits to be expected, but also costs. One would have to examine the balance between the two. Emerson put together a team of senior economists, including Jean Pisani-Ferry, Marc van Heuklen, and Daniel Gros, to study the subject. This led to a revival of the optimum currency area theory, developed in the early 1960s by Robert Mundell, setting criteria for establishing when giving up a national currency would yield benefits. Highly influential in academic circles, optimum currency area theory poisoned the debate on EMU for over a decade by focusing on why countries should *not* join a single currency.

The Commission sought to co-opt further professional economists into evaluating EMU in the following months (Dyson and Featherstone 1999: 724).[36] In this context, the activities of the AMUE also became useful. De Maigret had deepened his contacts over some time with the European Commission. His prime partner was the DG II under Commissioner Henning Christophersen. Thierry Vissol, as head of the unit dealing with the Ecu, was enthusiastic about the

Association's efforts to develop training seminars and remove other obstacles to Ecu usage, after having attended a Sherpa meeting of the AMUE. He considered that the involvement of major market players was a key to EMU success. Jean-François Pons had succeeded Mingasson as Director of Monetary Affairs after having served at the International Monetary Fund in Washington and as a member of the French Finance Minister Bérégovoy's Cabinet. Pons was more sensitive to the structural difficulties reported by some companies in using the Ecu and tended to favour a political approach to EMU. But they both quickly perceived that the Association could be a useful ally for the Commission in linking the Delors Report with Europe's companies, banks, and their professional organizations and render it more credible.[37] They also sought to develop the Ecu into a real competitor to the dollar in European and international markets and used the AMUE as a 'pilot fish to examine the reactions of the various stakeholders' (Vissol in private correspondence to authors).

The AMUE could complement the macroeconomic considerations about optimum currency areas or fiscal policy in EMU and provide a microeconomic foundation to the arguments for EMU. The political and institutional approach towards EMU needed to be imbedded into day-to-day economic practices. Together with Mingasson who had followed the work of the Giscard–Schmidt Committee, Pons and Emerson took a serious interest into the work of the Association. This led to a fortunate liaison. For while the Commission was working on *One Market, One Money*, the Association made a major step toward rejecting a common currency in favour of creating a single currency. Thus, the timing and the interest of the Commission's and the AMUE's reports created a powerful dynamic which tilted the dice in favour of the single currency. After the European Council in Madrid in June 1989 had formally endorsed the Delors Report and confirmed that the first stage should start on 1 July 1990, Pons and his team intensified their contacts with the Association in order to learn what European companies were thinking. When the Commission report *One Market, one Money* (European Commission 1990) appeared in October 1990, it combined three stances of thought:

1 The academic literature concerning *optimum currency areas* which has dominated macroeconomic debates on EMU ever since (see de Grauwe 1992; Gros and Thygesen 1992; Blejer *et al.* 1997; Eichengreen 1997).
2 The arguments by practitioners and businessmen who were primarily concerned with the contingent dangers of the inconsistent quartet (Padoa-Schioppa *et al.* 1987; Padoa-Schioppa 2000a,b).
3 The transaction cost argument, which provided a micro-foundation for the single versus a common currency.[38]

The AMUE provided input into the last two strands of the arguments, in particular by producing the report *A Strategy for the Ecu*. This made it influential with European decision makers, but less so in academic circles, which became obsessed with the first line of thought.[39]

A strategy for the Ecu

Early business views on EMU

For the private sector and companies in Europe, the theoretical subtleties of parallel currencies, or the distinction of a common versus a single currency seemed secondary. Their concern was saving costs. The basket-Ecu was useful to the degree that it could reduce uncertainty and, therefore, the cost of hedging against exchange risk. If it caused higher transaction costs, companies preferred national currencies today and saw benefits resulting from a single currency in the future.

But these microeconomic considerations were mitigated by the wider ideological consensus to which they subscribed in their respective home countries. Hans Merkle, for example, the chairman of Robert Bosch AG, always insisted that EMU only made sense if it created a stable currency in Europe. In his unique manner of rigidity and moral authority, the man who has been called the philosopher of the German business world declared: 'I hope that the realization of European Monetary Union will only take place if the independence of the ECB is guaranteed and if the economic and financial policies of European countries give priority to stability'. At one point when he felt that his colleagues did not pay sufficient heed to his concerns, Merkle was tempted to resign from the AMUE Board. He only stayed on because he felt obliged toward Helmut Schmidt, but the Association started to give greater attention to the arguments coming from Germany.[40]

The businessmen active in the Association understood that the Ecu had to be an important element in a more comprehensive strategy of promoting the EMU. In a programmatic speech Fiat chief Giovanni Agnelli summarized the Association's early thinking:

> 'A common currency is both symbol and means for guaranteeing that a market ruled by different legislative and fiscal situations will be irreversibly integrated. Just as it happened in the United States last century, when the dollar, issued by the Federal Treasury, was the factor that brought together several state markets with different economic and productive bases. A common currency is the way to give the businessmen, for their strategic planning purposes, the certainty that the internal European market is a consistent reality. The existence of a big domestic market means that industry must be able to invest all over Europe without any impediment to the free movement of capital. And that it must be able to enjoy equivalent credit conditions throughout the community based on a system of integrated, homogeneous and competitive financial institutions. But the aim of a free, integrated capital market providing backing for the industrial system can only be fully achieved if it is supported by a common currency. And last, by no means least, the single currency is essential to give Europe credibility and authority when the times comes to build a new international monetary order. European industrialists are acutely sensitive to this problem because they want to be able to tackle American, Japanese and Asian competitors in a clearly defined currency situation. The Bretton Woods agreements underpinned

> the growth of the market economies, the dollar being used as the principal reference currency until the United States had the strength to live with a system of fixed exchange. But, since 1971, we have been living in a climate of international monetary instability. It is no longer acceptable to saddle the United States with the sole responsibility for finding a solution to a situation that requires the co-operation of all world economic powers. But only the Ecu, as the currency of the whole European economy, will enable us to assume that part of responsibility which falls to us in the construction of a new monetary order, centred initially on dollar, yen and Ecu, but which could in future be extended to other currencies. Politics continues to harvest its electoral honours within individual nations, blandishing its electorate with notions of national pride and local and immediate interests. This does not always fit in with the interests of the community. The business community alone, in fact, is not in a position to solve problems that are the responsibility of the politicians. We believe that public opinion should be involved in these objectives so that it can apply greater pressure on the political class. As part of this framework, the Association is developing a series of measures within the business community so as to promote awareness and hence the more widespread utilisation of the Ecu.'[41]

At that time, Board members of the Association frequently referred to the Ecu as a *common* currency and publicly stressed its important strategic role for the European internal market. AMUE President Van der Klugt exhorted the Association: 'We must promote changes in mentalities and the adaptation of our staff to the large-scale opening of our borders to capital movements. After all, July 1990 is tomorrow!' In the October 1989 issue of *The Ecu for European Business*, Agnelli wrote: 'If we want an internal Community market guaranteed by the seal of the common currency, there are sufficient reasons for European entrepreneurs to resort to the Ecu as a currency for invoicing and accounting purposes and for the presentation of their financial statements'. Other companies followed with similar declarations. When Mikhail Gorbachev visited Italy in 1989, Fiat announced that future investment in the Soviet Union would be done entirely in Ecu.

Obstacles to using the Ecu

However, realities were different. The commercial use of the Ecu remained insignificant compared to traditional national currencies: less than 1 per cent of European trade was invoiced in Ecu. Although the Ecu had by now become the third largest currency in the world used to raise money, only a small proportion of this supply of Ecu was effectively kept in Ecu accounts.

At a meeting in the summer of 1989, the AMUE's Sherpas discussed why the Ecu was not functioning as money in a proper sense. Several of their chairmen had made flamboyant public statements about the Ecu while their troops had not followed. Some Sherpas were concerned that their company might lose public credibility. It was obvious that ignorance was not the problem, for the large European companies knew everything about financial instruments. Some participants suggested, in line with the European Commission's representative Thierry Vissol, that legal obstacles might be an important barrier, but nobody felt confident that they had fully understood what prevented greater use of the Ecu. On a suggestion of Agnelli, the Board decided that the Association should do a major study on how to remove the obstacles for the use of Ecu in European companies.[42]

In the meantime, political progress towards EMU had accelerated. Spain had joined the ERM of the EMS in June and the peseta and the Portuguese escudo were added to the Ecu basket in September. The Madrid European Council had restated the governments' commitment to achieve Economic and Monetary Union – much to the chagrin of Margaret Thatcher. It had endorsed the Delors Report and decided that the first stage should begin on 1 July 1990 although no dates were set for stages two and three. The heads of state and government had also asked the competent bodies[43] to carry out preparatory work for an intergovernmental conference (IGC) after the start of stage one. Ecofin had adopted the Directive on the Liberalization of Capital Movements in June 1989 and the Madrid Council had decided to abolish remaining restrictions in France, Italy, Belgium, and Luxembourg by mid-1990.

For the business captains on AMUE's Board, these were encouraging signs. At their meeting in Rome, Carlo Scognamiglio, Rector of the University Luiss, made the point: the chances for EMU were better than ever, 'because in the past, politicians had pushed in its favour, while industry was against it. This time industry was pushing forward, while governments seemed to block it'. Government resistance was linked with the fact that EMU could make them lose their fiscal and monetary autonomy. Therefore, European businessmen had to make a public case for a European currency.

A British counter-proposal

The difficulties that multiple currencies posed for European businesses re-appeared in September 1989, when the AMUE Board discussed a British alternative proposal for going towards EMU. In Madrid, Prime Minister Thatcher had hoped to have stopped the automaticity of all three stages of the Delors proposal (Thatcher 1993: 750–2). She now needed her own alternative game plan. After her return from Madrid she asked her Chancellor Nigel Lawson to produce an alternative to Delors. Lawson came up with a scheme around the idea of 'competing currencies'. Not surprisingly for a Tory politician, he opted for a market-led approach to EMU. The proposal called for the removal of all obstacles to the use of any European currency for domestic purposes. These obstacles were in fact substantial, as many countries in Europe insisted that company accounts, tax liabilities etc. had to be reported and paid in domestic currency. The proposal envisaged that, with equal opportunity, the strongest currency would become more widely used and would effectively become the common currency. Under the intellectual leadership of John Odling-Smee the UK Treasury worked during the summer 1988 with John Flemming, Michael Foot, and Chris Taylor of the Bank of England on a plan whereby the existing national currencies in the EC might compete for usage by consumers, firms, and institutions (Dyson and Featherstone 1999: 616). This idea was strongly influenced by the writings of the late Nobel prize winner Friedrich Hayek and by James Meade who had put forward a proposal somewhat similar to what later became the 'hard Ecu proposal'. It fitted nicely into the new emerging world of global financial markets after the abolition of capital controls in Europe. However, the plan came too late, was ill prepared and did not respond to industrialists' requirements. It had been presented orally at the informal Ecofin in Antibes in September, but a written version did not yet exist. At the AMUE Board meeting there was a consensus that competing currencies would make life more difficult for companies, not less. Paul Mentré, although always open to a market-led approach to EMU, called the British counter proposal 'inconsistent'. François-Xavier Ortoli, Chairman of Total, pointed out that, regretfully, the Ecu seemed to have been forgotten in the scheme. Some people objected that it effectively would turn the Deutschmark into Europe's common currency.

These propositions were also contradicting the Delors Committee, which had definitely rejected a parallel currency. For AMUE, they seemed incoherent with the logic of a monetary economy. Prices were expressed in money. Different monies would express different prices when exchange rates changed. Hence competing currencies were not compatible with the law of one price, which was the essence of a market economy. Above all, the British proposal had the weakness of not defining the institution and the final objective one wanted to attain. It is difficult to speculate on history, but had the British government been seen as supporting the goal of EMU, its market-led approach might have received a more favourable hearing. Had it even included the Ecu, as it did in the later hard Ecu proposal, the British government would have come quite close to the ideas of the Giscard–Schmidt Committee or the AMUE at the time. This was apparent from the ambiguous press release prepared by the AMUE Board on 20 September 1989. After emphasizing that European business strongly favoured monetary union and a large majority of them wished the introduction of a common European currency as an alternative to the present national currencies, the AMUE found that the Heads of State and Government at their Madrid Meeting in June 1989 ought to have gone further in their decisions. The Board then focused on the difficulties of developing the commercial use of the Ecu. It demanded that governments, banks, and businesses should aim to make the Ecu viable, thereby reducing the costs of 'non-Europe':

> Many of the technical and practical problems which companies face in using the Ecu result from the infant industry character of Ecu and will disappear once a critical mass of transactions has been reached, so that average transaction costs will progressively be reduced.[44]

To obtain this critical mass, AMUE referred to the Delors report demanding 'that there should be no discrimination against the private use of the Ecu and that existing administrative obstacles should be removed'. After noticing the positive steps made in several countries the AMUE Board made a bold jump:

> The most important step in removing administrative obstacles would be to attribute *the status of legal tender to Ecu* in all European countries, while maintaining its basket nature. This must go in pair with a process of general convergence in economic and monetary policies. Thus, the Ecu will not become a parallel currency, which might jeopardize economic stability. It will rather be the true *common currency*, an alternative option to the national currency in each country (...) In order to encourage an informal debate, AMUE has decided to undertake a comprehensive study in all European member states, analysing all existing obstacles and making suggestions for their removal.[45]

Thus, in September 1989, the Association was officially still pursuing a common currency approach to EMU. However, by the report it was now preparing, it started effectively to differentiate itself from the parallel currency approach of the Giscard–Schmidt Committee.

The study

The Board's decision to produce a study on *The Strategy for the Ecu* became a turning point in the Association's thinking. It gave the green light to the two-pronged approach of promoting EMU: removing obstacles to the private use of the Ecu, as requested in France and Italy, but linking it with the political, institutional and macroeconomic strategy that would ultimately lead to a unified monetary policy, as emphasized by the Germans and the Dutch. At the confluence of these market-led and institutional approaches stood the rapid replacement of national currencies by a single European currency. The Association thereby built on Delors' recommendations whereby the basket Ecu was to be the predecessor of the future European currency and to be issued by the ECB. Strictly speaking the two were not identical, but there would be a smooth transition and identity of value from one to the next. When it learned that the Bundesbank called this transition scenario from the basket to the single currency '*kongruenter Anschluß*',[46] the AMUE had found a consensual track. The approach had the advantage of building bridges. It took on board British preferences for markets, German tastes for institutions and plenty of scope for French pragmatism.

Work for the study became the Association's main activity between September 1989 and February 1990. By now, the AMUE was aware that the key to EMU success was the creation of a European-wide consensus on a single currency. In order to achieve this, it developed a unique methodology and involved opinion makers from all walks of European society, which was subsequently repeated by other studies. In a first step, it acted as a European think-tank, assembling the best experts from all over Europe around a table to produce evidence and study specific issues. The experts would formulate policy options and evaluate strategies to support the progress towards the European currency. In a second phase, the group's output would be discussed with representatives of the AMUE's member companies. The secretariat in Paris would facilitate the emergence of consensus among the different participants and subsequently make recommendations to the Board of Directors for approval. In a third stage, the Association would propagate the results of its research to policy makers, businesses and the media. As pushing for EMU meant lobbying for a public good, the costs and benefits were shared by all economic agents in the countries involved. The approach of the AMUE, thus, had to be a broader one involving more communicative efforts than if lobbying for a narrow interest.

The AMUE commissioned Ernst & Young Management Consultants to conduct research at company level. Head of the project was Malcolm Levitt, a former British treasury official who, after a stint at the European Commission in Brussels, had moved to the private sector as a consultant. Levitt was an EMU-agnostic. He was not particularly committed to creating EMU, but he was a perfectionist: if this is what politicians wanted, he would find out how to get there. His experience in the administration had taught him that, all too often, policy makers did not fully understand what they were talking about. He was in good company. Helmut Schmidt had once remarked: 'You have no idea by how much incompetence we are ruled'.[47] He meant this as a general statement, but it revealed the frustration by Schmidt, the intellectual, with politics, his profession. Levitt had experienced a similar disenchantment with respect to civil servants. He saw the AMUE project as the major and exciting European policy issue for many years to come and as an opportunity to think the logic of monetary union through. He wished to do a thorough, professional piece of work and he wanted to do it well.

Ernst & Young organized an extensive consultation of companies in order to find out what benefits they expected from a European currency. Very quickly, Levitt understood that it was not sufficient to just look at the microeconomic and legal obstacles to the Ecu. Economic convergence would determine not only how quickly EMU would become possible, but also how strongly the transaction cost obstacle would dominate the use of the Ecu. He enrolled the National Institute of Economic and Social Research (NIESR) in London to analyse the macroeconomic issues of economic convergence. External experts[48] were also asked to contribute in order to ensure that different European sensitivities were properly reflected. In addition the Association set up an external Advisory Board to give guidance on the general orientation of the project.[49] The purpose of the study was to find answers to these questions: what were the current obstacles to the wider use of the Ecu and how might they be removed? What was needed to alter the behaviour of firms so as to promote the wider use of the Ecu? What was required for policy making at the macroeconomic level?

The results were published in April 1990 as *A Strategy for the Ecu*, which came first in English, and was later translated into French, German, and Italian. In the foreword, Jacques Delors wrote 'given that the Commission will pursue its efforts in order to remove existing obstacles to the use of the Ecu, it is now up to the operators including governments and central banks, and to associations such as the Association for the Monetary Union of Europe to catch the ball and carry on the game' (AMUE 1990: 10).

The AMUE's message

The essential innovation of the AMUE report was a clear message: the single market required a *single currency*. The report merged the market-led and the institutional approaches to EMU by setting an institutional goal and spelling out a market-led strategy to reach it. EMU was not just an abstract political phantom, but a practical and concrete concern of private businesses. Yet, the work did not only address the precise difficulties firms were facing on their way to the completion of the internal market and the creation of Monetary Union, but it also placed these problems in a macroeconomic context, linking the microeconomic arguments to the broad political strategy pursued by political authorities.

The report opened with a dramatic statement: 'The single European market will not realize its full potential as long as multiple currencies remain'. Ernst & Young had undertaken a vast survey of firms in all twelve EU countries showing that the majority of companies anticipated greater cost savings and larger benefits from the single currency than the common currency. Over 50 per cent of companies felt that a single European currency would have a positive effect on their export, sourcing, marketing and distribution strategy and they did not perceive negative aspects on any part of their corporate strategy. On average, the expected benefit seemed to be 25–30 per cent higher with a single currency than with a common currency. Only 30 per cent of respondents felt that a common European currency would entail savings of 0.5 per cent of turnover or more; but 55 per cent felt that the single currency would produce such savings. Companies were also aware that the transition to a single currency and the replacement of national currencies would create transition costs; while over 55 per cent of the companies responded that they expected these costs to be negligible. Only 35 per cent felt they would be significant. For the first time, a report brought out significant evidence that European companies expected to benefit decisively more from a single European currency than from a thirteenth common currency.

While the corporate sector seemed to converge in the assessment of benefits from a single currency, the banking sector's view was quite different. They split into three approximately equal groups. One group felt that a single currency would increase income from the adoption of a European currency, a second group felt that there would be no such effects and a third group expected that there would be reduced income. Not surprisingly, banks felt much more threatened by a single than by a common, thirteenth currency. However, while over half of the respondents felt that they would lose income with a single currency, there was also a definite feeling that a thirteenth common currency would result in increased income opportunities in most banking products. As Bertrand de Maigret frequently put it: 'Banks thrive on monetary chaos'. This early survey by

AMUE and Ernst & Young threw light on the question why the City of London always kept a rather reserved and undecided attitude towards European Monetary Union.'[50]

The second major point in the report was the question of transition. The Ecu was *one* candidate for the European currency of the future, although *not the only* candidate. The simplest procedure would have followed Cooper's idea of declaring one national currency to be the European currency and abolishing all others. If one took money used by a large population, such as the Deutschmark, one would minimize changeover costs. However, this was psychologically unacceptable. Alternatively, the single currency could be an artificial *ad hoc* invention. Yet, this would make psychological identification rather difficult. By contrast, the Ecu was already fulfilling some of the functions of a European currency. This was the approach endorsed by the Delors Committee. The Association's research team now looked for ways to create a credible dynamic process for the transition to the single currency in order to overcome potential difficulties on the way. The European currency needed to be politically neutral to be accepted by the public; it had to enter people's habits, minds, and reflexes. It also had to be effective in all functions of money and that required confidence and trust, and raised technical issues about central banking. The report therefore emphasized a strategy that would turn the Ecu into a full-fledged European currency at the beginning of the final stage of EMU.

A question of credibility

Effectiveness as money meant that the European currency needed to serve as a good store of value, means of payment and unit of account. The basket-Ecu did not fulfil all these functions. As a store of value, the Deutschmark was better and as a settlement asset, the Ecu was not accepted by central banks. In essence, the Ecu was still little more than a unit of account. Macroeconomic convergence to price stability would improve the Ecu's qualities as a store of value. However, the survey found that firms had doubts about the political commitment by their authorities. They hesitated to use the Ecu as a means of payment in anticipation of the future currency as long as it did not have European central bank backing. As the Ecu lacked a privileged domain backed by history, law, and a central bank, companies found it difficult to take it seriously. The Association's report therefore recommended: 'Provided the political will exists, there should be a credible announcement that the Ecu will be the single currency of Europe'. This demand reflected the intellectual influence of the Rational Expectations School in Economics that was at the height of its prestige at the time. A credible announcement implied clarification of 'what?' and 'how?'. Unless governments clearly committed to a single currency, many firms emphasized that they would not be prepared to incur the considerable costs involved in changing the accounting and information systems, businesses, and financial operations and in staff training that were necessary to introduce the new currency. On the other hand, with a credible announcement that the Ecu would be the single currency of Europe they believed the necessary investment in learning and changing internal organization would take place during the transition period and the use of the Ecu would expand. The risk of an existing currency, such as the Deutschmark, becoming the common currency without having the political potential to be the single currency, might thereby be averted (AMUE 1990: 27).

A credible announcement for the Ecu to become the single currency also required a realistic timetable as the path of how to get there: 'A number of industrialists impressed upon us that unless a clear timetable is set down, they will be unlikely to take any announcement seriously. They also said that if the timetable is very long they would see no need to take any concrete steps until near the end of the proposed process, and only if the proposed target date looks credible. If such an announcement could be made within the next twelve months then, on the basis of the NIESR analysis, the end point (for the Ecu to become fully legal tender as the Community's single currency) could be 1997. The timetable could be: 1991, announcement made; 1991–92, agreement on overall strategy and Treaty amended; and 1997, completion by the end of the year' (AMUE 1990: 29). This timetable followed the European Internal Market programme, which had been announced in the 1985 White Paper, with an agreement in 1986 with the SEA and the completion targeted for 1992. Based on the NIESR simulations, the timetable assumed that EC economies could achieve the necessary degree of convergence so that all currencies could join the ERM. As it turned out, the process took two years longer; but the AMUE traced the path for what was essentially the Maastricht agreement.

To ensure the commitment of its members to their long-term objectives, the Association refused to evaluate or comment upon the various and very seriously held political viewpoints involved in the creation of a single currency. It did not see this as the responsibility of businessmen, and considered it strategically difficult as other representative organizations such as Unice had been paralysed by internal political antagonisms. The Association felt competent to talk about the single market, capital flows, and money; it did not want to take political partisan positions. This was also the reason for not getting involved in the discussion on political union. Thus it focused on microeconomic strategies and on the macroeconomic convergence *required* to make a single currency possible, *provided* the political will existed. The macroeconomic analysis by the NIESR suggested that by the late 1990s, the Ecu could be the single currency of Europe. Thus, economic convergence was not impossible.

The report also reflected the emphasis given to institutional arrangements by several members of the Association. Once a credible announcement was made that the Ecu would become the single European currency, an institution was needed to monitor and co-ordinate the practical steps. The AMUE gave credit to the arguments made by the Giscard–Schmidt Committee for a monetary authority during the transition to the single currency. An ECB should take up responsibility for monetary policy in the final stage and an IGC would have to make the necessary changes in the European treaties.

This suggestion was, of course, no longer an innovation. At the Strasbourg European Council, in December, a few weeks after the Berlin Wall had come down, the European Heads of State and Government had agreed to call an IGC dealing not only with EMU, but also, on German request, with political union. The disintegration of the Soviet Empire had disturbed geostrategic equilibria. The German chancellor Helmut Kohl, until then a little impressive politician, became a statesman of historic dimensions when he recognized that the long-term preservation of peace required an institutional backup to ensure the sustainability of Europe's strategic equilibrium. In the end he succeeded with EMU, and gave an impulse to political union. But the intellectual foundations and the general consensus on political union were far less developed than on EMU, which had already been deliberated for years. However, considerable uncertainty still persisted about the transition period. In order to increase confidence, the AMUE/Ernst & Young report saw the need that EC central banks lend support to the development of the role of the Ecu as a single currency and an institution that would back it. As it turned out later, the idea that the ECB could already operate before stage three and support the Ecu met with ferocious opposition by the Bundesbank which was concerned that a strong institution in stage two could interfere with their own stability orientated policies.[51] Thus, the *Strategy for the Ecu* did not endear the Association to the German authorities.

Once the recommended institutional arrangements were set up, the AMUE expected the private sector to review the opportunities and threats emanating from the development of the Ecu as a single currency of Europe. Companies would have to consider the impact on their customers, suppliers, competitors, and their own operations and systems. The political development of making a credible announcement by governments regarding the role and development of the Ecu was to stimulate major shifts in the behaviour of the private sector within the EC and in dealings with the rest of the world. A mutually reinforcing process would accelerate the political developments of adopting the Ecu as a single currency for Europe (AMUE 1990: 31). This statement effectively defined the philosophy, strategy, and actions of the Association for the next ten years. It turned out to be of crucial importance after the demise of the exchange rate system in 1994.

The Strategy's reception

A Strategy for the Ecu was an exercise in consensus building. Starting from sometimes widely differing positions, the research of facts and the exchange and weighting of arguments brought the participating experts, academics, industrialists, bankers, and policy makers closer to sharing similar views. The discussions usually reflected simultaneously business interest and political sensibilities with respect to the national debates. This helped to clarify the environment in which they all had to act with a common purpose and it created links of mutual respect and trust.

When the initial draft was presented to the Association's Sherpas in London early in 1990, there was a sense of excitement amongst the authors and discussants at having produced something new, making a difference. Most Sherpas from smaller European countries were delighted to see a coherent strategy to develop the Ecu into a fully blown European currency, while the French representatives appreciated the compatibility with their own government's strategy. The German Sherpas were satisfied with the macroeconomic aspects of the strategy. They understood that the Deutschmark would be politically unacceptable as a European currency and, therefore, agreed to the development of the Ecu as a politically neutral currency – provided it had the institutional backing of an independent European central bank that would ensure macroeconomic stability and low inflation. However, for some British members of the Association *A Strategy for the Ecu* looked like a provocation against their own government. They shared the economic logic underlying the analysis by Ernst & Young and the National Institute. But EMU was by now a highly political subject. Margaret Thatcher had made perfectly clear that her government would never agree to a single European currency replacing all national currencies. Already, the debate about joining the ERM had torn the government apart.[52] Chancellor Nigel Lawson had put forward his own plan for a market-led transition to EMU. It was in the interest of British industry and business not to make life *even more difficult* for this government. Heather Honour, the Sherpa for BAT's deputy chairman Sir Brian Garraway, was also worried that it would be difficult to develop membership for the Association in the United Kingdom with an agenda as radical as *A Strategy for the Ecu*. At first, she tried to resist the commitment to a single currency. But when she saw the strength of the arguments and the determination by her colleagues, she quickly realized that it was better to be amongst European leaders than being dragged behind. After a lengthy debate it was decided to put the report forward to the AMUE Board for approval in February 1990.

Geostrategic accelerations

While the AMUE *Strategy for the Ecu* was elaborated, the geostrategic balance of power changed dramatically. Developments in Eastern Europe had an accelerating impact on the EMU. In September 1989, Collignon and Ahnefeld visited Franz Schoser, the General Secretary of DIHT in Bonn, to talk about enlisting support for EMU from German chambers of commerce. Newspapers carried headlines about the mass exodus of East German refugees towards Hungary and Ahnefeld jokingly said: 'If they continue like this, we may even get German reunification'. Everyone laughed. The idea seemed too absurd. Two months later, the Berlin Wall came down. The Board members of AMUE saw this as both an opportunity and a challenge. In January 1990, François-Xavier Ortoli, Chairman of Total and Vice-President of the Association, wrote in *The Ecu for European Business*: 'In addition to looking forward to the single market of 1992, the Europeans are also contemplating the prospect of opening up the borders to the East – a fact that represents both an opportunity and a new challenge. The success of the single market might make it possible to turn the Community into an element of major importance in a wider European grouping taking in our neighbours to the East. To ensure such success, one must do three things: stimulate European businesses to regroup and to strive for technological excellence, consolidate financial Europe, and build economic and monetary Europe'. The need for an institutional backing of Europe's strategic equilibrium seemed natural to most businessmen in the Association.

Europe's Heads of State and Government, except Margaret Thatcher, shared this logic. At the European Council in Strasbourg in December 1989 they agreed to start the first stage of EMU as suggested by Delors on 1 July 1990 and to convene an IGC to work out the necessary revisions of the Treaty of Rome. However, the start of stage three was still undetermined. The Commission was charged to submit a paper by April 1990 on all aspects of the achievement of EMU. The AMUE quickly perceived this as an opportunity to provide their report on the *Strategy for the Ecu* as input for the Commission.

On 6 February 1990, the German Chancellor Helmut Kohl announced his decision for a monetary union between the Federal Republic and the German Democratic Republic. The manner of decision-making, and the uncompetitive convergence rate for salaries and wages, given the low East German productivity, came as a shock for Bundesbank President Karl Otto Pöhl who soon thereafter resigned. Although German Monetary Union (GMU) was in no way comparable with the lengthy process followed in Europe, it did influence the debate on EMU. The AMUE saw it as creating new risks, but also new opportunities. GMU increased risks, because a failure might have blocked EMU for a long time, if not forever. It offered new opportunities, because a success of GMU could serve as a model for EMU by proving less developed regions could catch up with wealthier ones under a tight regime à la Bundesbank. In the end, reality turned out to be painful: high interest rates nearly destroyed the European economic consensus, although the crisis of the mid-1990s also proved the need to unify Europe's economic management.

Interrogations

Giscard's doubts

Briefed by their Sherpas, all Board members agreed to the *Strategy for the Ecu* when the Board met on 15 March 1990. The single currency was the right step. However, it was also clear that the Association was taking a strategic orientation that was different from the Giscard–Schmidt CMUE. Prudently, van der Klugt had invited Valéry Giscard d'Estaing to the meeting held at the elegant premises of the Fondaçịon Juan March in Madrid. Van der Klugt had been aware that by swinging its weight behind the single currency, the Association was going a significant step further than the CMUE had previously suggested. Although van der Klugt had always insisted that the Association and the Committee were two separate organizations, he felt obliged to Giscard and to Schmidt, who was unable to attend the meeting.

The former President of the French Republic faithfully defended the philosophy developed by the Giscard–Schmidt Committee. Addressing the AMUE

Board, he first gave an eloquent overview of the rapidly changing developments in Europe on the background of the approaching German unification. He asked: 'Do we need to continue Europe's construction? Do we need to abandon more of our national powers?' Germany's attitude would be crucial. He expected progress on political union to be slower than on monetary union and thought that Germany's increasing weight would lead the British government to take greater interest in European affairs. Between full national sovereignty and its total disappearance, the true debate was different: by accepting a common currency, every state would lose part of its sovereignty, but gain other advantages. Giscard expected that Germany would become more preoccupied with herself as a consequence of unification.[53] Therefore, it would become difficult to set up a federal structure, that is, an ECB. Hence, he thought it necessary, in accordance with the Delors Report, to privilege the development of the Ecu. The words and references were carefully chosen, but remained vague. Giscard avoided a clear position between a single and a common currency. The Ecu was a common currency that would become a single currency when it was common to all. One participant commented afterwards: 'This was vintage Giscard – so intelligent that you do not understand anything'.

In fact, Giscard had doubts about the *Strategy for the Ecu*. He thought that European public opinion was far from being ready to give up national currencies. Too much history, too much prestige was attached to them. He understood the logic behind the Report, but he believed to know people better. He also was concerned about French domestic politics. The 'majority of the majority' in the Assemblée Nationale was in favour of a common currency. Finance Minister Balladur had favoured it at several occasions. Giscard was afraid that a premature promotion of the single currency could lead to a 'tactical clash', blocking the situation. He did not talk about this openly at the time, but it was on his mind.[54] The AMUE directors listened attentively to Giscard's comments and were confused: did he approve or disapprove? Van der Klugt, who had always a voluntaristic inkling, saved the situation. 'What we have learned from you and Helmut Schmidt when you built the EMS is that you have to do what you have to do and not listen to the experts who tell you why something cannot be done. Today businessmen say loud and clear, a single currency is what we need and it can be done'. The Board decided that the *Strategy for the Ecu* should be made public at the Association's annual conference in May 1990, well before the Commission would produce its own recommendations for the EMU preparation.

The choice of a single currency was a fundamental divergence of strategy from the CMUE, although not of the shared objective. By backing the institutional approach to EMU, European businessmen supported the 'fundamentalist' (Padoa-Schioppa 1998) requirements for EMU that were the very basis of German and Bundesbank thinking. This permitted the strongest possible arrangement for sustaining monetary stability in Europe and therefore substantially higher procedural gains from European integration than the 'softer' institutional solutions envisaged by the Giscard–Schmidt Committee, or the British governments. This choice allowed the AMUE to become a major player in the game that led to the euro as a single currency, while the CMUE became increasingly marginalized. After the conclusion of the Maastrict Treaty, the Committee's job of initiating ideas was done.

The UK's hard Ecu proposal

By coincidence, the British government put forward a second alternative proposal for reaching EMU by a market-led approach the very same day that the Association published its proposal for a single currency. The new British proposal suggested creating a 'hard Ecu', which would be as strong as the strongest existing EC currency by virtue of a 'no-devaluation' guarantee, implemented through the narrow ERM in the EMS (Taylor 1997). The scheme contained two complementary strands: a new currency as an optimal *standard of value* and a concept of how the new currency would be issued and managed. The first strand was originally put forward in a series of papers, only a few of which were published, by Paul Richards, a Director of Samuel Montagu & Co., in association with Sir Michael Butler, a Director of Hambros Bank and a former Head of the UK Delegation to the European Community in Brussels (see Richards 1990). Officials at the Bank of England and the Treasury later added the second strand.

The authors of the Hard Ecu proposal had learned from the failure of the 'competing currency' idea. They now focused on the fact that the Ecu as a basket currency by definition would always be weaker than the strongest component, that is, the Deutschmark. As a consequence, the weakness of the Ecu relative to the Deutschmark would impugn its acceptance as a reserve asset. This had been a frequent argument made by the Bundesbank against the basket Ecu. But with a no-devaluation guarantee, the hard Ecu would become the benchmark of stability and, therefore, attract investors' confidence. In a free competition between different currencies this should lead to a stronger demand for Ecu assets. The no-devaluation guarantee on the hard Ecu was to be implemented in the first instance through foreign exchange intervention within the narrow-band ERM, to which the new currency would be added. Thus the scheme's role in promoting monetary union rested heavily on the credibility of the international obligation to support the hard Ecu without limit and a *reciprocal obligation* accepted by the national monetary authorities to support their own currencies against it. If these obligations were strictly observed, there would be a powerful mechanism to induce convergence of national monetary policies on that of the country with the strongest currency, while leaving responsibility for policy still in national hands.

In this respect, the proposal had some similarity with the market-led approach put forward by the Giscard–Schmidt Committee. UK officials at the Treasury and the Bank of England were aware of Giscard's interest in a parallel currency approach, although they did not study the details worked out by the CMUE. European consensus building was inhibited by low mutual respect between the political and economic elites in the United Kingdom and on the continent. On the continent there was a feeling that Britain did not really want EMU. For British policy makers, Giscard was no longer seen as a major influence on French government policy. With hindsight it looks as if they underestimated his influence on the wider debate in France.[55] However, it also reflects the fact that the British members in the Giscard–Schmidt Committee never played the active role of promoting EMU and creating a Europe-wide policy consensus that most other CMUE members fulfilled.[56] There was little genuine interest in the United Kingdom or understanding of the motives that led continental actors to push for a European currency.

The UK scheme promised to add a new element of hardness to the existing narrow-band ERM: a new monetary standard with better anti-inflation credentials than the strongest existing currency, eliminating the risk of eventual depreciations that even the Deutschmark had to be subjected to. However, as discussions proceeded, ideas evolved: for example, increased stress was put on the automaticity of the obligation on national monetary authorities to repurchase central banks' excess holdings of their respective currencies with hard Ecu. More fundamentally, the idea gained ground that the hard Ecu's value against other currencies should be maintained through *interest rate policy*. This meant adding elements, which the original proposals initially lacked, principally an articulated concept of how the new currency would be issued and managed, especially how hard Ecu interest rates would be determined. At first the Treasury thought in terms of a currency-board institution to issue the hard Ecus, but this implied too passive and narrowly focused a policy approach to command wide support. Thinking at the Bank of England then went in the direction of an institution closer to a central bank, with powers to issue hard Ecu deposits as the reserve assets of a banking system for the new currency, and to set interest rates on them, thereby influencing hard Ecu interest rates in the market. That would provide the means to manage the hard Ecu as a currency in its own right and make the hard Ecu effectively a parallel currency. It is interesting that although British attitudes toward Europe often instinctively resisted institutionally binding commitments, when officials in London sat down to seriously think about Europe, they also had to come up with ideas on institution building. This was inherent to European integration.

The UK Government's proposal was, in part, a political manoeuvre to reconcile the pro- and anti-European factions in the Conservative Party. In that it succeeded, although it proved fatal to Margaret Thatcher's position as Prime Minister. In Parliament she admitted that 'in my view [the hard Ecu] would not become widely used throughout the community – possibly most widely used for commercial transactions. Many people would continue to prefer their own currency' (Thatcher 1993: 833). This statement led to the rebellion that brought John Major into office and probably prolonged the Tory era by five years. But it gave no credit to the European debate on the inconsistent quartet, the need for monetary stability, and institution building. In European politics, the hard Ecu proposal was less successful than in party politics as only the Spanish government actively supported the case. The Delors Report had already rejected a parallel currency, but left the content of the transition period open. The British Government did suggest real substance to stage two of the Delors plan and could have appealed to all those who saw a long transition period as essential for the preparation to EMU. The problem was that the scheme never pretended to offer an inevitable route to the single currency (Taylor 1997: 5) and, therefore, remained silent on the ultimate goal. This is why it was ultimately rejected. From a British point of view, the advantage of the hard Ecu proposal, at least in its initial form, was the absence of an ECB as it would have allowed every country to pursue national monetary policies. This contradicted what the Bundesbank had repeatedly argued: a monetary union needed a unified monetary policy.

The AMUE saw several fatal flaws in the British proposal. First of all, it ignored the transactional function of money as a means of payment. Having a hard Ecu as a thirteenth common currency would not avoid the problem of double transaction costs which was a barrier to the commercial life of a common currency. Therefore, one of the essential functions of money would remain underdeveloped. This handicap could only be overcome through replacing national currencies by a single currency. Second, the creation of an additional hard Ecu next to the already existing Ecu baskets would make companies' currency management even more complex than it was with thirteen currencies. Third, a parallel currency was politically unacceptable for Germany. Fourth, the hard Ecu offered no long-term protection against foreign exchange risk for productive investment, as costs and revenues would be set in other currencies.

The simultaneous publication of the British hard Ecu proposal and AMUE's more confident plea for a single currency was a stroke of luck for the Association. It instantly polarized the debate in Europe and turned the Association into an intellectual actor. It is likely that the British government never had a better chance to influence and change the course of action toward EMU than at this moment. The Giscard–Schmidt Committee should have been its intellectual ally. Paul Mentré certainly thought the hard Ecu proposal an interesting idea.[57] Giscard d'Estaing immediately called John Major and went to see him with Mentré in London. But nothing followed. Giscard felt that there was no real political commitment behind the British proposal to create a full-fledged EMU. He also was intrigued by Major's ambivalent positions as a 'hidden pro-European'.[58] Other actors were also disappointed. The Spanish government lent support to the hard Ecu for a few months. Even Hans Tietmeyer, at the time Vice President of the Bundesbank, came up with suggestions of strengthening the basket-Ecu. That, of course, was not the same as issuing a parallel currency. It all came to nothing. The basic reason was that the hard Ecu was seen as a bridge to nowhere by the architects of EMU. It could have been a solution to the 'empty shell' of stage two, provided it would have had a strong institutional commitment to full monetary union in stage three, as described in the Delors Report. However, this was clearly not what Margaret Thatcher had in mind. Her respect for Europe was vanishing rapidly and this influenced the whole debate in the United Kingdom.[59]

Political sensitivities

How politically sensitive the British debate on EMU had become was apparent when the AMUE secretariat in Paris tried to contribute to the UK debate as they did anywhere else in Europe. Soon after the hard Ecu proposal and *Strategy for the*

Ecu had been published, Collignon contacted Sir Michael Butler who had been, with Paul Richards, the driving spirit behind the proposal (Dyson and Featherstone 1999: 618–26). Butler had been a high-ranking diplomat and a strong advocate of Britain's role in Europe. He explained that the purpose of the hard Ecu proposal was to find a way to bring the UK government and especially Mrs Thatcher to a more positive attitude toward the EMU. AMUE was always looking for opportunities to build bridges, so he agreed with Butler to engage in a creative dialogue. A few days later he sent him a confidential draft paper where he suggested combining the single currency with a parallel currency. The trick was to give the Germans (and the Bundesbank) a single currency that would replace their national currency along the lines designed by the Delors Report. But if Britain wanted a parallel currency, they could take the single currency as an additional currency circulating in the United Kingdom. On 24 October 1990, Butler replied 'while it is theoretically possible to conceive of the totally different kind of transition envisaged in your [paper], I regard it as highly undesirable and unlikely to succeed. The EC has often accepted a temporary derogation for one or even two member states in relation to policies, measures or obligations, which the EC as a whole wishes to adopt. That contributes to more rapid progress and harmony between member states. But to begin such a major enterprise as EMU with only half the Community and contrary to the wishes of those left outside would be divisive and destructive. This is the British Government's position and I am quite confident that the British Government will not be alone in opposing such a solution.'[60]

A few days later, he leaked Collignon's paper to the press, calling the AMUE idea 'divisive and destructive' (*Sunday Correspondent*, 10 October 1990). The idea was dead, but the British members of AMUE were angry. Why did the Secretariat intervene in what was a British debate? Collignon was banned by BAT from events organized by the UK chapter of the Association and this banishment lasted for nearly a year. What was meant as an attempt to build bridges and create mutual respect failed and reinforced isolation. The incidence reveals a significant difference in the way the EMU debate took place on the continent and in the United Kingdom. The continental attitude was a free debate *in* Europe; the British was *about* Europe, from the outside. Only few pro-Europeans in the United Kingdom defined themselves with respect to the continental debate. Their pro-identity resulted from their opposition to the Eurosceptics.[61] This made the emergence of a cross-channel consensus much more difficult. Not surprisingly, in the subsequent political debate the British position remained marginalized.

However, for AMUE, the incident had a positive side effect. They appointed Christopher Johnson as UK Advisor to the AMUE. Johnson was an economist who had served as the Paris Correspondent for the *Times* and the *Financial Times* between 1954 and 1976. Thereafter, he was Chief Economic Advisor to Lloyds Bank (1977–91). He knew an extensive network of people in the City and in Westminster where he served as a Specialist Advisor to the Treasury Select Committee of the House of Commons from 1981 to 1997. Johnson was a convinced European by mind and heart, who soon helped the AMUE to find a respected place in the British debate on EMU.

4 The crises and the Phoenix

After the triumph with the Maastricht Treaty, which even defined a final date for EMU, many thought that monetary union would be achieved in a straightforward manner. However, the question of legitimacy was raised: Denmark did not ratify the Maastricht Treaty, which led to a severe crisis of confidence. The economic ratification through reading the convergence criteria was also put into question, when the EMS crises hit and the European economy slowed down. However, the crises confirmed the idea that further institutionalization was necessary to guarantee stability in the single market.

While national governments hesitated, the European Commission and the AMUE co-operated in giving the project a new perspective beyond political debates on EMU's pros and cons. They sought to find out which arrangements were needed for EMU to begin as agreed by the Maastricht Treaty. This work formed the background against which the Madrid Summit on 19 December 1995 settled a detailed technical transition scenario, restoring credibility to monetary union in the economic and political spheres.

The Maastricht Treaty

The gateway for a new epoch in Europe opened at the European Council at Maastricht on 10 and 11 December 1991. The new Treaty, which established the creation of European Economic and Monetary Union, was the most important act of European integration since the Treaty of Rome in 1957. Yet, for more than five years thereafter, it was never certain whether the caravan of countries would reach the promised city and whether all members would pass through the gate. A famous Sufi dictum says: 'Before you pray to Allah, tie your camels'. For the EU it turned out that the ties of the EMS allowed most member states to reach EMU despite devastating storms. Decisive were also the manifold links that had developed in and with the European business community – partly in day-to-day business, partly through determined efforts to clarify the path to making EMU work in practice.

Pre-structuring the negotiations

The negotiation of the Maastricht Treaty lay in the hands of governmental delegations which political science describes as hierarchically structured groups of officials who share collective preferences and represent national interests. These collective preferences reflect, among others, choices resulting from the democratic process, ideas and traditions as well as individual preferences of negotiating individuals.[1] All preferences have cognitive foundations, which permit the creation of consensus through communication, and a strategic dimension, which implies trade-offs in bargaining. In the course of European integration, governments bargained agreements concerning co-operation and thereby selected, created, and shaped institutions that would allow the long-term stability or reproduction of the negotiated consensus. For Moravcsik, the process of negotiation constitutes the essence of European integration (Moravcsik 1999: 5).

The negotiators of the Maastricht Treaty were operating in an already structured world (Dyson and Featherstone 1999: 19). In terms of our model in the introduction, these structures partly belong to the general context in which policy making takes place; partly they are the result of new evidence occurring by coincidence, experience, or deliberation. The historic background is constituted by a broad set of ideologies, institutions and conventions, the experience of two world wars, economic instability, hyperinflation, and unemployment in the 1920s and 1930s, the Cold War, the Bretton Woods System and its demise, but also European integration and the Single Market programme of 1987, the Werner plan of 1970, and German unification in 1989–90. The Delors Report provided specific new evidence in 1989; the experience of high capital mobility and the inconsistent quartet, and the emergence of a policy consensus favouring price stability.

The Giscard–Schmidt Committee and the AMUE also contributed to the pre-structuring process by providing relevant information and backing pro-EMU initiatives by active policy makers as we have shown in the two previous chapters. The Committee helped to re-launch the EMU process while the Association clarified the need for a single currency. Not even the Delors Report of 1989 had pointed out as clearly as the *Strategy for the Ecu* in 1990 that a parallel European currency would not bring the benefits of a single one. All these factors shaped collective preferences, although their weight varied according to national environments. As a consequence, national policy preferences were not uniform, even though new evidence contributed to their convergence. Hence, treaty negotiations between governments were necessary to find a settlement that would minimize the loss when the European agreement overruled the national consensus. During the Maastricht negotiations, the CMUE's and AMUE's impact was expectedly limited as public opinion and non-governmental actors have little impact during IGCs. Yet there was one exception: the setting of a final date for stage three of EMU. Since the publication of the *Strategy for the Ecu*, the AMUE had concentrated on three issues: observing the progress of the intergovernmental conference, improving the public acceptance of EMU and studying the external consequences of a single European currency.

Setting a date in the Treaty

The publication of the *Strategy for the Ecu*[2] had turned the AMUE into a heavyweight among the European NGOs. It had become a privileged dialogue partner for the European Commission. Commissioners regularly met with Board members, while the service staff in Brussels interacted with the Association's secretariat in Paris and frequently participated in working groups organized with AMUE's corporate members. At the same time, many member companies used their influential position to intervene in the domestic debate on EMU. The Association mediated horizontally between the national private sectors, between private and public sectors on all levels and vertically between the European and national levels of policy debates. It did so through the establishment of close personal contacts, a growing number of public meetings, seminars and conferences, the wide distribution of its newsletter, economic and political studies, as well as technical and practical brochures in all major languages of the community.

During the IGC, the AMUE at first only observed the negotiating process – although very closely. Progress was discussed with key policy makers such as Jean-François Pons, the Commission's Director for monetary affairs, Manuel Conthé, the Director of the Spanish Treasury, Horst Köhler his German counterpart, and with Commission Vice-President Henning Christophersen in March 1991. Central bankers in several countries and at different levels were contacted frequently. Forty of the French member companies met for lunch with Jacques de Larosière, the Governor of the Banque de France and with Elisabeth Guigou, President Mitterrand's trusted Sherpa and head of the General Secretariat of the Interministerial Committee for European Economic Relations and subsequently minister of European Affairs. Guigou was a key player during the Maastrict negotiations. After the Strasbourg European Council, she was charged to chair the group that prepared the setting up of the IGCs. Subsequently, she was the only member of the French government who participated in the two parallel IGCs; one establishing economic and monetary union, the other, on political union. She contributed to Mitterrand's decision in favour of a single and against a common European currency. Together with Joachim Bitterlich, she assured the close link between the French President and the German Chancellor. As a former official of the French treasury, Guigou had been involved with monetary issues since the mid-1980s and had followed the work of the Giscard–Schmidt Committee and the Association. She considered them as important voices of the European civil society beyond the usual political cleavages.[3]

For a long time, the IGC did not progress on three important issues: (1) the content and length of the transition period; (2) the progress of economic convergence and the dilemma of a multi-speed Europe; and (3) the commitment to the final stage of EMU. Even the AMUE board and the members were at first divided over the correct answers to these questions. Their discussion reflected the political debates across Europe. However, they were capable of reaching consensus quickly as they did not have to consider strategies to be re-elected and could thus regard the issues at stake from a more pragmatic point of view, and because they argued in a climate of mutual respect with facilitated consensus. This allowed the AMUE to act as an opinion leader, and to voice its position in a relevant stage of the negotiations.

While the Association quickly agreed that the ECB should already be established in stage two,[4] defining a position on the content of the transition period proved more difficult. A circle was to be squared between making the transition short as stage two had only limited policy content and was therefore politically fragile and, achieving effective convergence which needed time, while the political requirement of not splitting the community implied waiting for laggards. The Paris Secretariat referred to the *Strategy for the Ecu* as a solution. The study had outlined how convergence was possible by 1997, but now some Board members hesitated. Political considerations surfaced. Giovanni Agnelli and Sergio Pininfarina, who chaired the Italian employers' confederation Confindustria at the time, voiced Italy's concern that only a late start of stage two in 1994 allowed enough time for convergence and that there should not be a definite starting date for stage three. Although these precautions were not expressed explicitly at AMUE meetings, it was known that the Spanish and Portuguese governments harboured similar concerns and companies took these positions into account (Grant 1994: 146–7). Brian Garraway, with British pragmatism, pleaded for realism without making any constructive suggestion, while German prudence surfaced in Hans Merkle's concern that the Association should not get into binding timetables, as EMU should not start at all costs.[5]

The assessment of economic convergence remained equally controversial. It became more urgent in March 1991 as the economic shock caused by German re-unification showed that European economies could again diverge, a point Bundesbank President Karl Otto Pöhl emphasized at an AMUE meeting in London. While Xavier-François Ortoli, Hans Merkle, and Jacques Solvay agreed that the prerequisite of convergence could imply that not all countries would be ready on time, Belmiro de Azevedo, the Sonae Chairman, challenged the emerging consensus saying that price stability should not be the first aim, as this could delay peripheral countries in joining EMU. Business cared more about effective demand than price stability, he argued. What mattered for de Azevedo was the right policy mix. Inflation was wrong as it hit the poor, but too rigid stability policies would equally do harm.[6] This intervention led to a heated exchange with Merkle who insisted that his country would only join a monetary union if price stability and the independence of the central bank were preserved. 'In any case', the nearly eighty years old business patriarch added, 'for Robert Bosch AG the best years for business have always been those with price stability'. Van der Klugt tried to bridge the controversy by pointing at Spain as the best example for Portugal and Carlos March added that price stability in the long term was the key to the success of EMU. With the wisdom of a former President of the European Commission Xavier-François Ortoli suggested that there was a need to help weaker countries in the transition to assure economic coherence.

By May 1991, the Association's Board had found a consensus. To the great satisfaction of de Maigret, who had pushed the issue, the AMUE demanded, for the first time that 'the new Treaty should include a timetable for its implementation and a close deadline for the transition to a single currency. A clear agenda will induce governments to make the necessary political adaptations in a compulsory process, and that will encourage markets and companies to develop their use of Ecu widely'.[7]

The Board met again on 20 September 1991 in Paris to discuss the IGC. There was a change in mood and in leadership. The new AMUE President[8] was Etienne Davignon, now Chairman of the Société Générale de Belgique. In his first statement, he made two points: (1) The change in the international environment since the failed coup in the Soviet Union required that the EC proceed with integration; (2) The link between political union and EMU in the IGC was worrying. Negotiations on the first were badly prepared, overcharged, and without a guiding structure. EMU, by contrast, had a clear framework in the Delors Report, but governments still had not clearly indicated their intentions. Ortoli was concerned that the Maastricht summit would not commit the community irreversibly to move to full monetary union. The AMUE therefore should 'insist on the necessity for a clear signal from the European Council that the process will definitely lead to a single currency'. Jean-Réné Fourtou, chairman of Rhône-Poulenc saw a need to dramatize in a public declaration that 'we need to progress as fast as possible as regards deepening integration in the community'.

On 28 November 1991, two weeks before the negotiations at Maastricht were concluded, the CMUE Board became even more alarmed. It did not seem likely that the irrevocability of monetary union would be nailed down by a definite starting date. Davignon had attended the Giscard–Schmidt Committee a fortnight before, when it had discussed the outstanding issues in the negotiation with Commission Vice-President Henning Christophersen and the Belgian Central Bank Governor Alfons Verplaetse.[9] Schmidt and Giscard pressed for 1 January 1997 as the starting date of the third stage with the introduction of the single currency. They also warned that a generalized 'opting out' clause would entail a credibility loss. Finally, they emphasized that the European Monetary Institute should actively prepare the instruments of the unified monetary policy during stage two and consequently should be endowed with the necessary means and powers, while the Ecu should evolve in the direction of a strong and stable Ecu (CMUE 1992).

As the Netherlands was holding the European Presidency, the Committee charged its member Onno Ruding, a former Dutch finance minister and now Vice-President of Citibank, to transmit these requests to the Dutch finance minister and to Wim Duisenberg, President of the Dutch Central Bank. The next day, Giscard d'Estaing wrote with the same purpose in his and Helmut Schmidt's name to Prime Minister Ruud Lubbers who chaired the Maastricht IGC negotiations and to Commission President Jacques Delors. Etienne Davignon took the message to the AMUE Board. Together with Paul Mentré and de Maigret, he insisted on a clear commitment to the final stage of EMU and a date by which it was to be realized. They deemed this necessary for industry and capital markets to correctly anticipate future events and start preparing themselves. In view of this requirement, the draft Treaty of the Dutch Presidency showed three weaknesses, which Schmidt and Giscard had also previously observed in their discussions with the Commissioner. First, no date had been set for the start of stage three, which harmed the credibility of the transition process. Second, the significance and value of the Treaty was in doubt due to a generalized opt-out clause. Third, the efficiency of the European Monetary Institute as a body to prepare and plan the transition of stage three was not clearly established. The arguments seemed powerful, and a strong German–French consensus emerged in the following debate. This also convinced Agnelli, who had previously been reluctant to accept a precise starting date. This led to a final rewriting of the Board's press release:[10]

> The Treaty to be agreed at Maastricht is the most important event since the Treaty of Rome. European businesses wish to see the single European market crowned by a single currency, the Ecu. The Association insists on a clear procedure, based on adequate convergence, for the passage to the final stage. As business needs certainty, a precise starting date is essential to make people aware of the coming changes, which will necessitate several years of preparation. A Treaty without a deadline will not be able to increase confidence or prepare markets effectively. Therefore, a date for the introduction of the single currency should be announced by the Maastricht Summit, and all countries should start to implement the necessary policies immediately. It remains the Association's point of view that the year 1997 is a credible date.[11]

The AMUE and the CMUE had been the first pan-European organizations to voice criticisms and make precise suggestions regarding some of the open issues in the IGC. However, they were aware of the limited power unilateral declarations in press releases. So they lobbied the decision-makers directly before the IGC was concluded. It was the only time that the Association attempted concerted and direct influence on decision makers in several member countries rather than pre-structuring the general environment of policy making. The AMUE board members first pressed the claim for a date on Commission President Jacques Delors who was their guest for lunch that day. In the following days they lobbied their governments. For example, Agnelli spoke with the Italian Finance Minister Guido Carli. Davignon contacted the Belgian Prime Minister, and asked Hilmar Kopper, the chairman of Deutsche Bank, to intervene with the German chancellor Helmut Kohl. Two days later, Davignon also spoke to Kohl personally, pressing on him the need of a final date and irreversibility.[12] Kohl listened, but gave no indication of his preferences. He had already attained 'the level where he felt beyond all advice'. Kopper also spoke with the German finance minister Theo Waigel and his secretary of state Horst Köhler. They tried to cool his fervour, and did not seem particularly convinced.[13]

Chancellor Kohl had sent out confidential messages to Mitterrand, Lubbers, Andreotti, and Delors that he wished to make the process to EMU *irreversible*. However, he left it to others to suggest how that could be achieved. According to Dyson and Featherstone (1999: 421, 448), Kohl wanted *a date* for stage three so that the momentum to complete the process was not lost, but he did not go to Maastricht determined to set *one specific final date*.[14] While Delors was preoccupied with the difficulties of the IGC on political union, Tommaso Padoa-Schioppa, in Rome, who had been in regular contact with the CMUE and AMUE in the previous weeks, seized the initiative for a technical solution on an EMU date. On the flight to Maastricht, Padoa-Schioppa submitted a draft text on the date to Andreotti. Together with Umberto Vattani, previously an Ambassador to Bonn and now advising the Italian Prime Minister, he had marked out the double-date solution of a start of stage three in 1997 conditional on convergence in a majority of countries, but automatic in 1999 for any country that met the stipulated criteria. He had previously sounded out Elisabeth Guigou in Paris and Pascal Lamy, Delors' chef de cabinet and Giovanni Ravasio, Director General at DG 2 (Economy and Finance) in the Commission. Guigou indicated her agreement, given that she had already raised the issue two weeks earlier at the interministerial council of the French government. On 2 December 1991, the interministerial council agreed that the Treaty should include a date for an assessment before 31 December 1998 and the possibility of a qualified majority vote (Klau and Quatremer 1999: 180). However, Guigou was not certain that Mitterrand had retained the idea (Favier and Martin-Roland 2000: 103) and the fact that he endorsed her suggestion in Maastricht was unexpected. Apparently Andreotti obtained French approval for the formula suggested by Padoa-Schioppa at a private dinner with Mitterrand the evening before the summit that was to ensure 'automaticity' for the start of stage three of EMU.[15] The next morning, Andreotti and Mitterrand met with Kohl for breakfast. To Vattani's astonishment, Kohl accepted the formula without any hesitation 'as if he had been prepared for this suggestion'.[16] Klau and Quatremer point out that it was politically impossible for Kohl to support a fixed date before the summit as the Bundesbank and the Ministry of Finance were strongly opposed. However, he was open to accept this suggestion by the partners (Klau and Quatremer 1999: 183). Guigou recalls that Mitterrand was first to raise the issue in the formal council session and received immediate support from Kohl. It meant, as Mitterrand put it, 'we will have the single currency at the latest in seven years, that is, on 1 January 2001'. The decision came as a surprise for other prime minsters, but as a shock to many German officials and the Bundesbank who had worked hard to keep the option of not having to join EMU at all costs (Dyson and Featherstone 1999: 448; Heisenberg 1999: 186; Klau and Quatremer 1999: 183). According to Joachim Bitterlich, Kohl's Sherpa in the international negotiations, Kohl had himself come to the conclusion that a fixed date was necessary to make the process to EMU irreversible. Andreotti's suggestion was therefore well received.[17] He had kept the idea to himself, possibly because he feared that his finance minister Theo Waigel would have refused.[18] However, Waigel did in the end agree with Kohl because he found the double-date solution resolved the conflict between convergence and credibility.[19]

It is impossible today to evaluate the degree to which the CMUE, AMUE, and individual members of both groups of their network contributed to the consensus that a final date was crucial. Somehow, the idea 'seemed to be in the air'. Experts involved and close observers confirm, that the NGOs' pressure was certainly noticed. It had raised the awareness of the negotiators about the private sector's need to have a clear starting date, and secondly promoted the insight that political momentum through a fixed timetable was necessary to create political efforts for the convergence process. Finally, Padoa-Schioppa's double-date suggestion also allowed integrating those countries into the consensus, which had been afraid to be left out if there was a single and early starting date.

The insertion of a final date into the Maastricht Treaty has proven crucial for the final success of EMU. Without it, EMU may not have proceeded to the end after the two EMS crises and the failed first possible starting date in 1997 when convergence was insufficient.

Who will ratify?

After the signing of the Maastricht Treaty, the AMUE's attention focused on its ratification, which had two dimensions. Formally, ratification meant giving the signed Treaty legal validity through parliamentary votes or referenda. Substantially, ratification implied undertaking convergence efforts in order to meet the entry criteria. Both dimensions depended crucially on political will and public opinion. Germany was seen as the Achilles' heel. Would the Germans really agree to give up the Deutschmark? A year earlier, in October 1990, the AMUE had undertaken a comprehensive survey[20] about the attitudes of Europeans concerning the replacement of their currency by the Ecu. While respondents in the whole of the European Community favoured the replacement of national currencies by a single currency within the next six years at a ratio 61:39, only a tiny majority seemed to be in favour (51:49) in Germany. Of course, UK opinion was negative, but given the opt-out negotiated by John Major, this did not seem to endanger ratification. Interestingly, no one seemed particularly alerted by hostile Danish attitudes and their attachment to national sovereignty (see Table A2.1 in Annexe 2). The reasons for the approval in the other countries were based on a general interest in strengthening Europe, and to a lesser degree on the expectation of individual microeconomic benefits (see Table A2.2 in Annexe 2).[21]

An open question was whether public opinion would influence politicians in their ratification decision. Given that governments had negotiated the Treaty, the potential weak point was the opposition. Later, it became evident, particularly in Germany (see Chapter 5), that some opposition parties indeed had difficulties in defining their position on EMU without falling into an outright critique of the project in general. In order to get a clearer grasp of the situation in the EU countries, the AMUE questioned leading opposition politicians for the January 1992 edition of its newsletter *The Ecu for European Business*. Would they support their government? Some answers were surprising.

In the UK, Shadow Chancellor John Smith distinguished his party from the Conservative government by a favourable pro-EMU view:

> The Labour Party believes that progress towards monetary union is both inevitable and desirable. A single currency could offer many benefits to the European Community. Currency stability, low inflation and sharply reduced costs to business are the worthwhile objectives of EMU. A single currency would obviously strengthen the emerging single market and significantly

> enhance the Community's influence in the world economy. The task now facing Britain and the European Community is to achieve the levels of real economic convergence that are necessary for the successful adoption of a single currency. For the United Kingdom, that will require policies that favour investment in industry and in the skills of the workforce to ensure that we can compete with the best in Europe in the years ahead. In partnership with the Government, we believe that British industry can make the breakthrough to a truly competitive and productive economy. Provided we work for economic convergence and our investment performance improves, Britain has nothing to fear from a single currency. That is why the Labour Party regards the so-called UK 'opt-out' clause as unnecessary and irrelevant. It is important to realize that the 'opt-out' would only be relevant in circumstances in which Britain had successfully converged with the strongest European economies, but still objected in principle to a single currency. A Labour Government will not allow Britain to be left out.[22]

Smith's reaction to the Maastricht Treaty was the expression of a convinced European, and a subtle manoeuvre of an opposition politician. As a young member of Parliament, Smith had risked his career when he defied his own party leader Harold Wilson and, led by Roy Jenkins, voted with sixty-nine other Labour MPs for Britain's entry into the European Community. Without this vote, Prime Minister Edward Heath, whose own Conservative Party was also profoundly split on the issue, would not have managed to take Britain into Europe. For John Smith, it was an act of conviction. At an AMUE meeting organized for him in February 1992, Smith pleaded passionately for greater European integration, claiming that his native Scotland had greater links with Europe than England. While the Labour party had gone through a serious bout of euro-scepticism in the early 1980s, Labour leader Neil Kinnock and his shadow chancellor (and later successor) John Smith had converted the party to the benefits of Europe. They had been helped in this endeavour by Jacques Delors' presence at the Labour and Trade Union Confederation (TUC) conferences in 1988, where he had presented the European model of society as an alternative to Thatcherism. Kinnock was now determined to commit his party to the single currency (McSmith 1993: 165). He had set up the Institute for Public Policy Research (IPPR), run by Patricia Hewitt[23] and John Eatwell, to develop new policy perspectives in the monetary field. The IPPR engaged, among others, in a dialogue with Gavyn Davis, the pro-EMU chief economist of the merchant bank Goldman Sachs, and Hewitt was also in touch with the AMUE. John Smith's close policy advisor, David Ward, kept him informed about the Association's work. Smith's reaction to the Maastricht treaty worsened the troubles of the ruling Conservative Party less than four months before the general election. It positioned Labour as a pro-business party that sought to improve economic growth, employment, and stability in accordance with European standards. By contrast, John Major's government was portrayed as divided and isolated, capable of surviving only because it had negotiated an opt-out.

Another opposition leader, Paddy Ashdown, of the British Liberal Democratic Party, also shared his views in the AMUE newsletter:

> Historians will say that Maastricht was the moment when Europe put its history behind it and started to build a new kind of future, but Britain unfortunately remained trapped in its history and wanted to stay a little longer in the past. I cannot be certain that the great enterprise of monetary union in Europe will succeed. It will be brought under tremendous pressure in the next five or six years with growing internal problems to the European economies, the challenge of reforming the Common Agricultural Policy and of making sure that the emerging democracies of the East can join us. In my view, Europe will be plagued by ethnic and racial tensions and I think we will watch with horror the spectacle of the collapse of a supernova – the Soviet Union – on our doorstep. If Europe is not going forward, it will start to go back, and if it starts to go back, it goes back to a Europe built on partition and confrontation, not on co-operation. So Britain has to be at the heart of Europe, as Mr. Major has said. Unfortunately, while he said some of the right things, his actions have put us on the sidelines.[24]

Ashdown was also critical with regard to the opt-out clause granted to Britain on EMU: 'I believe that every citizen in Britain will pay a personal, direct and immediate price for the economic opt-out, because that will cause uncertainty – and uncertainty costs money.' This argument was not lost on the AMUE members. It was Malcolm Levitt, now at Barclays Bank, who was concerned about the uncertainty in the run-up to EMU and first started to push the Association to begin investigating the framework and conditions for the technical changeover to the single currency. This work prepared political decisions, which only became law after the Madrid European Council more than three years later.

In Germany, the abolition of the Deutschmark was greeted with public anxiety. The day Chancellor Kohl returned from Maastricht, he was received by a headline in the tabloid *Bild* read by 20 million Germans: 'Our DM is gone'. The next day it read: 'No Ecu, we want to keep our DM'. Norbert Wieczorek, spokesman of the opposition German Social Democratic Party (SPD), commented in the AMUE newsletter:

> The expressions of alarm in the rainbow press demonstrates a real concern in the population, but it is nonsense to say that the international currency, which we all want for the process of European unification, would automatically be inferior to the Deutschmark of today. The DM is certainly the symbol of economic progress and part of German identity. But there is no reason to assume that the future European currency could not play a similar role for a unified Europe. It could be catastrophic for a cohesive European Community if a minority of countries dominated the new currency, while others become independent of it while still being able to influence decisions in all other EC areas.[25]

Wieczorek also highlighted the difficulties, which could result from crash programmes for economic convergence:

> The consequences of a weakness in growth are unpredictable. The extraordinary boom of the 1980s is over and it has certainly contributed to convergence in Europe. But recently we have observed divergence and it is not certain whether the assumed conflict between stability policy and full employment would not reappear. Not everybody in France thinks like Mr. Bérégovoy.

Not everyone in the SPD shared Wieczorek's pro-European views. The party struggled over their position on EMU in the mid-1990s as we show in Chapter 5. There were also dissenting voices in the Bavarian sister party of Chancellor Kohl's Christian Democratic Union (CDU)s. To explain the benefits of EMU, the Bavarian Minister for European Affairs, Thomas Goppel, invited the AMUE to speak at a series of local conferences. Interestingly, beside media speculation to the contrary, there were no critical objections from citizens against the Maastricht Treaty in those early days.

The Danish referendum

In Denmark, all major parties, including Prime Minister Paul Schlüter's Konservative Folke Parti (16 per cent of the electorate) and Foreign Minister Uffe Ellemann-Jensen's Venstre Party (16 per cent) – as well as the opposition Social Democratic party (37 per cent) – were satisfied with the results of Maastricht. Some of the smaller centre parties, representing about another 11 per cent of the electorate were also in favour of the agreement. Only the two extreme left and right wing parties, Socialistisk Folkeparti (8 per cent) and Fremskridtspartiet (6 per cent) opposed the Maastricht Treaty.

The smugness of the early days after the signing of the Maastricht Treaty became apparent in the AMUE conclusion: 'A referendum on the ratification may take place in May/June 1992 and should not complicate the process of ratification'. However, on the 2 June, the Danish people rejected the Treaty by 50.7 per cent – a margin of 45,000 votes. For the first time it became obvious, that the population did not share the political elite's consensus on Economic and Monetary Union reached at the Maastricht summit. The so-called 'permissive consensus' by which the European population had consented to previous steps of integration had eroded. The reasons for the failed referendum were complex and multiple. The same government had been in power for ten years and the opposition Social Democrats were paralysed by internal power struggles. The government had difficulties getting the pro-campaigning going, assuming, however, that it was going to win in any case. The opposition, in contrast, was able to simulate fears about the future of the welfare state – an important argument in a country where four out of the five million workforce work for the public sector.[26] AMUE member companies like FLS were actively supporting the Yes campaign, but with a private sector of not more than one million work force, their leverage was small. Some well-known industrialists like Paul Svanholm, CEO of Carlsberg/Danske Bank, were opposed to the Treaty for various reasons: He foresaw that the EMU would lead to a dangerous field day for populism which would be hard to resist.[27] Hence, in view of the upcoming ratifications in France and Germany, serious doubts were arising whether the Maastricht Treaty would be implemented at all. After the Danes had said *No*, fears grew that the French could equally reject. There was a consensus among experts that EMU could start without Denmark. France – like Germany – however had to be among the first members of a single European currency.

The French referendum

In France, President François Mitterrand had declared after the summit: 'We have developed the prospect of an ideal Europe'. But when interviewed in the AMUE newsletter, his predecessor Valery Giscard d'Estaing did not agree:

> The Ecu will not have many defenders during the next five years, because the Germans don't want it, and that is understandable: they have a very good currency. The British are rather against it, so who is going to organize the promotion of the Ecu, who is going to be the Ecu champion? It is France. And here is the major plan of action for French European monetary policy: to make sure that we achieve EMU in 1997, France has to become the champion of the Ecu.[28]

However, before this could happen, and in response to the Danish referendum, Mitterrand decided that France would hold a referendum on the Maastricht Treaty on 20 September 1992. On the basis of largely positive opinion polls, he expected that a strong vote in favour would counter-balance the weak *No* in Denmark. It soon turned out to be the opposite. Public opinion deteriorated and began to oscillate around the 50 per cent mark in the weeks before the vote. As a consequence of the deepening economic crisis, rising unemployment, and uncertainty after the EMS crisis, France was split over the question whether to surrender the French franc in favour of the single currency or not. As in Denmark, the specific referendum question was very much confused with a vote over other issues, in particular for or against Mitterrand's presidency (Hayward 1996: 16). Only nine months ahead of Parliamentary elections, the debate on Maastricht became as highly politicized as French Presidential elections normally were (*L'Express* 4 September 1992).

The Conservatives were deeply divided over the issue: Giscard's liberal–conservative UDF supported closer European integration and had no problems lining up with the Socialists on this issue. In fact, Giscard appeared on the same panel as Elisabeth Guigou, by now Minister for European Affairs, at one conference organized by the AMUE in France, and at the AMUE's Annual Conference in Frankfurt. Some members of their Gaullist partner RPR accused the UDF of 'treason' (*Neue Züricher Zeitung* 21 June 1992) – a delicate situation for party leader Jacques Chirac. He had been in rivalry with Giscard for years, but now decided to support a *Yes* to Maastricht. Anything else would have undermined his credibility for the forthcoming presidential elections. Yet, the Treaty's critics and self-declared saviours of the French nation in the RPR such as Philippe Séguin and Charles Pasqua were growing stronger. Although the party leadership was supporting ratification, 72 out of 127 RPR MPs in the Assemblée Nationale supported a *No* vote. The active RPR anti-Maastricht campaigners found themselves in a remarkable coalition with populists, left-wing socialists, anti-capitalist communists, and nationalists of Jean-Marie Le Pen's radical National Front. Only three weeks before the referendum, three national papers expected a *No*, while opinion polls forecast a 50:50 outcome in the following days (*Sondage Ifop* 11 September 1992).

Linking with the CNPF

Not only were parties divided over the issue, the same was true for trade unions and other organized interests. The French employers federation, the Comité National du Patronat Français (CNPF),[29] remained for a long time distant towards EMU despite individual initiatives to bridge the gap. Already in March 1989, at a friend's house, Bertrand de Maigret had met Pierre Bellon, Vice-President of the CNPF, who showed enthusiasm about a co-operation with the AMUE. De Maigret had told him about close co-operation with Confindustria, the Italian employers' federation, which had already led to a number of joint seminars on EMU and the use of the Ecu. In October 1989, François-Xavier Ortoli had written to CNPF President François Périgot, inviting the French employers to participate actively in the work of the AMUE. He cited the Presidents of the Italian and Greek federations who had meanwhile joined as Board members. Périgot had publicly spoken in favour of EMU and had welcomed the Delors report (e.g. *Le Monde* 28 April 1989), although this reflected more his personal views than those of the CNPF.[30] In the following months, de Maigret was invited to working groups on EMU and an active exchange took off. However, in those days, he remained an outsider. When he suggested to one CNPF member that the organization should participate in seminars designed to prepare companies for the use of the Ecu, he received a cold shower. In a note to Ortoli, de Maigret wrote that discussions were 'tough' in particular because some people had had disappointing professional experiences with the Ecu. He 'doubted that they would play an active role for the time being.'[31] In its publications, the CNPF gave priority to issues of tax harmonization, the status of a European enterprise and the accomplishment of the single market, without linking it to a single currency. At the time, de Maigret worked closely with Yves-Thilbaut de Silguy, then International Director at Usinor, a leading French Steel Company. They prepared a draft resolution favouring a single currency over a common currency, which was rejected by a CNPF committee. In July 1991, Périgot, speaking as the CNPF president, said rather undecidedly: 'The currency is the priority. Single? Common? I will not engage in this debate because once the European currency is common, it will become a single one' (*Le Monde*, 16 July 1991: 16).[32] Reading an internal CNPF document of 26 July 1991, de Maigret perceived the risk that the CNPF would wait for the future development of a European currency, without taking a lead. There were several reasons for this: Some companies, especially small and medium-sized enterprises which were mainly operating in domestic markets, did not see an interest of a European currency if the price for this were high changeover costs. Exporting companies in uncompetitive sectors, such as textiles, were hostile to fixed exchange rates as they wanted to keep devaluations as an instrument to improve their competitiveness.[33] Finally, some entrepreneurs had political preferences that seemed to prevail over economics. For example, many Gaullist entrepreneurs favoured Edouard Balladur's ideas on a common currency. For Périgot this was a minefield. Although he personally saw the need for a single currency (a few years later he became a member of the AMUE Board as President of the European Employers' Association UNICE), as CNPF president he had to reflect the sentiments of all his members. For him, the AMUE was an intelligent lobby for stable exchange rates that was capable of acting because it reflected the views of committed personalities without the need for compromise.[34] This view confirms our analysis in the introduction, whereby the AMUE resembled more an epistemic community, capable of building public consensus by providing convincing evidence and arguments, than a narrow interest group lobbying for economic rents.

De Maigret persisted in convincing French industry and through them, public opinion. During the referendum campaign, he wrote to the new Vice-President Sellière pointing out the considerable progress in the CNPF working groups: 'I think our country can only win if the CNPF takes a progressive and public position on the monetary subject' (Letter to Seillière, 19 August 1991, AMUE archives). As the referendum came closer, private sector organizations became more supportive of EMU, because they started to fear the economic risks of a *No* to Maastricht.[35] The CNPF only fully backed the single currency after the Treaty was ratified.

Also beyond the industrial sector, the Association took an active part in the French referendum campaign. It organized forty-seven interviews and/or articles by major businessmen in favour of the Treaty. Its French board members, particularly Jean-René Fourtou, the Chairman of Rhône-Poulenc,[36] spoke at numerous public meetings. In the Paris secretariat, Marie de Saint Cheron[37] looked after the daily, and sometimes nightly, practical organization. The arguments put forward covered mainly the need for exchange rate stability in a single market, and the benefits of macroeconomic stability for growth and employment. While many of these pro-Maastricht arguments were valid for all EU countries, the debate in France also had to address specific concerns. Some related to the future of the common agricultural policy or the status of the franc zone in Africa, aspects which, in reality, were hardly affected by the new treaty. Concerns about a too liberal market-driven project were countered by pointing out the chances EMU offered for economic policy co-ordination and employment gains through stability.

This argument was more convincing in France than later in Germany because the French public was receptive to explanations that building EMU meant cutting down Germany's influence in monetary matters.[38] As this aspect gained considerable importance in parliamentary debates and in the media, the AMUE argued: 'Monetary sovereignty will be exerted jointly by the member countries, while it is today largely an appendage of the Bundesbank. [...] The Bundesbank has the task to serve German interests, but what is good for one is not automatically good for the others'. The Association also pictured a dark scenario of what would happen if the French said *No*. The arguments concerned the economic and political fragilisation of Europe and, again, Germany: 'If France refuses to go ahead, the temptation would be large for Germany to consolidate its influence in the North and in the East, and to build new alliances it would control entirely. It is clear that the Germans have no desire to give up the Deutschmark for the Ecu. They only agreed because the Maastricht Treaty contains political perspectives which insure the consolidation of Europe and long-term peace'.[39] Analysing this statement with the concepts we developed in Chapter 2, the argument was that substantial gains were more important for France than for Germany, but EMU reflected a stable equilibrium because the procedural gains were important for both countries.

A few days before the referendum, the AMUE changed its communication strategy. With a 50 per cent chance that the French would say 'No', the Association became more careful and pointed out how integration could proceed in case of a refusal:

> Should the French follow the example of the Danish negative vote, the dynamics of the European Community and the prospect of an early economic recovery would be badly damaged. But after a short period of turmoil, there would still exist a broad new single market consisting of 340,000,000 consumers, the newly constructed European Economic Area, and the 13 year old European Monetary System which has clearly proved its efficiency and which will deserve a rapid return to its former strength. More importantly, there would still be the same deep attachment by European citizens to an environment, which has brought them modernity, peace, and prosperity. And so they would start again and build a Europe which would still head towards greater economic integration, but which would entail more internal decentralisation and democracy.[40]

In the end, the French did say Yes, by a narrow margin of 51.1 to 48.9 per cent. The close result showed that the worries had been justified. Looking back, Padoa-Schioppa wrote: 'In the forty years since the rejection of the Treaty for a European Defence Community by the French Parliament in 1954, European countries have never retried the route of common defence. This would have been the fate of the monetary union had the Maastricht Treaty failed to pass the hurdle of ratification' (Padoa-Schioppa 2000b: 200–1).

After the ratification, the AMUE did not cease its activities in France. The debate on the single or common currency continued, while the private sector hesitated to use the Ecu and to prepare for EMU. The French Board members Ortoli, Mentré, Lagayette, and Fourtou were influential voices, their Sherpas, notably Thierry Walrafen, were active in financial circles. De Maigret monitored activities in the National Assembly and the Senate, and often spoke in Committees and Conferences. On an individual level, he held close contacts with MPs in the relevant committees and tried to spread the Association's positions. The correspondence (AMUE archives) gives evidence that the exchange mounted to substantial debates. For example, in September 1993, Laurent Dominati, a member of the National Assembly, reacted to a manifesto, which de Maigret had sent him a few days before. He questioned the sense of a single currency: 'Wouldn't it be more realistic to promote monetary union by privileging the creation of a common currency, without waiting for the birth of a single currency?' (Letter by Dominati, dated 6 September 1993, AMUE archives). The point had been made by the CNPF before and, therefore, de Maigret replied in detail, sharing the arguments that had led AMUE member companies to opt for the single currency. Many examples of close interaction can be found in the correspondence, which permitted de Maigret to introduce his ideas into the two French chambers. Having been an MP himself, he knew how to convince former colleagues to put questions to Ministers by providing them with background information.[41]

Ratification in Italy

In Italy, the Treaty ratification was never really in doubt, given the very pro-European sentiments in public opinion. However, an initiative by Giovanni Agnelli demonstrates how policymaking had become border transcending. Agnelli, who was also one of the few Senators for life in the upper chamber, was well aware of the domestic Maastricht debate in France and the AMUE's activities there. On 4 August 1991 he published an article in the newspaper *Il Sole/24 Ore* under the title: 'Now Italy must quickly ratify Maastricht'. He argued that the Italian Parliament should help to overcome the political uncertainty after the Danish *No* and give a positive signal for the French referendum. Despite the summer holidays, this initiative led to a close co-ordination between the President of the Republic, Oscar Luigi Scalfaro, Prime Minister Guiliano Amato, the Presidents of the Senate Giovanni Spadolini, and the lower chamber Giorgio Napoletano, and the different parliamentary party leaders. Amato asked the Senate to approve on 20 September, the day of the French referendum, not only the Maastricht Treaty, but also health and insurance system reforms, and budget consolidation measures. The purpose was to send a message to the rest of Europe, especially to French voters that Italy was serious about moving to EMU. Amato had already articulated this concern when he met the French Prime Minister Pierre Bérégovoy on 30 August 1992. Agnelli also contributed to these political developments because he was aware of the dangers of the emerging currency crisis, which led to the lira devaluation on 13 September. Thus, Agnelli helped to build an understanding between Italy and her European partners in order to strengthen the policy consensus for EMU.[42]

Pushing practical preparations

In parallel to political lobbying activities or promoting pro-European public opinion, the Association pushed practical preparations for the transition to EMU. This had been a concern of its members since the early work for *Strategy for the Ecu*. In a statement to the press on 13 December 1991, the day after Maastricht, Davignon had welcomed the Treaty and declared:

> The next move is for national governments to take the necessary steps to meet the criteria by 1996, and to remove legal and institutional obstacles to the use of the Ecu, so that it will be more widely used by companies and naturally accepted by the public as the single currency of the Union within the following seven years. The Association will intensify its action during the ratification process. It will soon publish the results of a study group of its members which will offer clear guidelines as to how banks and companies can prepare themselves for the introduction of the Ecu as a single currency.

The idea of a new study group had first come from the European Commission. Officials had learned from the AMUE work leading to the *Strategy for the Ecu* that companies had to look at an enormous amount of practical details if they wanted to make greater use of the Ecu. The need to develop the use of the Ecu, which was now destined to become the single currency, was more urgent than ever. It now had the potential to develop a life of its own. However, due to German resistance, the Maastricht negotiations about stage two had been difficult.[43] As a result, the practical role of the European Monetary Institute, other than setting up the future central bank, was still not fully worked out.

The Treaty on Economic and Monetary Union had enhanced the credibility of the Ecu considerably. An important role in this development was taken by the Ecu Banking Association and its President Dominique Rambure. The volume of transactions in Ecu had rapidly grown and the Ecu had progressively taken on an autonomous existence. This was greatly enhanced when the notion of a 'hard Ecu' appeared in the summer of 1990. The decision in Rome to make the Ecu the single currency precipitated this development and at the end of 1990 the Ecu was quoted at fifty base points above the theoretic value of the basket, while its interest rate at three months was nearly 100 points lower. It was time to reduce these erratic variations in rates and value, the scale of which resulted both from the political analyzes of speculators on the Ecu's future and from structural modifications of the Ecu market. The rapid growth in the volume of loans in Ecu was another reason for believing that the Ecu needed institutional support. It was becoming necessary to harmonize at EC level the schedule of the biggest issues in order to avoid saturation of the markets, hindering their proper operation.

Yet, after the negative Danish referendum in 1992, the Ecu-market collapsed. With rising doubts about the political feasibility of EMU, financial operators saw little need to put their trust into an anticipated currency that might never come. In this context, the European Commission saw the need to eliminate obstacles to the use of the Ecu. This was to be put into the perspective of companies preparing themselves for the replacement of national currencies by the Ecu.

In late 1990, the Commission suggested that the AMUE should chair a high-ranking working group to analyse the best ways for a smooth transition to the single currency as a follow-up to the *Strategy for the Ecu*. However, the Association's directors thought it too heavy-handed to have large company CEOs chair a study group, although they appreciated becoming a sparring partner of the Commission.[44]

The external consequences of the single currency

In the aftermath of Maastricht, the AMUE also turned to geostrategic questions. Since the creation of the Giscard–Schmidt Committee the world had been transformed. The Soviet empire was dissolved, Germany united, and Europe committed by Treaty to a single currency. Although the story of EMU went back far into time, there is little doubt that the acceleration in the monetary integration process was due to the political dynamics resulting from the fall of the Berlin wall.[45] Suddenly, there was an opportunity to bring central and Eastern Europe into the grand strategic equilibrium that had brought peace and prosperity to Western Europe. It was also clear that Europe had to consider the larger world of which it was part. The looming Gulf war was a reminder. Agnelli had formulated the strategic vision that many of his friends in the AMUE shared:

> The crisis in the Persian Gulf, the unification of the two Germanies and sterling's entry into the EMS Exchange Rate Mechanism are recent events which have had a decisive effect on the prospects with which, at the start of the summer, we began to work toward the inauguration of the Inter-governmental Conference on Economic and Monetary Union. The Gulf crisis has brought to the fore, first of all, the crucial problem of the lack of any effective, ready-made structures with which to co-ordinate the foreign and defence policies of EEC countries. [...] During the Seventies, Europe trembled before the inconvertibility of the dollar and soaring oil prices. The Werner plan for a European economic and monetary union in 1970 failed, and European countries entered such a cycle of recession and instability that the EEC risked dissolution. This time, those EC member countries that are willing must take a stand in favour of courage, because the European currency, and the establishment of a 'democratic government' of the European economy, is the decision that will eventually make it possible to push political union forwards. The alternative is to risk the dissolution of the EEC, in a climate of 'everyone for himself'.[46]

Against this background, the Association increasingly discussed matters of international monetary relations. At the Board meeting in Brussels in March 1991,

François-Xavier Ortoli who, as chairman of a French petrol company, was keenly aware of geostrategic concerns, declared: 'We need world monetary stability. Five years ago, nobody thought it would be possible to have the discussion we now have about EMU. Let's start to do the same for yen, Ecu, dollar relations. The co-operation between central banks is one first step in this respect'. Also, for Hans Merkle, 'world-wide stability was much more important for business than just European stability. The first goal of a European single currency should precede a second step which is imperative to assure Europe's power'.[47] Jean-René Fourtou, chairman of Rhône-Poulenc, gave one of the most convincing explanations why business needed stable exchange rates:

> Differences in national monetary and fiscal policies have led to significant interest rate variations. They have allowed the persistence of some remarkable internal and external imbalances between the three major international trading blocks, in particular in respect of the US dollar zone and the DM or European currency block. Inflation is still a national plight and flexible exchange rates rather seem to condone lax monetary policies. As for exchange rate misalignments, they are hardly avoided in the present regime, as US dollar movements remind us every day. Far more important, however, is the general climate of uncertainty in world markets. An exchange rate that serves as a basis for investment and other calculations today may be utterly changed in a month. Nobody would dare anticipate where it will stand in five or 10 years' time. Yet businesses need certainty. In a competitive world economy, profit margins are tight. Already small exchange rate variations may be able to wipe them out. Under these circumstances, it becomes increasingly risky to allocate important financial funds to long-term productive investment. More often, short-term financial investment is preferred. Long-term growth is therefore less than optimal. What is to be done? Greater worldwide monetary stability is required, in particular with respect to the exchange rate between dollar and the Ecu-composing currencies of the European Monetary System (EMS). This, of course, is a difficult task. The Bretton Woods System failed because institutional arrangements cannot survive if policy aims between partners are contradictory. A stabilization of international exchange rate fluctuations must start with greater co-ordination of economic and monetary policies. This implies, first of all, an acceptance of the fundamental norm that the elimination of inflation is a priority in any monetary economy and necessary to ensure long-term growth. Furthermore, it is probable that the creation of European Monetary Union (EMU), including an independent European Central Bank and the Ecu as the single currency of the Community, will facilitate greater convergence towards international monetary stability. This is because a single currency, the Ecu, will become an attractive and powerful competitor to the US$ and the Japanese yen. Europe will speak with a single voice in monetary matters. The consequent rebalancing of the international monetary system will need greater policy co-ordination.[48]

These considerations were increasingly reflected in the AMUE's activities, although they never overshadowed the main purpose of making the single currency happen. While political initiatives like exchange rate targeting seemed out of reach for the moment, the AMUE engaged in research related to the international dimension in order to structure debates and generate insights. Consequently, the Association's Annual Conference in 1991, organized with the Royal Institute of International Affairs in London, took the title: *European Monetary Union in a Turbulent World Economy*. Speakers included Toyoo Gyohten, former Vice-finance Minister of Japan, Rudi Dornbusch, Professor at MIT, Jacques Attali, President of the newly created European Bank for Reconstruction and Development, Bob Hormats, Vice Chairman of Goldman Sachs International (New York), and Jacob Frenkel, Director of Research of the IMF.[49] The fundamental message was: EMU can and should contribute to greater monetary stability world-wide, but this required greater monetary co-operation and co-ordination between the major countries.

In later years, the Association sought to improve links with Asia. It organized conferences with local members or partners in Tokyo, Beijing, Bangkok and in 1996, in partnership with the French Research Institute CEPII and the Korean Institute for Finance, an academic conference on exchange rate management in Asia in Seoul. Six months before the Asian crisis the contributors made clear that Asian pegs to the dollar were unsustainable.[50]

Central and Eastern Europe

A second question that preoccupied businessmen was Central and Eastern Europe. Hans Merkle repeatedly encouraged the AMUE to spend more time on working with these countries in order to avoid them being tied too closely to Germany.[51] Merkle, at the time over eighty years old, was personally worried about Western Europe's strategic post-war equilibrium falling apart. He insisted on the importance of a greater, united Europe as he saw the danger of a future confrontation between the three monetary zones – the Ecu, dollar, and yen. It was important to make progress step by step without discrimination in order to avoid domination by one country. The integration of Eastern Europe was not a short- but a long-term project and Merkle thought it important to offer incentives for these countries as one could not be certain that the end of Communism had been definitely achieved. In response to Merkle's request, but also to a number of contacts in Warsaw, Prague, and Budapest, the AMUE suggested how to integrate these former Communist countries into the Western European process toward EMU. It was designed to help fast-reforming countries of Central and Eastern Europe gain currency convertibility and to facilitate their convergence to EC economic and monetary standards. The proposal to create an Ecu Zone for Eastern Europe was modelled on the EMS and contained three main elements: An Eastern European Stabilization Fund, convertibility standby facilities, and a soft ERM. The idea was to gradually strengthen exchange rate commitments during the process of transition to a market economy.

The proposal was launched on 13 November 1991 in Berlin.[52] It was, as Ortoli put it, an important contribution to a public debate and was discussed by a panel including, among others, Jiri Jindra, an advisor to the President of the Czechoslovakian Central Bank, Werner Riecke, advisor to the President of the Hungarian Central Bank, who later became deputy President of the Hungarian Central Bank, and Walter Romberg, the last finance minister of the GDR, now a member of the European Parliament. Riecke welcomed the Ecu Zone as a realistic solution to many of Hungary's economic problems. Jindra indicated that the Czechoslovakian Central Bank would take part in further discussions. Experts from the financial sector greeted the suggestions. For example Harry Schröder, Vice President of Commerzbank, drew attention to the positive results of pegging the Swedish currency to the Ecu, which had reversed capital flows back into the country. Larry Anderson of Deutsche Bank Capital Markets in London interpreted the proposal as a continuation of an international trend in the transition from flexible exchange rates to a more stable tripolar international monetary system. At a later meeting with the AMUE Board, Jacques Delors became interested in the proposal. However, the practical realisation of the idea became a victim of the EMS crisis when the idea of giving intervention guarantees fell into discredit.

In 1992, the AMUE was at the height of its success. It seemed to have achieved its main mission, was a respected dialogue partner, and acted as an intellectual powerhouse for European policy makers. All this was to change suddenly, when the Danish people once again confronted Europe with the essential question: to be or not to be?

The European Monetary System in crisis

On 2 June 1992, the Danish people said 'No' to the Maastricht Treaty of in a referendum that shocked Europe. This triggered a crisis of legitimacy that nearly prevented the Treaty's ratification. Financial markets played havoc and effectively blasted away the EMS, thereby confirming the worst fears about the inconsistent quartet. Exchange rate volatility created severe distortions in the single market. As the EMS crisis confirmed the need for a strong institutional backing for monetary co-operation in Europe's single market, it deserves to be analysed in some detail. The AMUE took a particular interest in the issue when preparing a report for the European Parliament.

A short history of the EMS

The EMS had finally evolved into the 'zone of monetary stability' that Helmut Schmidt and Valery Giscard d'Estaing intended to create in 1978. This evolution had taken place in four phases. Between 1979 and 1983, the system resembled largely the previous snake system. Central parities were realigned seven times in a period of only four years. National economic policies remained inconsistent, with high and diverging inflation rates. There were no clear rules on the size of the realignments, but broadly inflation differentials were accommodated.

However, realignments were increasingly supplemented by meaningful adjustment packages.

From 1983 to 1987, the EMS entered calmer waters. Significant nominal convergence in costs, wages, and monetary aggregates was realized. The Deutschmark emerged as the dominant currency in *phase two*, serving as the anchor for bloc floating.[53] The use of the Deutschmark for EMS interventions reinforced its function as an international means of payments and reserve asset. Hence, the external monetary relations of ERM countries were increasingly determined by the dollar–Deutschmark policy of the Bundesbank (see Funabashi 1988; Ungerer 1990; Henning 1994). International capital flows increased dramatically during the period, rendering the system more vulnerable.[54] The last realignment of phase two, in January 1987, was of a new type, prompted by speculative unrest in currency markets linked to the dollar's weakness, rather than by macroeconomic divergence among EMS participants (Gros and Thygesen 1992: 84). It therefore reflected the increased role of world-wide capital flows and of the Deutschmark as an international reserve asset. Better co-ordination of monetary polices, in particular with regard to interest rates, was required to stabilize the system. This led to the so-called Basle–Nyborg agreement, in September 1987.

Phase three from the Basle–Nyborg agreement to the Maastricht Treaty of 1992 was one of remarkable exchange rate stability. Hence it has often been called the 'hard EMS'. No exchange rate realignment took place during this period.[55] However, the stability of exchange rates was achieved by significant interest rate differentials (see Figure 4.1), which converged only gradually and put stress on the conduct of economic policies in member countries. Tensions between the US dollar and ERM currencies during 1988 and 1989 led to rumours about realignments and to debates on the appropriate economic and financial policies in the United States and Europe. Although inflation rates had come down, they had not converged everywhere to German levels. Real exchange rates consequently appreciated and the competitiveness of high inflation countries like Italy and Spain weakened. In these countries, many companies considered German policies as a strait-jacket. EC member states also increasingly implemented the policies related to the Single European Act, which was signed early in 1986 and had set the end of 1992 as the starting date for a single market in Europe. Of particular importance was the liberalization of capital movements. By mid-1990, remaining restrictions had been abolished by France, Italy, Belgium, and Luxembourg. Germany, the Netherlands, Denmark, and the United Kingdom had done so long before.

The debate on the creation of the Economic and Monetary Union was renewed during this period, partly in response to the SEA and its monetary implications. At the end of the period, the EMS was enlarged by several currencies. Spain joined the ERM in June 1989, the United Kingdom in October 1990, and Portugal in April 1992, at a fluctuation band of ±6 per cent. The EMS also became a reference for outside currencies.[56] These pegs were voluntary and unilateral. Although there were no supporting commitments from the EMS central banks, they had symbolic value.

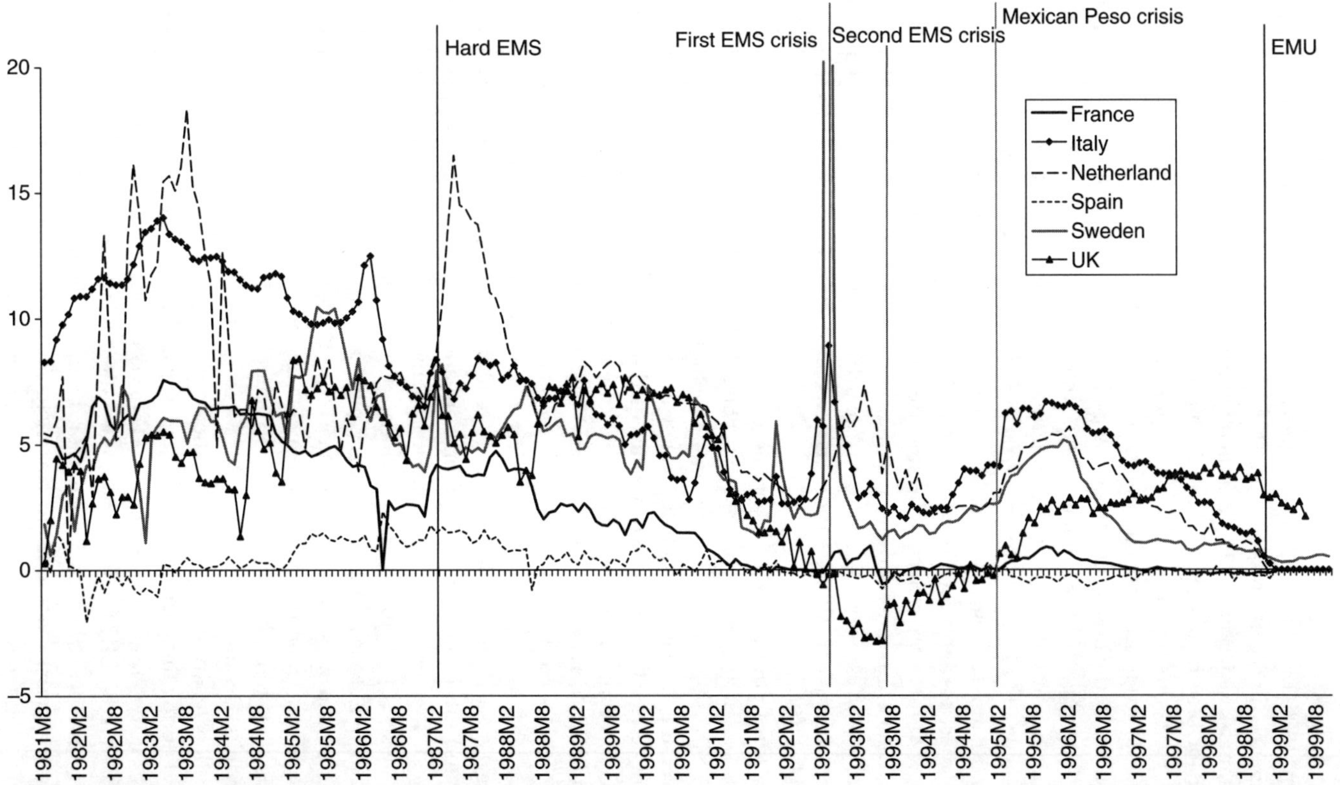

Figure 4.1 Short-term interest rate differentials to Germany (source: IMF).

Phase four of the EMS (1992–99) was marked by crisis, turmoil, and the final run-up to EMU. The inclusion of new and large currencies meant that the contingent intervention obligations by the Bundesbank increased substantially. Furthermore, the new members were all high inflation countries relative to Germany. Between 1989 and 1992, the price *levels* diverged from Germany by 6.6 per cent in Italy and the United Kingdom, by 7.8 per cent in Spain, and 22.3 per cent in Portugal. By contrast, the French price level fell by 2.4 per cent below the German level as a consequence of competitive disinflation (Collignon 1994).[57] Thus, domestic economic and monetary policies were still not really converging. It also has been widely acknowledged that the United Kingdom had joined the ERM at too high a rate, which exacerbated the subsequent difficulties.[58] Hence, the question of realignment was not unrealistic. Many analysts thought about it, but the official consensus in Europe was not to talk about it. The AMUE board raised the topic on several occasions, as the concern about deteriorating competitiveness grew, but each time it was decided to support governments in their commitment to the existing ERM exchange rates by keeping silent. In Italy, Agnelli insisted on the need to bring down inflation. Real exchange rate misalignments had to be corrected by 'virtuous policies', not by exchange rate adjustments. The policy consensus was so strong that it could not be destroyed by words. For example, the German information service for investors *Plato Brief* reported in May 1992 remarks of Bundesbank President Schlesinger, made at the Annual Meeting of the AMUE in Frankfurt, that the exchange rate for the Italian lira was grossly overvalued and would necessitate a devaluation before Italy could join the EMU. Although the remarks were made publicly and the information was processed in investors' media, markets only considered the realignment scenario seriously several weeks later, when the first Danish referendum rejected the Maastricht Treaty.

By the early 1990s, the EMS had become brittle: a heavy load was attached to the German anchor, which threatened the Bundesbank's capacity to control domestic money supply. On the other hand, competitive disinflation was not a collective solution for fundamental disequilibria. The real depreciation of one currency requires the appreciation of another. With fixed nominal exchange rates this would only have been possible, had Germany been willing to accept higher rates of inflation than its partners. As this would have undermined the Deutschmark's anchor function in the system, it was out of question (König and Willeke 1998: 25).[59] In fact, the EMS suffered from a dilemma that also undermined the Bretton Woods System: the inconsistent roles of an anchor currency in performing a national and an international function simultaneously. As Padoa-Schioppa noted: 'The policy conflict that accelerated the decline of the Bretton Woods System arose from the accommodating policy stance of the anchor currency, whereas in the case of the ERM the policy of the anchor currency was restrictive. In both cases the problems caused by the attribution of international status to a national currency and responsibility for running a monetary policy for a group of countries to a national central bank proved to be insurmountable' (Padoa-Schioppa 2000b: 197). The only logically coherent solution to this dilemma was to make the international function of money national, that is, to eliminate the currency barriers and create a single currency for Euroland.

The EMS was hit by one political and two economic shocks. The first resulted from the rejection of the Maastricht Treaty by the Danish voters on 2 June 1992. The latter consisted in the adjustment of the Deutschmark to the economic consequences of German unification, and the very weak US dollar prior to the American elections.

The Danish credibility shock

Within fourteen months the EU switched from manic Europhoria into a deep Eurodepression. What had happened? The EMS had been seen as a smooth 'glidepath' to EMU (Connolly 1995: 130), a 'funnel' that would facilitate economic convergence (Collignon 1994: 41). In the early 1990s, academic economists appeared to agree that the role of the Deutschmark in the EMS had contributed to disinflation in all member states (see Collignon 1994: 54, 123). Although there was empirical evidence for this claim, the underlying causal mechanism was not clearly understood. The favoured explanatory model was monetarism plus rational expectations. Membership of the EMS provided additional 'discipline' to monetary authorities in inflation-prone countries. The two channels of discipline worked through increasing the credibility of central banks or government austerity programmes. Without perfect credibility, financial markets require a risk premium on interest rates over and above the anchor currency and this was an indicator of the stability commitment.

By 'tying their hands', public authorities demonstrated their intentions. This applied to monetary policies as much as the credibility of austerity packages, mostly incomes policies plus fiscal consolidation. By pegging a highly visible exchange rate, governments could not easily renege on their policies. Some authors have argued that the higher reputation resulting from the peg to the Deutschmark would lower the cost of stabilisation policies, notably in terms of unemployment (see, e.g. Artis and Ormerod 1994). However, academic research has never been able to prove this claim convincingly. In fact, it seems that disinflationary policies in the EMS did not work through the credibility of the exchange anchor *alone*, but rather that exchange rate policies were part of traditional stabilisation packages, focused on incomes (wage) policies and fiscal consolidation (Collignon 1994: 133). 'Homework needs to be done at home', the Bundesbank used to say. This proved to be crucial in the 1990s, when all countries made significant efforts to reach the Maastricht convergence criteria.[60]

When the Maastricht Treaty was signed, it was expected that the EU countries participating in the ERM[61] would converge rapidly to the Maastricht criteria and join a single currency within a relatively short period. As a consequence, financial markets expected the high yields on long-term securities in high inflation countries to come down to German levels. Such developments opened significant potential for capital gains and investors poured money into Italy, the United Kingdom, Spain, and Portugal. These portfolio investments were called *convergence plays*. The IMF has estimated that approximately US$ 300 billion were transferred to high-yield ERM currencies, prior to the Danish referendum (International Monetary Fund 1993).

However, the negative vote in Denmark's June 1992 referendum put a big question mark on the feasibility of a rapid transition to EMU. It was no longer clear that the Treaty would or could be implemented politically. Observers agreed that EMU would not be able to start, if Germany or France decided to keep out – and the French referendum was due only three months later. As a reaction to the credibility crisis, financial markets re-positioned themselves. Huge amounts of money flowed out of Spain and Italy, later also the United Kingdom. While both Mediterranean countries had previously accumulated foreign exchange reserves with the exchange rate near the ceiling of the EMS band, the situation now reversed dramatically. Despite little or no 'news' about the fundamental facts of the Spanish or Italian economies, their currencies fell to the bottom of the ERM fluctuation band and needed support by the central banks, especially the Bundesbank. This situation would not necessarily have been unsustainable, had it not happened against the background of a profoundly destabilized German economy.

The German unification shock

Although the way German unification was pushed through by Chancellor Helmut Kohl in 1990 had been criticized by Bundesbank President Karl Otto Pöhl and the opposition leader Oskar Lafontaine, it may well be true that there was no alternative. Nevertheless, the economic facts were a 'disaster', as Pöhl put it. The sudden access by the East German population to hard purchasing power caused a major demand shock in Germany and to some of its ERM neighbours.[62] German real GDP increased by 5.7 per cent in 1990 and 4.5 per cent in 1991 – unheard of since the early 1970s. Domestic demand was the prime factor behind these developments.[63] Government transfers amounting to nearly Ecu 225 billion went from West to East Germany, representing 65 per cent of GDP in the former GDR.[64] The conversion of eastern money balances into Deutschmarks increased money wealth effectively by a factor of five.[65] As a consequence, consumer demand for Western goods exploded. German imports increased by 9.4 and 12.1 per cent in 1990 and 1991, respectively, pushing the import share from other EU countries up by nearly two percentage points of GDP, while imports from the rest of the world remained stable. Thus, German unification had the effect of directly stimulating economic activity in Europe.[66] Due to the sudden demand shock consumer price inflation increased from 2.0 per cent in 1990 to 3.8 and 4.0 per cent in the two following years.[67] Rising inflation in a tense (Western) labour market[68] led to higher wage claims. Nominal wages increased by 4.7, 5.8, 5.4, and 3.3 successively from 1990 to 1993. The Bundesbank considered that this contributed to an inflationary wage–price spiral, which needed to be broken. Hence, from February 1991 on, it increased interest rates. With hindsight it appears that the Bundesbank overreacted. As it is often the case in an economic boom, labour productivity also improved. Consequently, unit labour costs, which are the appropriate variable to measure cost pressure, increased in 1992 by only 0.4 per cent and in 1993 by 0.2 per cent. But in each of the three years before and after that period, they had fallen by more than 0.6 per cent (European Economy No. 60,

1995: 225). Hence, German price increases reflected a profit-inflation, which would have petered out gradually by increasing supply, rather than a wage-push inflation, which would have required a stabilization–recession as the Bundesbank believed. However, after monetary tightening, business activity cooled down rapidly in the second half of 1992, reinforced by the deteriorating international climate after the Iraqi invasion of Kuwait. The darkened economic outlook with worries about jobs made the public acceptance of Maastricht more difficult.

The dollar shock

On 2 July 1992, the US Federal Reserve Board reduced its discount rate to 3 per cent to combat the recession, while the Bundesbank raised its discount rate to a record 8.75 per cent two weeks later – the highest level since the creation of the Federal Republic after the war. The short-term interest rate differential between Germany and the United States widened to 6.75 percentage points and caused massive capital inflows into Germany that upset the Bundesbank's monetary targeting. In the late 1960s, the Bundesbank had lowered its rate in a similar situation. Not so this time. On 4 September 1992, the US Federal Reserve reduced its rates again, and the dollar fell to a historic low of DEM 1.3870. The extremely tight monetary conditions with high interest rates and an overvalued Deutschmark bloc became unbearable for Europe. They led to one of the most painful recessions since Second World War, extremely high levels of unemployment and a dramatic deterioration of public finances. In 1993, GDP in the EU fell by 0.5 per cent, in Germany and the Netherlands by 1.2 per cent (West Germany 1.9 per cent), in Spain by 1 per cent, and France and Italy 0.7 per cent. The aggregate budget deficit in the EU increased from 3.7 per cent in 1990 to 6.3 per cent of GDP in 1993, and throughout the European Union unemployment shot up. On average, it increased from 8.1 to 11.3 per cent between 1991 and 1994.[69] Only the United Kingdom regained sufficient policy margins after leaving the ERM that helped to bring down the unemployment rate from 10.1 per cent in 1992 to 8.4 per cent in 1995.

The demise of the hard EMS

The ERM crisis brought severe instabilities to the single market as it provoked exchange rate developments, which had nothing to do with fundamentals. The effect of the crisis on selected currencies is shown in Figure 4.2. The bilateral exchange rate to the Deutschmark in June 1992 is chosen as the base of the index. While the French franc stayed close to the DEM, the lira, peseta, and sterling were substantially devalued. All devaluing currencies *overshot* their long-term steady state level, but while Italy and Spain reintegrated into the system and finally locked into the euro at these equilibrium rates, the United Kingdom remained outside the ERM, causing a new currency overvaluation. The hard EMS's demise started at the periphery, where institutional backing was weakest. When tensions increased in the financial market, Finland abandoned the unilateral peg to the Ecu on

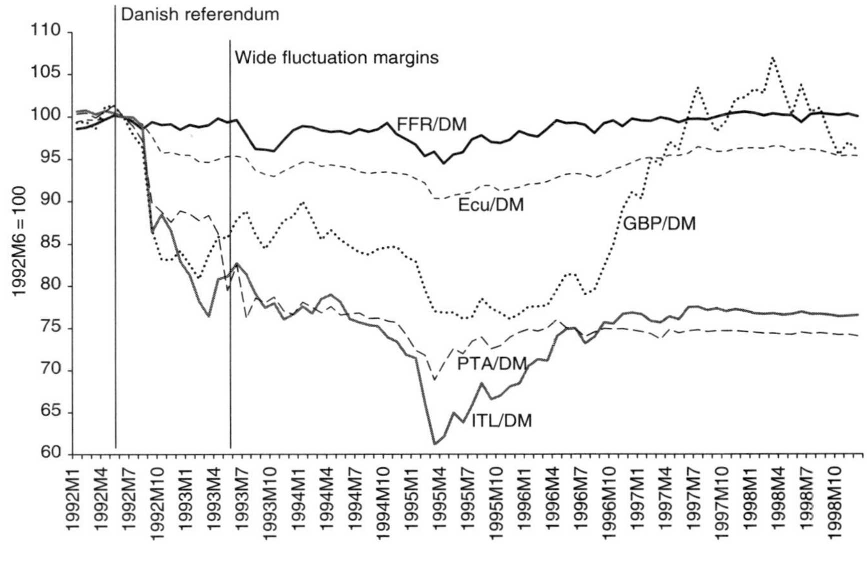

Figure 4.2 ERM exchange rates in crisis (source: IMF).

8 September 1992. Swedish marginal lending rates were raised, first to 75 and then to 500 per cent. This was proof of a growing credibility crisis. On 13 September, after intense speculative attacks, the Italian lira was devalued by 7 per cent and the Bundesbank lowered its interest rates marginally the following day. Although this devaluation should have corrected the price level divergence of 6.6 per cent since 1989, two days later the Italian lira dropped below its new central ERM parity. Financial markets were no longer concerned by fundamentals, as they were now convinced that they could make money by ripping the system apart, instead of betting on convergence. Soon sterling also fell to its lowest point against the Deutschmark and the Spanish peseta started to soften. Additional insecurity came from the uncertain outcome of the French referendum. On 16 September 1992 (Black Wednesday), the pound was suspended from the ERM and the lira followed the next day.[70] The United Kingdom announced that it would not return to the ERM until 'faultlines' had been reformed. The Spanish peseta was devalued by 5 per cent within the ERM on 17 September, and again on 23 November 1992, this time together with the Portuguese escudo, both by 6 per cent. The French franc, Danish krone, and Irish punt all came under heavy selling pressure. On 20 September, the French referendum narrowly approved the Maastricht Treaty by 51.01 per cent, which removed some of the political uncertainties. However, under market pressure Sweden abandoned its unilateral peg to the Ecu in November, and Norway in December.

On 1 January 1993, the Single Market came into force and with it banking regulations concerning the capital and liquidity of credit institutions. Monetary turbulences continued unabated. On 1 February, the Irish punt was devalued by 10 per cent in the EMS because Ireland was heavily dependent on imports from the United Kingdom (42 per cent) and the dramatic devaluation of sterling risked creating significant distortions.[71] After some cooling down in financial markets in early 1993, the Spanish peseta was again devalued on 13 May, followed by the Portuguese escudo by 8 and 6.5 per cent, respectively, without any accompanying economic adjustment.

In July 1993, massive speculative attacks developed against the French franc, the Danish krona, and the Belgian franc, which led to the widening of intervention bands in the system at the emergency meeting of the Community Finance ministers and Central Bank governors on 1 and 2 August 1993 in Brussels. However, by simply widening the margins rather than abolishing the EMS, the Ecofin council maintained the formal policy framework for the Maastricht Treaty. Interestingly, it was the British Chancellor of the Exchequer, Kenneth Clarke, who saved the day. The crisis meeting had been going on for two days, chaired by the Belgium finance minister Philippe Maystadt (who at the same time was absorbed by a domestic crisis after King Boudoin's sudden death). All participants were aware that if they did not produce a solution by Sunday night, private operators in the financial market would cause havoc the next day. By 10 PM that night 'discussions had gone terribly wrong'[72] and an exhausted Maystadt proposed that they should 'agree to fail to agree'. After a short break, the meeting was reconvened and Maystadt formally announced that there was no solution: 'We have to see what happens in the markets tomorrow'. Kenneth Clarke, who had been less exhausted and involved in the negotiations as the United Kingdom no longer participated in the ERM, listened with disbelief to what he considered 'the death warrant of Maastricht'. He was a convinced European, although of a pragmatic kind, and more concerned how things worked out concretely than by high philosophical thinking on integration. After Maystadt's declaration, which usually would have terminated the session, Clarke took the floor and made a passionate plea to his fellow ministers, urging them not to give up and to widen the intervention bands in the ERM. To his surprise, all his colleagues suddenly agreed with his urgent plaidoyer. The meeting finally decided that the central rates, which had been in force since 14 May 1993, remained unchanged, but in response to speculative movements, the obligatory bilateral marginal intervention limits for all currencies participating in the ERM were widened to ±15 per cent.[73] The widening of the bands was supposed to be of limited duration, but remained in force until EMU started in 1999. Clarke's contribution to the survival of EMU was an impressive demonstration of the power of ideas. Convincing arguments, put forward by disinterested individuals, could alter collective preferences.

EMU's loss of credibility

Although monetary authorities restated their commitment to price stability and all member states reaffirmed their determination to put the Maastricht Treaty into operation, including pursuing policies of economic convergence, the credibility of the EMU project was shattered. Especially in the Anglo-Saxon press, few commentators believed that the Maastricht Treaty should or would be implemented. David Marsh had commented in the *Financial Times* during the crisis: 'A treaty ostensibly mapping the road to EMU now appears to contain built-in roadblocks. [...] Western Europe reacted [to the fall of the Berlin Wall] by trying to speed up, through the Maastricht treaty, moves towards EC unity first launched in the 1950s and accelerated by the process of creating a single European market. That was always a debatable choice. In retrospect, it looks like the wrong one' (*Financial Times*, 8 April 1992). As the hard EMS was de facto suspended in August 1993, speculations rose whether the EMU project would eventually also be abandoned. Ulrich Cartellieri, Board Member at the Deutsche Bank, criticized this view in a German weekly: 'Doubts and confusion as a consequence of the monetary crises blend with nationalistic trends, not only in Germany. John Major has made the critique a political topic: According to him the EMS has failed, the concept of Monetary Union has been unrealistic from the start, an Economic and Monetary Union cannot be realized'. Yet, Cartellieri insisted, 'EMU was without an alternative' (*Die Zeit*, 20 October 1993: 36).

With hindsight, the EMS crisis had two consequences: It reinforced the political commitment to EMU on the Continent and blocked the UK's adhesion. For the AMUE, it became a close encounter with death.

Reinforced political commitment

After the widening of the bands to ±15 per cent in August 1993, many observers expected that national monetary authorities would use their new freedom to lower interest rates to stimulate economic growth. However, European governments and central banks followed policies that remained consistent with the implementation of the Treaty.

Figure 4.2 shows the developments of some large currencies with respect to the Deutschmark. After the Danish 'No', sterling and the lira were first devalued, then left the ERM. The Spanish peseta remained in the system which kept short-term volatility subdued, compared to Italy or the United Kingdom, but frequent devaluations led to a readjustment in the exchange rate that was close to that of Italy. On the other hand, France and the other smaller currencies in the hard core, such as the Belgian franc, the Dutch guilder, the Danish krona, and the Austrian schilling remained remarkably close to the German currency. This stability was partly achieved by widening the bands and thereby removing the incentive for financial markets to speculate against authorities, partly by greater flexibility in the actual conduct of monetary policy: whenever required by foreign exchange market conditions, central banks would raise (or lower) interest rates. This underlined authorities' determination to maintain a close link with the Deutschmark and deterred speculative attacks (Verplaetse 1997).[74] In Italy, the return to stability took longer than in the countries that remained in the ERM. Although Italy and Spain seemed to have reached a fundamental equilibrium exchange rate by the end of 1993, roughly a quarter below its pre-crises level, speculative market pressures in early 1995 pushed the lira into a further devaluation of 20 per cent from which it recovered only in 1996.

The devaluations in 1995 were a spillover from the Mexican crisis in December 1994, but the dramatic amplitude in Italy reflected home-made distrust in financial markets about the sustainability of Italy's public debt. Rumours expected the Italian government to default. Matters were complicated by the budget plan announced by the Berlusconi government in 1994 and the social unrest its pension reforms caused. After Berlusconi's fall, the transitory technical government by Lamberto Dini started to improve the situation and solved the pension crisis, but only with the election of the Prodi government in April 1996 did Italy regain the confidence of financial markets.[75] At the end of November 1996, Italy returned into the ERMs of the EMS and from then on, the lira remained stable with respect to the Deutschmark until it became a member of the euro-zone in 1999. For sterling, the development was different. Although the initial devaluation of approximately 15 per cent seemed to have corrected the previous overvaluation, allowing growth to come back in the United Kingdom, sterling started to appreciate by mid-1996 to reach pre-1992 levels within one year. Policy makers responded to the turmoil with renewed commitment to the single currency.

This had political and economic reasons. Politically, the EU had looked into the abyss of 'co-ordination failure' (Padoa-Schioppa 2000b: 193) and seen how this endangered the stability of the strategic equilibrium on which Europe's freedom and prosperity were built. Most continental policymakers learned that the answer to the crisis was a stronger institutional set-up for monetary policy, not a weaker one. This was also true for the Bundesbank. When its president Hans Tietmeyer was asked why Europe needed the EMU since the EMS had been functional for years, he gave a long explanation of the need for European stability. He described his personal involvement in Mitterrand's decision in 1983 not to leave the ERM and concluded: 'It is not in Germany's interest that such an important decision by our largest trading partner can be taken by one man alone'.[76]

The solution to the 'inconsistent quartet', whereby free trade, unrestricted capital flows, fixed exchange rates and autonomous national monetary policies cannot coexist in the long run, required delegating monetary policy to the European level unless the single market was there to be given up. During the crisis, this became clear with early signs of erosion in the single market appeared. While 1000 Italian lira cost DEM 1.33 before the crisis, this price fell to 80 Pfennig in April 1995 – a devaluation of 40 per cent. The British pound fell from DEM 2.95 to DEM 2.21 in 1995, a loss of 25 per cent of its value. Yet, by 1999 the lira was back up to DEM 1.01 and the pound to DEM 2.79. These gyrations caused havoc in the single market. Carl Hahn, the former Chairman of Volkswagen, reported at one AMUE meeting that the car manufacturer effectively lost DEM 2000 with every Golf car sold in Italy at the then prevailing exchange rate. However, the Fiat Chairman was also critical about a lira devaluation, although at first sight they seemed to benefit his company: 'We have tried devaluations so many times. They never work'.[77] In France, political voices on the right and the left asked for protection of the domestic market against 'dumping imports' from Italy and Spain.

French industrialists in the textile sector openly questioned the single market: 'In the present conditions of monetary disorder, it is appropriate to install monetary or customs compensations with respect to countries that do not have the political will or technical capacity to respond to the convergence criteria which would allow them to reach a single currency. This is the only means within reach of our economy to compensate for abnormally obtained advantages' (Georges Jollès, *Le Figaro*, 20 April 1995). The Works Council of Ford Europe complained about interfactory price distortions that were unrelated to productivity.[78] The chief economist of Saint-Gobain, Albert Merlin, wrote: 'There cannot be a single market that deserves this name, if one does not put an end to the multiple price distortions which pollute the principle of competition and undermine the rationality of the effort made by companies to play the big interior market' (*Le Figaro*, 3 September 1993).

The AMUE referred frequently to the 'inconsistent quartet' and re-emphasized that 'a true Single Market requires a single currency to be successful. Without full EMU, neither European business nor consumers will reap the full benefits. Investment will remain distorted by regional risk considerations, and growth and efficiency will continue to be sub-optimal' (AMUE press release, 10 December 1992). In June 1993, it declared: 'Monetary disorder would lead to protectionism and exacerbate the recession. The EMS remains the natural foundation for monetary stability and it is imperative that its functioning be improved, in giving more authority to the European Monetary Committee and to the future European Monetary Institute. Competitive devaluations should be prevented and price stability should remain among the primary aims in order that convergence can be accomplished, since this is an essential prerequisite to Economic and Monetary Union' (AMUE press release, 11 June 1993). After the EMS crisis, the AMUE increasingly shifted its focus to economic convergence as the necessary public policy to achieve a large group of EMU members and to practical issues of the preparation for the changeover to a single currency within companies (see next section). The promotion of the Ecu was restricted to market-led niches in the business sector, as the Association now avoided promotion campaigns that had been envisaged in the early days of the Giscard–Schmidt Committee.[79] They were now convinced that the Ecu as a parallel or common currency could not meet all expectations of European companies, and focused instead on the message 'the Ecu as a single currency'. However, the Ecu remained useful to maintain political momentum, helping the broad public to accept a single currency, which was still widely refused.

The problem with the United Kingdom

For a long time, the Association did not give up hope on the United Kingdom and Denmark. In April 1994, it published a manifesto where it invited the two countries 'to opt in' to EMU in order to avoid splitting Europe. However, the political situation in the United Kingdom had deteriorated. John Major had built his career by taking Britain into the ERM, despite the resistance of Margaret Thatcher.

He subsequently won a surprise victory in the general elections of April 1992. Yet, when the EMS crisis broke out, his authority was seriously damaged and never recovered in the five years of his Prime Ministership. The Conservative Party started to disintegrate over the divide between pro- and anti-Europeans (see Turner 2000).

On several occasions, it seemed uncertain whether the United Kingdom would ratify the Treaty. With hindsight it appears that the Maastricht Treaty's ratification and ultimately EMU was also saved by another important pro-European politician, namely by John Smith, who had succeeded Neil Kinnock as Labour leader after the elections. Smith once confided: 'I have ensured the survival of the Maastricht Treaty by deciding that we would not ask to have it ratified by referendum. That would have killed it'.[80] However, the actual ratification process in parliament was difficult and ran a serious risk of defeat.[81] The main reason was the bitter war amongst Tories over Europe and Labour sought to benefit from their divisions. However, on several occasions, John Smith signalled to AMUE not to worry, Labour would help to ratify Maastricht. Nevertheless, the ERM experience also discredited EMU for the left in the United Kingdom. Given the unsustainably high exchange rate at which the United Kingdom joined the EMS and the severely restrictive monetary policies in the early 1990s, the ERM was associated with institutional rigidity, recession and high unemployment, while Labour's motivation for joining Europe had been stable growth and higher employment. After the crisis, the British economy seemed to be better off with a less constraining framework for monetary policy although little credit was given to the ERM experience for bringing down inflation from over 7 to less than 2 per cent. The UK establishment therefore reverted to their traditional instincts for discretionary policy making. Rather than seeing a single currency as the solution to the problems, which had caused the ERM crisis, EMU was discredited for many years.

Ups and downs for the AMUE

The AMUE was increasingly concerned as the crisis unfolded; yet still tried to spread optimism. Two days after the Danish referendum the Board had declared in a press release that this was 'not the first set-back that Europe had known and it will be overcome as others before. European Monetary Union meets a clear need, as it will consolidate the Single Market and foster development of stability in Europe. It must therefore be pursued as an important priority for business'.

However, the mood darkened in the following month. Rising unemployment, the loss of public confidence, political instability in several countries, uncertainties about the Danish situation, and the consequences of the US elections weighed heavily on progress toward full EMU. While the difficulties of the ERM required more policy co-ordination, the Ecu market had also collapsed as a consequence of the devaluation of the basket against the strong currencies.[82] At a Board meeting on 6 October 1992, all participants[83] expressed their concern for the future of the EMU. Their doubts were less about technicalities, but about basic questions, such as the role of nationalism and the difficulties of economic convergence. In this context, a two-speed approach to EMU became more acute.

The Board unanimously emphasized the need for greater stability for European business and called on authorities to avoid the Community 'breaking into two unions'. The Association made a distinction between countries 'having the will to proceed to full EMU and those who do not'. Europe *à la carte*, that is, without rules to bind *all* members, was considered 'disastrous, as the content of the Community would disappear'. On the other hand, several speeds of transition for those countries, which had the political will to proceed, could be useful. A year later,[84] the Board re-iterated this view by stressing that 'the progressive constitution and enlargement of the hard-core will be a strong incentive for all countries to converge'. The assessment turned out to be realistic. It was exactly this kind of peer-pressure that pushed Italy to change domestic policies in order to meet the convergence criteria.[85] Following this logic, the AMUE stated in March 1993: 'The French–German co-operation is the rock of credibility of European interpretation and in the present circumstances this is more important than ever'.[86] When the French franc came under significant speculation attacks, the Board also emphasized 'that if the EMS went, we would have to start again from scratch'. It made a call to 'demystify' the arguments against a hard-core group.

The wild fluctuations within the single market, radically changing relative prices, and competitive positions without any link to companies' efficiency, were intolerable for European businessmen. *Le Monde* commented that only few businesses 'had in effect taken precautions. Many had to react hastily or were ambushed. The monetary turmoil mixed up the business plans of their companies'.[87] Risks were not only related to the commercial performance, but also to the costs side and asset values. It could have been expected that these problems strengthened the position of the AMUE, as companies now brutally experienced how exchange rate instabilities hampered the single market. However, the contrary was the case. The crisis deeply affected the day-to-day business conditions of the Association. With the credibility of EMU in a shambles, many of the larger and high fee-paying member companies, who suffered from the recession, cancelled their membership. Figure 4.3 shows the evolution of membership fees of the Association. After the initial contribution to the foundation of the organization, income stayed for several years close to Ecu 900,000. With the crisis it dropped by 20 per cent and in 1994 it seemed as if the AMUE was heading for bankruptcy. In emergency, Davignon, Agnelli, Kopper, Sheehy, and de Maigret met at Le Bourget Airport in Paris to resolve the crisis. They embarked on a recruitment campaign for new members that would bear fruit in the following years. Beyond the ideological motives supported in particular by the early AMUE members, soon very practical considerations gained importance. By focusing on the necessity for practical preparations of a single currency the Association was able to re-establish the credibility of the EMU.

Reporting to the European Parliament

By the end of 1993, the Association's directors responded to the increasingly negative public opinion on EMU by shifting the emphasis of its public message to the

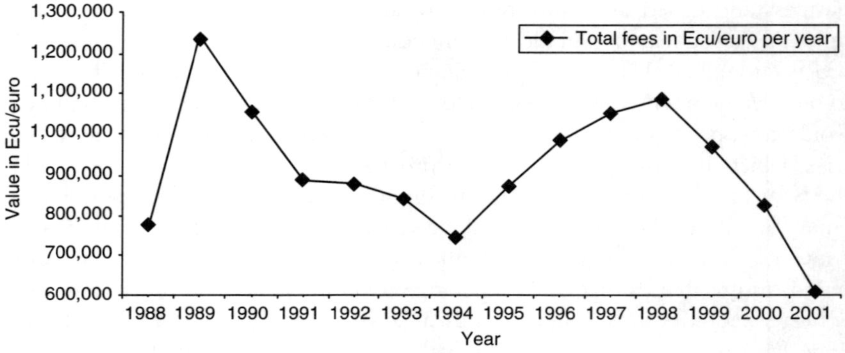

Figure 4.3 Membership fees received by the AMUE, 1987–2001.

welfare aspects of EMU. It stressed that European integration was providing a solution to unemployment, and was not its cause.[88] This message was developed in a report written at the request of the European Parliament. After the crisis in September 1992, Christa Randzio-Plath, the chairwoman of the Parliament's Subcommittee on Monetary Affairs, had asked the AMUE to evaluate the functioning of the EMS since its creation and to provide policy recommendations to improve the EMS in the transition to the EMU. The study reviewed the EMS experience from a theoretical and empirical point of view. It analysed the mechanics of the ERM, concentrated on the important developments in European and world capital markets and reviewed the fundamentals of economic convergence and divergence. The initial draft[89] was subsequently validated by different working groups, which the Association had set up for the project. The academic working group assembled leading economists,[90] while the working group with sixty-four participants from companies and banks gave them practitioners' feedback. A group of 'wise men', among them Helmut Schmidt, Renato Ruggiero,[91] Etienne Davignon, and François-Xavier Ortoli gave a final validation.

Two aspects were highlighted: (a) improving real convergence by linking macroeconomic incomes policies to general productivity increases; and (b) protecting nominal convergence by strengthening voluntary central bank co-ordination during stage two by 'broadening the anchor'.[92] Both suggestions were also thought to contribute to the fiscal consolidation necessary in several countries to reach the Maastricht convergence criteria. One originality was the discussion of economic convergence in the context of 'non-integrated labour markets'. The report stated:

> The trap of tight money, low growth and high unemployment could be overcome, if the pressure to combat inflation is taken off central banks by social partners agreeing on a 'co-operative game' where all parties win and nobody loses. This would be achieved by productivity-orientated wages policies for the economy as a whole. Ideally, if nominal wages were increased by the

> same rate as general productivity growth, price stability would be guaranteed. The central bank could then relax monetary policies, reduce interest rates, and thereby simultaneously stimulate investment (supply effect) and effective demand. At the same time, economic growth would improve the fiscal position of the government.[93]

The passage reflected discussions with Heiner Flassbeck, then chief economist at the German research institute DIW, one of the external experts contributing to the project. The suggestion that incomes policies may have a useful role for convergence and combating unemployment gave rise to a heated debate. Christopher Johnson, UK advisor to AMUE, pointed to the spectre of the British 'winter of discontent', when the Labour government of James Callaghan was confronted with the rejection of British incomes policies. Thus, calling for 'incomes policies' would be unacceptable in the UK. A compromise was reached by calling for 'macroeconomic policies *for* incomes'. Johnson also explained that the notion of 'social partners' did not exist in the English language, whereupon David Croughan, Chief Economist of the Irish employers' association replied: 'We speak English in Ireland and we *have* social partners'.

The report was transmitted to the European Parliament on 30 July 1993, two days before the ERM fluctuation margins were widened to ±15 per cent. As a consequence, the report's recommendation of providing unlimited credit facilities for non-sterilized central bank interventions in the EMS for the entire transition period prior to stage three never found its way into official policy debates. However, the idea of supporting growth-orientated monetary policies by appropriate wage settlements remained a subject the AMUE pursued for years. In November 1995, it organized a conference on European Monetary Policy in Kronberg near Frankfurt, where Nobel Prize winner Franco Modigliani explained the rationale for such policy (Modigliani 1997). To strengthen the political viability of this approach, Modigliani and the AMUE had also invited the two chief social partners in Italy, Innocenzo Cipolletta from Confindustria and Sergio d'Antonio, head of the trade union federation CISL, who shared their experience of Italy's social pact, which had laid the foundations for Italy's disinflation in the 1990s.[94] In 1997, the theory was further developed in the Association's Sustainability Report. After the start of EMU in 1999, the idea reappeared in the form of the Macroeconomic Dialogue institutionalized at the European Council in Cologne when Flassbeck and Collignon assumed European responsibilities in the German Finance Ministry (see Dyson 2002: 180–1).

Preparing the changeover

In 1995, the European Commission started to consider the practical challenges of the currency changeover in much more detail. 'I remember how we learnt that Commissioner Yves-Thilbaut de Silguy suddenly wanted to bring the publication of the Green Book forward', a Commission official recalls. 'His decision to have the draft of the transition scenario ready by May was a bit of a surprise and led to a couple of frantic weeks of work. There were many aspects of the changeover where we had no clear idea how to proceed'.[95] Initially, the Directorate General Economy and Finance (DG 2)[96] which had been working on the practical aspects of EMU since the Delors report, was asked to prepare the Green Book up to September 1995. But the new Commissioner for Economic and Financial affairs was pressuring his staff to present a paper a few months earlier.

There were at least two reasons for this rush. First, the political credibility of the EMU had been lost after the EMS crisis. De Silguy was worrying that the EU member states would not stick to their signatures under the Maastricht Treaty, which could provoke a fundamental political crisis with far-reaching economic consequences.[97] Second, the best way out of this situation seemed to be regaining credibility by focusing on practical issues, answering the open questions in the transition scenario and by encouraging practical preparations in the private sector.[98] The Madrid Council in December 1995 was a good occasion for a new commitment to EMU by the member states by agreeing a changeover scenario. Given the high sensitivity of the issue, the Green Book had to be ready well before.[99] De Silguy had a long experience in European affairs. Before becoming European Commissioner he had worked in this field for over twenty-five years, both as an advisor to Jaques Chirac and Eduard Balladur and as a director of large French companies. A few years earlier he worked closely with Bertrand de Maigret in the monetary subcommittee of the employer's association CNPF. He was therefore perfectly aware that the private sector faced a load of practical adaptations.

De Silguy's staff in DG 2 needed partners, that is, a network of experts who could help them find the answers to practical questions they were supposed to put forward in the Green Book.[100] Given previous co-operation with the AMUE and personal ties between de Maigret and de Silguy, it was natural that the Commission turned to the AMUE. Before, the Green Book was developed the Commission had commissioned a study on the general change-over for firms to the business consultants McKinsey, it had co-operated with selected firms and banks and diffused a questionnaire in September 1994. The head of the Ecu unit, Thierry Vissol, had been involved in the proceedings leading to *Strategy for the Ecu* and various related workshops which were partly financed by the Commission as part of their strategy to understand the practical aspects.[101] He had also attended the workshops that led to the AMUE report on *How to Prepare Companies for EMU*, which had given him more detailed impressions of the practical consequences of the changeover (AMUE 1992). Before the Maastricht Treaty entered into force, this expert group had concluded that 'thinking and planning for the single currency needs to start now'.

Two reports frame the issue

The study group was directed by Malcolm Levitt who had previously steered the *Strategy for the Ecu* at Ernst and Young and who had now become EU advisor to the Chairman of Barclays Bank.[102] In 1992, it presented a report about the practical implementation of the single currency in terms of the necessary systems, legal and market implications.[103] It equally pointed out what governments and EU institutions should do: decide rapidly on the timing of the changeover, encourage the use of the Ecu and remove legal obstacles. However, Levitt was disappointed by the work of the group, as he felt many banking participants 'were more concerned to sell Ecu-denominated bonds than to focus on the real issue'.[104] Even worse, he was preoccupied by the fact that senior bankers were unaware of technical details and believed modern computer systems could be switched over to the Ecu just by writing a little program: 'I clearly recall a dinner in Brussels with a number of Continental bankers at about Chairman level who held this view and they struck me like the man in the back of the chauffeur-driven Rolls Royce who did not understand the difference between the spark plug and a cigar lighter'.[105]

A second report followed in May 1994, again based on the results of a cross-sectoral, pan-European working group directed by Levitt. The Commission again supported the work as it shared Levitt's discontent. It concentrated on systems, treasury, legal, and market matters and managed to pin down timescales and tasks involved in the conversion. Discussions with experts from the banking sector revealed that the large banks were not prepared to commit resources to the preparation until there was a clear timetable and greater certainty which countries would participate. Its principal new insight was that stage three could not start with the use of Ecu cash in mass retail transactions: 'The introduction of the single currency cannot be implemented by public authorities without the early participation of everyone involved in making, receiving, processing, accounting and finally settling payments: in particular banks, companies in every sector of economic life, and the general public' (AMUE 1994).

The report requested that public authorities clarify the still-to-be-taken decisions on the changeover scenario and other legal and practical details. Companies insisted that many of their choices actually depended on a general framework, which, governments still needed to determine. For example, how would the changeover to the new currency be enforced? Would it be gradual or instant? Would there be a long or short period for parallel circulation of old and new currency? What was the legal status of the currencies? Did debt contracts need to be altered and at what point? Another important insight of the work involving lawyers and corporate treasurers as well as bankers was that there was the need for a regulation to ensure continuity of financial contracts to be denominated in legacy currencies. The conclusions and the time scale and costs for conversion of systems and the legal issue surprised many senior officials in national authorities and the Commission as well as the EMI. While some people at first thought these results were a British intrigue to delay EMU, they were eventually convinced by the arguments on bank lead times. As for the legal issues, Levitt later had to make extra efforts to get the point across.

In 1994, the AMUE also set up a working group to study the change of currency, which took place in Brazil on 1 July 1994 and was quicker and less costly than envisaged in the EU. By the time the AMUE had produced its third document on the transition and changeover, while no other organization had yet issued any clear assessments about the tasks to be completed and the needs of business as far as timetables etc. were concerned. However, the AMUE tried to entice other organizations to tackle these issues. It always saw its role as that of an ice-breaker, opening the passage for other, larger operators to follow. The Banking Federation of the EU was the first who followed and came forward with a survey *A First Contribution on the Practical Aspects* in March 1995 (Banking Federation of the European Union, 1995).

Dialogue with the AMUE in the two working groups and the two reports inspired the first Commission memorandum, which described the transition problems and outlined changeover scenarios. In the Communication on 'Practical problems involved in introducing the Ecu as the EU's single currency' published in June 1994, the Commission expressed itself on the microeconomic and sociological effects involved in introducing the single currency, and proposed a formal Commission initiative to contribute to the practical implementation of the single currency. 'It is clear that the highly complex nature of such an undertaking justifies a lengthy period of preparation – of the order of several years – and the prior adoption of an overall strategy setting out the practical steps to be taken in introducing the Ecu as the single currency' (European Commission 1994a: 177). The project was urgent as the Maastricht Treaty stipulated that the Ecu should be transformed into 'a currency in its own right' at the beginning of stage three, that is, between 1 January 1997 and 1 January 1999. 'The deadline – the precise date of which remains open – demonstrates the need to examine without further delay and in detail the practical problem involved. [...] The launching of an initiative of this kind is made all the more urgent by the number and scale of the problems to be overcome and by the time needed to introduce the essential changes in the Community countries'.

In contrast to national governments and officials, the Commission was determined to take a leading role in preparing the introduction of the single currency. In order to be able to present recommendations to the Council, the Commission formally decided to set up a technical group responsible for studying the practical steps involved in moving to the single currency. This group was supported by an interdepartmental working group and later became known as the Maas Group.

An expert group on the transition scenario

The Group's President was Cees Maas, formerly Treasurer General at the Dutch Ministry of Finance and at the time of the working group member of the Executive Board of the ING Group. He seemed a good choice as he represented a private sector bank, but had held political responsibilities in one of the countries, which – like the other reticent EU members – had to be convinced to take practical steps to prepare the launch of the single currency. Among the twenty members of the Maas Group were several AMUE representatives, for example Etienne Davignon who chaired the meetings when Cees Maas was absent, Philippe Lagayette, then CEO of the Caisse des Depôts et Consignations, and Tom Hardiman of IBM Ireland who also chaired the Irish employers' confederation. Heinz-Joachim Neubürger of Siemens also participated actively and soon joined the AMUE. Other members were representatives of professional organizations, consumers, central banks, and European administrations.

In January 1995, the group presented its first report. Many of its observations, such as those regarding the needs of banks, the corporate sector or necessary political decisions, had been stimulated by the AMUE studies. The report also suggested that the ECB should conduct its monetary policy in the single currency straight away – rather than operating in the various national currencies, which according to the Maastricht Treaty remained a theoretical option.[106] It recommended a transition in half a year, 'because a long and undefined period would seriously impair EMU's credibility and thus the willingness to accept it among the public at large and politicians'.[107] However it remained unclear about how to prevent undesirable speculation.

The Maas report was in line with a view published in July 1994 by Thiery Vissol (Vissol 1994). This first scenario ever put forward by a Commission official had suggested a transition in two stages, with a 'double big bang'. In the first, the Ecu should become the European accounting unit for all economic actors apart from consumers. The banking and the public sector should henceforth operate entirely in Ecu, apart from tax payments and direct client relationships. The firms should also adopt the Ecu, sparing retail pricing. Notes and coins should then be introduced in a second 'big bang', after which the Ecu remains the only legal tender in which all transactions have to be done. This two-step scenario should avoid double accounting, pricing and treasuring. While the scenario did not mention a timetable for the first and second big bang, Vissol explained later that the Commission at that time was convinced that a year's time between the start of EMU and the introduction of coins and notes, at the end of the transition, would be sufficient. However, the Monetary Committee of the EU Finance Ministries and Central Banks did not react favourably to either of these plans. The Ecofin at that time was not yet so advanced that it could deliver a consensual judgement – in particular Germany resisted a rapid end to the Deutschmark.

The Commission's strategic re-launch

Malcolm Levitt remained concerned that a lack of political commitment could hamper the transition. While officials in the European and domestic administrations seemed to have accepted that – for practical reasons – it was impossible to fully replace national currencies at the start of EMU, they had not fully grasped the need for full political determination. Levitt repeatedly pointed out that if the politicians were determined to implement Stage three, then the Ecu had to be used for the denomination of all Government debt, for interbank transactions and settlement accounts at the Central Bank, and for all money/foreign exchange operations by the Central Bank. Retail transition should be phased in over the following two or three years. However, his proposal met with the remark from very senior Commission and EMI officials that the German population would never accept the replacement of bonds by Ecu denominated government bonds in advance of the introduction of the single currency. Moreover, it was rumoured that the Bundesbank was proposing to start stage three simply with the locking of national currencies and with the Ecu to be phased in gradually over a fairly extended period. Levitt recontacted very senior officials at the EMI and the European Commission emphasizing that, 'unless the single currency was used for government debt denomination, Central Bank–commercial bank transactions, and monetary/foreign exchange operations, it would appear as if the authorities themselves had no confidence in the durability of Stage III'.[108] The political reactions to the suggestions on the changeover had confirmed de Silguy's view that a new initiative was needed to re-launch the process. The Maas scenario was proving to be too narrow and risked being rejected by some countries. Hence, de Silguy requested his services to elaborate a document, which was to take a more prudent approach: 'The purpose of the Green Paper is to help create a consensus on the final scenario among the competent authorities' (European Commission 1995).

For de Silguy's new strategy contact with people who had direct practical experience and were able to drum up support from business for the EMU became of urgent importance to the Commission. Apart from the AMUE working groups, DG 2 had no real close relationship with the business community at that time, because its work had previously concentrated on monetary and macroeconomic issues. Other Directorates General, such as those responsible for the Internal Market, Competition Policy, Industry, or SMEs did indeed have close interactions with the private sector. However, for the DG 2 they were not useful in providing practical input for the new strategy to move towards EMU.

Compared to other business organisations and associations, the AMUE was an appealing strategic partner for the Commission.[109] First due to its neutrality: Party politics did not seem to matter, as the founding fathers had been a German Social-Democrat and a Conservative Frenchman and the Association's personnel constituted a deliberate mixture of nationalities and political sympathies. Also, the AMUE did not defend sectoral or national interests: It was a trans-European organization fighting for a public good: the successful move to the single currency. The Commission discovered that some sectoral lobbies were 'less helpful', as they were primarily trying to ease the specific burden of the sector they presented – a few even asking for compensation for the changeover through tax breaks. The AMUE combined a large network of companies and banks, which could provide input and spread information alike. It had a high degree of operational flexibility, which the Commission services and larger organisations with a stronger hierarchical structure such as the Federation of Chambers of Commerce or national Industrial Federations were lacking. The partnership between DG 2 and the AMUE became so intimate that de Silguy's monetary advisor Jacques Lafitte discussed the essentials of the Green Book with the AMUE Sherpas meeting in London, a month before its publication. Co-operation became increasingly closer so that Yves-Thilbaut de Silguy concluded in 2001: 'The AMUE was central in making the strategy work'.[110]

The Green Book's scenarios

In its suggestions, the Commission took a more prudent approach than the Maas Group. It discussed three scenarios for the transition period and explored the potential risks the changeover could involve. The suggested timetable of the final changeover was more relaxed. Periods were longer, and no immediate changeover of all book money was implied, taking into account the AMUE's warning that the banking sector would not be able to assure full operations in Ecu from the start. De Silguy had chosen not to consult the governments prior to the publication, and awaited their feedback attentively. However, in the summer of 1995, the debate remained calm, although the choice of the transition scenario preoccupied many in economic policy circles and especially the private sector, which was keen to obtain clarity.

Experts were notably concerned with the question how the Ecu and the national currencies should be distinguished in stage three[111] – the period in which exchange rates were irrevocably fixed, a single monetary policy existed, yet national and European monies still existed in parallel until national notes and coins were completely withdrawn. Two scenarios dominated the debate in 1995: The *big bang scenario* implied that all money functions should be changed from national currency to single currency from day one of EMU. The *mounting wave scenario* acknowledged the impossibility of affecting all changeovers the same day, recommending a sequence of staged changeovers for different money functions. One possible variant could be the *double big bang* the Commission had put forward in 1994.

Either way, the discussion raised fundamental questions about the nature of money: when was the currency effectively 'single'? What was the legal status of currency (notes and coins) versus central bank money (high powered or base money)? How important was the role of legal tender? What, in fact, was money? Because some of these questions were not really thought through, some rather Byzantine debates developed. For example, some observers, including officials in the Commission, thought for a while that if the national currencies continued to exist in stage three, there could be speculative attacks against these currencies, threatening the sustainability of the monetary union. Early in 1995, the Commission asked the AMUE to write a short assessment of these issues that could help them to structure their thoughts in preparation of the Green Book. The paper, presented to DG 2 in March 1995 (see Collignon 1995), focused on three points: (1) Money was a settlement asset whereby debt contracts were definitely extinguished. Hence, the physical manifestations of money, such as notes and coins, were not essential for the definition of a single currency. It was the legal status that mattered, and therefore a single currency required a *lex monetae*. However, such law was a necessary and not sufficient condition for the existence of money. A Ecu could not be created 'by decree'. It was an endogenous phenomenon emerging from the conclusion of private credit contracts in an environment of uncertainty; (2) The unity of a single currency was manifested in the conduct of monetary policy. In order to set interest rates at a desired level, the central bank has to provide liquidity for the money market. In a monetary union, access to this supply of high-powered money has to be the same for all participants in this market that was used by banks for refinance purposes. This meant that the European System of Central Banks had to effectuate all operations in the single currency from day one, although financial institutions could denominate some of their debt contracts in previous denominations. Hence the re-denomination of all outstanding financial assets was less urgent than the complete integration of the money market and an efficient payment system across borders. (3) If the critical mass for the irrevocability of the new currency was the money market and a *lex monetae*, the mounting wave scenario was less urgent. In fact the AMUE report expected that the spontaneous use of the single currency in phase three (a) would hit similar barriers as had been analysed in the *Strategy of the Ecu* five years before. It therefore took a more cautious approach than the Maas Group and suggested a *Tiger Wave*, which mounted first to the low requirement of monetary policy integration and would then leap to a big wave at the end.

The paper written by the AMUE for the Commission was in many respects close to the work done by the EMI and the different national central banks and helped to bridge understanding between the two European institutions – which was not obvious at first. It clarified that the full integration of the money market made any form of speculation between national currencies and the euro impossible. In fact national currency became simple sub-denominations of the euro – like cents, but at a non-decimal rate.[112] The paper was useful input for the legal team in the DG 2,[113] but went against some of the ideas pursued by Thierry Vissol who sought currency re-denomination in all European financial markets. In his view, if EMU was completed in more than one step in the transition stage, the challenge was to structure the sequence in such a way that they maintained market pressure towards reaching the final stage of a single currency in stage three. Hence, an old idea dating back to the Giscard–Schmidt Committee reappeared in a new incarnation. This was not only crucial to encourage private sector preparation. There was also a political dimension to this argument: The mounting wave scenario involved some kind of dual currency running during stage three (b). Those who favoured this approach, insisted on the normative force of facts: by using the new currency as book money in the transition, the possibility of reverting to national currencies was reduced. This seemed particularly important given the negotiating behaviour of German officials (see below and Chapter 5). On the other hand, while the big bang seemed impossible from a practical point of view, the mounting wave scenario de facto laid the grounds for new political debates: 'Once the idea of dual currency running is admitted, it is not surprising that some observers find advantages in an indefinite period of dual currency running. In this scenario, stage three (c) would never be attained. With some sophistication an argument can be construed how this might be compatible with the Maastricht Treaty' (AMUE 1994: 7). It looked as if Europe was again falling into the old discussions on the parallel versus single currency, which had already overshadowed the Delors Report in 1989 (see Chapter 3). Hence, whenever possible, the AMUE spoke out for a transition scenario, which would have a definite termination point in stage three (c). The Association still saw the political need of the irrevocable step towards a single currency, but in addition, it was also concerned about the economic downsides of parallel currencies, which were 'clearly against the interest of European industry and the requirements of a transparent single market'. This was the lesson it had learned when developing the *Strategy for the Ecu*.

The second, and probably even more important decision was the handling of exchange rates between national currencies and the Ecu in stage two

(b) – a particularly sensitive period. In this stage, the starting date of EMU and the first-round members had already been selected by the European Council while the ESCB was being set up, but exchange rates would not be locked yet. According to the Maastricht Treaty, the European Council had to choose the date and announce at which exchange rates national currencies would be converted into the single currency, yet the actual fixing would take place only at the beginning of stage three, not during the intermediary phase. In this period, gigantic capital movements were feared: Speculations in the financial markets could hamper the smooth transition and endanger the whole start of EMU.[114]

The fear of speculative attacks in the transition stage led to extreme suggestions, such as Sir Edward Heath's: 'I always visualize our ministers of finance, meeting quietly one Saturday, five minutes before midnight. They agree, "we are going to have a single currency at the existing rates". And at five minutes past midnight they tell the world "Europe now has a single currency". That is how it has got to happen, and it cannot happen any other way. And I hope that all those that are now responsible here for the single currency will keep this in mind. When it is done, it will have to be done like that, otherwise all the speculators will do us in again' (Heath 1994). Sir Edward Heath's ten-minute transition scenario did not find its way into the Council decisions in Madrid. Neither did the suggestion to attempt keeping exchange rates within a (nominal) target zone, which narrows with economic convergence, as the AMUE has recommended to the Commission in March 1995. Central bankers informed markets in time that market rates close to ERM central rates would become conversion rates and this led to stabilising market movements. Yet, as it was suggested in the same study, the European central banks did indeed co-ordinate interest rate levels in the run-up to stage three in order to avoid instabilities.

Pinning down the transition scenario in Madrid

The Green Book and the various other studies prepared the grounds for the European Council of Heads of State and Government in Madrid in December 1995. Rather unexpectedly, the summit adopted a definite transition scenario and further technical details related to the single currency. For several reasons, this gave the realization of EMU in 1999 a strong push (de Silguy 1998: 136). First, it was a signal to the markets and the private sector that EMU was a credible and irreversible project, well on track to be launched at the latest in January 1999. It gave a clear timetable and legal certainty to enable the private sector to prepare for monetary union. Second, it helped national governments to pursue convergence efforts and to counter those voices, which were openly doubtful whether EMU should and would be implemented. Third, it gave the single currency its future name: the 'euro'.

The Madrid Summit settled an important legal issue: an EC-regulation guaranteed legal certainty and also the continuation of contracts denominated in legacy currencies. For a long time preceding the summit, Commission officials and national authorities seemed convinced that the *lex monetae* was sufficient to solve these problems, even though the AMUE, wholesale market associations, and major law firms had been trying in vain to convince Commission officials that such law had nothing to do with the continuity of contracts. When Malcolm Levitt saw the neglect of this issue, possibly out of ignorance, he renewed his efforts to impress on officials why the private sectors needed a regulation guaranteeing legal certainty. 'A final breakthrough was achieved at the eleventh hour and senior Commission officials convinced Delors that the issue had to be on the Madrid agenda, where it was then agreed that a Regulation was needed; I was telephoned a few days later by the extremely senior people concerned to ask whether I was now happy!'[115]

Although most decisions of the Madrid Council were of a technical nature, political tensions emerged. As Levitt had expected earlier, Germany was a particularly difficult partner in negotiations. One of the problems for Germany was the name of the single currency. While most people in Europe assumed that the new currency would be called Ecu, Germany argued that the German version of the Treaty did not clearly establish that the single currency would be called Ecu. Rather Ecu stood for a neutral European Currency Unit. This, as de Silguy (1998: 136) points out, was not due to an error in the treaty's translations, as has often been said. 'The inconsistent writing of the expression Ecu witnesses the negotiators' intention not to settle the name of the single currency in Maastricht'. In early 1995, the German government suggested to use 'Euro' in connection with the national currency, that is, the 'Euro-Mark' in Germany, or the 'Euro-Franc' in France (de Silguy, 1998: 136, also *Welt am Sonntag*, 9 April 1995: 1). As German public opinion was euro-critical, the government argued it needed to make the loss of the Deutschmark less painful for the German public. Not surprisingly, many AMUE members saw their earlier concerns about political neutrality re-emerge.[116]

Underlining the German opposition, Bundesbank chief Hans Tietmeyer had stated repeatedly that the Ecu would not gain the trust the new single currency needed – as the Ecu basket had lost about a third of its value in relation to the DEM since its creation in 1979. A second argument against the name Ecu was the fact that in the middle ages there had been gold coins circulating freely in France and elsewhere in Europe which were called 'Ecu' – and that Germany would not accept a European currency with a French name. However, this argument was somewhat inconsistent with the claim that the German public still remembered the Ecu as 'Esperanto-money'. The AMUE publicly spoke out in favour of the name 'Ecu' as it understood that this was laid down in the Maastricht Treaty.[117] The AMUE Secretary-General was asked to raise this issue in his next co-ordination meeting with the Director General of the EMI and with the European Commission's Director General for Economic and Monetary Affairs, Giovanni Ravasio. However, even within the Association consensus was not obvious. Four months earlier, the two German Board Members Hilmar Kopper, of Deutsche Bank and Carl Hahn of Volkswagen, had shared the German government's concern. In the presence of Ravasio, they had concluded: 'The Ecu has too artificial an image, including its name, and does not inspire trust.

The presence of the future Central Bank in Frankfurt is not enough to show that the Ecu is as strong as the DEM and its very name should be changed when it becomes the single stable currency'.[118]

The Commission along with the French government and Valéry Giscard d'Estaing had argued that the single currency should indeed be called Ecu. This, the French Commissioner Yves-Thilbaut de Silguy had explained, was more convenient for French speakers than the expression 'euro' which Germany promoted. The French view is summarized by Jurgensen: 'Undeniably, the name Ecu is a success. It is short and sounds nice. It has a sense in French and in English, the first charged with history and symbolism, the second more prosaic and pragmatic, conform with what is often described – a little abusively – as the soul of the two people. In fact, the Ecu is an old French and European money (cf. the Portuguese Escudo and even the British or Danish crown) as it is the technocratic name of the European currency unit' (Jurgensen 1991: 120). However, at the informal meeting of Finance Ministers and Central Bank Governors in Valencia in October 1995 the decision was taken with a majority of 12 countries to call the new currency 'euro' (*Frankfurter Allgemeine Zeitung*, 30 October 1995: 13). Two months later at the European Summit in Madrid, the Heads of State and Government confirmed this decision, along with a scenario for the changeover. This decision may have made public communication on the euro easier in Germany, at least technically, given that the political debate was far from being solved. For many other countries, which had assumed that the single currency would be called Ecu and communicated accordingly, this decision was another bitter pill they had to swallow in order to accommodate German demands.[119]

Another contentious issue in Madrid was the legal nature of the European currency in stage two. The German delegation questioned the Commission's suggestion that from the day, the ECB takes up its single monetary policy for the euro-zone 'the ECU ceases to be defined as a basket of currencies and becomes a currency in its own right, for which the national currencies are perfect substitutes, i.e. different denominations of the single currency' (European Commission 1994a). The Maastricht Treaty said that, 'at the starting date of the third stage the Ecu will become a currency in its own right' (Art. 109 L4). However, it remained unclear whether national currencies should at the same time cease to be legal tender. Germany, did not agree that the Deutschmark should legally be abolished from day one of EMU. 'The German anxiety re-emerged to commit itself to something the nature of which was not entirely known. If the Deutschmark kept it status as legal tender after the start of EMU this meant keeping a way out open for Germany', one EU-official involved in the lengthy negotiations with the Bundesbank before the Madrid summit recalls. For many observers, it seemed politically dangerous to keep a backdoor open, as Chancellor Kohl came up for re-election in 1998 and the opposition SPD had not yet clearly pronounced themselves in favour of a European single currency. Many felt reminded of the discussions about a common currency and the promotion of the Ecu before the Maastricht Treaty had come into force.[120] In the run-up to Madrid, the German government and the Bundesbank finally had to agree that the national currencies would not persist as legal tender after the launch of the single currency. However, this happened not without side-payments. Germany was granted a 'no coercion'-rule, thus leaving the use of euro in phase IIIa to the private sector – although some countries such as Belgium saw this as 'apartheid'. The rule stated that no one could be forced to use the single currency before the transition was completed, and that contracts in national currencies could be fulfilled in national currencies. However, this was only cosmetic. Germany finally had to agree that EMU meant it really had to give up the Deutschmark.

Launching communication on the single currency

Shortly after the adoption of the Green Book, the Commission defined a first budget for communication on the single currency, which was to be renewed and increased up to the introduction of notes and coins in 2002. Again, it was de Silguy and DG 2, which, took on the responsibility while the Directorate General for Communication was only marginally involved. The AMUE quickly became a significant recipient[121] of funds for projects developed in close co-operation with the Commission services. It often acted as an initiator of new ideas, but was conscious of supporting the Commission's needs that it considered as an ally. Being fully aware of the importance of communication, the AMUE thought about the messages to be conveyed. Although the European Summit in Madrid clarified the transition scenario to the single currency in December 1995, the practical details still had to be filled in. EMU rapidly became a very practical issue for the business community in general and for banks in particular. Without their full support the introduction of the single currency would be impossible anyway and a timely preparation of the changeover was essential. The AMUE was convinced that by starting preparations early, companies could avoid bottlenecks, reduce cost, and even gain competitive advantages. Smaller and medium size enterprises could afford to take more time for the preparations, as long as banks, large corporations, accountants, and consultants would start the changeover process in time.

The Commission's *Green Paper on the Practical Arrangements for the Introduction of the euro* recommended the creation of national platforms to coordinate the smooth transition to the euro. The business community, however, requested that national governments continued to show commitment to realize EMU according to the agreed deadlines associated with the Maastricht Treaty. This implied the fulfillment of convergence criteria, ensuring that the institutional and legal framework would be in place and that the public administrations would be ready in time.

Some active members of the AMUE (e.g. Siemens, Philips, Daimler Benz, or Fiat) had started their preparations even before an official timetable was agreed. These companies had decided to changeover to the euro at the earliest possible date. The Association benefited therefore significantly from their experience, for example from Philips' Dutch board member Dudley Eustace and his Sherpa Ton Ruhe. In the first half of 1996, the AMUE brought together 135 European business executives to discuss how to prepare companies for the accounting, finance, marketing, communication, and Information Technology (IT) implications.

Information available on agreed timetables and on legal issues were the starting point, but the debate rapidly evolved into discussions about more technical, more difficult and sometimes also more sensitive issues such as price transparency in the common market, business implications for the financial community or IT consequences. There was a broadly supported view that the changeover to the single currency should be viewed by organizations as a major project and that a strong project management was needed throughout the whole changeover process. Chaired by Ton Ruhe and assisted by Guillaume Lepecq of the AMUE, a large group of executives produced the report *Managing The Changeover to The Single Currency*. Translated into different European languages, more than 100,000 copies were distributed across Europe in a relatively short period of time and published on the newly created website of the AMUE.

Soon the AMUE occupied a leading position in what became a transnational debate, by organizing working groups and conferences, assessing technical and strategic issues such as cross-border marketing within EMU, psychological price points, rounding issues, triangulation, and truncation etc.

The main challenge however was getting the euro accepted by the man-on-the-street as a useful leap forward to improve European competitiveness and public welfare. With the primary objective of maintaining price stability, a single currency was a necessary condition to improve Europe's world-wide competitiveness, to raise investments and to accelerate growth and job creation. Businesses had to play a significant role in information campaigns along with the public authorities. In June 1996, the Association published a brochure entitled *Europe United Through a Single Currency, which* was translated into several languages and widely distributed to the public at large. Previously, general explanatory brochures had been produced on the initiative of national member groups. Thus, in the United Kingdom, Christopher Johnson helped to write 'Questions and Answers about Monetary Union in Europe'. In Italy, a similar booklet, written by Alfonso Sabatino with the help of Giorgio Bodo, Giorgio Guarena, and Mario Massazza of Fiat, received a contribution by Prime Minister Lamberto Dini and found a wide circulation through Confindustria and *Il Sole/24 Ore*.

Many of the strategic questions were highly relevant for larger companies in the mid-1990s. For example, Daimler Benz organized changeover workshops for group top management. Siemens joined the AMUE board during this period because Heinz-Joachim Neubürger found the work so useful that he convinced the company's financial chief Karl-Hermann Baumann to get personally involved. In Fiat, Giorgio Guarena worked out a changeover plan to the euro for all industrial group activities involving over 2000 managers. It became a leading model for other Italian companies. However, work in AMUE study groups also changed the Commission's perception of what EMU meant for small- and medium-sized enterprises. Chambers of Commerce had tried to convince them that EMU was 'a disaster' for SMEs. The direct contact with EMU experts from small- and medium-sized companies via the AMUE, however, showed that EMU was feasible for SMEs, if only preparation was started early and in a pragmatic way.[122]

The Association distributed information on the euro in twelve different languages, well before private or public institutions in European countries had developed their own material. Soon, banks, companies and other organizations were buying AMUE's brochures, offering them to their own clients. In this way co-operating with the Association was another advantage for the Commission: AMUE's members provided a European network for the publication and distribution of euro information. Member banks voluntarily bought and distributed AMUE material to their private and corporate clients. In total, more than four million guides were distributed, irrespective of the free downloads form the AMUE website, which received up to 600,000 hits per month.

Nearer the starting date of the EMU, the information needed to be more detailed and more specialized. The Association, and especially its assistant director Guillaume Lepecq, was instrumental in turning AMUE to sectoral studies, such as the retailing sector or tourism. AMUE assisted many banks, companies and other organizations in learning how they were affected by the changeover to the new currency and how to communicate about it. All of the publications were based on findings resulted from working groups or conferences in which the European Commission participated.

The Phoenix flies – into a new storm

The early euro communication activities by the AMUE and the Commission had the merit of galvanizing the private sector around the practical preparations for EMU, well before national governments started their own communication. Early initiatives created important spillovers for banks, companies, industrial associations or national ministries, which used or were inspired by the AMUE material when they began launching their own communication campaigns. This facilitated the spreading of information on the final run-up to EMU.

With the Commission's Green Book and the Madrid Council's decisions, the project of EMU had arisen like a Phoenix from the ashes of the EMS crisis. It had received new credibility through the renewed political commitment by all EU Heads of State and Government in Madrid, and with the definition of a timetable for the run up to EMU and a clear changeover scenario it had become a neat and feasible project. EMU had successfully been put back on the European and domestic agendas after the political and economic crises of credibility. It is important to understand the role of these technical, bureaucratic and apparently 'apolitical' decisions for the creation of a broader political consensus on EMU. After the Danish referendum and the EMS crisis, political dialogue between advocates and opponents of the single currency had nearly broken down. Mutual respect for the other side's point of view became weak. This carried the risk of dissensus turning into conflict, of rejecting the essence of the Maastricht agreement. Some may have pondered the option of imposing the new currency by the force and power of the state.[123] However, in a democratic society the introduction of a new currency had to be supported by a more fundamental consensus. In this context, the focus on practical issues for a vast, European-wide deliberative process aimed at finding the best technical solution was crucial for restoring mutual respect. This process started with the technical working groups, where purpose orientated rationality (Zweckrationalität) aimed at regulating daily business activities had the unintended consequence of creating a European policy consensus, which was then institutionalized by the European Commission. This process was facilitated by the AMUE's network as an epistemic community where mutual respect was high. The consensus within the group then took a larger dimension because the individuals and the organizations they represented were seen by many other actors and individuals in society as worthy of respect. This led to the adjustment of their own views and preferences thereby facilitating the emergence of a European-wide consensus, which incorporated many policy dimensions, including macroeconomic convergence.

However, the success to relaunch EMU by technical efforts did not prevent deep political doubts about EMU in the following years. With the difficult path to convergence, the question of 'why monetary union?' re-surfaced in many countries. As we will see in the next chapter, dissenting voices regained weight that criticized the design of EMU, asked for a postponement, or put the entire project into question. Despite the new dynamics, the start of EMU could still not be taken for granted in the mid-1990s.

5 Campaigning for EMU

With the Green Book and the decisions of the Madrid summit, European governments and the Commission had hoped to re-establish EMU's fragile credibility. However, the real test was convergence to the Maastricht criteria. As this proved to be economically painful, public opinion became increasingly hostile. Even mainstream political parties were tempted to capitalize on the fears and doubts of euro-sceptical voters. The populist EMU critique had some parallels with the populist movement that emerged in North America when the US single market was created in the 1890s; both shared anti-liberal rhetoric, irresponsible economic promises, and a latent xenophobia. In some countries, especially Germany, there was a real risk that EMU could fail because of a lack of political support from the population and among the Members of Parliament. The German government, therefore, hardened the conditions for EMU membership and also for fiscal policy making in EMU, although in other countries serious and painful convergence efforts were under way. The most spectacular example is Italy, where the price of convergence was high in terms of growth losses and unemployment, but also France. As public opinion and political rhetoric deteriorated in the climate of economic recession and political distrust, the AMUE focused on explaining the reasons for EMU, especially in Germany. Its communication strategy tried to overcome populist EMU criticism by rational arguments, providing new evidence for the need for a single currency. This has contributed to an environment that allowed governments to pursue their objectives in achieving EMU and achieve convergence.

The populist temptation

On 24 March 1996, the German Social Democrat Dietmar Spöri lost the regional elections in Baden-Württemberg while the right wing Republikaner Party entered parliament for the first time. Spöri had fought and lost his election battle with an anti-euro campaign. Many critics in the media, his political opponents, and even those within his own Social Democratic Party had criticized it as 'populist' as it had provided credibility for extremist arguments. By coincidence, the same weekend most German Social Democratic Members of European Parliament (MEPs) were meeting in seclusion to study facts and arguments about monetary union, just 100 km from Stuttgart. Christa Randzio-Plath, the chairwoman of the European Parliament's Sub-Committee for monetary affairs, had organized the meeting and sought the AMUE's help to base the debate on the euro on more rational foundations. Eighty per cent of the population harboured doubts about the stability of the European currency (see Frankfurter Allgemeine Zeitung, 5 January 1995). Political entrepreneurs within the established parties and those outside them were starting to capitalize on the population's fears and confusion. Randzio-Plath feared that the forty-year achievement of political, economic, and also monetary integration could unravel, unless the EMU supporters won the battle of ideas.[1]

European populism

After the negative outcome of the first Danish referendum in 1992, European policy and business elites seemed to have lost touch with the public. Although the Maastricht Treaty was ratified by very large majorities in the legislatures of all member states of the Community, public opinion did not follow (Bogdanor 1996). Of the twenty-five statesmen who signed the Treaty in December 1991, fourteen were no longer in office a mere twenty months later (Dahrendorf 1996). Europe was hit by a crisis of legitimacy, in addition to its economic problems. In this environment, a wave of New Populism built up and swept across Europe (Taggart 1996: 41). It focused particularly on immigration and on EMU, although the phenomenon was much larger and had profound socio-economic roots.

As a political movement, populism goes back to the creation of the People's Party in the United States in 1892. The party was founded by a heterogeneous coalition of mid-west and southern farmers, urban workers, and small and medium entrepreneurs as a reaction to the emerging single market on the American continent. Populist movements also emerged in the late nineteenth century in Russia as a reaction to capitalist industrialization (Fitzpatrick 1994), and in Latin America during the twentieth century (Dornbusch and Edwards 1991). Populism is an expression of anxieties and frustrations, which are created by structural transformation and hard economic times and are felt particularly severely by social groups suffering from declining relative prices or competitiveness in the economy. Populists often fail to understand the distinction between a general deflation and relative price changes (Freedman forthcoming), and as a consequence propose incoherent economic policies, such as the use of expansive monetary and fiscal policies, an over-valued currency to accelerate growth in non-tradable goods, and a redistribution of income (Dornbusch and Edwards 1991: 7). Given the inconsistencies and contradictions of populist ideas, their politics and economics are ultimately unsustainable. Populism translates into manifold political ideologies and economic concepts, but is distinct from fascist or communist ideologies, which also respond to social tension resulting from rapid modernization. With reference to Hirschman (1970), we may say that populism is a 'voice' solution: the expression of discontent within the political system respecting the rules of the game. Communism and fascism, in contrast, are 'exit' solutions as they imply overturning the political democratic system.[2]

The common features of different forms of populism across countries and time consist of: (1) the formation of a political movement, by charismatic and paternalistic leaders who claim to speak for 'the whole of the people' or the undifferentiated mainstream of society (the 'silent majority', the 'little and forgotten people'); (2) nostalgia for the traditional economy and inconsistent economic policy proposals that promise redistributive effects (Kaufman and Stallings 1991: 38);[3] (3) an overtone of defensive intolerance or latent xenophobia. This third element is the complement to the unstructured notion of 'the people': an undifferentiated mass can only be defined by whom it excludes rather than by whom it includes. Populism is also opposed to 'the establishment', which runs the system and pushes for modernization. Populists prefer a vision of the 'heartland' from which they derive what is 'normal' in a traditional sense and, consequently, comfortable (Taggart 1996: 33). The populist inclination to exclude others and value their own undermines the emergence of social consensus. The low degree of mutual respect maintains dissensus and potentially creates conflict that can lead to violence and the physical elimination of the enemy.

EMU became a crystallization point for populist ideologies, when the elite consensus on which the Maastricht Treaty was based was put into question by the broader public. The euro was taken as the symbol for liberalized European markets, which threatened traditional economies. Yet, in reality the transformation had its roots in the forces of globalization, and the European response to it which took the form of the SEA of 1986: the freeing of capital markets and increased cross-border competition. The decision to create a single European currency – against the background of the single-market programme whose consequences started to be felt in the early 1990s – gave rise to populist ideas throughout the EU and particularly in the richer industrialized countries of the North. With the exception of Portugal and Greece, productivity growth in the tradable sector accelerated significantly relative to the non-tradable sector. This created a social cleavage between the international and the domestic factions of society, which was exploited by populists. Their criticism focused on the dangers of giving up monetary sovereignty, which meant the capacity to inflate for some (southern populism) and achieve overvaluation ('strong currency') for others (northern populism). Either way these policies were inconsistent with long-term economic stability. Inter-European fiscal redistribution also became a dominant issue in some countries. Furthermore, the expected loss of the national currency – a strong symbol of identity in many countries – was used to mobilize latent xenophobia.

For European monetary integration, populism posed a double threat. Its xenophobic dimension made mutual respect and the creation of cross-border consensus and a European culture difficult. Meanwhile, playing with unsustainable policy promises undermined the orthodox policy objectives on which EMU was based. After the formal ratification of the Treaty by parliaments, achieving convergence now required a material ratification. To understand the difficulties of this second step, it is useful to look at the larger context within which the debate on EMU took place. This is also relevant for our study on the private sector involvement for EMU, because the member companies of the AMUE were clearly opposed to populism, not only for philosophical and political, but also for reasons of economic consistency.[4]

Structural transformations and populist ideology

The strategic equilibrium in Western Europe after Second World War was based on a liberal market economy, combined with the welfare state and Keynesianism as a theory of macroeconomic management. This consensus was shared by Christian Democratic parties, who usually gave more emphasis to economic liberalism, and by Social Democrats, who stressed the idea of material equality.[5] Both political movements shared a commitment to political liberalism and economic sustainability. In its heyday, the model worked in a corporatist fashion where triangular arrangements between labour, capital, and the state became the dominant form of political–social organization (Streeck 1993).

With the demise of the Bretton Woods System and the two oil shocks in the 1970s, this system reached its limits. Economic growth had become insufficient to finance the growing demands by the welfare state, thereby destroying the distributive consensus of corporatism. Keynesianism seemed helpless in the face of irreducible inflation. At the same time, structural changes toward a service economy and increasing globalization loosened the traditional links between political and social organizations. The emergence of new left and green parties was one response to the crisis of the social democratic consensus in numerous West European countries (see Taggart 1996: 21–30). Another was a more radical form of economic liberalism, which became dominant as conservative governments in many parts of Europe took over. In some countries, like Spain and France after 1983 and in Greece after 1995, social democratic governments applied orthodox conservative policies. Influenced by the neo-liberal Reagan and Thatcher model of monetarism, deregulation, and increased competition, the 1980s saw far-reaching reforms within each EU member state, but also through the creation of the single market on a European scale in 1992. While this initiative gave new impetus to overcome eurosclerosis, it was also at the root of the emerging new populism.

To understand the social impact of the European single market and globalization, it is useful to look at the American precedent at the end of the 1890s. American populism was a direct response to the economic grievances, which followed the industrial transformation of the United States and the emergence of an interior market (Pollack 1962). The growing railroad system in the United States facilitated low-cost transport. New communication technologies like telegraph and telephone increased information flows and lowered the costs of transcontinental payments. The resulting economies of scale allowed the creation of huge trusts and oligopolies, which squeezed small businesses out of the market.[6] When hard times struck, farmers[7] tried to protect their old economic practices and attacked the institutions that curtailed their income and represented the most significant elements of their production costs: railroad freight schedules, mortgage lenders, high interest rates, and an appreciating dollar (Parsons 1973). Their programmatic demands focused on three areas: (1) nationalization of land, railroads, telegraph, and telephone systems; (2) opposing the 'sound' and 'hard' money advocates (mostly bankers and merchants), demanding instead the expansion of the amount of currency by free unlimited coinage of silver; and (3) forbidding land ownership by illegal aliens.

A 100 years later, these three essentials of populist ideology reappeared in the European debate. Challenges to the policy consensus focused on: (1) regulation instead of liberalization; (2) expansive demand policies instead of tight money; and (3) moderate xenophobia focusing on immigration. Similar causes seem to have produced similar effects: progress in transport and telecommunications facilitated the global opening of markets for goods, services, labour, and capital (de la Dehesa 2001). Europe also removed a large amount of non-tariff barriers by the creation of the single market. The Commission and European governments 'sold' these policies by insisting on the economies of scale and related growth effects and benefits for consumers. However, although they acknowledged the related increase in competitive pressures, the fall-out for small- and medium-sized companies with less investive capacity, lower productivity increases, and working in previously protected market niches was covered by silence. Having overcome the turbulence of the 1960s and 1970s, income distribution had become a taboo in Europe. It re-emerged at the populist fringes, particularly when monetary conditions became tight after German unification. The similarity to American populism is striking – starting with the macroeconomic deterioration, economic pressure on the non-tradable sector by international competition, critical discussion of monetary policy, and finally even the fact that the interests of AMUE member companies in the single market resembled US east-coast trusts to a fair degree.

The single market and new populism

It can be shown that the competitive pressures and distributional conflicts between large international companies and small businesses have increased in the early 1990s as a consequence of the Single Market programme. Job insecurity also loomed large, especially in traditional sectors. These tensions, perceived as national threats, served as a basis for populist argumentation.

In 1990, the European Commission studied the impact of the Single Market on the industrial structure in Europe (European Commission 1990).[8] It showed that the removal of trade obstacles led to sectoral specialization and competitive advantages. Germany, France, and the United Kingdom had competitive advantages in Research and Development, while Germany, France, and the Benelux performed well in capital-intensive sectors. Portugal and Greece were mirror images to these European 'core' countries, while Spain had witnessed substantial growth around two poles: labour-intensive industries having advantages within the Community and capital-intensive sectors showing competitiveness with respect to the rest of the world (especially Latin America). Italy represented a special case. It was weak in capital-intensive industries (many in the south), but held a strong position in a fragmented labour-intensive sector, dominated by small firms in the north.

The single market apparently led to the following adjustment: Spain and Portugal attracted significant amounts of domestic and foreign capital, accelerating interindustry specialization and reinforcing relocation of investment away from Europe's North towards the South.[9] As a consequence, in the most industrialized member states in the North, firms have grown and internationalized their operations. While the less-developed countries have Europeanized, the highly industrialized core countries have globalized.

We can also go on a different route to capture the structural changes. Krugman (1987) has pointed out that European integration offers opportunities for gain resulting from economies of scale, but they are likely to be unevenly distributed because of oligopolistic rather than perfectly competitive markets. In Annexe 3 to this chapter, we present a formal model on how productivity increases in the modern European sector squeeze the profit margins in the traditional sector, if relative wages do not change. Although this is a microeconomic argument about markets and firm structures, we can try to find evidence by comparing a typical sector of non-tradable goods, such as building and construction, with the tradable sector of manufacturing. We have looked at the full range of variables: relative prices, wages, productivity, profit margins, and gross value added per person employed. The picture is similar in all cases and is well summarized in Figure 5.1

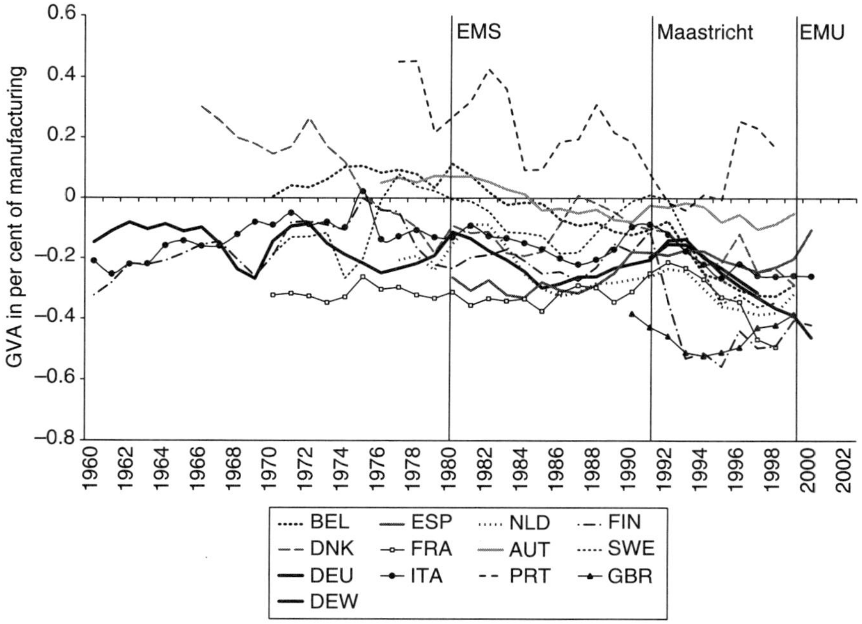

Figure 5.1 Relative gross value added per person employed: construction versus manufacturing (source: European Commission, AMECO data, and own calculations).

for gross value added (GVA) per person employed.[10] A fall of GVA per employee in the traditional industries relative to modern ones will reduce its distributive margins, thereby putting pressure on wages or profit margins and leading to job losses in the traditional sector. While relative values between the two sectors were reasonably stable in the 1960s and 1970s, there was a rapid deterioration in the 1990s with the exception of Portugal, Spain, Austria, and Greece.[11] Interestingly, the United Kingdom also experienced such deterioration, but turned the corner after leaving the ERM in 1992.

These trends have produced winners and losers. Surveys for the Commission study have demonstrated that relocation effects were limited to a small number of sectors, but were particularly relevant in traditional industries of the industrialized countries where labour costs account for a large proportion of total production costs. Our own data would justify the assumption that the non-tradable sectors of the economy must have felt competitive pressures and a deterioration of living standards most strongly. This may have fuelled populist ideologies. The hypothesis that tensions resulting from structural change served as a basis for populist ideas is supported by the electoral strength that New Populist parties found in the first half of the 1990s, particularly in the northern, more industrialized countries of Europe as documented in Table 5.1.

The data in Table 5.1 reflect populist mobilization in national elections.[12] Local elections sometimes showed even stronger performances by populist parties. For instance, in Germany, the right-wing Republikaner Party was elected to the local Parliament in Baden-Württenberg in 1996, with over 9 per cent of the votes,

Table 5.1 Levels of New Populist mobilization

	Country	*Best vote*	*Year*
High	Austria	16.6	1990
	Denmark	15.9	1973
	Norway	13.0	1989
	France	12.4	1993
	Finland	10.5	1970
Medium	Italy	8.7	1992
	Sweden	6.7	1991
	Belgium	6.6	1991
	Switzerland	6.5	1991
	Germany	2.4	1990
Low	Luxembourg	–	–
	Netherlands	–	–
	United Kingdom	–	–
	Ireland	–	–
	Greece	–	–
	Spain	–	–
	Portugal	–	–
	Mean	5.8	

Source: Taggart (1996: 50).

while other populist parties on the left (PDS) and right (DVU) fared well in the new Länder of East Germany.

However, election results are only a very imprecise proxy for public opinion because parties and the supply of policy programmes structure them. Also, populist ideas permeate all public debates and cannot be ascribed to one specific group or party alone. Thus, in the United Kingdom, the Conservative Party became a prisoner of right wing anti-European factionalism whose rhetoric fits our definition of populism (Turner 2000). Also in Germany, 'mainstream political parties became interested in capitalizing on the disaffected voters' (Heisenberg 1997: 152). Senior politicians from Schröder to Stoiber all used populist arguments at times. In Italy, Berlusconi was a master of blending typically populist elements with mainstream right wing neoliberalism. In France, several political groups manifested different degrees of populism, from Jean-Marie Le Pen's *National Front* to Jean-Pierre Chevènement's *Mouvement des Citoyens*.

According to the Eurobarometer, support for EU membership dropped from over 70 per cent on average in 1990 to 48 per cent in late 1996. In Germany, it plummeted to 39 per cent and in the United Kingdom to 35 per cent. Italy remained significantly more pro-European than the EU-average with a 75 per cent support in 1996,[13] as did Luxembourg, Greece, and the Netherlands. The eurobarometer also shows that nationalist resistance to European integration was fuelled by fear of uncontrolled imports from other member countries, economic dislocations, economic crisis, the disappearance of small and medium sized enterprises, and the loss of jobs (Eurobarometer No. 45 1996). The hostile attitudes toward the euro reflected the structural change in the European economy. Table 5.2 shows the potential impact of structural change on public approval of the EU. The first three columns indicate that support for European integration has fallen everywhere, with the exception of Italy and the new member states that joined in 1995. The fourth column shows by how much GVA per person employed has fallen in the non-tradable construction industry relative to the tradable manufacturing sector. The elasticity gives the factor by which the opinion of EU approval responds to structural change. Public opinion is highly sensitive in Sweden, Belgium, Germany, and Austria. It seems indifferent in Spain, the United Kingdom, and Luxembourg. After weighing this elasticity by the correlation coefficient and taking into account the structural change, we can calculate the theoretical or expected change of EU approval. It is extremely high in Sweden, followed by the unified Germany (West Germany alone resisted better), and Belgium. Of course, many other factors will also affect people's view on the EU. Particularly in Sweden and Finland, but also in Italy, did EU approval move in the opposite direction from what the economic factors would have led us to expect. It is, however, remarkable that in countries with high populist votes, the structural transformation seems to explain a larger part of opinion change than in the others. Interestingly, Austria, ranking top in the list of electoral populism, appears here at the bottom. The phenomenon of Haider cannot be related to European integration or globalization.

Table 5.2 Explained change in EU approval due to change in relative GVA

	Approval of EU (%)			*Change in relative GVA (%)*	*Elasticity*	*Correlation coefficient*	*Expected change in EU approval (%)*	*Expected/ actual (%)*
	Actual 1990	*Actual 1999*	*Change (%)*					
Luxembourg	84	71	−15	−49.2	−0.0581	−0.07458	−0.2	1
Germany	70	64	−9	−38.8	1.2455	0.64383	−31.1	363
Sweden[a]	32	37	16	−33.5	−4.3537	−0.68357	−99.6	−638
Finland[a]	38	47	24	−22.8	0.6986	0.48933	−7.8	−33
Denmark	61	47	−23	−19.8	0.5759	0.33961	−3.9	17
France	70	59	−16	−18.2	0.2584	0.21240	−1.0	6
Belgium	75	54	−28	−16.6	1.4824	0.80678	−19.9	71
Italy	79	81	3	−16.1	0.8131	0.74892	−9.8	−387
Germany(W)	70	48	−31	−9.6	2.2426	0.61641	−13.3	42
Netherlands	89	42	−53	−4.7	1.0273	0.70483	−3.4	6
Spain	78	44	−44	−2.2	−0.0072	−0.00108	0.0	0
Portugal	79	68	−14	−1.9	0.2848	0.19236	−0.1	1
United Kingdom	58	29	−50	−0.2	0.0172	0.00428	0.0	0
Austria[a]	32	54	69	2.8	2.5388	0.40042	2.8	4
Greece	76	60	−21	48.6	0.2531	0.52436	6.4	−31

Source: AMECO; Eurobarometer.

Note
a Series starts with accession in 1995.

Economic and political criticism of EMU

Of course, populism was not the only expression of anti-EMU sentiments. Euroscepticism had many facets, some of which were based on rational arguments. We can distinguish objections for economic and political reasons.

Orthodox economic criticism of EMU reflected the traditional cleavages of strong currency countries with a balance of payments surplus versus weak currency countries. We have seen in Chapter 2 that this conflict goes back to the economic divergence between Germany and France. In strong currency countries fears about inflation dominated. This fear had profound historical roots, particularly in the German and Austrian experience of hyperinflation in the 1920s. It was the result of a learning process after the instabilities of the 1970s (Collignon 2002: chapter 1), especially in the smaller countries, the Netherlands, Austria, and Denmark. The Bundesbank prominently defended this line of argument before and after the Maastricht negotiation. It was reflected in the insistence on the convergence criteria, central bank independence, and led to the institutional add-on of the Stability and Growth Pact, all being institutional arrangements to preserve price stability. Attachment to macroeconomic stability did not necessarily lead to anti-EMU positions, but the conditionality of EMU-support created a Janus-headed ambivalence, which was often interpreted as hostility to EMU. In essence, this Euroscepticism resulted from a lack of trust and low respect for European neighbours. Many German officials, but also the media, treated other European officials and economic cultures as insufficiently committed to price stability, despite evidence to the contrary. These economic concerns were distinct from populist arguments. They aimed for coherent policies with the declared objective of long-term sustainability, while economic populism activated inconsistent policy claims.

Eurosceptics on the left criticized the *neoliberal* economic and monetary policies, particularly in view of rising unemployment. They feared that EMU would require greater flexibility in the labour market[14] and a dismantling of the welfare state. They also questioned the Bundesbank's hegemony over Europe as the tight policies after German unification had contributed to the overvaluation of the Deutschmark and the EMS crisis, reinforcing the deep recession in the 1990s. Some challenged *la pensée unique* (e.g. Fitoussi 1995) and favoured less restrictive monetary and fiscal policies suggesting even leaving the German straitjacket of the ERM and EMU.[15] If the ECB acted in a similar way, these EMU-critics argued, then EMU was not worth it. In response, the pro-European political left called for a better policy-mix that would re-stimulate economic growth and employment creation (Strauss-Kahn 2002). They demanded an Economic Government as a counterweight to the independent and stability-oriented ECB. In a soft form, this was finally realized through the creation of the so-called *Euro-group* at the Amsterdam European Council in 1997. The idea that EMU offered an opportunity to improve the policy-mix for the euro-zone, favouring growth and employment, was particularly influential in France. It found an echo in some smaller member states, in Italy, but also in Germany's SPD and in most

European Trade Unions.[16] They sought to revive the European post-war consensus, although they were now aware that macroeconomic policies needed to be complemented by structural reforms. The centre–left criticism of the neo-liberal interpretation of EMU was different from left-wing populism because it focused on *achieving* an economic equilibrium and the return to full employment. It, therefore, presented an alternative to the dominant German approach of macroeconomic policies with the sole objective to keep inflation down. After Social Democratic parties had swept into government in most EU member states in the late 1990s, this philosophy became the dominant consensus at the European Council in Lisbon in 2000.

A third argument against EMU was that it would imply fiscal transfers, as Europe did not fulfil the conditions for an Optimum Currency Area (Mundell 1961; Eichengreen 1997). Since the Maastricht Treaty restricted national fiscal policies and labour markets were perceived as rigid, some economists and politicians argued that transfers on an EU level had to accommodate economic shocks in the EMU. This worried critics from net-contributing countries who were expecting to see their countries' contribution rise. The transfer argument lent itself to populist agitation linking redistribution issues with xenophobia.

Criticism was also expressed for political reasons. Geostrategic considerations motivated those who feared a split in Europe between a 'hard core' and a destabilized periphery. It would have put into question the strategic equilibrium on which European integration was founded.[17] On the other hand there were those who emphasized the need to fulfil the convergence criteria stipulated by the Maastricht Treaty.[18] German insistence on a rigid interpretation of these criteria was often understood as a desire to exclude Italy as this country had particular convergence efforts to make.[19] This seems to have been the true intention of some German officials in the Bundesbank (see Jochimsen 1998) and in government who wished to start EMU with the small group of countries belonging to the narrow Deutschmark zone.[20] Another factor was the incomprehensible style and language in the debate about the convergence criteria. The emphasis was on the proper functioning of the monetary union and the implications for financial markets. Little was said about the need to reduce debt and deficits to make pension schemes and the European Social model sustainable and achieve a fair intergenerational distribution of the tax burden.

Probably the most powerful political argument against the Maastricht Treaty was the insufficient democratic legitimacy of European integration. Since the days of Jean Monnet, Europe's unification had progressed by bringing more and more policy areas into the European domain.[21] However, with the growth of policy functions, and the common management of European public goods, a democratic deficit emerged. The legitimacy of European policy making was derived from national governments and their administrations, but not from a genuinely public European consensus. A broad pan-European debate about European policy objectives was missing. The European Parliament could not fill this gap as its powers were too restricted.[22] Therefore, Eurosceptics, especially in the United Kingdom, focused their campaigns on the democratic deficit, which would result from giving up the sovereignty of their elected parliaments for an un-elected bureaucracy in Brussels. A similar sensitivity was reflected in the Maastricht ruling by the German Constitutional Court, which ruled in 1993 that it was unconstitutional to move to the final stage of EMU without a previous vote by the two Houses of the German Parliament.[23] Although, these concerns were discussed at the 1996 intergovernmental conference, which concluded the Treaty of Amsterdam, the issue remains unresolved, even after the new Treaty of Nice (rejected by the Irish in a referendum in 2001).

All these arguments were reflected in the euro-debate, with different weights depending on countries, political orientation, etc. They mingled with doubts about the feasibility of EMU as economic convergence lagged behind. The developments in public opinion had threatened the formal ratification of the Treaty, as we have seen with the referenda in Denmark and France, and the opt-out of the United Kingdom. This decision by the German Constitutional Court perpetuated this danger by turning the two chambers of the German Parliament into key players: they could stop the final transition to EMU if public opinion turned too negative. Furthermore, the growing 'confidence gap' (Lipset and Schneider 1983) between citizens and politics made it increasingly difficult to implement substantial economic reforms necessary to converge to the stability criteria. Especially in France, this became a serious obstacle for the Juppé government. Hence, there was a danger that populist temptations in a broad sense could derail the train to EMU either politically or economically. In the mid-1990s, the media were speculating about postponement and cancellation of the start of stage three, while politicians found it increasingly difficult to implement the reforms necessary to reach sufficient convergence.

The AMUE's communication strategy

Observing these developments, the AMUE changed its strategic orientation. While it had previously worked behind the scenes with decision-makers in public institutions and private companies, it now started to take on public opinion. The new institutional set-up had to be grounded in a broad public consensus. Monetary management required legitimacy as a resource and the rejection by the Danish voters, just like the narrow success in France, had shown that the creation of elite consensus was not enough to formally legitimize the agreements. As Pascal Lamy, Delors' *Chef de Cabinet* said after the initial Danish *No* to the Maastricht Treaty: 'Europe was built in a St. Simonian way. From the beginning, this was Monnet's approach. The people weren't ready to agree to integration, so you had to get on without telling them too much about what was happening. Now St. Simonianism is finished. It can't work when you have to face democratic opinion' (quoted by Eriksen and Fossum 2000: xii). As part of its post-Maastricht strategy, the Association sought closer contacts with national and European institutions, including the newly founded EMI, and for the first time engaged in broad public communication initiatives. It also started to see its role as an advocate for economic policies that facilitated economic convergence. At the same time it developed activities to spread these ideas across Europe. Given its limited resources, it focused at multiplier functions and linked up with other institutions. A mission statement in 1994 summarized the Association's thinking.

> The European Monetary Institute (EMI) and Central Banks may now play a determinant role in the implementation of EMU and should be supported and assisted in this process to a greater extent as the Association is in a position to facilitate direct contact with businesses and diffuse information from the EMI.
>
> Consequently:
>
> - Discussions will be conducted by President Davignon with President Lamfalussy to organize a close co-operation with the EMI on the preparatory work for full Monetary Union.
> - Co-operation with the European Commission will be maintained.
> - Co-operation with national Central Banks will be developed with the objective of obtaining their official moral support.
> - Bank membership will be sought in order to increase the number of AMUE members and benefit more actively from Bank expertise and participation in the transition to EMU.
> - Constructive co-operation will be maintained with the Ecu Banking Association, which has become more technically orientated.
>
> Concerning the enlargement of AMUE to EFTA countries currently negotiating EU membership (Austria, Finland, Norway, and Sweden), President Davignon will endeavour to gain the national governments' support for this extension. AMUE Board members will assist in selecting and inviting pro-European businessmen to become active members.
>
> Activities to be developed:
>
> - Major public meetings with prestigious speakers will be multiplied in order to spread the message of the Association more actively amongst economic and monetary leaders and politicians. Local meetings and seminars will be continued as in the past. Periodic meetings or work sessions will be organized to attract bank membership, in such financial centres as London, Frankfurt, Paris etc. where there is a strong concentration of foreign banks.
> - Publications with strong content will be preferred to widely distributed newsletters, as the efforts to promote public knowledge of AMUE may now leave room for more direct communications to officials, opinion leaders and Association members.
>
> (Conclusions of the AMUE steering committee on strategy and financial matters, 16 February 1994, AMUE Archive)

While the Association had always abstained from taking a partisan political position, the need to enter the political arena grew, the closer the start of the EMU came. In January 1996, a comprehensive memo on *AMUE strategy and communication policy* prepared a change in strategy:

> Economic and Monetary Union is our main objective, in an environment simplified by the ratification of the Treaty, but complicated by the convergence obligations and the depreciation of certain currencies, notably the Italian lira and the US dollar. A world dialogue in the monetary domain remains thus a complementary objective. [...]
>
> Difficulties met by most countries to fulfil the Maastricht criteria raise questions on the final date of Monetary Union or on the possibility of loosening the criteria. In the climate of uncertainty, which we have had since mid-1992, the strategy of the Association has always been to stick to the Treaty of Maastricht, which leaves room to appreciate long-term tendencies when the compliance of countries with the convergence criteria will be scrutinized, in early 1998.
>
> Also the Association has always built on decisions taken by the European Council to make sure that their practical implementation would reduce the possibility of political drawbacks.
>
> On a political front, our intervention will remain necessary at least until we have the final list of countries initially participating in the EMU. It will then be necessary with respect to peripheral countries and future members of the European Union to oversee the maintenance of their convergence efforts and to avoid all forms of distortions (monetary, fiscal or social) affecting the EMU or the single market.
>
> With regard to technical aspects of the currency conversion, it is possible that our intervention be useful up until the substitution of coins and bills, in 2002. There is reason to fear that after EMU has provided large businesses with exchange rate stability in 1999, it might be more difficult to implement in 2000–2002 the costly adaptations, which the transition to the single currency will necessitate. Resistance might arise at the level of retail and other small businesses, which do not participate in international trade.
>
> AMUE has limited financial capacities in comparison to the number of European citizens to convince and educate on the currency changeover. However, AMUE has the capacity to generate arguments and proposals, which can then be widely publicized by others.
>
> (AMUE Strategy and Communication Policy, 22 January 1996, AMUE Archive)

The initiatives that followed encouraged learning processes on a European level – among very different actor groups. By working with European companies on the practical issues of the changeover to the euro, corporate elites started to learn from each other and take into account the opinions and experiences of their partners. Regularly, representatives of European and national administrations participated. These intense encounters contributed to the emergence of shared norms in the European corporate world and to the *identity building* of a European

Civil Society. This was subsequently spread to small- and medium-sized enterprises in all EU member countries. Gilbert Lichter reports the same phenomenon arising from his work with banks in the Ecu Banking Association. He attributes it to the role of 'round tables' where people from different countries and companies met in order to discuss their practical problems. In order to do so, they had to be prepared, which meant involving other staff at home. By meeting at a neutral place, away from home, they felt free to listen, talk, and leave behind the constraints of their domestic consensus. They thereby were able to give credit to arguments outside their domestic cultural context. They could 'out' themselves with pro-European ideas and take them back to their companies as manifestations of a larger European consensus.[24]

The contribution to a border-transcending European policy consensus among political decision-makers and the broad public was more difficult, but followed a similar method. AMUE representatives used public meetings to explain the reasons for a single currency and argued with those who had different ideas. Commission President Jacques Santer has acknowledged this role:

> The Association has been a major driving force behind the EMU project. Many of your companies have played a leadership role by clearly advocating the advantages of the single currency for the private sector and society as a whole. This has required considerable courage in the face of widespread scepticism about the euro. Investments and public announcements in favor of the euro by headline companies have had important demonstration effects, sending a clear wake-up call to less prepared companies on the need to start getting ready for the euro.
>
> (Jacques Santer at the AMUE Board meeting, 27 February 1998, Brussels. Quoted in Report on the Annual General Meeting Held on 31 March 1998 in Paris, p. 6, AMUE archives)

The AMUE effectively became a small-scale European *agora*, that is, a discussion forum for the exchange of ideas and preferences. Figure 5.2 shows the number of meetings where members participated and spoke as representatives of the AMUE.[25] These reunions, often co-financed by the European Commission, had several objectives. First, they challenged the speakers to develop arguments at all levels – macro- and microeconomic, political, and societal. This made them experts in their respective environments. Second, the AMUE reached millions of professionals and citizens through distributing invitations, and still more via reporting in the local and often also specialized press. This created a public-relations effect, which signalled that EMU was not dead. Finally, at every opportunity they offered a candid and rationally argued presentation of evidence in favour of EMU, offering an alternative to the passion of the populists and eurosceptics. The AMUE was thereby able to hold the ground and set the agenda. This work was not highly visible, but it helped to mobilize businesses, banks, chambers of commerce, professional organizations, elected local bodies, even

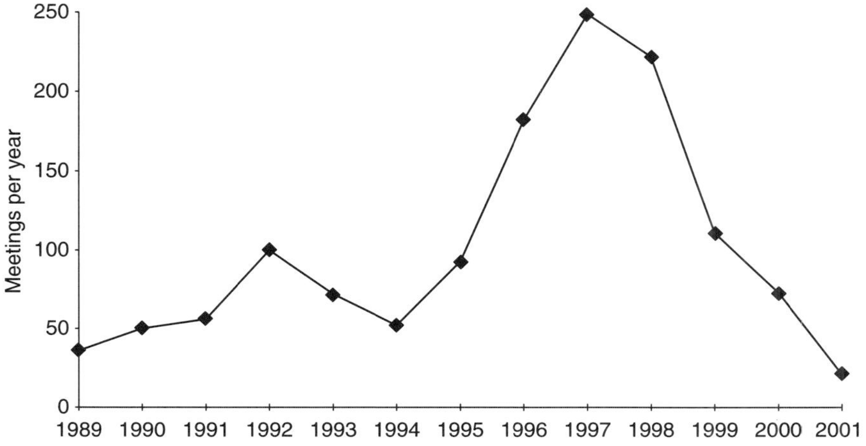

Figure 5.2 AMUE participation in meetings on EMU, 1989–2001.

central banks, etc. Although these meetings took place in all member states of the EU, Germany received particular attention.

In the following, we take a closer look at Germany and Italy; two countries with a key role in the run up to EMU. Both had very different starting positions: (1) Germany was the country that had influenced negotiations on EMU most, but it was also a country whose political commitment to EMU had come under doubt in the second half of the 1990s. Yet, its membership was crucial, as nobody could envisage starting the European currency without this largest EU member. (2) In Italy, a large founding member of the EC, public opinion was highly positive with regard to European integration and the euro. However, convergence indicators suggested in the mid-1990s that Italy could not be part of the first wave of EMU members. Excluding Italy would have caused enormous political problems including a backlash in Italy and for European integration in general. Looking at the communication processes in and between these two countries, and against this background at the AMUE work provides evidence for the difficult process of turning dissensus into general agreement.

German dissensus over EMU

In the mid-1990s, German public opinion towards EMU turned overtly hostile. The public reactions following the Maastricht summit gave a first impression of the anti-euro polemic that would develop in the following years. When Chancellor Helmut Kohl and his finance minister Theo Waigel returned from Maastricht in 1991, tabloids, especially *Bild*, thrived on an anti-EMU mood. Peter Gauweiler, the Bavarian minister for the environment and a party colleague of Waigel, made it into the news by declaring that Germany did not need artificial Esperanto-money.

The nature of scepticism in the German public

For many Germans, the fear of losing monetary stability blended with national pride in the Deutschmark as a symbol of Germany's post-war economic success and rehabilitation. The argument that only Germans had the 'right' policy preferences and would have to pay for others' mistakes, played into the hands of populists mobilizing latent xenophobia. Connotations of *us* against *them* appeared in the attributes 'tricksters', 'Southerners', 'Club Med', 'inflation community', 'Weichei' (soft egg), etc., in the public debate.[26]

Memories of currency reforms, after the two world wars, through which many Germans had lost their life savings, resurfaced. '*Währungsunion*' was often confounded with '*Währungsreform*', either due to a lack of knowledge or voluntarily for demagogical reasons. Few people remembered that the introduction of the Deutschmark had also met with significant resistance, opposition, and even demonstrations in the streets when it was introduced on 19 June 1948 (Roeper and Weimer 1996).[27] In Eastern Germany, the situation was even more difficult than in the rest of the Federal Republic. 'The people had just got used to the D-Mark, a symbol of wealth and freedom many had longed for. They did not want to give this up only ten years after they had received it', Norbert Wieczorek, MP and spokesman for the Social Democrats on monetary affairs in the Bundestag explained.[28]

Critique and scepticism was also reflected in the media. Many commentators, in line with euro-sceptics in the major parties, doubted that EMU would come at all. Although the timetable was confirmed and details had been settled in Madrid, the daily economic paper *Handelsblatt* wrote in May 1996: 'there will be no European single currency in this decade. Even if enough EU-members fulfil the convergence criteria of the Maastricht Treaty – the dates cannot be met' (*Handelsblatt* 8 May 1995: 27). Two major papers were openly euro-sceptic. The founder of the weekly magazine *Der Spiegel*, Rudolf Augstein, repeatedly treated Mitterrand as a swindler and accused Kohl of having traded the Deutschmark against German re-unification and of blindly following French interests: 'It is in his nature to give in to the French. Afterwards no one ever knows when and where he did it' (*Der Spiegel* 21 July 1997: 26). The *Frankfurter Allgemeine Zeitung* concentrated on the ordo-liberal critique of EMU, questioning the stability of the new currency. In June 1992, it published a manifesto with German economists criticizing the agreements concluded at Maastricht. The advocates of EMU were less numerous. But in 1997, the *Manager Magazine* published a manifesto signed by sixty German economists – this time in favour of EMU. The most favourable paper towards EMU was probably *Die Zeit*, the German left-liberal weekly of which Helmut Schmidt had become an editor in 1982.

The public scepticism was fed by the worsening economic situation after the EMS crisis and a debate about the *Standort Deutschland* developed. This had two consequences. For some it was proof of the necessity to complete EMU, for others it led to a withdrawal to domestic issues. After the deterioration of the exchange rates in late 1994 and 1995, the appreciated Deutschmark created problems for the export sector. The German private sector was divided over EMU matters, especially over the question of internal and external stability. After the EMS crisis, the German Federation of Industry (BDI) feared an overvaluation of the Deutschmark more than the risk of inflation. It criticized the high exchange rate for harming German export competitiveness; 'Taking into account the current upward pressure on the D-Mark exchange rate this question is disturbing for companies [...] The differing capabilities and needs have to be acknowledged' (BDI quoted in *Die Zeit* 14 July 1995: 20). This concern echoed similar views in France and other member states where currencies had remained closely tied to the Deutschmark. In Germany itself, however, it raised severe objections. For example, the German employers' federation (BDA) or the Association of German Chambers of Commerce (DIHT), who represented many small and domestically oriented companies, criticized the BDI for not caring sufficiently about price stability and regularly issued statements on central bank independence and price stability as a prerequisite for EMU. Those with vested interests in importing and non-tradables were more concerned about maintaining their purchasing power and, therefore, favoured policy autonomy for the Bundesbank. Given that their economic position deteriorated significantly in the 1990s, especially in Eastern Germany (see Figure 5.1), these positions dominated the debate in Germany. Yet interestingly it raged over issues of structural reforms and not over exchange-rate management or capital mobility.[29] Although exporters suffered from *Standort Deutschland* (location Germany), they called for economic reform and greater labour market flexibility, that is, lower wages, but hardly ever for a weaker Deutschmark. In fact, a depreciation without further reforms would have increased the pressure on the non-tradable sector. Hence, representatives of the Government and the ruling conservative–liberal coalition emphasized that EMU was a 'fitness programme for Germany'. Inadvertently, they thereby disenfranchized those sectors of the economy and society that suffered from the increased competitive pressures. This fuelled the emergence of populist ideas in Germany.

In the financial sector, only few institutions were actively favouring EMU from the beginning.[30] Most in favour were the members of the German Banking Association (Bundesverband deutscher Banken) whose clients were mostly concentrated in the tradable sector. Among the most active were Deutsche Bank and Dresdner Bank, who were also AMUE founding members. From the beginning Deutsche Bank enriched the debate with detailed studies on conceptual and practical aspects of the EMU. Commerzbank, Germany's third largest bank, was initially a member of the AMUE but decided on a strategy of differentiation and became more cautious, publicly doubting the start of EMU and whether France could become a member in the second part of the 1990s. The other sectors of the German banking system, especially the savings banks, with a strong exposure in the small- and medium-sized non-tradable sector, were at first, focusing on the defence of clients' asset value. However, subsequent to the ratification of the Maastricht Treaty they 'played the game'. After 1995, when Horst Köhler,[31] the former secretary of State in the Ministry of Finance, who had negotiated the Treaty, became chairman of the *Sparkassen und Giroverband*, the local savings banks became an important network explaining the benefits and practicalities of the euro to a sceptical German public. At that time, the private sector was so reluctant to use the Ecu that German AMUE members had serious doubts about the Commission strategy of promoting EMU by replacing political–ideological debates with the technicalities on practical preparation.[32] The chairman of Deutsche Bank, Hilmar Kopper, said at a Board meeting: 'Money remains a very emotional issue and so far public opinion has been underestimated by European and national authorities. There is no point in business promoting the Ecu if the level of unfavourable opinion remains high.'[33]

The Social Democrats' problem with monetary union

The Social Democrats in the opposition remained undecided on EMU during the second half of the 1990s. This reflected less a general dislike of EMU than the strategic dilemma of any opposition party: Why should they support the government, in this case Helmut Kohl and the Christian Democrats, who claimed to be the instigators of the EMU project? How could Social Democrats identify with an EMU whose construction had been shaped by neo-liberal thought? The SPD needed to find a way to distinguish their support for EMU from the Conservative Chancellor Kohl's positions.

Rudolf Scharping, at the time party chairman, referred to EMU in October 1995 as 'just some idea or other'.[34] In autumn 1995, Gerhard Schröder,[35] Prime Minister of Lower Saxony, suggested the defence of the Deutschmark as a national issue for the next election battle. Several SPD members on the Board of the Bundesbank, like Wilhelm Nölling and Reimut Jochimsen, doubted the trustworthiness of their European partners in honouring their commitments to price stability and sound public finance in EMU. They played with fears that the euro would be less stability prone than the Deutschmark, harming the savings of the 'small people' and reducing the purchasing power of wages.

There was a danger that the Social Democrat populists would line up with populists from the right and attack the conservative–liberal government as 'betraying German interests'.[36] Two of the four German professors who called upon the Constitutional Court to stop EMU, Nölling and Hankel, were well-known Social Democrats, who both previously had senior responsibilities.[37] Hankel regularly used a rhetoric, in line with the historical concept of populism defined earlier in this chapter. In an article in the *Handelsblatt* he linked the single currency to social instabilities: 'The strongest earthquake will happen in Germany, the EMU country with the highest wages and the strongest social system. […] As soon as low-wage-workers of all our Western and naturally also our Eastern European neighbours will pour into our country – thanks to Waigel's and Kohl's Deutschmark-sacrifice – German wages can only develop in one direction: downwards. […] Our social system can only do one thing: collapse' (*Handelsblatt* 12 October 1995 quoted in Meier 1996). The appeals to latent xenophobia strikingly resemble the nativist rhetoric in the US a century earlier. From an economic point of view the argument is inconsistent. There is no reason why wages in high-productivity countries should fall as competitiveness is about unit labour costs, not nominal wages. Even mainstream Social Democrats were affected by these ideas. In the context of rapidly rising unemployment and structural changes in the German economy after unification, they saw EMU as a giant neo-liberal project for deregulation where wage flexibility remained the only instrument to adapt to economic shocks. This argument also found an echo in some trade unions, especially of the building and construction industry. With regional elections in three important Länder in 1996,[38] followed by national elections in 1998 and given the highly euro-critical public opinion, the risk remained high that the SPD would now turn against EMU. Observers say that some SPD members were even developing a communication strategy against the euro.[39] However, not all Social Democrats had forgotten the party's tradition of 130 years of internationalism[40] and the commitment of its two chancellors Willy Brandt and Helmut Schmidt to European integration.[41] Particularly vocal supporters of EMU were Christa Randzio-Plath, member of the European Parliament for Hamburg, Klaus Hänsch, President of the European Parliament, and Heidemarie Wieczorek-Zeul, the party's European spokeswoman. After some hesitation, Oskar Lafontaine who became party chairman in November 1995 joined them.

Those in the SPD who were concerned about the anti-EMU tendencies were so for essentially two reasons. First, a commitment to EMU was crucial to building their credibility as a future government party. Heide Simonis, SPD Prime Minister of Schleswig-Holstein, warned: 'If we do not structure the debate early, we may only have to answer the question: Are we going along with the masses, or against them? And then, we will not only lose the next elections, but will also have a European disaster'.[42] It seemed irresponsible to create a *Scherbenhaufen*,[43] which would subsequently make governing Germany very difficult. In this respect they faced a similar dilemma as the British Labour party in 1990, when Neil Kinnock and John Smith backed the Conservative government's decision to join the ERM and later to resist a devaluation. Second, they were aware that Germany's acute problems were largely aggravated by the dramatic overvaluation of the Deutschmark. This was publicly explained by Heiner Flassbeck from the research institute DIW, who also was an advisor to Oskar Lafontaine. The argument was strengthened by the support of important trade unions, particularly from export-oriented sectors, such as metal and automobile industries, and who suffered from the overvalued Deutschmark. Hoping EMU would prevent costly competitive devaluations by export partners, they also aimed at creating 'a European Economic and Employment Policy'.[44] This brought their position closer to the view, popular in France, that an economic government should complete monetary integration.

Training members of the European Parliament

The critical situation in the mid-1990s had a parallel in history. In 1957, the SPD had hesitated to ratify the Treaty of Rome. At the time, Erich Ollenhauer, the opposition party's chairman, had wanted to delay the vote in the Bundestag, but

Jean Monnet personally convinced him to vote for the Treaty negotiated by the Christian-Democrat Chancellor Konrad Adenauer – just as the French Socialists would, who had negotiated it under Guy Mollet (Monnet 1976: 497). In the mid-1990s, it was not enough to convince the party chairman. The SPD needed a well-argued position in the debate on EMU.

One of the decisive initiatives in rallying the SPD to EMU came from the German Social Democratic members of the European Parliament. Christa Randzio-Plath[45] who chaired the sub-committee on Monetary Affairs in the EP since 1992 and other MEPs had harshly criticized Spöri's anti-euro campaign in Baden-Württemberg (*Stuttgarter Zeitung* 5 February 1996: 5). On the election weekend in 1996, Randzio-Plath and her EP colleagues had come to Karlsruhe, not far from their parliament in Strasbourg, for a workshop with the AMUE. The purpose was to train the MEPs in explaining the EMU project, and in dealing with EMU objections. 'We were regularly discussing Monetary Union in the European Parliament. But, most MPs were not specialized in this field. They needed advice, information and arguments concerning the politics, economics, history and social dimension of the project in order to cope with the demands of party members and the civil society', Randzio-Plath explained.[46] For the MEP from Hamburg, this was not just a matter of business as usual. Christa Randzio-Plath had become a passionate European in her adolescence even before she joined the Social Democrats. When still at school, she had visited the museum and concentration camps of Auschwitz. The brutalities of fascism and nationalism had convinced her that only a united Europe could prevent the repetition of violence and crimes against humanity. Monetary union had now become a key element to stabilize European integration. As chairwoman of the European Parliament's Subcommittee on Monetary Affairs, Randzio-Plath had become a respected expert on monetary and financial matters. In winter 1995, however, her small office in the Parliament could no longer respond to the increasing requests for material on EMU that came from her MEP colleagues and the public at large. She was also increasingly concerned about the debates in Germany where populist rhetorics reinforced xenophobic tendencies and prominent politicians openly argued against EMU putting implementation of the Maastricht Treaty into doubt. Many critics, including the media, showed astonishing misperceptions about the developments in Europe. In December 1995, Spöri had said it was not imaginable that the EU summit in Madrid at the end of the month would decide on details of EMU according to the Maastricht Treaty: '1999 is dead'. Although the Madrid summit produced exactly the opposite (see Chapter 4), German doubts undermined confidence in neighbouring countries. In 1996, the political elite in France, including President Jacques Chirac, was convinced that Germany no longer wanted EMU and they therefore sought to put the blame on their German counterparts 'like a hot potato'. Only at the end of 1996 did Chancellor Kohl seem to prevail and French authorities became again confident in Germany's commitment to EMU.[47] A socialist member of parliament, former and later minister, Charles Josselin, said; 'The perspective of monetary union has moved far away. We did have doubts whether it could be realized in 1997, but can we say now, only two years before the final date, that it finally will start? This is a question that all Europeans ask themselves urgently'.[48]

In December 1995, Randzio-Plath asked the AMUE to write a handbook for the Social Democratic Group of German MEPs, an overview of the arguments why Europe needed EMU, why it was good for Germany, and what Social Democrats could find in the project. She had witnessed the Association's work for years and made use of the report on the EMS crisis, which had helped her and other members of Parliament two years earlier. In January 1995, she had been invited to a Board Meeting in Paris, where she discussed European unemployment problems, the link between unemployment, and monetary policies and public acceptability with the business leaders.

The Association shared her judgement that Germany was in danger of turning away from the commitments it had signed in Maastricht. It welcomed the initiative to build consensus for EMU together with the MEPs and to integrate potentially disaffected groups. It was also concerned that the debate on postponing EMU or the widespread doubts about convergence and feasibility, depressed the private sector's motivation to prepare for the changeover. According to the DIHT, in 1995 only 24 per cent of German companies believed that EMU would start on 1 January 1999. Eighty-eight per cent stated they had not taken any measures in view of the euro. It was, therefore, important to re-establish the EMU's political credibility.

After four months, the AMUE delivered 200 pages of facts, figures, and arguments supposed to enable MPs to survive public debates, and to fight for the euro on economic or political grounds and to prevail against emotional nationalistic populism. The handbook appeared in three editions and was distributed in the EP and to all Social Democrats in the German Bundestag, and later published electronically on the web.[49] In a meeting of the party's National Executive in 1998, it was called 'the best available document on EMU'. The European Commissioner de Silguy requested a shorter English version for internal usage. Subsequently, prominent SPD members such as Heidemarie Wieczorek-Zeul, Peter Struck, Otto Schily, and party chairman Oskar Lafontaine wanted contact with the AMUE.[50] Not only the handbook, but further contributions, such as speech writing or summaries on various aspects of EMU were requested and allowed the AMUE to provide direct input to the ideas of high-ranking SPD members.

Social-democratic arguments for the euro

Discussions with leading national politicians, the Commission, Helmut Schmidt's office, and the private sector had convinced the AMUE staff[51] that the public debate on monetary union should include economic reasoning as well as geopolitical and strategic considerations of tying Germany into Europe or strengthening Europe *vis-à-vis* the United States. Over the years the AMUE had developed arguments that EMU was about stability, wealth, and peace. The document requested by Randzio-Plath, however, had to describe a genuine SPD approach to EMU. Picking up on arguments previously developed by John Smith for the British Labour party and by Dominique Strauss-Kahn in the French Socialist Party, the SPD handbook emphasized economic growth, employment, and the chance to create an optimal policy mix. This distinguished it from the ordo-liberal view that dominated the German government's and Bundesbank's positions. Stability counted heavily, but not only the German model of price stability. The need for long-term social stability on the European continent was also emphasized. The EMU candidates already effectively shared a consensus on stability that had allowed the agreement on the Maastricht Treaty. Because of its independence, the ECB could pursue monetary policies as stability-oriented as the Bundesbank. But at the same time EMU could become a tool to regain the capacity for macroeconomic policy. Policy co-ordination in Europe opened opportunities for joint action that were not available to individual member states. Additionally, the elimination of exchange-rate fluctuations brought stability to the single market. It greatly reduced the risk and uncertainty for investment and thereby contributed to growth, which was necessary to sustain the welfare state. EMU could also help to stabilize the social system in the era of global capital mobility. The idea that unfair competition through discretionary exchange-rate reduction could be abolished by creating EMU convinced many, employers and trade unions alike. It appealed to car manufacturers in Schröder's Lower Saxony and to Bavarian farmers who were subjected to Prime Minister Stoiber's populist attacks against Brussels. By developing this argumentation, the AMUE was able to introduce ideas into the German domestic EMU debate that were common in other countries, but received little credit under the rigid ordo-liberal policy consensus that dominated Germany.[52]

The broad view of EMU, including the social dimension, made it possible to accommodate fears over liberalization, globalization, and the dissolution of the social system. These were not only linked to EMU, but also to a parallel debate on German competitiveness, which was unprecedented domestically and abroad.[53] This debate focused almost entirely on the question of cost competitiveness leaving aside exchange-rate questions. Employers strongly criticized high labour costs and especially the level of social contributions and company taxation. Although the rising tax pressure was a consequence of German unification, discussing its financial and economic implications remained a taboo. Instead, liberal and conservative opinion leaders attacked high labour costs and employer's surcharge and questioned the German *Sozialstaatsmodell*. Understandably, this was interpreted as a threat by those who ran the danger of losing their job or social protection. When the government sold EMU as a 'fitness-programme', many ordinary people blamed Europe for their growing insecurity. They did not see that the problem of German price competitiveness in the world resulted from the continuous appreciation of the strong Deutschmark *vis-à-vis* the currencies of main trading partners. This had not been a problem while Germany's neighbours had much higher inflation and therefore the 'strong Deutschmark' had become an object of pride and a symbol of virtue. However, the stability consensus spread in Europe and as inflation disappeared, the real appreciation of the Deutschmark caused an increasing deterioration of competitiveness for the German export industry. Public opinion remained attached to the old idea of a 'strong Deutschmark'.

Some Labour Unions backed by a few Social Democrats did point at the exchange-rate effect on price competitiveness. However, for some time they failed to link this issue prominently to monetary union and to establish clearly that EMU was an opportunity to escape the detrimental effects of the strong Deutschmark. The AMUE handbook now provided evidence and detailed arguments which were also given weight by the Association's founder Helmut Schmidt in 1996: 'The Bundesbank is even proud of the instability of our hard currency. But the rise in German labour costs, so large in international comparison, is at least in half caused by the most incredible appreciation of the Mark *vis-à-vis* the currencies of almost all our competitors in the world markets'.[54] This argument had the potential to counter populist anti-EMU rhetoric playing with fears of flexibilization and adaptation. It was able to integrate those who were critical of the neo-liberal fitness project without speaking against EMU. Just as the conservatives managed to get their right-wing EMU critics on board, the Social Democrats could integrate their left-wing. Both thereby prevented populist movements within their parties from growing stronger.

The arguments put forward by the AMUE were also designed to generate an understanding of the situation in other EU member states. Many countries had made significant efforts to reduce inflation and public deficits to fulfil the Maastricht criteria. What would happen if the prospect of EMU vanished? Would not the Deutschmark bloc break apart? Who would want to make sacrifices in terms of growth and employment, if the promised Euroland disappeared? This was especially true for France, which had shadowed German monetary policy since 1983. Especially after German reunification, the French economy had borne considerable costs: in order to maintain exchange rate stability, the French Central Bank and Finance Ministry[55] raised interest rates in line with the Bundesbank, but in addition, financial markets asked for a risk premium as the ERM was not perfectly credible. This made credit in France more expensive than the domestic economic situation would have called for. The price for not leaving the D-Mark bloc was a recession of unprecedented dimensions.[56] It only made sense in the perspective of building an ECB responsible for all countries – and not only the German situation. During the years of high Bundesbank interest rates in the mid-1990s, growth stagnated in most member states or even turned into recession. The EMS crisis was proof that the Deutschmark-bloc was not sustainable in the long run. Hence, EMU would protect Germany against further losses in competitiveness. A unified monetary policy also provided an opportunity to improve welfare and employment, without implying populist 'easy money' policies. Other left-wing parties in Europe also defended this line of thinking. For Oskar Lafontaine, meeting as the new party leader with his European colleagues in Madrid soon after, this was the decisive argument which made him back the euro, after having previously also been tempted by a populist defence of the Deutschmark.[57] By giving credit to arguments in other member states' political debates, the SPD effectively became an agent of European integration, while the insistence on a 'strict' application of the Maastricht criteria by the conservative–liberal Kohl government unintendedly reinforced long-standing prejudices about 'foreign' countries.

These arguments were part of an approach slowly but steadily developed by SPD after 1995. The AMUE is said to have had an important input delivering information and evidence to decision-makers within the party at the highest level.[58] This, of course, was only part of a broader process, which involved long discussions and many conferences and meetings. Many MEPs who had been trained at the seminar in Karlsruhe played an important role in developing the party opinion on the euro. Randzio-Plath as a member of the party's national executive was an opinion leader on EMU. MEPs contributed to a pro-EMU shift as they spoke up in the regional groups and spread their views about EMU. AMUE founder Helmut Schmidt also put pressure on the SPD. As an editor of the renowned weekly paper *Die Zeit*, he regularly published his opinion on the importance of EMU and the euro. Party leaders had to fear that he would criticize them openly in *Die Zeit*, if they became more critical on EMU.[59]

The Kohl government and the CDU

In contrast to the social-democratic opposition, most of the ruling Christian Democrats,[60] who formed the coalition government with the Liberal FDP, supported the pro-European strategy of Chancellor Helmut Kohl. However, especially in the Bavarian CSU, resistance within the party increased as the public mood turned sour. Edmund Stoiber, Prime Minister of Bavaria, provoked an open dispute with Kohl when he publicly accommodated anti-EMU sentiments in Bavaria.[61] Several MPs spoke privately about their doubts 'that we can pull it off'.[62]

In face of the fierce public criticism, the governments' main line of argument was defensive, focusing on the stability of the single currency. Official communication emphasized that the euro would be as good as the Deutschmark.[63] Additional benefits from EMU were of second order. With the support of the Bundesbank, the government took several initiatives to ensure the monetary stability of the future currency. For instance, it prevented decisions that could harm the independence of the central bank, it fought for stronger mechanisms to control fiscal deficits and argued to keep the legal identity of national currencies[64] as long as possible. In 1997, the federal government published a brochure whose title summed up this concern: 'Der euro, stark wie die Mark' (The euro – as strong as the D-Mark). The government also linked the issue of monetary union to the debate on structural reforms. Future competitiveness was seen as subject to deregulation, moderate wage bargains, and more flexible labour markets. No connection, however, was made with the appreciating Deutschmark exchange rate.

The Christian Democratic Union/Christian Social Union (CDU/CSU) was able to integrate populist ideas by identifying with a 'strong currency' that favoured domestic purchasing power. It did so by taking a restrictive position on all measures connected to the stability of the future currency. Euro-scepticism and

EMU-populism from the conservative side was likely to focus on the strength – or rather weakness – of the single currency. While populists in France, Italy, Sweden, and elsewhere focused their criticism of EMU on restrictive monetary policies, confounding relative prices with the absolute price level, in Germany they concentrated on the erosion of purchasing power in the traditional, non-tradable sector. Hence, demands for 'weak' or 'strong' currencies were two faces of the same populist coin. Sustainable policies require a 'stable' currency.[65]

A key role in the German government's strategy was assumed by the Bundesbank. When Jacques Delors was President of the European Commission, he occasionally said; 'In Germany maybe only few believe in God, but everyone believes in the Bundesbank'. Indeed, the central bank had earned an extremely high degree of prestige and credibility among the German public, politicians, and even abroad. The Bundesbank was able to turn this credibility into strong political influence over the government's Maastricht and post-Maastricht positions (Heisenberg 1999). But its political weight was further increased by the Maastricht ruling of the German Constitutional Court. The ruling prevented an automatic start of EMU by obliging the two chambers of the German Parliament to assess and vote on the degree of convergence. Given the bank's high reputation, and the technicality of the subject, MPs strongly relied on the Bundesbank's judgement. However, it was never entirely clear whether the Bundesbank was actually supporting EMU or only paying lip service with the secret agenda of spoiling it. In order to pre-empt a potentially disruptive verdict, and to silence the Bundesbank, Finance Minister Theo Waigel proposed the Stability and Growth Pact on fiscal discipline in 1995, and subsequently argued for the strictest interpretation of the convergence criteria.[66]

From Maastricht to the start of EMU, hardly anybody in Germany dared to criticize the Bundesbank. There seemed to be a consensus that it was doing its best to safeguard what Germany had achieved in terms of monetary stability. Only few pointed to the interest inherent in almost any organization not to give away power.[67] One of the few exceptions was an open battle between Helmut Schmidt and Hans Tietmeyer. The former Chancellor and founder of the EMS harshly criticized the Bundesbank President in an open letter in *Die Zeit* for being 'the most prominent opponent of EMU' whose rigidity and punctiliousness was harming Germany's interests. Apart from a handful of economists, Schmidt was alone in questioning the economic sense of the convergence criteria and Tietmeyer's insistence on their strict interpretation. Few people in Germany were aware of the silent embarrassment among European central bankers, when Tietmeyer harangued and lectured his colleagues on this subject in the EMI Council.[68] Schmidt's critique was observed with gleeful interest abroad: *Le Monde* published the text in full and papers from all over the world as diverse as the US news magazine *Time*, the *Financial Times*, and *L'Humanité* reprinted or quoted parts. At home, it had little impact.

When it became clearer in 1996/97 that the first round of members could include the so-called Club Mediterranée (Italy, Spain, Portugal) the government, backed by the Bundesbank, set out to harden the stability requirements. Minister of Finance Theo Waigel, and other German officials started to insist that '3 per cent means 3.0 per cent' and thus limited the scope for interpretation of the deficit criterion. Harsh rhetoric against 'cheaters' and 'soft-currency countries' clouded the view that the southern European partners had come a long way and were in fact sharing the European stability consensus. While people in many European countries had high respect for Germany's economic success and the role of the Deutschmark, and had, therefore, agreed to the efforts to comply with both Maastricht and Germany's restrictions, the Germans gave little credit in return. The AMUE applied itself to overcome this comprehension gap through its work with the SPD, but also with the CDU via personal contacts and public conferences. Ulrike Guérot, who had directed Karl Lamer's office in the German Bundestag, held close and regular contacts with the Christian-Democratic MPs in Germany, and with their conservative counterparts in France, as well as with the Konrad-Adenauer-Foundation, which developed intensive seminar and publication activities around the issue of EMU. Davignon spoke to a meeting of the CDU Economic Council; politicians and Bundesbank officials were invited to AMUE internal and public meetings. The Association also started to attend regular meetings on euro-issues set up by the BDI, the confederation of industrialists.

Convergence and dissent in Europe

When the Maastricht Treaty came into force in 1993, most observers in Europe expected that even if EMU started at the latest possible date on 1 January 1999, not all member states would be able to qualify for participation. It seemed hardly imaginable that the 'Club Med' would be part of the first wave of EMU members. These Southern-European countries, just like Belgium, were far from meeting the convergence criteria in 1993. It seemed hardly imaginable that they could converge in only four years, as the 1997 data were relevant for the assessment. However, these countries made unexpected efforts. The most dramatic and difficult adjustments took place in Italy. After years of unsustainable economic policies, Italy finally adopted the orthodox consensus institutionalized in the Maastricht Treaty and qualified for the introduction of the euro in 1999. It was no coincidence that this adjustment paralleled the profound political crisis, which opened the transition from the first to the second Italian Republic. To understand this complex process, we first recall the specificity of Italy's development before the 1990s, then briefly sketch the policy adjustments after Maastricht, and finally analyse the role of the European debate for domestic changes.

Eccezionalismo Italiano

After Second World War Italy turned from an underdeveloped country into a modern industrial state. When Monnet suggested the European Coal and Steel Community in 1950, Italy's steel production was no higher than Luxembourg's. Subsequent industrial modernization was government-supported in heavy industry, but found its full dynamism in the large private sector of small and medium sized companies. Italian capitalism long remained state-centred and oligopolistic. In 1992, only two (Fiat and Iveco) of the eleven largest companies and only five of the thirty largest (Fabbrini 2000: 46) were privatized. Fiat occupied an intermittent role in the Italian industrial tissue. It was always a private company, but was dependent on the government for the infrastructure that facilitated its development (roads and railways).

The rapid economic growth in the 1950s and 1960s caused far-reaching social transformations: migration from south to north of biblical dimensions, the secularization of society, and an attachment to freedom and democracy. The main political agent was the Christian Democratic Party, but the social changes also fuelled support for Italy's Communist Party, the largest in the Western world. During the Cold War, and given Italy's role in NATO, the strong position of the Communists made the alternation between governments and opposition effectively impossible, despite the fact that they shared the legacy of the anti-fascist 'founding myth' of the Italian Republic (Leonardi and Weitman 1989: 11). As a consequence, Italian institutions found it difficult to adjust to a world in transformation. Italy's crisis can be explained by the ideological and political resistance to the dynamic changes of the environment that resulted from the political blockage during the cold-war equilibrium (Fabbrini 2000). European integration was both a cause and a solution of this crisis. It contributed to the transformation of the 'environment', but it also 'Europeanized' the governance of the state.

As Padoa-Schioppa (2001b: 34) recalls, the 'four freedoms' – freedom of circulation of goods, services, capital, and persons – that constitute the basis of the Treaty of Rome were not even realized within Italy in the mid-1950s.[69] Membership of the EC forced the government to abolish these regulations. Italian governance was transformed through European legislation, common objectives, and by integration into Europe's discursive culture (Fabbrini 2000: 200–2). The EU encouraged policies to overcome economic backwardness in the Mezzogiorno and other parts of Italy. For many years, Italy was a primary recipient of EIB loans, and the EU was a prime source of funds ear-marked for the Mezzogiorno, although until 1989 it was not always certain they had actually arrived there.

In the 1980s, domestic politics were still characterized by *immobilismo*. The geopolitical blockage and domestic political resistance explain why Italy was not able to adjust to a new economic environment with the same flexibility as other European countries. The United Kingdom or Germany both changed their political majority and implemented new policies to react to the oil shocks and combat inflation in June 1981. The Italian Christian Democrats had to accept for the first time since 1945 that the leader of another party, Giovanni Spadolini, became prime minister of a five-party coalition (Leonardi and Wertmann 1989: 86). It was a sign of political weakness and led to an uneasy competition with Bettino Craxi's Socialist Party. Each side tried to outbid the other with promises to the electorate. Italian authorities accommodated inflationary wage demands and adopted social legislation in the field of labour relations, pensions, and health care that increased wage costs and public deficits. The comparison with France is poignant where a strong Communist party prevented the necessary adjustment in the 1970s. As we have seen in Chapter 2, de Gaulle's, Pompidou's, and Giscard d'Estaing's difficulties to implement more radical austerity measures kept France behind Germany's performance. Only with the election of President François Mitterrand and the structural weakening of the Communist party was the political blockage finally overcome and, after the French EMS crisis of 1983, a pro-European adjustment strategy opened the way for monetary union in the 1990s. However, in France, the political resistance was much lower than in Italy[70] and consequently the final adjustment process was less dramatic.

It is tempting to call Italy's policies in the 1980s 'populist'. Macroeconomic policies had a Latin American taste and Bettino Craxi's system of governance has been called 'soft Peronism' (Flores d'Arcais 1996). However, although macroeconomic policies were inconsistent, some significant elements of populism cannot be traced. First of all, the causes for macroeconomic disequilibria had a foreign-policy dimension (the oil crisis) and were not only determined by structural transformation in the domestic market. Small- and medium-sized enterprises were, in general, more competitive than the state monopolies. Considering Europeanization opened markets and reduced the role of the state, Italy's business seemed to benefit and not to suffer from Europe. Second, xenophobia was never a dominant theme in Italy's political culture, even if immigration from Africa and Albania became an issue in the 1990s. Anti-European sentiments were mostly absent in the domestic debate. Famous Christian Democrats, like Alcide de Gasperi, Emilio Colombo, and Giulio Andreotti, the man at the centre of Italy's post-war system, made important contributions to European integration, especially in making the SEA and the Maastricht Treaty possible. In fact, some have argued that to be Italian is to be European.[71] Third, the first steps towards economic adjustment were already taken in the 1980s. Italy's monetary market economy was effectively suspended in 1975 when Guido Carli, then governor of the Banca d'Italia, agreed to monetize budget deficits. Government bills that could not be sold at a given interest rate in the financial markets were bought by the bank. As a consequence, inflation rose to high levels and real interest rates became negative. Once Carlo Ciampi had become governor and Italy joined the EMS in 1979, financial management returned in July 1982 to a market-led system of setting interest rates. The government now had to borrow funds at positive real rates. Hence, the servicing of public debt required a positive primary surplus of the national budget.[72] However, the necessary adjustment did not start until the mid-1980s and even then it was slow. The primary surplus[73] only became positive in 1991. As a consequence, the debt/GDP had shot up: to over 120 per cent in the 1990s and the public debt position was contained only in 1997. Thus, Italy's macroeconomic disequilibrium was long lasting and does not really fit the typical boom–bust cycle of populist economics (Dornbusch and Edwards 1991). Instead, Italy's *vincolo esterno* to Europe contributed to Italy's financial stabilization. This contribution was relatively weak during the times of the EMS, as were the binding commitments of this system. With the perspective of EMU, and the danger of being left out, the pressure to change policies increased substantially. This development supports our analysis in Chapter 2 that institutions matter for the sustainability of fundamental strategic equilibria.

Italian adjustment

Italy converged to the parameters of Maastricht in three steps. The first was disinflation, the second a change in governance, and finally a quantum leap in deficit reduction. As we have seen in Chapter 4, the persistent positive inflation differential to Germany hampered Italy's competitiveness during the 'hard EMS' period (1987–92). It kept interest rates above German levels (see Figure 5.3), which rendered fiscal consolidation more difficult. Italy's inflation performance in the 1980s was strictly related to the dynamics of the labour market and to the behaviour of manufacturing firms (Fantacone *et al.* 1999). In a climate of crisis, the Amato and Ciampi governments (23 April 1992 to 14 April 1994) made a first major step in consolidation with the Agreements on Wage Performance (July 1992 and July 1993). They replaced backward inflation indexation, the so-called *scala mobile*, by forward-looking collective wage agreements pegging rises to expected inflation. This transformed the inflationary habits in Italy's 'real' economy.[74] It literally started at the moment when the ERM fell apart and the lira devalued substantially. While previously such devaluation would have re-ignited inflation, the new wage regime kept inflation under control. The shift in the price level in 1995, due to imports, was not reflected in a price–wage spiral (see Figure 5.4). Firms' pricing policies had adjusted to Europe's stability-oriented post-Maastricht environment; they even expected a decline in price *levels* (Fantacone *et al.* 1999). Productivity growth jumped up, as a consequence of the transformation taking place in the European single market. Hence, unit labour costs were stabilized. The revival of social concertation and income policies in Italy was a crucial feature of the political system and management of the Italian economy during the transition from the first to the second Republic. It stands in

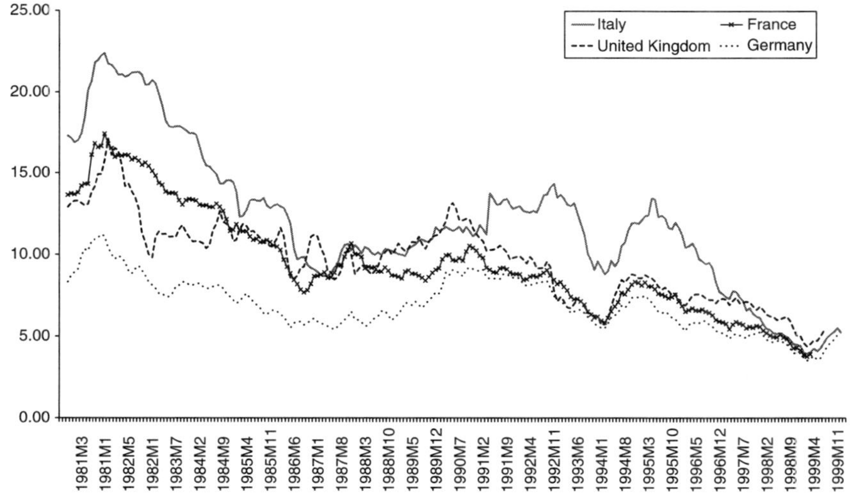

Figure 5.3 Nominal interest rates on government bonds (source: IMF).

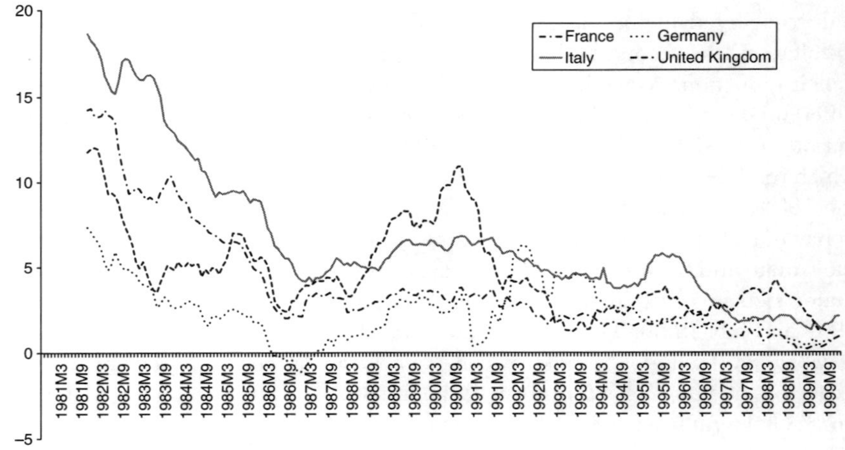

Figure 5.4 Inflation in large EU countries (source: IMF).

sharp contrast to the crisis of centralized bargaining in countries like Sweden and the United Kingdom (Regini and Regalia 1997: 212). Its success supported the recommendations on wage bargaining made by the AMUE over the years (see Chapter 4: 129).

The second step was fiscal consolidation. Reforming public finances required a fundamental transformation of the Italian state. Starting with the referendum on electoral laws in June 1991, followed by the juridical prosecutions of *mani pulite* in February 1992, within days of the signing of the Maastricht Treaty, a political crisis broke open. It destroyed the established party system and ultimately brought Italy back on track to the economic and political equilibrium of Europe. This transition from the first to the second Republic, which was completed with the formation of the Prodi government in April 1996, accelerated the process of EMU and opened the possibility of alternating governments in Italy and a clean-up of the political elite. Clientism was replaced by expertism and 'technical governments', often staffed by the Banca d'Italia – one of the few Italian institutions with a high reputation. Prime Ministers Carlo Azeglio Ciampi and Lamberto Dini both were previously Governors of the central bank. Both were aware of Italy's need to join Europe's stability culture. Ciampi had personally followed the work of the Giscard–Schmidt Committee since he had hosted one of their meetings at the Banca d'Italia in 1987. He also attended several meetings of the AMUE in Rome and in Paris.

The early consolidation successes of lower inflation and improving (positive) primary budget surpluses were soon faced with the obstacle of high European interest rates as a result of the German monetary policy after unification. Especially, small- and medium-sized companies suffered from low operating profits (Regini and Regalia 1997: 212). This put pressure on businesses to rationalize production and increase productivity. The effects were unequally distributed.[75]

Not surprisingly (see Table 5.2), Italy had a genuine attack of populism in the form of the regional *Lega Nord* and subsequently Silvio Berlusconi's creation of *Forza Italia* (Biorcio 1997: 196). During the short period of Berlusconi's first government (May 1994 to December 1994), which included the post-fascist *Alleanza Nazionale* and Umberto Bossi's *Lega Nord*, there were, for the first time, critical statements from ministers about Italy joining EMU. Berlusconi was elected on a platform of economic populism and nationalism.[76] For ordinary people, Europe remained part of the solution of Italy's problems; contrary to other countries public opinion did not reject Europe. The European orthodoxy was inconsistent with Berlusconi's promises to create 'one million more jobs' and not to raise taxes. His attempts to reduce the budget deficit turned out to be built in part on 'smoke and mirrors' (e.g. one time revenue increases by settling pending tax cases at a discount), partly on cuts in pensions and social services. This conflictual approach mobilized the largest demonstrations in Italy's post-war era. The government backed down on spending cuts and presented a budget law to Parliament, which projected a deficit of 9.07 per cent of GDP for 1995. Two days later, Berlusconi resigned (Katz and Ignazi 1996: 23–4).

He was succeeded by the technical government of Lamerto Dini and following the election victory of the centre left alliance *Ulivo* by Romano Prodi. The new government did not result from a sudden shift in public opinion to the left. The balance of total numbers of voters did not move significantly between 1994 and 1996. Prodi's victory was due to the strategic alliance 'to save democracy' against populism (the 'Latin American drift') and anti-Europeanism. It included all major political and social groupings, from ex-communists to the 'noble world of entrepeneurship' (Mastropaolo 1997: 100) and banking. Giovanni Agnelli, in his function as 'Senator for Life', voted for the Prodi government. He took a very active role in Italy's convergence process, because of his political functions and his influences on the governments as Italy's major business leader. He also had an important public role. For instance, he was a speaker at most AMUE annual conferences, and his ideas on EMU and the way to achieve it were covered in most Italian media. As Marletti put it: 'The victory of the *Ulivo* was not due to a change in demand, but in the supply of representation, which the parties offered to the voter' (Marletti 1997: 62). The two main reasons for this political realignment were the prospect of EMU and the new freedom for alternating governments after the end of the cold war. This change was the pre-condition for Italy meeting the Maastricht criteria. Berlusconi ultimately failed because he was not able to create a consensus around the issue of pension reform. His successor, Lamberto Dini, was able to accomplish this task, by obtaining the support of left-wing parties. He filled the transition until new elections and allowed Romano Prodi to 'take Italy into Europe'.

The leap

For the Prodi government, joining EMU in the first group became an imperative, especially after an important meeting with the Spanish Prime Minister Aznar during 23–24 September 1996. According to Giorgio Fossa, President of

Confindustria and a board member of AMUE, 'Aznar was the prime protagonist of the Italian way to the euro' (*El Mundo* 1 May 1998). The meeting, which has attained a quasi-mythical status, is remarkable not only for its impact on Italy's consolidation strategy, but also because it confirmed that Spain was intending to join the euro from the beginning. Only half a year before, José Maria Aznar had expressed doubts that Spain could be part of the first euro-group. After an election rally, at a dinner with Valéry Giscard d'Estaing and Rodrigues Rato, the future Finance Minister, he thought it 'impossible' to reduce inflation to the required levels. The constraints were unbearable. Giscard argued against this view.[77] Aznar also came under pressure from his socialist challenger José Borrell and he rapidly drew the conclusion. After his election as prime minister in May 1996, he used the euro challenge to justify a policy of wage restrictions, stimulate economic growth by tax reductions, and implement a number of structural reforms that helped to reduce unemployment. When Aznar met with Prodi in September 1996, he had become confident that Spain would achieve the required Maastricht criteria. Prodi's Finance Minister Carlo Ciampi had already set out the plan and prepared a substantial budget adjustment.[78] The Italian government's strategy was outlined in the graphs shown by Carlo Ciampi to his German colleague Theo Waigel in October 1996 and reproduced here as Figures 5.5 and 5.6. The primary surplus was increased to 6.7 per cent of GDP. Economic growth had also returned and the debt/GDP-ratio started to fall (see Figure 5.5). The crucial variable was now the level of interest rates. Ciampi needed to reduce the risk premium on Italian government bonds. If the debt service could be reduced to 6 per cent of GDP and the primary surplus was kept above 5 per cent, public-sector borrowing requirements could be practically eliminated (Figure 5.6).

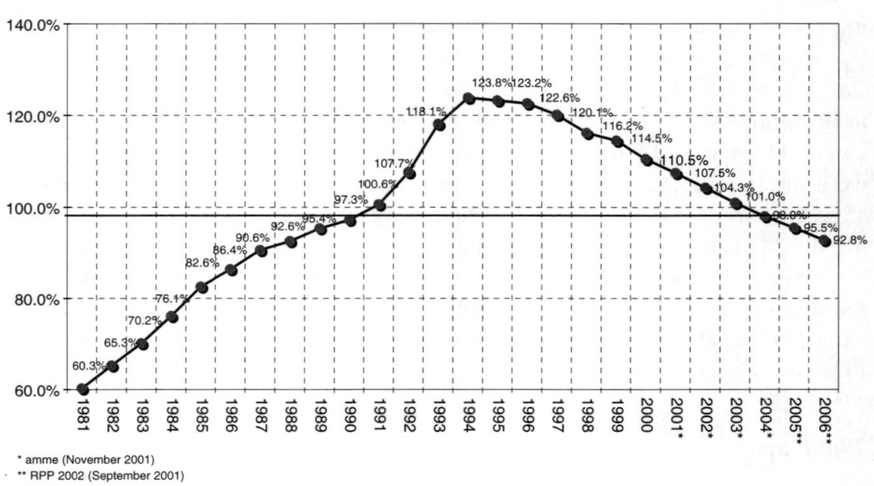

Figure 5.5 The Italian general government debt/GDP ratio, 1981–2006.

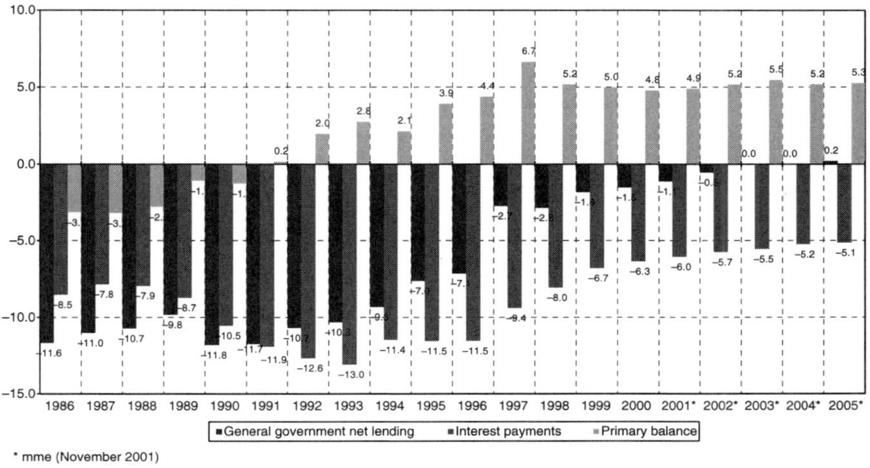

Figure 5.6 The Italian deficit and its components (as a percentage of GDP).

Ciampi's plan was to reach the 3 per cent deficit ratio in 1997, as he explained to Waigel. Waigel thought it nearly impossible to achieve the target given that Italy's official deficit ratio was still 6.7 per cent in 1996.[79] The German Finance Minister was concerned with the credibility of the EMU project with the German public and insisted publicly on the absolute requirement to reach the deficit target of 'three point zero'. However, he admits in retrospect, that there was a distribution of parts between him and Chancellor Kohl. While the finance minister insisted on the rigid implementation of the Maastricht criteria, Kohl sent out messages to Prodi that Germany would not object to Italy's membership in EMU.[80] Hence, the Italian Government needed a singular effort to bring the deficit down from nearly 6.7 to less than 3 per cent. This was achieved by a budget revision in September 1996 with a combination of long-term structural measures, the imposition of short-term cash limits on government spending, and by postponing expenditure in the critical year of 1997.[81] In the end, the fiscal adjustment from 1996 to 1997 amounted to 4.0 per cent of GDP of which 1.6 per cent was due to permanent and 1.1 per cent to one-off measures in the primary surplus (including the imposition of a special euro tax). The rest came from a reduction in interest rates, as financial markets finally became convinced that Italy could indeed join Euroland. Ciampi's manoeuvres were more than 'a trick' by which Italy cheated its way into the first circle of virtuous countries. They amounted to a bet, whereby short-term extra efforts were rewarded by long-term consolidation gains. The lower interest rates prevailing in the euro-zone made a more permanent consolidation of public finances possible, without further increases in the tax burden on the Italian economy. As President of the Republic since 1999, Carlo Azeglio Ciampi has taken an active role in ensuring that this has remained the guiding principle for all governments since Italy joined EMU.[82]

On various occasions, German politics interfered with the convergence process in Italy. In the summer of 1994, two close allies of Chancellor Helmut Kohl, Wolfgang Schäuble and Karl Lamers, put forward their paper arguing for a 'core Europe' to advance in integration, which clearly saw Italy in the group of late joiners. The paper not only caused an outrage in the Italian establishment, just like the Italian interpretation of the German Finance Minister's comment in Parliamentary Committee that Italy would not join EMU,[83] it also pushed the risk premium for government bonds up. Italy's relations with France also deteriorated, when President Jacques Chirac stated that Italy would not be in the first wave. It is not established whether he did so in order to put pressure on Italy, which he had criticized for the low lira exchange rate, or whether he was allying with Germany to keep Italy out of the first wave (Quaglia 2001a: 9). With hindsight it is clear that these comments contributed to the change in Italian policy objectives.[84]

The Stability and Growth Pact

The turning point in the political dynamics and the relations between Germany and other member states was the creation of the Stability and Growth Pact, a process that took nearly two years. As mentioned above, in September 1995, the German Minister of Finance Theo Waigel called for additional measures to secure budgetary discipline. Suddenly, the treaty provisions agreed in Maastricht seemed no longer to suffice. On 10 November 1995, Waigel outlined his ideas in a speech to the Bundestag,[85] which aimed at strengthening the limits to public deficits and debt by imposing non-interest-bearing deposits and fines on countries which had a budgetary deficit above 3 per cent of GDP. In a monetary union, expansive fiscal policy by one country can create negative spillover effects for others, for example, by creating inflationary pressure. By suggesting automatic sanctions for excessive deficits and a quicker implementation of the Excessive Deficit Procedure already laid down in the Maastricht Treaty, Waigel was hoping to increase pressure on future fellow EMU governments. The fear was that once the convergence criteria were fulfilled and the ultimate sanction of EMU membership being denied had vanished, governments would have little incentive for fiscal discipline as they shared the costs with other EMU members.

Many of the European partners were at first shocked by the proposals. The idea of a 'Fiscal Schengen' outside the community institutions seemed to indicate that Germany wanted to keep Euroland small. Or worse, it could have been a ruse to put the blame on others for failing EMU. As Heisenberg (1999: 161) put it: 'the harsh nature of Waigel's sanctions met with alarm in several member states and seemed to reflect the degree to which Germany distrusted its partners to maintain correct economic policies within the single currency'. Apart from France and the Netherlands, all EU member states and the European Commission opposed the suggestion on political and/or legal grounds although they were careful not to give Germany a pretext to pull out of the euro-project.

Economists throughout Europe challenged the logic of the Stability Pact. As the motive was not macroeconomics, but that of a politician with an eye on public opinion and mistrust for the other possible EMU members, these arguments did not find much weight in the debate. The AMUE, witnessing the reactions outside Germany through direct contact with officials and corporate decision-makers, was concerned that there was no constructive transnational debate on the question of how fiscal discipline should be assured in EMU. In order to contribute to a pan-European consensus, the AMUE sought to make the other side heard in Germany. With the backing of the Bertelsmann Foundation, Stefan Collignon wrote the book: '*Geldwertstabilität für Europa*'.[86] It was not only suggesting a different model of how policies could be co-ordinated in the EMU, but also elaborated the aspects of macroeconomic management, which were hotly debated in France.

After months of debate and a negotiation marathon at the European Council, the Pact for Stability and Growth was adopted by the European Council in Dublin in 1996. Waigel's proposal had been modified in several ways. Most importantly, the Pact became part of European legislation, rather than a separate Schengen-like agreement. Second, the unrestrained automaticity of sanctions was given up as it was incompatible with the EU Treaty. Sanctions were now subject to a political choice by a qualified majority vote in the Council. Third, the new focus of the pact was on prior planning, surveillance, and commitment, rather than on ex-post sanctioning.

Why did the German government wish to move towards more rigidity in fiscal policies, when fellow EMU members were already struggling for convergence? In a letter to the *Financial Times Deutschland* on 14 May 2001, Waigel wrote: 'The definition of an exact deficit quota was the decisive tool to build up political pressure, in order set the monetary union on a stability track. Indeed, insisting on exact quotas, the scientific foundation of which might be difficult, was a contested means. Yet, in my opinion this was the only way to win the necessary trust of the financial markets as well as the legislative institutions in the Monetary Union'. There were further domestic concerns, which made Waigel push for the Stability Pact. First of all, there was Waigel's situation as chairman of the CSU, the Bavarian branch of the Christian Democratic Party, who had always been tougher and more populist on EMU than the rest in the country. Waigel kept a delicate balance with the state Prime Minister Stoiber who played with populism on the right. But Waigel was a deeply convinced European. When he joined the CSU and all through his political life, he was inspired by the party's founder Joseph Müller (called Ochsensepp) who had survived the concentration camp in Flossenburg. Waigel frequently quoted from a speech given by Müller in 1946, where he said: 'If the European peoples wish to have security today, then I would see the best security in having a single (!) currency. If there is only one currency in Europe, no country can mobilize against another. That is the best guarantee for the security of the European people' (Müller 1946). As party chief and successor to Müller, Waigel carried this tradition within his party. The Stability Pact was his response against populist temptations and slippages.[87] Second, the Stability Pact was a strategic move by the German government to silence the Bundesbank. This was particularly important in order to reassure the German public when the convergence efforts were to be assessed in 1998. Third, the Pact was seen as a reaction (partly even in anticipation) to those who would criticize the conservative/liberal coalition for not doing enough to ensure that the euro would be as strong as the Dentschmark.[88] This argument was later used by four professors in their Maastricht complaint before the Constitutional Court. Fourth, the Pact reassured the members of Parliament in their vote on EMU. Waigel's strategy seemed to work. In a spring 1997 survey, 58 per cent of the responding MPs said the Stability Pact was a significant factor in their EMU decision and only 2 per cent said it was insignificant (Heisenberg 1997: 13).

Three per cent is 3.0

For the German government it was still not sufficient to set up mechanisms to ensure the long-term stability of fiscal policies. While most political observers had been expecting a small EMU of six states when the Maastricht Treaty finally came into force in 1993, suddenly up to eleven countries seemed to be able to fulfil the convergence criteria in early 1997. The unofficial German credo, however, was: 'Small is beautiful' – a sharp contrast to the position the new Socialist government in Paris took in May 1997. Theo Waigel started to insist on the so-called '*Punktlandung*' leaving no doubt that the German government would make sure that only those countries could become members of EMU whose deficit did not pass the limit of 3.0 per cent of GDP. Also, Bundesbank President Tietmeyer insisted that EMU could only start when convergence was sustainable. Against the background of latent distrust and increasingly open xenophobia in German public opinion, the government passionately insisted that 'three per cent means 3.0 per cent'. This tactic was supposed to show that the German government was doing all it could to prevent an unstable euro. It had the side effect of seeming to exclude Italy and others from the first round of EMU countries, even if they only narrowly missed the 3 per cent target. Distrust grew when the French, the Italian, and other governments tried to improve their deficit in 1997 through what the press rapidly named 'creative accounting'. Many people in countries with a tradition of monetary stability and sound budgetary policies such as Germany and the Netherlands feared these countries would quickly revert to expansive fiscal policies, if they did not even do their homework now. In the end, the German government itself had to recur to creative accounting. In 1997, Germany ran into trouble in fulfilling the fiscal convergence criteria. Waigel asked the German Bundesbank to revalue the gold reserves, a step which would have created additional revenue in 1997 – the year that formed the basis for convergence assessment. Thereafter, this debate disappeared.

Meanwhile the debate on postponing EMU had gained ground. The German government started to insist that convergence was more important than the timetable. The Bundesbank repeated at every possible occasion that political union should precede monetary union. The news magazine *Focus* concluded: 'There shall only be a common money if there is a common tax and fiscal policy, a common security and foreign policy. These – if at all – will only exist late in the next century. And up to then, the Bundesbank would reign over the D-Mark, alone. This tactic of delay can be successful, because EMU in 1999 is not automatic. The Council of Ministers can decide at any point that a common currency is not reasonable' (*Focus* 15 April 1995: 18). Similar analyses were published in daily papers. Economists and politicians such as Gerhard Schröder, then Prime Minister in Niedersachsen,[89] spoke openly in favour of a postponement. These statements, naturally, troubled Germany's partners who feared that Germany might still in the end, refuse monetary union. The AMUE only started to see clearly in early 1997, when Bertrand de Maigret had a conversation with Wim Duisenberg, then President of the EMI. Over lunch after a meeting of the EMI council, Duisenberg responded with a cheeky smile to Maigret about German trustworthiness: 'I believe in it since this morning, because Bundesbank President Tietmeyer has insisted that we rent offices for the European Central Bank with a capacity up to 1000 people and not – as others have suggested – only for 100 or 150'.

French–German dissent

France's path to convergence was also difficult. Populism has a long history in France, on the left as on the right. The structural transformations of France during the 1990s were nothing short of dramatic; productivity in the tradable manufacturing sector grew by over 37 per cent faster than in the non-tradable construction sector between 1992 and 1998. Relative mark-ups deteriorated later by 20.9 and relative wages by 7.1 per cent. Hence, while the international sector of the economy improved its competitiveness, the domestic sector was under severe pressure. Populism, during the 1990s, affected particularly the political right who attempted to recover voters from the National Front. Not only did populist ideas gain ground, but also the breakaway factions from the UDF (Philippe de Villiers) and the Gaullists (Charles Pasqua) undermined the coherence of the political centre right. On the left, Jean-Pierre Chevènement's *Mouvement des Citoyens* and the resurgence of Trotskyite parties had a similar effect. Under these circumstances, it was not easy to steer France into EMU. Before and after its difficult Maastricht referendum, which only very narrowly brought about a *yes* to the Maastricht Treaty,[90] France had to cope with high public deficits. These were, in part, a consequence of the economic downturn after the German high interest rate policy, in part a result of uncontrolled spending by the Balladur government. But for the sake of exchange-rate stability, France had also tolerated high interest rates, which strangled domestic demand and increased the cost of the state's debt service. With a fiscal deficit of 6 per cent in 1994, the government decided on drastic spending cuts after Jacques Chirac's election to the Elysée. A three-week strike in December 1995 signalled a rejection of this policy, which hit the economy during a period of global downturn. In 1996, similar strikes generated enough public support to force the government to retreat from plans to reform pensions (Hall 2001: 181). The classical effects of deflation creating unemployment then hampered the intended consolidation of public finances. As a consequence, France requested – in line with the Maastricht Treaty – a 'dynamic interpretation' of the deficit criterion. It did so not to pave the way for irresponsible fiscal behaviour, but to avoid measures, which were inappropriate in the economic situation (Guérot 1997: 231).[91]

However, the efforts by the Juppé government were hardly more successful than Berlusconi's in Italy. In May 1997, the Socialist Lionel Jospin won national elections in a surprise landslide. Gaullist President Jacques Chirac had brought the election date forward by almost a year as he wanted to disentangle national elections and the convergence assessment for EMU membership. The day before the elections, the news leaked that France was heading for a 3.8 per cent deficit in 1997, requiring extra austerity measures. The French voters decided thus to give the socialists a chance.

With the arrival of Jospin as Prime Minister, the discourse changed. He set out four conditions for the start of EMU: an immediate participation of Spain and Italy; a 'dynamic interpretation' of the criteria; the creation of a '*gouvernement économique*'; and a pact for growth and employment. 'With this position, Jospin expressed the French displeasure, shared by a majority, with the way Germany had pushed through its stability model irrespective of social realities. It seemed as if Germany was refusing to subject its monetary policy to employment objectives, and France refused to orient its whole economic policy on a stable inflation rate' (Guérot 1997: 234). German perceptions of France radicalized, disregarding the facts. The more the French emphasized the social consequences of EMU, the stronger grew the impression in Germany that even France could not be trusted.[92] However, in the end nothing speaks louder than facts. The new government stimulated consumption and growth, voluntarist measures supported youth employment and created a new environment of trust and confidence, while the previous Juppé government had punctured the economy.[93] Within a year, Jospin's Finance Minister Dominique Strauss-Kahn had increased the rate of corporate tax to 42 per cent, doubled the supplementary income tax (CSG) to 7.5 per cent of earnings, raised funds from selling nationalized companies (like France Telecom and Air France). France qualified as expected for the new currency (Hall 2001).

Mediating across the borders

In the climate of mistrust and deteriorating credibility, the AMUE increased its transnational mediation efforts and its broad public communication. This included three lines of action: (1) producing evidence about the sustainability of EMU; (2) strengthening the broad public respect for the efforts made reaching the convergence criteria; (3) building up the credibility of the project by getting companies to prepare for the practical change-over to the euro.

The Sustainability report

As the critical decision date of 1997 approached, resistance against EMU intensified, particularly in Germany. While anti-euro activists mobilized public opinion against the 'laxist southerners', Bundesbank President Hans Tietmeyer insisted that what mattered for a sound currency was not a one-off achievement of the

Maastricht criteria, but long-term sustainability in economic developments. The Bundesbank's chief economist, Otmar Issing, compared the high-deficit countries with an alcoholic who has to prove that he had 'kicked the habit' (Issing 1996). The AMUE decided that one had to take these arguments seriously.

In 1996, it set up a group of twenty-five experts[94] to study the 'Sustainability of the euro and the Convergence Criteria':

> It looks as if the debate on EMU is now focusing on the dangers of a bad Monetary Union. Convergence may increase but labour markets are not reforming. The time bomb of unfunded state pensions that will be exploding into the budgets at a rapid pace should also be integrated. President Davignon emphasized that the basic issue on EMU today is the question on sustainability. It is not enough to pass the examination alone. EMU must maintain stability in the long run. He suggested the AMUE deal with the issue of sustainability of EMU in order to avoid an ideological debate about future policies and form group to discuss it openly.[95]

The AMUE sought to assess the sustainability of EMU not only from the point of view of the convergence requirements set out in the Treaty. It was looking for criteria, which would determine the conditions necessary for EMU's success in the long run. It did so by a number of theoretical and empirical papers. First, it considered that the sustainability issue could be addressed in terms of who would wish to leave the EMU? This meant turning the optimum-currency area argument of Robert Mundell on its head. It concluded that an optimum-currency area was sustainable if price stability was maintained. The monetary set-up in the Maastricht Treaty was therefore coherent with long-term sustainability. Yet, monetary stability was only a necessary, but not a sufficient condition. Did the public debt dynamics put stability in question? A paper by Collignon and Mundschenk (1999) looked at the theoretical and empirical issues. It found that while public debt had been unsustainable in most countries during the 1980s, they had all returned to sustainable debt dynamics at the end of the 1990s. It also emerged that fiscal consolidation was not only a question of finance ministers doing their homework, but also of the macroeconomic environment. As one of the most spectacular results, the paper found all the public debt would converge to the Maastricht benchmarks of avoiding excessive deficits as long as governments responded to a deviation from targets by a correction in the primary surplus of more than the growth-adjusted interest rate. Historically, this had always been the case and the Stability and Growth Pact was likely to improve this reaction. Hence, it was unlikely that fiscal policies would undermine the stability of the future currency. Finally, the report looked at the question of unemployment, as a potential cause of political destabilization. The report sought a rule for monetary policy that would avoid the super-conservatism that prevailed in the 1990s. It found that if wage bargainers increased wages in line with aggregate productivity, thereby stabilizing unit costs, monetary policy could become more accommodative and stimulate investment and economic growth.[96] In the empirical part, Piercarlo Padoan analysed substantial achievements made by Italy in eliminating inflation.

To the surprise of some economists in the group, it emerged from the empirical evidence presented that not Italy, but Portugal gave reasons for concern. The increase of unit labour costs seemed to create inflationary pressure and endanger Portuguese competitiveness. Theresa Cardoso, formerly at the Portuguese Central Bank, attempted to cool down the debate by arguing that unit-labour costs were in a catch-up process. Some group members, including Collignon, were prepared to issue a warning to Portugal, but political prudence let other members refrain from this. George Hay of Banco Hispano-Americano settled the dispute by saying; 'we in Spain would be happy if we had the same degree of wage flexibility as Portugal'.

The publication of the sustainability report was not a major media event, but did stimulate discussions amongst policy makers. It was sent to all central banks, the EMI, the Commission and key parliamentarians in all member states and the EP. For Hervé Carré of the European Commission, who participated in the meetings, the discussions were an eye-opener. Later, Otmar Issing favourably commented on the public debt analysis, but said to Collignon; 'you will have to do more to convince me that wage bargainers are responsible for price stability and the central bank for unemployment'. Even if, or maybe because it did not only repeat mainstream opinions (see Annexe 1), the sustainability report helped to give credit to the idea that it was safe to venture into EMU.

Broad public campaigns

In an initiative to stabilize public opinion in Germany, the AMUE sent a letter to all MPs in the Bundestag in early 1997, offering them to organize euro conferences in their constituencies with AMUE speakers. With some marginal financial backing from the Commission and later also from the Bundespresseamt, the AMUE organized the programme with speakers, while the MPs provided local infrastructure and organization. Usually the AMUE also co-operated with local banks (Sparkassen) and invited a speaker from the Bundesbank. Peter Struck, General Secretary of the Social Democrats in the Parliament, was the first to encourage the MPs of his party to invite AMUE speakers. Possibly because of the AMUE link to Helmut Schmidt, the Christian Democrats were initially hesitant. Only after Friedrich Merz[97] had visited the AMUE office in Paris, seeking allies against Europessimism, and after Karl Lamers, the foreign policy spokesman of the CDU/CSU, mobilized Christian Democrats did the initiative reach cross-party dimensions. The liberal party FDP also accepted the AMUE offer. The Greens, however, remained reluctant. When Collignon visited Joschka Fischer in Bonn to invite him to an annual meeting of the Association, his first reaction was: 'what, big business is interested in us now?'

In 1996, the Association participated in forty-eight public events in Germany. A year later it reached a peak of almost ninety conferences and still participated in over fifty in 1998. The vast majority of the conferences included the participation of German MPs with demand peaking in autumn 1997. The AMUE's communication strategy followed three objectives. First, it wanted to send a positive signal to the public by explaining why EMU was good for Germany. Second, it sought to contribute to the emergence of a European-wide consensus by giving credit to what was happening in other EU countries and overcoming the nationalistic overtones in the German EMU debate. Third, the purpose was to convince political decision-makers, especially the Members of Parliament. Before they set out for the first conferences, Collignon explained: 'The audience is the one thing. It's nice if we can win them over. But whom we really want to convince is the MP. They have to sit on the panel with you, otherwise you will never manage to have their ear for an hour'. AMUE speakers were invited by almost a quarter of all members of the German parliament. 'The offer was clever', the Christian Democrat Karl Lamers judged looking back. 'You gave the members of Parliament the chance to set up an interesting evening conference many people would attend. And you helped them out on a topic most were not firm in'.[98] Credibility was increased by the fact that the AMUE speakers represented a non-political private sector organization, which would only be in favour of EMU if monetary union was going to be a success. Second, the presence of the Bundesbank inspired trust, and forced the Bundesbank speakers to comment publicly on what they thought of the AMUE position on EMU. A relationship of mutual respect thereby ensued.

For the AMUE, it was important to counter xenophobic perceptions of reliable and unreliable countries, and to build confidence especially with respect to Italy and France. To this purpose, the AMUE also asked Dominique Bocquet, a German-speaking French *Inspecteur des Finances* and former Secretary-General of the European Movement, to participate in conferences. Guillaume Lepecq, Luc Moulin, and many executives from AMUE member companies and banks followed with an educational campaign to help companies with the change over to the new currency.

The main task was to broaden the picture of a purely German debate and counter mistrust and prejudice. Aggression was rarely openly expressed. Only in Munich, a meeting of 600 people organized by the local CSU MP Erich Riedel with a debate between the leader of populist anti-euro movement Manfred Brunner and Stefan Collignon for the AMUE got high-jacked by the neo-Nazi party NPD. But mostly, the AMUE speakers were successful.[99] For example, in November 1998, AMUE speakers frequently travelled to Eastern Germany, speaking at large conferences, but also in local pubs, where political groups convened evening sessions in the back room. One evening, Daniela Schwarzer was invited to a small town not far from Leipzig. The room was packed with over 300 people. After listening to the presentation, an animated discussion broke out bringing forward all the mistrust German public opinion projected on the euro. The tension reached a peak when one gentleman stood up and shouted: 'No wonder, you are for the euro. You live in France. And all the Latin people just want soft money. They are all cheating their way into EMU, the French are just like the Italians'. Little of the arguments developed in the last hour seemed to have reached the participants. Yet, she was not on the point of giving up and shouted back. 'Yes, the Italians have introduced a one-year extra tax. Yes, they have done so to get their budget right. But have you ever thought about the question, why the Italian people accepted this? It is because they want to be in EMU – even if they have to pay for it personally. They have understood that the euro is a historic chance and they support their government in pursuing it. This goes as far as accepting a higher income tax. For me, this is not a bad trick. It is a commitment to European integration, which deserves acknowledgement. Think about it this way for a minute'. She sat down, waiting for a further challenge from the audience. There was a moment of silence. Suddenly, someone started to clap his hands, others followed. The local MP had difficulties in believing his constituency was applauding for Italy. But he got the momentum and spoke up for the first time since he had rather hesitantly introduced 'the young lady from Paris' earlier this evening. Probably for the first time he publicly agreed that the euro was a chance for Europe. Yes, there were challenges and risks, but that the advantages and long-term prospects were probably even bigger.

Helping companies change over to the euro

While Germany was certainly the main focus of political AMUE activities in 1997 and 1998, the Association also expanded its euro communication for businesses throughout the EU with over 200 own conferences per year. Often invited by other organizations, Bertrand de Maigret spoke at 374 meetings out of a total of 1317. Collignon spoke at a series of conferences organized by Confindustria in major Italian cities (Bari, Naples, Rome, Florence, Bologna, Pesaro, Venice, Genoa, and Milan) explaining the need for monetary stability. The AMUE also produced printed material. One of its early initiatives was the brochure *'Europe united through the Single Currency'*, which, requested by BAT Chairman Sir Patrick Sheehy, was first published in English in 1996. Other languages followed, as officials in Brussels and national administrations explicitly encouraged the AMUE to intensify communication efforts towards the broad public. The French Prime Minister's office wrote on 4 December 1996: 'It was with great interest that I looked at your brochure, which presents the objectives, the stakes and the practicalities of the changeover to the Single Currency in a very clear way. I am convinced that a French version of the text would respond to a very large demand among our citizens'.[100]

With its monthly newsletter '*The Ecu for European Business*' later renamed '*EMU for Business*', the AMUE spread EMU-related information into the business sector but also to political decision-makers and journalists in all EU countries. The website of the AMUE became a privileged source of practical information and received record hits in the second half of the 1990s. However, these initiatives were never purely technical. They always emphasized the broader dimensions of acceptance, identification, and political leadership. In this endeavour, AMUE was ready to join forces with other organizations, offering them an international platform. For example, a group of 300 French business leaders, elected representatives, and civil servants were invited to comment; 'The contest for the euro is a contest relating to good management of public affairs, it is an economic contest and a political contest. Countries in which public opinion has been the best informed, the best alerted and the best at accepting the necessary changes and managing their effects – will also be the best adapted to the euro, whatever other technical or accounting problems are encountered. But in which European country do those responsible for communicating on the euro know how to say it, how to share this conviction and this evidence with the users of the euro – you, us, everybody? [...] The real promise of the euro lies in gaining back sovereignty. From that will come economic and financial power. That will feed the values of civilisation. It will reinforce the rediscovered freedom of the individual and stimulate the rebirth of a policy of European power. The silence of the politicians over this promise is a measure of their collective failure' (Groupe Equinoxe in *AMUE Newsletter* 21, 18 April 1997).

As the start of EMU came closer, the AMUE communication activities increasingly focused on the private sector. The AMUE never questioned that EMU would start on 1 January 1999. Its concern was to contribute to a timely and successful changeover. Campaigning for the practical introduction of the single currency had been a strategic move in the early 1990s to circumvent the political and ideological debates on EMU, which seemed to block the whole project as explained in Chapter 4. In the second half of the 1990s, the promotion of euro-preparations had become an urgent practical necessity. We can identify various phases of the AMUE's work on practical issues involved in the changeover to the single currency.

1 In the early 1990s, the AMUE started assessing the practical issues involved in the creation of a monetary union. Internal working groups established the most important problems for the company and banking sector. This work had a double objective. First, the exchange among the members permitted mutual learning and helped to identify best practices. The challenge was to reach a basic understanding of what the changeover to a new currency actually meant: which parts of companies would be concerned to what degree, which delays would be necessary to achieve the changeover, and which budget had to be allocated. Euro project leaders from all over Europe needed a forum to discuss the issues at stake – not only technical ones, but also management problems, such as the question of how an early euro transition could be completed most efficiently in a multinational group or an international bank, when inner-organizational resistance in this change project was to be expected. The second objective was to use this knowledge to influence the political decisions on the transition framework such that the private sector could manage the changeover in a cost-efficient way. As we have explained in Chapter 4, the Maastricht Treaty left important details of the transition scenario open. The AMUE shared its know-how with the European Commission, developed it further in working groups and provided input for the Green book on the changeover scenario, which the Commission put forward in 1995.
2 Once the scenario had been settled at the Madrid summit in December 1995, many AMUE members developed their own changeover strategies and started internal communication on the euro. Some AMUE members

declared officially that they would start using the euro as early as possible, that is, as of 1 January 1999, and engaged in communication with their business partners. Only a limited number were eventually in a position to do so as their business partners were not yet prepared. Member banks started to distribute AMUE information material to their corporate clients. Communication thus started to develop beyond the immediate members into the broader private sector. In April 1996, the AMUE reconsidered its own role: 'Its political role may diminish. [Yet, t]he preparation of the major economic protagonists – banks and businesses – will have a powerful driving effect. This evolution leads us to give priority to the service provided to our members and beyond them to all European businesses'.[101] In 1996, the AMUE also started to monitor[102] the state of euro preparations throughout the EU, and made this information accessible to political decision-makers.

3 While the AMUE was among the very first organizations to provide information and advice on the transition to the single currency, euro information material released by other institutions (such as the Commission, Euro Info Centres, banks, chambers of commerce) mushroomed from 1997 onwards. However, the need suddenly seemed bottomless and the European Commission asked the AMUE to continue and broaden the campaigns. This involved educating multipliers and providing them with information material as well as direct information of companies that were not part of the AMUE network. The AMUE also intensified its efforts to set up conferences and workshops for SMEs – in 1997, it organized one per working day throughout the EU.[103] It also distributed information in print and through the Internet. A key document was a practical guide for small- and medium-sized enterprises that illustrated the early need to start preparations, recommended a methodology to manage the project, and included a 'euro-audit'.[104] The AMUE members supported[105] these initiatives, because they were concerned about the acceptance of the euro although this did not offer direct benefit for them. 'Those who do not travel and who do not trade with other countries might well consider in 1999 that the major companies have received most of the benefit expected from the stability of exchange rates. Why then oblige others to make changes whose profitability will be perceived as collective rather than individual? If care is not taken a popular demand may arise after the year 2000 calling for a halt to this changeover of banknotes and coins which are going to temporarily complicate the daily life of citizens. This popular reaction, politically sensitive, could be reduced, or even transformed into dynamic support, if it were to be correctly anticipated by companies and their representative organisations'.[106] After the start of EMU, communication related to the introduction of coins and notes, especially retail and consumer issues, gained importance. As national regulations on details of the introduction of notes and coins remained to be finalized, the AMUE attempted for a last time to influence political decisions on the changeover framework through active participation in European or official national working groups.

4 The AMUE subsequently engaged in countries that were not immediately part of the euro-zone. First initiatives were developed in the 'pre-in' countries, that is, the United Kingdom, Sweden, Denmark, and Greece. The objective was twofold: first, to raise the awareness of local companies of the arrival of the euro, as they could be confronted with the new currency, for example, in sales or procurement operations although they were not part of the eurozone. Second, there was the political motive of increasing support for EMU membership in the two Scandinavian countries and the United Kingdom. In 1999, the AMUE, financed by the European Commission, also engaged in a euro project in Central and Eastern Europe.

Throughout these four phases, the AMUE developed and refined its communication approach and its tool-kit. Up to the end of its activities an important pillar was its monthly newsletter *EMU for Business*. It reported on political and economic developments in the candidate countries, intending to establish a transnational dialogue, and made outstanding speeches or articles available to an international public. By summarizing, for example, best-practice reports of companies' euro preparations and reporting on changeover scenarios in candidate countries, it aimed at contributing to an exchange of information and facilitating the technical changeover. Benchmarking was essential to a number of businesses, which had confidence in the experience of other business leaders. It also gave updates of major political events, regularly reviewed the state of national regulations and distributed excerpts of relevant documents. The magazine also provided summaries of major conferences and listed upcoming euro events from throughout the EU. While the Newsletters were at first a service reserved to the AMUE members, they were published on the Internet from 1997 onwards. Here, the AMUE developed a euro-platform with information in thirteen countries. In 1998, the site was re-launched, part of it as an intranet reserved for the members, but the larger part of it available to the broad public. Most AMUE documents were immediately published online and other organizations were invited to provide material. The site also hosted official documents relevant for the changeover in the future EMU countries.

As it became apparent that euro preparations were lagging behind in all future member countries, the AMUE increasingly worked with organizations which could act as multipliers. It was actively encouraged to do so by the European Commissioner Yves-Thilbaut de Silguy, and then by Pedro Solbes, with whom it had confident contacts. The Director of Monetary Affairs, Hervé Carré, was also very supportive. In the second half of the 1990s, the AMUE established close contacts with regional partners, such as Chambers of Commerce or sector specific organizations. The urgency had grown: in spring 1998, less than a year before the launch of the single currency, for example, 57 per cent of the German companies had still not made any effort to prepare for the euro (DIHT 1998). Businesses were ill-informed about the changeover necessities: 'Many business people still believe that the transitional period will last until 30 June 2002, so that they assume to have plenty of time to get ready. Others do not understand that payments in (NCU) National Currency Union bank notes may still be made in January–February 2002 while the use of NCU as book money and accounting in NCU will be forbidden. Many businesses will then be surprised at the need to have in early 2002 the accounts underlying VAT declarations and payments in euros' (AMUE Newsletter June 2000). However, working groups addressing issues of euro preparation (such as, accounting, treasury, IT) existed throughout the European Union, many of which had been initiated and expanded with the help of AMUE members.[107]

It soon turned out that sectoral federations and associations, chambers of commerce, or public bodies were not the only organizations that could convince SMEs to start their euro preparations. In its internal working groups, the AMUE discovered that its large member companies were making important efforts to educate their smaller business partners. After reviewing their strategies and recognizing an important success, the AMUE was invited by the European Commission to co-organize a public conference[108] on this issue. With the participation of the Commission and the EP, the AMUE brought together more then 150 large companies and some small suppliers or distributors who had already started the changeover in co-operation with a larger business partner. The objective of the conference was, first, to establish and demonstrate best practices, that is, how the smaller business partners could best be helped. Early movers including, Siemens, Elf, General Motors, and Philips, explained their strategies to help smaller business partners. A second objective was to raise 'awareness among large companies of their self-interest in having small- and medium-sized enterprises adequately prepared for the euro' (AMUE newsletter). The AMUE explained its increased efforts to work with SMEs as follows: 'Firstly, because they are our natural partners, because their competitivity translates into their prices and so our own. Secondly, because the use of the euro after 1999 by major companies could hamper small businesses if they are not prepared. And thirdly, because it is in all of our interests to encourage the support of Small and Medium sized enterprises for Economic and Monetary Union'.[109] At the conference, presentations, for example, by Opel and the French retail chain Auchan[110] operating in eleven countries and working with 8,000 suppliers made clear that a smooth transition of SMEs was crucial for large corporates. The SMEs commented how they had experienced the support and gave advice and pointed out where difficulties had remained. While General Motors and Elf invited their distributors to participate in internal euro seminars, Siemens distributed 20,000 copies of a euro CD-Rom. It also informed all its distributors in two successive letters about the general euro framework and the company's changeover plans, and managed to conclude 35,000 agreements with its distributors on a coordinated changeover. Optimus, the Portuguese telephone company of Sonae added one-to-one co-operation schemes to direct mailings and euro seminars. All large companies tailored their information according to the national changeover scenarios and business branches of the smaller business partners. The conference showed that the efforts of the large companies not only raised SMEs' awareness of the euro in general, it also helped them to recognize that the currency changeover was not only a technical problem but had strategic implications in the new market situation created by enhanced price transparency.[111] The SMEs reported that they were strongly influenced in their euro strategy, for instance, as far as dates were concerned.[112] The interdependence of large companies and their suppliers and distributors created further momentum in the changeover process, despite the 'no compulsion–no prohibition' rule for the period from 1999 to 2002. The conference also highlighted the possibilities of private–public partnerships: other players involved in the euro preparation of SMEs, such as public authorities in the member countries, the Euro Info Centres set up by the European Commission, Eurochambers or networks like the European SME association UEAPME, had successfully started to co-operate with large companies such as IBM. In order to help multipliers informing small- and medium-sized enterprises on the euro, the AMUE started to provide power point slides on its website, which could be downloaded for presentations in euro workshops, it put electronic checklists online, which could easily be used and adapted for workshops, and it sent its printed euro guides to conference organizers on request. If a local organization wanted to set up a euro conference, the AMUE gave advice for setting up the programme and sent speakers to the event, if the organizers felt they needed external expertise. With the European Commission, IBM, and the European Accountants Federation,[113] the AMUE launched the 'Euro Trophies' in several member countries in 2000, a competition selecting small- and medium-sized enterprises, which prepared successfully and innovatively for the euro. While the winners received a prize of up to 5,000 EUR, their stories were widely publicized throughout the EU as examples to enterprises still considering their future course of action.

As an increasing number of companies started to believe that EMU would start on time,[114] demand for tailored information shot up. It had become clear that there were not only important differences in the degree of information of large and small companies, but also across different sectors and in different regions. While information on the transition framework was now easily accessible, communication material had to be adapted to specific needs. In order to understand the sectoral specificities, the AMUE again set up working groups with companies, sectoral organizations, and business consultants. As a starting point, the AMUE established the need of sectors that were likely to be early users. It turned its attention to the tourism industry where business to business and also client relationships were likely to be invoiced in euro as early as possible. As the date for the introduction of coins and notes came closer, the AMUE started working on the retail sector. Shops were not only bearing the bulk of work during the changeover period, they were also the place where customers made their first experience with the new currency. In order to ensure their confidence, the transition to the euro had to work as smoothly as possible. A first guide aiming at larger retailers was published in 1997. Two years later, a lack of information material for small shop owners such as bakeries, grocers, shoe shops, or hairdressers became evident. So a second euro guide for retailers was written. It gave simple and hands-on advice to shop owners on how they could cope with the changeover and the dual currency period as easily and cost-efficiently as possible, while meeting the customers' need for transparency and information.

On 8 December 1997, the AMUE presented its first euro guide in Greek language at a conference in Athens. Although Greece would only join the EMU in 2001 (which was not even deemed a realistic date in 1997), the interest was high – politically and practically.[115] In 1998, the Swedish EU Bureau for Industry and Commerce in Stockholm joined the AMUE. Together with other AMUE members, such as SE Banken and the Foundation of Swedish Industry, the Bureau set up various conferences. The European Commission and its President Jacques Santer encouraged this work, because their own capacity to intervene was limited by political considerations.[116] In spring 1999, five euro conferences[117] were held in five Central and Eastern European countries Poland, Hungary, the Czech Republic, Estonia, and Slovenia. Even though EMU had started on 1 January 1999, information on the euro was scarce. For example, in 2001, a truck loaded with electronic equipment got stuck at the Czech boarder because the customs officers had not been instructed on how to administer and tax imports priced in euros. Meanwhile, banks were registering an increasing demand for euro-related banking services. The interest of Central and Eastern European companies was growing as they noted that the start of EMU did not only require them to technically be able to work in euros, they also learned that the arrival of the new currency had changed the competitive situation in the market they were soon hoping to integrate and in which many of them were already doing business. In June 2000, the AMUE held a workshop in Frankfurt on the introduction of notes and coins. At that time, national regulations remained to be finalized: according to the subsidiarity principle, each country could define the rules for the exchange of the currency within the framework defined at the Madrid Summit 1995. The workshop finalized recommendations for the smooth introduction of notes and coins.[118]

The need for further integration

For populism to remain a 'voice' option, it is important that the 'progressive' forces in society remain capable of integrating some of the social discontent, partly by creating a new collective identity. This is what happened in the United States at the end of the nineteenth century. The large trusts, which operated in the continental market became sponsors of American culture, such as Ivy League universities or the Metropolitan Museum. Established political parties became advocates of social progress and welfare. In Europe at the end of the twentieth century, similar tendencies were perceptible.

The large European companies, which supported the AMUE, were all motivated by stability in the Single European Market. This is why it made sense for them to introduce a single currency. But at the same time, these companies were the prime agents of social change. Therefore, they also had an interest in preserving the cohesion of the emerging European civil society. These objectives were not compatible with populism. Macroeconomic stability was a pre-condition for the sustainability of European monetary union and the single market. Whether this was achieved by a centre-right or centre-left government was, from this point, of lesser importance. This explains why the alliance between Valéry Giscard d'Estaing and Helmut Schmidt could so easily find the support of the most powerful business leaders in Europe. But at the same time, the Association never hesitated to swim against the stream of established ideas if new evidence could enrich the European public debate.

For political parties and leaders, the issue of EMU was like a litmus test: it would prove their suitability for government responsibility. The particular articulation by which political formations would bundle the different and often contradictory ideas into a general consensus often depended on the specific environment in which they operated. In the late 1980s this was more efficiently done by centre-right parties, in the late 1990s by centre-left parties. However, what was new and unique in Europe was a network of people in civil society who shared ideas and the means to bring them together across borders of states and cultures. Companies and their chairmen lobbied for a monetary union, which had the characteristics of a common good. The unintended consequence of their engagement was the emergence of a European economic culture. This is why the men and women who were committed to making EMU happen are the true foundation of European unification.

Epilogue

This book has analysed the involvement of the private sector in the creation of the euro from a very special angle: the activities of the Committee and the Association for the Monetary Union of Europe. This perspective is certainly incomplete, as the private sector is much larger. Also, our study does not privilege representative organizations but tells the story of the involvement of individuals, rather than of the whole sector. Nevertheless, the history of the two organizations and our interpretation of it challenges some fundamental assumptions of integration theory. We will now draw some theoretical and practical conclusions.

Methodological challenges

Our first criticism concerns the concept of agency. As we discussed in Section 1, traditional integration theory focuses on collective actors such as governments or supranational institutions. Different theories attribute different weights to different actors (national governments, the Commission, the European Parliament, the European Court of Justice) and identify different constraints imposed on these actors (such as electoral accountability or functional requirements). The motives of these actors are naturalistically derived from exogenously given interests and pay-offs. This interpretation ignores important developments in modern sociology and philosophy: the linguistic turn following Wittgenstein's work on speech acts. Most established integration theory is based on a purposive concept of agency. European integration is the result of policy making, which is identified with intentional acts known or believed by agents to yield a particular outcome. However, what is missing from this perspective is the notion that certain intentional acts may release a whole series of unintended consequences (see Giddens 1993: 83). Social facts are partly a subset of such unintended consequences. Historical–institutionalists works (e.g. Pierson 2000) have pointed to the unintended consequences derived from formal institution building. However, we were interested in the opposite phenomenon: the emergence of institutions as social facts from micropurposive individual acts. In this book, we were not only concerned with the intended acts of the individuals active in the AMUE/CMUE although they needed to be told, we also paid attention to the unintended consequences of the network's activities, which contributed to the creation of the euro as an institution. Interpreting European integration and the creation of the single currency as a purposeful series of acts naturally leads to an assessment of success or failure of actors and their strategic interactions. This preoccupies (liberal) intergovernmentalism and functionalists alike. By broadening the analytical horizon to a network of individuals around two NGOs we have introduced a new dimension: the building of trust, consensus, and institutions as the unintended consequence of individual acts in daily life. When business people met to discuss the reduction of transaction costs by a single currency or the design of an efficient changeover strategy, they did not do this in order to create trust, although this was the result. The emerging policy consensus was the foundation on which formal institutions like the Maastricht treaty, the Lex monetae, etc. were based. We have analysed this particular process with respect to the business world but we also investigated its impact on the political and public spheres. This justified our focus on actors in the epistemic community of AMUE/CMUE as a paradigmatic case. We used the Lehrer and Wagner consensus model to describe the mechanism through which the transformation from intended individual acts to unintended (epistemologically objective) social structures via consensus takes place. In a given group or society each individual may have specific prior desires or rational preferences, but in the process of social communication a consensus emerges as the weighted average of individuals' assessments and their mutual respect for each other. This consensus produces frames of meaning whereby individuals organize their experiences of life and create the social reality of 'Europe'. Hence, European integration should not only be seen in terms of technical rationality (*Zweckrationalität* à la Weber) leading to formal institution building, it should also be considered in terms of communicative rationality (Habermas 1996), which leads to informal institution building, some of which may subsequently become codified and formal. Informal institutions such as norms and identities are not only relevant for preference information, but also for the sustainability of formal institutions.

This leads to our second criticism of traditional integration theory. It neglects normative aspects of mutual respect, trust, and consensus as a necessary foundation of European unification. The norms we are interested in are not superimposed onto people's behaviour as are obligations within a system of domination. They are the essence of rule-governed behaviour and, therefore, have a constitutive role for the creation of social facts and institutions. Without such norms, there are no reproduced practices. Therefore, there are no European institutions without European norms. For example, we have seen that the European continental consensus is centred on the norm of preserving lasting institutional equilibrium via mutual respect and trust, while in the UK distributive aspects of costs and benefits of integration seem to carry a greater weight in public deliberation. As a consequence, the British commitment to European institutions may not be the same as elsewhere. The object of modern integration theory should be the nature, creation and development of such underlying norms.

Finally, the emergence of norms as consensual functional agreements is the unintended consequence of individual behaviour that follows communicative rather than teleological rationality. This requires channels and media, which allow the production and exchange of information across borders in Europe. The Giscard–Schmidt Committee and the AMUE functioned as one such channel, but many others need to be researched. The creation of a single market and a single currency have contributed to daily practices that are consequently transforming the life-world background of Europeans. Our discussion of populism has shown that this transformation is not without danger for its own sustainability and European integration.

To summarize, we consider that research on European integration would benefit from broadening the horizon of the analysis of regional integration by governmental and supranational actors and the formal and intended consequences of their joint decision-making. It should include the unintended consequences of social interaction.[1] Our study has shown that the private sector has not only defended its interests and attempted to influence preference information in the formal constitutive and legislative process, it has also acted as a transnational consensus builder and is thus part of the foundation of Europe's civil society. Although our story may appear to be elite-centred, it is important to notice that the process of Europeanization would be impossible without networks of private actors. Representative and deliberative democracy work through structures of trust. We consider that the elites described in this book were influential because they deserved and received respect. The AMUE and CMUE were a particular manifestation of this phenomenon. Studying other organizations, like the Ecu Banking Association, UNICE, ETU, or even the European Parliament in this perspective may yield further and new insights.

Political implications

These theoretical considerations have implications for constitution building and policy making in Europe. If we understand policy making as choosing or maximizing collective preferences, then an essential question is how these preferences are formed. We have modelled preference formation as a stochastic process of consensus building. With European monetary union, the scope of issues subject to European collective preferences has significantly increased. This was correctly anticipated by neo-functionalist theories. Yet, it ignored that decision-making must draw on legitimacy as its fundamental resource. Without it, no social institution is sustainable. Decision-making in Europe does now require the democratic deficit between policy-scope and its legitimation be addressed. The cumulative effects of many integrative structural changes warrant a new qualitative step to formalize institutions of European governance. This has been acknowledged by the European Council in Laaken in December 2001, where Valéry Giscard d'Estaing was appointed President of the Convention on the Future of Europe, charged with elaborating a European constitution. It is important that it takes into account the lessons learned in recent years.

The hitherto dominant approach to European integration, with the intergovernmental mode of creating common practices and the technocratic regulation in Brussels, only uses output-legitimacy as its source. That is to say governments and administrations are supposed to deliver optimal results given their constraints, and people must gratefully accept them. This model seems to have worked for nearly half a century in European integration. European unification was accepted because it seemed to deliver peace, freedom, and prosperity. However, this acclamatory consent to policy making is pre-democratic. European citizens are reduced to the status of belonging to their 'people' as part of the social corps and not as autonomous individuals or active citizens. This is reflected in the EU's tendency to what Schlesinger and Kevin (2000: 206) call 'pronunciamentism', that is, top–down communication rather than dialogue. Citizens are allowed to assent (*'fiat, fiat, dignum et justum est!'*) or resist; Grotius and Pufendorf described this traditional relation between the sovereign and the people in the seventeenth century (Rosanvallon 1992). Modern democracies, by contrast, are dependent on input-legitimacy, that is, active citizens who do not only choose between alternatives of collective preferences, but also participate in preference formation by contributing to a debate among respected equals. This is why the Lehrer and Wagner (1981) consensus model requires more than only attributing weight to the opinion of authorities. It also needs the deliberative aspect, which we modelled by Baysian preference transformation. The political implication is that the EU needs better structures allowing active European citizens to participate in the management of common affairs. The substance of European citizenship and a European demos is then not the identification with a cultural background that remains relevant in the framework of the nation-state and the definition of nationality, but a commitment to the shared values of the Union, to the duties and rights of a civic society covering a discrete area of public life (Weiler 1997; Koslowski 1999).

Democratic input-legitimacy has two sources: the habits, conventions, and certainties of the pre-structured life-worlds and the rational insights that emerge from communicative action. Both dominate democracies in nation-states. Yet, providing input-legitimacy to European policy making requires transcending the 'honey-combs' of nation-states. Active European citizens must be able to deliberate reflexively on the optimal policy options regarding decisions, which affect potentially all of them. In today's multilevel governance, policy consensus is primarily achieved through mutual respect and connectedness within the nation-state. But the mechanisms of connectedness across borders are weak. Preferences derived from national backgrounds dominate policy debates at the national level, while different cultural contexts are reflected in disagreements at the European level. This way of operating disqualifies the essence of European integration, which is the creation of mutual respect and trust. What is needed are transborder structures for communicative action. Private sector organizations like the AMUE and CMUE fulfilled exactly this function. However, they were spontaneous, *ad hoc* institutions and disappeared when their task had been achieved. Other organizations like large companies, European social partners, or even the European Parliament may in the long run play a similar, but more stable role.

It is occasionally affirmed, particularly from a populist perspective, that a European democracy requires a European demos which does not exist. Hence, further integration would hit the barrier of legitimacy. This argument suffers from an insufficient distinction of the two sources of input legitimacy. With proper structures of pan-European communication, that is, with a commitment to mutual respect and formal mechanisms to thicken connectedness across borders, European consensus on policy issues is possible, as this book has shown. The integrative structures in Europe's civil society described here were primarily working on the level of European elites. They have nevertheless contributed to the emergence of a European democracy because they brought the public sphere into the even more exclusive sphere of intergovernmental negotiation. They had an integrative impact by strengthening mutual respect across borders and cultures. But it is doubtful that this function can be permanently assured by such relatively weak organizations as NGOs. A deeper analysis of the construction of a European public sphere would require a book on its own.[2]

It seems to us that in the future, only a fully fledged European government, accountable to all citizens, will provide a sustainable focusing point for the deliberations from which a European consensus may emerge. Some have argued that 'sub-units are better able to secure shared interests, particularly if shared geography, resources, culture or other features make for similar interests and policy choices among members of the sub-units' (Føllesdal 2000: 98–9). In our view, this vision of subsidiarity reinforces European *dis*integration because it strengthens consensus on national preferences, and therefore, European dissensus, rather than a pan-European consensus that unites people. The logic of our stochastic consensus model leads us to the conclusion that European citizens as individuals need a bigger say in decision-making than their governments.

Informal structures of cross-border and cross-cultural communication are necessary, but not sufficient for the institutional production and reproduction of input-legitimacy. They need formalization to prevent dissent turning into conflict. Majority voting contributes to social stability if consent on the procedure provides the foundation for the toleration of dissenting preferences. This is only possible if the decision-making institutions and processes are simple and rapid. Otherwise, the Lehrer and Wagner weight matrix takes a form that perpetuates dissent and potentially leads to conflict. Therefore, the unintended consequence of European integration is now the need for structures of European policy making that resemble effectively a European government. Europe's public goods, the European *res publica*, can no longer be left to national governments alone. The normative content of European integration is simple: Europe belongs to its citizens, not to its governments.

Annexe 1 Introduction

In this annexe we describe collective preference formation as a three-step process. Each step is considered separately under ceteris-paribus assumptions. In reality the time-sequence may approach simultaneity.

Individual preferences

We distinguish between desires and individual preferences. A preference is a positive evaluation of a desire. Desires are mental states whose intentionality is directed toward the objects of desires among which an individual has to choose. The intensity of desires is described by a utility function assigning a value between zero and one to each desirable option. We may describe this intensity as the personal or subjective probability that an individual will choose an object from a set of options (s),[1] given his or her background. The background may be culture, convention, habit, commmon knowledge,[2] cognitive frames, etc. Formally, if there are k options (s_k), the intensity of desire δ_j is the probability of option s_j being chosen by an individual, given background B:

$$\delta_j = p(s_j \mid B) \tag{A1.1}$$

We will also call this desire for j a 'naturalistic preference' because the background is assumed to be exogenously given 'by nature'. A primitive choice function would select options with the highest intensity of desire: max $(j)\delta_j$. However, rational decision-makers will not act on all desires. They will re-evaluate and actualize their desires in the light of alternative evidence, arguments, or generally – *any kind of* information. We will call the evaluated desires *rational preferences* (π_j). The evaluation can be modelled by Bayes' theorem.

$$\pi_j = p(s_j \mid B \text{ and } E) = p(E \mid s_j \text{ and } B)\frac{p(s_j \mid B)}{p(E \mid B)} = \frac{p(E \mid s_i \text{ and } B)}{p(E \mid B)}\,\delta_j \tag{A1.2}$$

The rational preference for state j by a given individual corresponds to the intensity of desire, modified by the likelihood $p(E \mid s_j$ and $B)$ or *reliability* of the argument E and normalized by the probability of the argument arising given the background. Hence, a rational *individual preference* reflects the posterior probability of option δ_j being chosen, given the argument or evidence E and the background B. We may interpret $p(E|B)$ as the value of an argument providing new information,[3] while $p(E|s_i \text{ and } B)$ reflects the probability assessment or weight that is attributed to the *reliability* of an argument given the background. Hence, the modification of naturalistic desires depends on the reliability of an argument and its innovation over the existing informational background in the process of evaluation.

The rational choice rule is: max $(j)\pi_j$.

Social preferences

The second step is to extend the conversation to other members of a group or society. First, we note that different individuals have different backgrounds and, therefore, also different desires and individual preferences. Hence, we re-write Equation (A1.2) with an index i for individual i:

$$\pi_{ij}=p(s_{ij}|B_i \text{ and } E)=p(E|s_{ij} \text{ and } B_i)\frac{p(s_{ij}|B_i)}{p(E|B_i)}=\frac{p(E|s_{ij} \text{ and } B_i)}{p(E|B_i)}\delta_{ij} \tag{A1.3}$$

Individuals notice the differences in their preferences that are due to their individual backgrounds and their evaluations of arguments and evidence. As social beings, they will communicate in many ways about their preferences and their evaluations of evidence. This communication leads to part of the individual backgrounds becoming common knowledge, and this will reduce the variance of individual preferences.[4] Furthermore in the process of communication and reflexive deliberation they will reconsider their own assessment in light of other individual's opinions and preferences.[5] This fact will lead to *preference change*. We will assume that the adjustment process consists in modifying one's previous preference by a fraction of the difference in two individual's preference intensities.[6] However, they will not attach the same weight to all other individual's opinion. There will be some individuals that they trust more or respect more than others. As a consequence, they will change their own preferences to a larger or smaller degree. As we will see, the speed of preference change depends on the weight of respect that individuals attribute to each other. In order to keep the mathematics simple, we will first demonstrate the two-person case. Hence, individual one $(i=1)$ adjusts his preference for option $(j=1)$ as follows:

$$\pi^1_{11}=\pi^0_{11}-\alpha(\pi^0_{11}-\pi^0_{21}) \tag{A1.4a}$$

and person two does something similar:

$$\pi^1_{21}=\pi^0_{21}-\beta(\pi^0_{21}-\pi^0_{11}) \tag{A1.4b}$$

Thus, person 1 adjusts his previous individual preference by a fraction α of their difference in opinion and person 2 by the fraction β. We assume α and β to fall into the interval $0 \leq \alpha, \beta \leq 1$. If the adjustment coefficient is zero, the person does not change his opinion; if it is 1, he totally aligns his views on the other person's previous preference. Equations (A1.4a) and (A1.4b) are identical with:

$$\pi_{11}^{1} = (1-\alpha)\pi_{11}^{0} + \alpha\pi_{21}^{0} \tag{A1.5a}$$

$$\pi_{21}^{1} = (\beta)\pi_{11}^{0} + (1-\beta)\pi_{21}^{0} \tag{A1.5b}$$

In this form, the adjustment coefficients in the process of deliberation can simply be interpreted as the relative weights that members of a group attribute to each other's opinions and preferences. This statement is easily generalized to a group of n members forming an $n \times n$ weight matrix **W**. Social preference assignments for option s_j are represented by the product of the weight matrix **W** with the vector of n member's previous individual preferences:

$$\pi^{1} = W \times \pi^{0} \tag{A1.6}$$

Thus, the social preference vector $\boldsymbol{\pi}^1$ reflects both the variety of individual preferences based on background and evaluative capacities, but also a judgement about each other's backgrounds and capacities.[7] As long as different individuals take each other's opinion into account, they attribute a positive weight to each other including themselves, and this means they respect each other. We therefore call the condition $0 < \alpha, \beta < 1$ *mutual respect*. Mutual respect is a necessary, but not sufficient condition for social preferences to converge to a unique equilibrium, which we call consensus.

Collective preferences

Equation (A1.6) describes a dynamic system of preference adjustment. For, as soon as one individual's preference has been changed, all those who respect her will also adjust their preferences because they trust her evaluation of new evidence. This is the nature of deliberation. It does not matter whether the initial change originates in new evidence ($p(E|s_j$ and $B)$), or in a change in reputation.[8] Either way, all social preferences will be affected. But how? deGroot's algorithm[9] shows that if the weight matrix **W** is a stochastic matrix (a square matrix whose columns are probability vectors adding to 1)[10] in a system of first-order difference equations, this system converges under certain conditions to a unique equilibrium vector. In equilibrium the process of preference adjustment is complete, because there is no new information forthcoming, which would make people reconsider their preferences. The convergence conditions are, in the terminology of Lehrer and Wagner: (a) mutual respect; and (b) connectedness. The latter implies a 'chain of respect' such that each individual can be shown to be connected by positive respect to at least one other (and himself). Formally this implies that the weight matrix **W** can be represented by a Markov matrix. The unique equilibrium vector indicates the consensual weights within the group; it summarizes available information about each individual's expertise and reliability within that group or society.[11] Thus, different people may receive different consensual weights, but every individual will use these same consensual weights in his evaluation of himself and others.[12] This vector is a numerical summary of background knowledge.[13] However, in this formulation, background does not only reflect naturalistic conditionings but also an evaluation of evaluative capacities.

Deviation from the equilibrium weights is a sign of disagreement or *dissensus*, indicating that the exchange of information has not yet been optimized. Hence dissensus is the result of incomplete deliberation. This is a consistency argument, for if a person refuses to aggregate the knowledge about other individuals beliefs and preferences into his own preference assignment, although assigning a positive weight to other members in the group, he is acting as if he were assigning a weight of one to himself and a weight of zero to every other member of the group.[14] However, in this case the chain of mutual respect is broken and *conflict* prevents consensus. Hence, the rationale of mutual respect in a connected context logically leads to a dynamic process of preference adjustment that tends to consensus as a unique equilibrium. Only if the condition of mutual respect is not fulfilled, as in the case of moralist righteousness, religious, or ideological fanaticism, political tyranny, would disagreement have other causes than insufficient exchange of information and incomplete deliberation.

The algorithm leading to consensus is as follows. If we extend Equation (A1.6) to the k options under consideration, we can describe the social preference matrix as Π with the dimension $n \times k$:

$$\Pi^1 = \mathbf{W}\,\Pi^0 \tag{A1.7}$$

where $\boldsymbol{\Pi}^0$ is the matrix of all π_{jk} elements. We assume for simplicity and without loss of generality that $\mathbf{W}$ is constant. The adjustment dynamics require that

$$\Pi^t = \mathbf{W}\,\Pi^{t-1} \tag{A1.8}$$

Given our assumption of non-negative entries and unit row sum, Equation A1.8 describes a stochastic process known as finite homogenous Markov chain. As is well known, with $t \rightarrow \infty$, the process tends to converge[15] to a unique weight matrix $W^t = \overline{W}$ *with identical rows*, which lead to the consensual preference assignments:

$$\Pi^* = \overline{W}\,\Pi^0 \tag{A1.9}$$

The matrix Π^* has n rows for each individual and k columns for the number of available options. The unique feature of this equilibrium matrix is that each row contains identical values for the probability assessment of accepting a given option. Hence, in consensus, there is apparently unanimity about collective preferences – and choices. One may object that 'the fact that all members of a community come to *accept* a certain social situation does not necessarily mean that it is unanimously *preferred* to other social alternatives'.[16] However, this dichotomy is implied by our modeling of collective preferences as being derived from naturalistic desires, but subsequently re-evaluated by evidence and mutual respect for others. The point is that consensus does not require unanimity in desires, beliefs and feelings, but a unanimous commitment to evaluate all available information in society (including institutions, ethical norms, etc) in the context of mutual respect and trust. The interesting result of this theory is that social *consensus* can be modelled as the equilibrium value of a stochastic process. *Dissensus* reflects the variance in preferences from equilibrium at any given moment of time.[17] *Conflict* implies absence of equilibrium, that is, a disjunctive sets of preferences.

The speed of convergence of each individual's opinion to consensus (i.e. the number of iterations necessary to reach an infinitesimal deviation) depends on the characteristic equation of the weight matrix – that is, an *n*th-degree polynomial equation. Convergence requires that every root of the characteristic equation is less than 1 in absolute value. The closer it is to zero in absolute value, the faster is the speed by which consensus is obtained. In general this means that fast convergence and *little dissensus requires reciprocal weights of respect.* In the specific case of the two-person system in Equations (A1.4) and (A1.5), characteristic roots are given by

$$r_1 = 1, \quad r_2 = 1-(\alpha+\beta)$$

so that the solution is:

$$\pi^t_{11} = C_{11} + C_{21}(1-\alpha-\beta)^t \qquad \text{(A1.10a)}$$

$$\pi^t_{21} = C_{11} - C_{21}(1-\alpha-\beta)^t \qquad \text{(A1.10b)}$$

where C_{11} and C_{21} are constants.

As $t \rightarrow \infty$, the system converges to the consensual preferences $C_{i1} = C_{11}$, which are in this special case $C_{11} = (\pi^0_{11} + \pi^0_{21})/2$. $C_{21} = (\pi^0_{11} + \pi^0_{21})/2$ reflects initial disagreement, which is partly a function of new evidence (see Equation (A1.3)). The measure of dissensus in a group or society is the variance of their preferences. In our special case of $j=1$ options and $n=2$ members of the group:

$$\text{Var}\ (\pi_j) = \frac{1}{n}\sum_{i=1}^{n}(\pi_{i1} - C_{11})^2 = C_{21}(1-\alpha-\beta)^{2t} \qquad \text{(A1.11)}$$

With the number of deliberative steps increasing $t \rightarrow \infty$, initial dissensus will disappear. If both individuals respect each other equally, that is, if the expression $(1-\alpha-\beta)$ is close to zero, convergence is fast; if they have no or little respect for each other, that is, the bracket is close to one, convergence is slow and dissensus is high. Yet, as long as the general conditions of mutual respect and connectedness are fulfilled, communicative action and the process of deliberation will tend to create consensus.

The occurrence of new evidence can be interpreted as a stochastic shock, which will increase dissensus, but will also 'disappear' in the background, as it becomes part of the common knowledge in the process of deliberation. Hence, the systematic production of new evidence in favour of one argument will shift the consensual preferences in the direction of this evidence, although it also increases noise. Contrary to conflict, a high degree of (tolerated) dissent is therefore a sign of intellectual creativity, while a highly consensual society converges toward conformism. The 'noise' created by new evidence manifests in dissensus, and may overshadow consensual collective preferences. Although the nature of deliberation is such, that ultimately consensus will be reached, it may appear that a consensual equilibrium is far from being achieved if the noise is high.

Because collective choice requires taking a decision at some stage, procedures are necessary to shorten the process before unanimity is attained. With full consensus on collective preferences, the choice rule $\max(j)\pi_j$ is a formality. With stochastic noise, the visibility of collective preferences is blurred and consequently choice makers (governments) may pick from a range of options. This fact allows for leadership to affirm itself, especially when powerful leaders benefit from high values in the weight matrix **W** as this may help to swing consensus in the direction of their own preference.[18] *Voting* is the standard procedure to terminate the deliberative process *before* full convergence to equilibrium is achieved: when the *mean* of the preference distribution is unobservable due to stochastic noise, the *median* may be second best. By contrast, *constitutional rights* are a mechanism to deal with conflict, when there is no mutual respect for certain issues but an agreement on procedures rather than substance is possible.

The function of epistemic communities can be analysed in terms of the described consensus model as follows:

1 As a provider of evidence, epistemic communities affect the evaluation $p(E|s_j$ and $B)$ of naturalistic desires.
2 As a community with a high degree of internal respect, an epistemic community accelerates consensus within the group (thick weight matrix within the epistemic community).
3 Because individual representatives of the epistemic community command high respect in their larger societies, they reduce dissensus between societies (thicker matrix between countries).

Annexe 2 The crises and the Phoenix

Table A2.1 Opinion on the replacement of national currencies by the Ecu in October 1990

Question: Discussions are underway to replace the twelve currencies of the European Community with a single currency, the Ecu, in five or six years' time. This means that your everyday purchases, among others, will be made with Ecu notes and coins and no longer with national money. Would you be strongly in favour of, in favour of, indifferent to, against, strongly against this replacement?

Response: Percentage of persons who answered.

	Twelve EC countries	*Belgium*	*Denmark*	*Germany*	*Greece*	*Spain*	*France*	*Ireland*	*Italy*	*Luxembourg*	*Netherlands*	*Portugal*	*UK*
In favour	61	76	31	51	80	75	73	74	66	79	56	76	37
Against	39	24	69	49	20	25	27	26	34	21	44	24	63
Total	100	100	100	100	100	100	100	100	100	100	100	100	100

Details of the responses for the whole community:

Strongly in favour	22	
In favour	24	46/61
Indifferent	19	
Against	14	
Strongly against	15	29/39
No answer	6	
Total	100	75/100

Table A2.2 The importance of the consequences in replacing national currencies with the Ecu (Percentage of persons who answered 'really important'; the other choice was 'not really important'.)

	Twelve EC countries	*Belgium*	*Denmark*	*Germany*	*Greece*	*Spain*	*France*	*Ireland*	*Italy*	*Luxembourg*	*Netherlands*	*Portugal*	*UK*
There will be a strong, stable currency for all countries	85	93	70	80	85	88	88	93	88	94	87	77	80
The community will be stronger and better united	84	95	72	79	87	86	93	94	87	92	85	79	68
The European market will function better	83	88	69	81	85	90	87	90	85	91	81	79	69
It will be possible to compare prices instantaneously	81	87	66	83	78	81	86	82	87	91	72	76	78
Exchange fees and commissions will be cheaper	77	84	55	72	75	83	81	84	80	86	73	32	72
Journeys will be easier within the EEC	76	80	53	72	80	86	74	83	78	80	72	86	69
This changeover to a single currency will be expensive for companies	69	75	70	60	68	75	76	67	72	77	73	66	68
It is an experiment with risks	67	66	69	62	66	70	70	64	79	77	69	68	69
It will be necessary to do a mental calculation for the conversion	52	45	48	43	57	52	53	56	55	49	44	50	61
This will cause the loss of a part of national sovereignty	51	49	66	43	56	54	56	41	50	74	56	51	59

Annexe 3 Campaigning for EMU

A two-sector model of profit margins

We assume an economy with two sectors, one operating with new technologies and/or economies of scale (the modern sector) and the other with traditional technology. As a consequence labour productivity increases faster in the modern than in the traditional sector.

Each sector sets prices by adding a mark-up (c) over unit labour costs, that is, the ratio of nominal wages (w) to productivity (λ). The two price equations in log form are:

$$p_m = w_m - \lambda_m + c_m \qquad \text{(A3.1)}$$

$$p_t = w_t - \lambda_t + c_t \qquad \text{(A3.1)}$$

The rate of inflation is the weighted average of the first difference of the two sector prices

$$\pi = \alpha \Delta p_m + (1-\alpha)\Delta p_t \qquad \text{(A3.3)}$$

We also assume:

$$\pi = 0 \quad \text{(price stability)} \qquad \text{(A3.4)}$$

$$\Delta w_m = \Delta w_t \quad \text{(efficient labour market)} \qquad \text{(A3.5)}$$

$$\Delta \lambda_m > \Delta \lambda_t \quad \text{(definition of modern sector)} \qquad \text{(A3.6)}$$

Furthermore, to simplify matters we assume that the modern sector keeps its mark-up constant:

$$\Delta c_m = 0 \qquad \text{(A3.7)}$$

After inserting Equations (A3.3)–(A3.7) into Equations (A3.1) and (A3.2), we obtain:

$$\Delta c_t = \frac{1}{\alpha}\Delta p_t - (\Delta \lambda_m - \Delta \lambda_t) \qquad \text{(A2.8)}$$

This means that the mark-up in the traditional sector depends on its price setting power and the productivity differential between the two sectors.

If the mark-up in the traditional sector is to remain constant, it has to increase its prices in proportion to the productivity growth differential between the two sectors:

$$\Delta c_t = 0 \Rightarrow \Delta p_t = \alpha(\Delta\lambda_m - \Delta\lambda_t) > 0 \tag{A3.9}$$

On the other hand, if the traditional sector finds it difficult to raise prices, its mark-up will fall at the rate at which productivity increases faster in the modern sectors

$$\text{if } \Delta p_t = 0 \Rightarrow \Delta c_t = -(\Delta\lambda_m - \Delta\lambda_t) \tag{A3.10}$$

Hence, technological progress in the modern sector squeezes the profit margins in the traditional sector and explains the demand for more accommodating monetary policies.

Annexe 4 List of interviewees

Interviews

Francesco Alfonso	Rome
Joachim Bitterlich	Madrid
Marco Buti	Brussels
Hervé Carré	Brussels
Declan Costello	Brussels
Alvaro Cuervo	Madrid
Etienne Davignon	Brussels
Belmiro de Azevedo	Porto
Jacques de Larosière	Paris
Bertrand de Maigret	Paris
Yves Thibaut de Silguy	Paris
Dudley Eustace	London
Elisabeth Guigou	Paris
Valery Giscard d'Estaing	Paris
Daniel Gros	Brussels
Ulrike Guérot	Berlin
Heather Honour	London
Christopher Johnson	London
Karl Lamers	Berlin
Malcom Levitt	London
Gilbert Lichter	Paris
Nader Maleki	Frankfurt
Paul Mentré	Paris
Friedrich Merz	Berlin
Philippe Moutôt	Frankfurt
Birgit Nielsen	Copenhagen
François-Xavier Ortoli	Paris
Tommaso Padoa-Schioppa	Frankfurt
François Périgot	Paris
Karl Otto Pöhl	Frankfurt
Jean-François Pons	Brussels

Christa Randzio-Plath	Hamburg
Klaus Regling	Brussels
Michael Röskau	Paris
Helmut Schmidt	Hamburg
Niels Thygesen	Copenhagen
Cornelis van der Klugt	Eindhoven
Umberto Vattani	Rome
Thierry Vissol	Brussels
Theo Waigel	Munich
Norbert Wieczorek	Berlin

Informal discussions

Jaques Delors	Paris
Günter Grosche	Brussels

Annexe 5 List of expert groups

Study for the European Parliament on EMS reform

The academic working group

Prof. Michael Artis	Manchester University
Prof. Philippe Bacchetta	Universitat Autonoma de Barcelona
Prof. Christian de Boissieu	Paris I
Dr Harvey Chen	LSE
Ms Teodora Cardoso	Consultant/Banco Portugues de Investimento
Prof. Rüdiger Dornbusch	MIT
Prof. Barry Eichengreen	University of California, Berkeley
Dr Heiner Flassbeck	DIW
Prof. Wolfgang Gebauer	J W Goethe Universität
Mr Matthias Müller	J W Goethe Universität
Mr Klaus J. W. Schmidt	J W Goethe Universität
Mr Michael Thiel	J W Goethe Universität
Mr Andreas Worms	J W Goethe Universität
Mr Alberto Giovannini	Columbia University
Prof. Charles Goodhart	LSE
Prof. Paul de Grauwe	Katholieke Universiteit Leuven
Dott. Stefano Micossi	Confindustria
Prof. Niels Thygesen	Copenhagen University
Prof. Brendan Walsh	University College Dublin
Prof. Charles Wyplosz	INSEAD

The market working group

Mr George Arebalo	Chargé de Mission/Caisse Centrale de Coopération Economique
Mr Massimo Baldi	Economist/San Paolo Bank
Mr Graham Bishop	VP/Salomon Brothers
Mr Olivier de Boysson	Economist/Banque Paribas

Mr Bernard Bricheux	Directeur Adjoint/Matif
Mr Trevor Brown	Partner/Clifford Chance
Mr Jean Carrel-Billiard	Sous-Directeur/Crédit Lyonnais
Mr Michael Clayton	Finance Director/Smirfit
Lord Cobbold	MD/Gaiacorp
Mr Jaime Correa	Finance Director/Companiha Portuguesa Radio Marconi
Mr Alan Davies	Chief Economist/Barclays Bank plc
Mr Michel Demont	Partner/KPMG Peat Marwick
Mr Christian Franck	VP/Commerzbank
Mr Jonathan Hoffman	Director Economics/CSFB
Mr John Iliopoulos	VP/J Boutari & Son
Mr Laurent Jonckheere	Treasurer/Solvay
Mr Taoufik Kharroubi	Chargé d' Etudes/Matif
Mr Soeren Kristiansen	Chief Analyst/Burmeister & Wain Finans A/S
Ms Gisela Kurtz	Senior VP/Deutsche Bank Research
Mr Roger Lomax	Finance Advisor/BAT Industries
Mr Ruis Martin dos Santos	Banco Portugues de Investimento
Dr Carlo de Meyer	Senior Economist Treasury/ABN Amro Bank
Mr Eric Müller	Chief Economist/CCF
Ms Ana Munera	Economist/Banco Centrale Americano Hispano
Mr Torsten Ottens	Trading Manager/Europa Bank
Mr Giulio Pampuro	Financial Planning/Pirelli
Mr Richard Parlour	Partner/Clifford Chance
Mr Peter Praet	Générale de Banque
Ms Vicky Pryce	Partner and Chief Economist/KPMG Peat Marwick
Mr Derek Scott	Director/Barclays de Zoete Wedd
Ms Florence Sirel	Economist/CUME
Mr Andrew Shilston	Group Treasurer/Enterprise Oil plc
Mr Krishna Tampoe	Partner/MTI European Software Technologies
Mr Richard Urwin	Divisional Director/S G Warburg
Mr Gawain Wilson	Economist/CCF

Wise men advisory group

Mr Etienne Davignon	Chairman/Société Générale de Belgique Former VP/EC Commission President/AMUE
Mr François-Xavier Ortoli	VP/AMUE Former President/EC Commission Former Minister of France Honorary Chairman of Total

Mr Alain Prate	VP/European Investment Bank Former Dep Governor/Banque de France
Mr Amb R Ruggiero	Board Member/Fiat Former Minister of Foreign Trade Former Italian Negotiator for EMS
Mr Helmut Schmidt	Former Chancellor of Germany

Daphne Josslin assured the administration of the research group.

The Sustainability Report working group

In 1997 the Association for the Monetary Union of Europe (AMUE) set up a working group on 'Sustainability of the euro and the Convergence Criteria'. The following experts participated in the work:

Mr Peter Bofinger	University of Würzburg, Würzburg
Mr Willem Buiter	University of Cambridge, Cambridge
Mr Stefan Collignon	AMUE, Paris
Mr Christian de Boissieu	Chambre de Commerce et d'Industrie de Paris
Mr Hans-Peter Fröhlich	Institut der Deutschen Wirtschaft, Köln
Mr Andrew Hughes Hallett	University of Strathclyde, Glasgow
Mr Pier Carlo Padoan	CER-Roma, Rome
Mr Jean Pisani-Ferry	CEPII, Paris
Mr Nils Thygesen	University of Copenhagen, Copenhagen
Mr Angel Torres	Ministerio de Industria, Madrid
Mr Martin Weale	NIESR, London

The meetings were also attended by members of the AMUE and guests:

Ms Teodora Cardoso	Banco Portugues de Investimento
Mr Hervé Carré	DG II – Monetary Affairs, European Commission
Ms Antonia Colomba	Confindustria
Mr Antonio Cortes	Banco Central Hispanoamericano
Mr Jens Dallmeyer	Deutsche Bank Research
Mr Bertrand de Maigret	AMUE
Mr Mikhail Ekdahl	Skanska AB
Mr Fernando Fernandez	Banco Central Hispanoamericano
Mr Jorge Hay	Banco Central Hispanoamericano
Ms Daniela Israelachwili	UNICE
Mr Per Jedefors	Skandinaviska Enskilda Banken
Mr Christopher Johnson	AMUE UK
Mr John Kirschen	Fiat Sp. A.
Mr Jussi Mustonen	Confederation of Finnish Industry and Employers

Mr Alvaro Nascimento	Universidade Catolica Portuguesa
Mr David Naudé	JP Morgan
Mr José Neves de Almeida	Sonae Investimentos
Mr Nigel Newman	Barclays Bank
Mr Giovanni Palladino	Confindustria
Mr Thierry Walrafen	Caisse des Dépôts et Consignations

Susanne Mundschenk assured the administration of the research group.

Three working meetings were held, in Paris (8 April 1997), Madrid (10 June 1997), and Rome (10 October 1997).

Annexe 6 List of former AMUE board members

Mr Giovanni Agnelli	Chairman/Fiat
Mr José Maria Amusategui de la Cierva	Chairman/Banco Central Hispanoamericano
Dr Karl-Hermann Baumann	Chairman Supervisory Board/Siemens
Rt Hon. Kenneth Clarke	Dep Chairman/BAT
Mr Antonio D'Amato	President/Confindustria
Mr Etienne Davignon	President/Société Générale de Belgique
M Belmiro de Azevedo	Chairman/Sonae SGPS
Mr Georg Ehrnrooth	Chairman/Wärtsilä
Mr Dudley Eustace	Exec. VP and CFO/Philips
Mr Georges Faber†	Chairman/Arbed
Mr Carlos Ferrer†	President/Unice
Dott. Giorgio Fossa	Chairman/Confindustria
M Jean-René Fourtou	VP/Aventis
Mr Paolo Fresco	Chairman/Fiat
Mr Brian P. Garraway†	Dep Chairman/BAT
Dr Carl H. Hahn	Chairman/Volkswagen
Dr Tom Hardiman	Chairman/IBM Intl Treasury Services
Mr Jan Hommen	Exec. VP and CFO/Philips Electronics
Mr Georges Jacobs	President/Unice
Mr Joseph Kinsch	Chairman/Arbed
Mr Hilmar Kopper	Chairman/Deutsche Bank
Mr Max Kothbauer	Dep Chairman/Creditanstalt-Bankverein
Mr Philippe Lagayette	J P Morgan SA
Prof. Alexandre Lamfalussy	Former President/European Monetary Institute
Dr Spiro Latsis	Chairman/EFG Bank European Financial Group
Mr André Leysen	Chairman/AGFA-GEVAERT
Mr Luigi Lucchini	Chairman/Confindustria
Mr Bertrand de Maigret	Secretary General/AMUE
Mr Carlos March	Chairman/March Group

Mr Patrick McEvoy	Committee Chairman/Confederation of Irish Industry
Mr Paul Mentré	Executive Secretary/CMUE
Mr H.L. Merckle†	Managing Partner/Robert Bosch Gmbh
Ms Birgitte Nielsen	CFO/FLS Industries
Mr François-Xavier Ortoli	Chairman/Total-CFP
Mr Theodore Papalexopoulos	Vice Chairman/Titan Cement Co
Mr Gonzalo Pascual	President/Spanair
Mr François Périgot	President/Unice
Mr Sergio Pininfarina	President/Confindustria
Mr Uwe Plachetka	Executive Secretary/CMUE
Mr Birger Riisager	President and CEO/FLS Industries
Mr Cesare Romiti	Chairman/RCS Editori
Mr Karl-Erik Sahlberg	President and CEO/Skandinaviska Enkilda Banken
Mr Melker Schörling	Chairman/Skanska
Sir Patrick Sheehy	Chairman/BAT
Mr Feijo Sickinghe	Chairman/VMF Stork
Mr Jacques Solvay	President/Solvay & Cie
Mr Poul Svanholm	President/Carlsberg
Dr Björn Svedberg	President and CEO/Skandinaviska Enkilda Banken
Mr Martin Taylor	Group Chief Executive/Barclays Bank
Mr Emmanuel Tesch	President/Arbed
Mr Cornelis van der Klugt	Chairman/Philips
Mr Alexandre Vaz Pinto	Vice Chairman/Caixa Geral de Depositos
Dr Franz Vranitzky	Former Chancellor of Austria/Westdeutsche Landesbank
Mr Jacob Wallenberg	Chairman/Skandinaviska Enkilda Banken

Notes

1 Introduction

1 Dyson and Featherstone (1999) is the standard reference for a detailed historical analysis of the way to EMU.
2 An exception is Frieden (1991). Verdun (2000) very briefly touches upon the interest of the employer organizations and trade unions in Britain, France, and Germany. She does not, however, indicate or show whether and how these organizations engaged for or against EMU.
3 See, for example, Frieden (1991: 441), which is the most important reference; Dyson and Featherstone (1999: 243, 246, 336, 628, 640, 693–4, 711, 734, 737); Moravcsik (1999: 393, 434, 440); Balanyá *et al.* (1999: 79f); Verdun (2000: 167–71); McNamara (1998: 39) confounds the business and the elder statesmen's group. In general, few of the many studies on EMU put the private sector in the centre of analysis.
4 The AMUE archives can today be consulted at the Centre Historique des Archives Nationales (CHAN), 60, rue des Francs-Bourgeois, F-75141 Paris cedex 03, France.
5 For example, political leaders may search 'support' of interest groups, if this makes their reelection more likely. On the EU scale, however, no empirical evidence has been presented that interest groups offer public support with electoral relevancy or the votes of their own members in exchange for positions defended by governments in EU Treaty negotiations. Second, decision makers may, explicitly or implicitly react to discomfort with the nature of EU integration, which has taken protest to the streets; since 2000, EU summits have been accompanied by NGO-led demonstrations. It is likely that these social movements have prepared the grounds for an easier acceptance of social issues as part of the integration agenda.
6 The private sector is a whirlpool of ideas and actions, intentions and obstacles, successes and failures and is constantly interacting with the political sphere. It is structured by institutions, rules, and conventions, but its fundamental nature is complex. The appropriate description of the role and influence of the private sector embedded in a polity and society would be an *n*-dimensional vectorial space. As such a model cannot be delivered by political science, the number of actors has to be reduced. Modelling influence and interaction necessarily implies severe simplification.
7 We thank Kevin Featherstone for pointing this idea out to us.
8 See note 66.
9 Below, we develop our model of preference formation in more detail.
10 In this respect, we agree with Greve and Jørgensen (2002: 54–75) that the Maastricht Treaty must be seen as an 'instant of emergent European constitutional politics which is embedded into wider societal processes'.
11 Our analysis relies on expert interviews, on the AMUE and CMUE archives, on an evaluation of official policy documents in which we trace the input of both groups, and our own insider knowledge.

12 On lobbying in Europe see Mazey and Richardson (1993). A review of the literature on how interest groups affect outcomes in elections and in legislatures through contributions, lobbying and other informational activities is given by Austen-Smith (1997). Balme *et al.* (2002) investigate the Europeanization of collective action.

13 Concern for business interests and support from the private sector has become important for the reputation of governments, particularly before national elections, and in times of high unemployment. Economic performance also receives more public attention, as the media have developed economic reporting and increasingly more people feel directly concerned as shareholders.

14 Drazen also noted: 'legislative lobbying has so far played little role in political economy in macroeconomics because it is much more common to lobby for trade or other microeconomic legislation than for macroeconomic policy', Drazen (2000: 96).

15 The effect of creating constitutional-orientated institutions are less visible than the effects of legislation, not only because of the greater complexity, but also because of time lags and higher probability of unintended consequences.

16 This distinction has also been used by Bartolini (2002: 4ff), who differentiates among *functional issues*; that is, 'political issues which are congruent with national issues but discussed at the EU level', and *constitutive issues* which 'pertain to the process of European integration per se'. For a definition of regulative rules see also Searle (1995: 27; 1998: 123).

17 For an overview of what 'goods' interest groups can offer to political decision-makers and the administration in their lobbying activities is given by Buholzer (1998: 97).

18 Fossum (2000) has raised the issue of societal acceptance of European institutions. He discusses the constitution-making aspects of treaty revisions and the non-governmental sector ('individual members of a community') from the perspective of 'legitimation through values'. Although this allows to assign a role to the process of deliberation ('the republican view of democracy'), he does not show the empirical manifestations of the process. As a consequence, 'values' remain exogenous. In our approach values emerge endogenously as consensus resulting from deliberation.

19 AMUE members who were familiar with the work in other European associations often pointed this out; see, for example, the comment by François Périgot (Chapter 3).

20 A similar confusion appears in Goldstein (1993), who notices a 'dual role' for ideas in the explanation of protectionism. When ideas and beliefs affect policies 'by influencing decision manners', they are usually reflecting preferences for regulative rules. On the other hand, when they are 'encased or embedded in institutions' they reflect constitutive rules.

21 Throughout the book, empirical evidence is provided for this view. Chapter 1 outlines the strategic vision in more detail.

22 By contrast, in the United Kingdom – and contrary to Denmark – the redistributive aspect of exchange rate variations became more dominant after the exchange-rate mechanism (ERM) crisis in 1992.

23 For an overview see Rittberger *et al.* (1999).

24 These were, for example, representatives of other companies and banks, EU Commission officials, national politicians, researchers, and representatives of interest groups.

25 See, for example, volume 46 of *International Organisation*, Issue 1, 1992, which is dedicated to epistemic communities. See also Verdun (1998) who finds that the Delors Committee fulfils the criteria, or Kapstein (1992), who argues that Central Bankers' co-operation as such does not.

26 This point was especially raised in discussions with Dieter Wolf.

27 This argument is developed later where we discuss and criticize the naturalistic concept of preferences in the main-stream integration theories.

28 Around these reports, many further communicative activities were developed, often involving multipliers. These were, for example, seminars and conferences gathered

as diverse groups, for example, corporate euro-project leaders or teachers in political education or experts in national euro-preparation committees. The reports' ideas were also published – often in a simpler and shorter form via newsletters and newspapers.

29 Each strand of literature has brought about many theoretical works and has inspired probably even more empirical works. Here, we only list a very small selection of leading authors in each domain. Governance studies: Wallace and Wallace (2002). Integration theory: Moravcsik (1999), Haas (1958). Constructivism: Checkel (1999), Risse (2000).

30 Of course, there are also multiple descriptive–historical analyses. With respect to EMU, *The Road to Maastricht*, by Dyson and Featherstone (1999) is probably the most valuable and most complete to date. Their book is one of the main references for our work as far as historical events up to the Maastricht Treaty are concerned. It constitutes the context for our more narrowly defined analysis of the private sector, as we are not attempting to re-write the history of EMU. It describes the two main dimensions of EMU negotiation, which are cognitive and strategic (1999: 13). Our claim is that the AMUE as an epistemic community had a significant role in structuring the cognitive dimension of EMU. As Adler and Haas (1992: 371) put it: 'If we define the role played by epistemic communities as one of policy co-ordination, then, the task is to show not only the structural characteristics of the co-ordination game but also the process by which agents and their expectations are created and by which the alternatives and outcomes of games are defined'.

31 For an explanation of EMU, see pp. 379–471.

32 Moravcsik's concept of liberal intergovernmentalism explicitly departs from the realist assumption that national interests are determined by the structure of the international system.

33 'Business incentives were translated directly into political demands. Public pressure for EMU came from business and unions ...' Moravcsik (1998: 393).

34 As Scharpf (1999) pointed out, this simplification treats state actors as proxies for the underlying social forces.

35 'Preferences for such policies emerged from a process of domestic political conflict in which specific sectoral interests, adjustment costs and, sometimes, geopolitical concerns played an important role. Consistent with modern theories of foreign economic policy, I argue that the specific conditions under which governments were willing to liberalize trade reflected their international economic competitiveness; the conditions under which they accepted monetary integration reflected prevailing macroeconomic policies and preferences', Moravcsik (1998: 3).

36 A typical example for this kind of spillover is the argument of the 'inconsistent quartet' leading to the conclusion that the single market required a single currency.

37 This is clear when neo-functionalists postulate that private action is most likely to contribute to integration when it remains de-politicized.

38 For an overview of the literature on bureaucracy, technocracy, and the politics of expertise as well as profound case study of technocracy in the EU policy-making process, see Radaelli (1999).

39 Freeman (1990: 134) defines a social contract as 'a uniform public rule applying equally to all persons'.

40 This view is usually attributed to Thomas Hobbes.

41 Following Max Weber, Habermas has called this *Zweckrationalität*, which he distinguishes from *communicative rationality* that he explains in terms of the conditions for a communicatively achieved, reasonable consensus. See Habermas (1987: 86; 1996).

42 A naturalistic epistemology assumes that beliefs have a causal connection with corresponding states of affairs. Hence, beliefs and knowledge are a direct function (one-to-one relation) of external facts. The logical status of a belief does not fix its justification status. Hence, naturalistic theories eliminate normative aspects of beliefs and preferences.

In Annexe 1, we show how new evidence, arguments, and normative considerations can modify naturalistic desires in a Bayesian context.

43 Freeman distinguishes between an 'agent-centred' conception of reasoning, which corresponds to the view outlined above, and a 'right-based' contract view.

44 In fact, Macpherson (1962) shows that Hobbes himself did not have the isolationist view that is usually attributed to Hobbsianism.

45 In Annexe 1, we show how this can be extended to *n*-dimensionality of preference formation.

46 See note 68.

47 See, for example, Risse-Kappen (1996), Marcussen (2000). As the constructivist turn in international relations and in the study of integration has not yet brought about a comprehensive theory, it makes sense to investigate how their argument can be hooked into existing integration theories. Checkel (1999) discusses the implications of the social constructivist understanding of institutions as constitutive for the analysis of European integration.

48 We may consider Keynes as an early precursor of this approach. In the *General Theory*, he wrote 'the ideas of economists and political philosophers, both when they are right and when they are wrong, are more powerful than is commonly understood', Keynes (1936: 383).

49 Habermas (1984) is, of course, the outstanding counter-programme.

50 An exception is the work on European public opinion, which may be interpreted as revealed preferences. See Niedermayer and Sinnot (1995).

51 Also, Amy Verdun in her book *European Responses to Globalisation and Financial Market Integration* asks why 'this particular design of EMU came about' (Verdun 2000: 3) against the background of the single market and increasing globalization. The book focuses on four actor groups in Britain, France, and Germany: central banks, Ministries of Finance, employers' organizations, and trade unions. Yet, in contrast to Marcussen and McNamara, Verdun is more interested in the actors' interests, than in the ideas underlying them. She distinguishes between national interests and the interests of these national actors and asks: 'What are the perceptions of interests of different actors towards EMU, and how, in their view, does EMU serve or frustrate their policy objectives?' (Verdun 2000: 9). But, of course, interests derive from preferences and these reflect competing ideas.

52 See especially Chapter 5 in this book.

53 The economist-centred approach.

54 Our emphasis.

55 Epistemology deals with *judgements* about entities and our *knowledge* about them. Ontology deals with entities or groups of entities that *exist*.

56 These distinctions are inspired by Lehrer (1997).

57 See note 42.

58 Liberal intergovernmentalism as developed by Moravcsik provides a micro-foundational model for preferences by investigating the domestic dimension of national preferences. While this provides a deeper root for state preferences, it is still based on naturalistic assumptions.

59 These writers justify their view by referring to empirical hypothesis testing, reason, or rationality. Realism and its descendants stand in an empiricist, functionalism, and rational choice theory in a rationalist tradition of epistemology. For the philosophical tradition of empirical and rationalist foundation theories of knowledge, see Lehrer (1990: Chapter 3).

60 See also the work by Kahneman and Tversky (2000) on 'framing effects'.

61 Coherence establishes the validity of propositions, it does not 'establish some sort of causal link between ideas, beliefs, etc. and policies' as a number of political scientists claim. See Yee (1996: 76) for a discussion of 'congruence' and 'process tracing procedures' to link ideas to the content of policies.

62 For example, see the contributions in Hall (1989) on how Keynes' ideas were accepted in very different ways in different countries.

63 Giddens discussed this under the label of double hermeneutics: 'original ideas and findings in social science tend to "disappear" to the degree to which they are incorporated within the familiar components of practical activities' Giddens (1993: 15).

64 On social learning and European identity change, see Checkel (2001).

65 Of course this only applies to ideas that are coherent with the existing stock of knowledge.

66 What we call naturalistic preferences can be shown to correspond to an 'internalist' interpretation of rationality, whereby the rationality of a choice function depends on its internal consistency with different parts of its domain, see Basu (2000: 9). This line of thought goes back to Samuelson's Weak Axiom of Revealed Preference. Sen (1987: 13–14) has pointed out that 'it is hard to believe that internal consistency of choice can itself be an adequate condition of rationality. [...] Since what we regard as consistent in a set of observed choices must depend on the *interpretation* of those choices and on some features *external* to choices, for example, the nature of our preferences, aims, values, motivations'. Hence, the rationality of a choice function depends on how well it matches up to something external to the choice function (Basu, 2000: 36). This second approach of 'externalist' rationality corresponds to the coherence theory of acceptance as knowledge. It implies to *analytically separate choices from preferences* and to analyse preference formation against the structure and transformation of background. In this context, normative considerations become salient.

67 Jean Monnet formulated this brilliantly in the phrase: 'Nous ne coalisons pas les Etats, nous réunissons les hommes.' Chapter 2 provides evidence that these ideas certainly motivated Valéry Giscard d'Estaing and Helmut Schmidt in their efforts to create a European currency.

68 Institutional facts are often described as 'intersubjective' relations, which create 'objective' reality. However, this begs the question of the ontological status of such relations. Searle's distinction between the ontologically subjective and epistemologically objective status of facts is a clarifying step forward.

69 Because observer-dependent institutional facts are partly constituted by an (ontologically subjective) set of attitudes and beliefs, although forming an epistemically objective social reality, they become the founding stone of coherence theory. However, this statement goes beyond our purposes in this introduction. Given that language is an institutional fact (like money), the statement can be understood as the pivot for the 'linguistic turn' in modern philosophy.

70 In fact, any liberal theory of European integration should take this approach: for modern liberalism is based on what Arrow called the axiom of 'unlimited domain', that is, the condition that no individual should be excluded from the establishment of a collective choice.

71 A large part of this book is an account of how people came to accept the euro as money. There were several incidences where it was uncertain whether rules could be accepted or implemented. The Bundesbank frequently referred to the dangers of the single European currency not being accepted as money by the people.

72 For the general statement, see Searle (1995: 35).

73 Collective intentionality may seem mysterious to methodological individualists. Yet, the concept is perfectly rational when interpreted as ontologically subjective and epistemologically objective.

74 Searle's notion of background gives meaning to acts, without individuals having to reflect on the constitutive rules which define such meaning. In this respect, background resembles what Habermas calls 'Lebenswelt' (life-world). See Habermas (1984: 335–7), and the translators' introduction, p. xxv–xxvii, Habermas (1982: 541–607).

75 See note 66.

76 The five conditions are: (a) collective rationality; (b) Pareto principle; (c) the independence of irrelevant alternatives; (d) non-dictatorship; and (e) unrestricted domain.

(No individual should be excluded from contributing to the establishment of a collective choice.) For a simple textbook exposition, see Cullis and Jones 1998.

77 Essentially, this is a stochastic model of consensus. For a technical description see Annexe 1.

78 This idea is not new. It goes back, at least to J. S. Mill (see Holmes 1995: 181). But it has consequences, which have not been sufficiently acknowledged and are formalized in the deGroot and Lehrer and Wagner models.

79 This does not imply that each individual needs to be aware of *all* other individuals' preferences. It is sufficient that they are socially connected.

80 In this respect the Lehrer and Wagner model of consensus converges to Habermas' model of communicative action where the conditions of communicative rationality create 'the rationally binding force of criticisable claims to validity', Habermas (1987: 77). Jane Braaten (1987) has claimed that the Lehrer and Wagner model and the Habermasian models of argumentational consensus procedures are contradictory. We believe that our interpretation of Lehrer and Wagner as a stochastic consensus model in a Baysian framework (see Annexe 1) overcomes this objection. We may also say that in this model consensus is the unintended consequence of agents' purposive acts to gather information for making optimal decisions. See Giddens (1993: 82–4).

81 The distinction between dissensus and conflict in social sciences, therefore, resembles the distinction of persistence and histeresis in economics.

82 These are the minimal conditions. It is, of course, possible that individuals change the assignment of weights 'jumping' therefore towards the equilibrium.

83 Interview, François Périgot, 20 August 2001.

2 Foundations

1 Born in 1926, Valéry Giscard d'Estaing was French Finance Minister under Charles de Gaulle (1962–6) and Georges Pompidou (1969–74). He was elected President of the Republic from 1974 to 81. He served as a member of the European Parliament from 1989 to 93 and since then at the National Assembly.

2 Helmut Schmidt, born in 1918, was German Defence Minister from 1969 to 72 and subsequently Finance Minister. In 1974, he was elected Chancellor of the Federal Republic of Germany and served until 1982.

3 Interview, Valéry Giscard d'Estaing, 14 November 2001.

4 Interview, Valéry Giscard d'Estaing, 14 November 2001.

5 They were each assisted by only one advisor. Helmut Schmidt's advisor was his Secretary of State, Horst Schulmann. Giscard was assisted by Bernard Clappier, then Governor of the Banque de France. He was one of the founders of the Schumann Plan in 1950, when he served as the prime mediator between Jean Monnet and Robert Schumann.

6 Interview, Helmut Schmidt, 6 July 2001; interview, Valéry Giscard d'Estaing, 14 November 2001.

7 In 1982, the Christian-Democrat Helmut Kohl suceeded Schmidt. The Socialist François Mitterrand was elected French President in 1981.

8 Helmut Schmidt has acknowledged that Monnet and his proposal of a European Reserve Fund were one of the sources of inspiration that led him and Giscard to the creation of the EMS. See Duchêne (1994: 335).

9 Paul Mentré (interview 27 August 2001) remembers that Giscard's proposal was a very daring and risky venture, given de Gaulle's attachment to strengthening the French franc by increasing France's gold reserves.

10 Interview, Valéry Giscard d'Estaing, 14 November 2001.

11 Interview, Valéry Giscard d'Estaing, 14 November 2001.

12 For more details, see Chapters 3 and 4.

13 Interview, Paul Mentré, 30 August 2001.
14 Hervé Carré, interview, 19 July 2001. The Monetary Committee was set up in 1958 to monitor the monetary and financial situation of each member state and of the Community as a whole. With the start of EMU in 1999, it was replaced by the Economic and Financial Committee (EFC).
15 We will argue in Chapter 5 that there was an inherent logic between these two events, which applied even more strongly to Italy.
16 The 'inconsistent quartet' means that the policy objectives of free markets for goods and capital, fixed exchange rates and national monetary autonomy were inconsistent.
17 Valéry Giscard d'Estaing, speech at the Bremer Tabak Kollegium, Heidelberg, 13 November 1986.
18 We discuss later why Britain often experienced difficulties in sharing the German–French consensus.
19 A 'stroke of luck'. This is Schmidt's expression (interview 6 July 2001). Giscard d'Estaing (1988: 724) saw it in a similar way: 'The natural and trustworthy intimacy that existed between Helmut Schmidt and me is without any doubt unique for the relationships of political leaders in today's large European member states. It has allowed us to advance Europe's unity'.
20 Interview, Schmidt, 6 July 2001; interview, Valéry Giscard d'Estaing, 14 November 2001.
21 In November 2001, Schmidt and Giscard were awarded the Jean-Monnet Medal for their achievements in bringing forward monetary integration.
22 Jean Monnet had been invited by President Giscard d'Estaing to the Elyseé on several occasions and when Helmut Schmidt was German Chancellor, he asked Monnet for advice at least twice (interview with Helmut Schmidt, 6 July 2001).
23 In terms of our consensus model in the introduction, Monnet's method aimed at both the transformation of background by common practices and common knowledge and the emergence of consensus by strengthening mutual respect between people.
24 The creation of the European Coal and Steel Community of course was also pushed by the motive to pool sovereignty in the sectors which formed the basis of warfare.
25 The Committee for the Monetary Union of Europe (CMUE) also became known as the Giscard–Schmidt Committee. In this book, both expressions are used interchangeably.
26 A difference, however, was that the Monnet Action Committee brought together representatives of different institutions and political decision takers, while the Giscard–Schmidt Committee assembled prominent business leaders as well as former statesmen (some of whom returned to office later, making it easier to feed the ideas developed in the Committee into day-to-day politics).
27 Schmidt has returned the compliment by writing that Giscard d'Estaing had been very involved in defence issues during his Presidency and had also become an expert (Schmidt 1990: 284).
28 The detailed knowledge he had gathered as legislator proved useful when, as Chancellor, he was engaged in a power struggle with the Bundesbank over the EMS; interview, Schmidt, 6 July 2001.
29 In the 1990s this led Schmidt to a major clash with Hans Tietmeyer, then President of the Bundesbank, see Chapter 5.
30 Moravcsik (1998) concentrates on substantial benefits. That Schmidt had more in mind is revealed by his formulation: 'Comprehensive strategic concepts must go beyond the economic and strategic domains'. See Schmidt (1990: 274).
31 In game theory this is called a Nash equilibrium.
32 Interestingly, this also explains Schmidt's support for NATO's deployment of American intermediate-range missiles in Europe that ultimately cost him the chancellorship. Kissinger (1994: 775) points out that Schmidt tried to 'couple' American defence

with Europe because of doubts whether 'Western Europe could count on the United States' using its nuclear weapons to repel a Soviet attack that was confined to Europe.

33 For Robert Schumann, economic and industrial co-operation meant that wars became 'not merely unthinkable, but materially impossible'. Helmut Kohl stands in this tradition when he claimed in the 1990s that EMU was necessary to prevent wars in Europe. Compare this with Margaret Thatcher's Secretary of State for Trade and Industry who declared in 1990 that EMU was a 'German racket to take over the whole of Europe.' EMU meant losing British sovereignty to Germany and 'you might as well give it to Adolf Hitler, frankly.' As for the French, they were merely 'Germany's poodles' (Dyson and Featherstone 1999: 568).

34 In the seventeenth century the Whigs were a political party which stood for a limited monarchy after the English revolution of 1688 and wanted to subordinate the power of the crown to that of Parliament.

35 Kissinger, a friend and intellectual sparring partner of Schmidt, shows the difference between the British and Continental strategies that already appeared in 1812, 'when it became evident that Europe was not to be organized by force'. Because 'Britain was threatened only if Europe fell under domination of a single power, Castlereagh was primarily concerned with constructing a balance of forces. Because the balance of power only limits the scope of aggression, but does not prevent it, Metternich sought to buttress the equilibrium by developing the doctrine of legitimacy [...]'. Interestingly, this difference of philosophy is also apparent in domestic economic and monetary policy. While in Germany an independent central bank was obliged by law to maintain the stability of the currency, government in the United Kingdom still keeps the option to set policy objectives for the Bank of England.

36 France also had a 'Legacy of Greatness' but given the traumatic experience of German occupation, it was not so strongly expressed in the political sphere, but in the economic field – in the form of dirigisme and protectionism (interview, François Périgot, August 2001).

37 Turner also quotes Amery and Churchill.

38 Edward Heath was Prime Minister from 1970 to 1974 and was succeeded by Harold Wilson.

39 Interestingly, the French military doctrine since de Gaulle has effectively been free-riding on the security provided by NATO. (For a critical assessment, see Schmidt 1990: 271–82.) There is a lot to be said for the interpretation that in today's Europe, *national independence* or *sovereignty* is a polite expression for *free-riding*.

40 Assume, for example, that a given exchange rate reflects a fundamental equilibrium between two economies. If this equilibrium is disturbed by a shock in such a way that it leads to inflation and/or unemployment, the economic system has become unstable. If intervention rules allow the exchange rate to return to a level that is consistent with internal and external balance (which was the idea behind the EMS), they minimize deviations from the fundamental equilibrium. Therefore, such exchange-rate interventions create what we have called procedural gains. Alternatively, a freely floating exchange rate, which follows a random walk, will not necessarily return to equilibrium and may cause persistent distortions in the form of inflation and unemployment, as the 1970s and 1980s have shown.

41 Great Britain – James Callaghan, former Prime Minister and MP; David Howell, MP. Italy – Mario Schimberni, Industrialist; Rinaldo Ossola, President of Creditor Version. Spain – Miguel Boyer Salvador, former Minister and President of the Banque Espagnole du Commerce Exterieur; J.A. Sanchez Asiain, President of the Banco de Bilbao. Federal Germany – Wilfried Guth, President of the Conseil de Surveillance, Deutsche Bank; Manfred Lahnstein, former Minister of Finance, Director of the Bertelsmann Group. France – Renaud de la Geniere, former Governor of the Banque

De France, President of the Compagnie Financiere de Suez; Pierre Beregovoy, former Minister, Deputy. Holland – Jelle Zijlstra, former Prime Minister, former Governor of the Dutch Central Bank, former President of the BIS. Belgium – Etienne Davignon, former Vice-President of the Commission des Communautés Européennes, Director, Société Générale de Belgique. Denmark – Niels Thygesen, Economic Institute, University of Copenhagen. Portugal – Jose Silva Lopes, former Minister of Finance. Greece – Xénophon Zolotas, former Governor of the Bank of Greece. Ireland – Anthony O'Reilly, President, Heinz Corporation. Luxembourg – Gaston Thorn, President of the International Bank of Luxembourg, former Prime Minister, former President of the Commission des Communautés Européennes. Secretaries – Uwe Plachetka, Economist, Bonn; Paul Mentré, President Crédit National, Paris, general rapporteur for '*An Action Programme*'. Although James Callaghan, the former British Prime Minister at the time when Schmidt and Giscard set up the EMS, was formally a member of the Committee, he never took a very active part in its work, to Schmidt's personal disappointment. Apparently, the reasons were not unrelated with the fact that the CMUE had no budget for travel expenses (communication by Uwe Plachetka, 30 October 2000).

42 Interview, Giscard d'Estaing, 14 November 2001.
43 Interview, Helmut Schmidt, 6 July 2001.
44 After the conclusion of the Maastricht Treaty, the Committee stopped its activities. The Association for the Monetary Union of Europe continued its work.
45 The CMUE had a direct (via the *Tresor*) and indirect (via political rivalry between Giscard's centrist UDF and Balladur's gaullist RPR) influence on the Balladur Memorandum, which echoed most of the issues discussed by the group (Dyson and Featherstone 1999: 165–6). The Genscher memorandum and Chancellor Kohl's position were influenced by leading figures at the Deutsche Bank. See Chapter 3 for details.
46 Minutes of the CMUE; Archives Helmut Schmidt.
47 Speech at the Annual General Meeting of the Ecu Banking Association, Rome, 20 March 1987.
48 Interview, Valéry Giscard d'Estaing, 14 November 2001.
49 The manifesto was published on 1 November 1975 by *The Economist*. It was signed by: Pascal Salin, Herbert Giersch, Giorgio Basevi, Michele Fratiani, Peter Korteweg, Paul de Grauwe, Michael Parkin, David O'Mahony, and Niels Thygesen.
50 Interview, Niels Thygesen, 26 September 2001.
51 In 1998, Padoa-Schioppa became a member of the Board of the European Central Bank.
52 The SEA constituted an important reform of the European Community Treaties, introducing, among other things, the Single Market Programme and institutional reforms.
53 The other one was the Swiss National Bank. See Bofinger *et al.* (1996: 279).
54 Interview, Helmut Schmidt, 6 July 2001.
55 See minutes of CMUE meeting in Bonn, 28 March 1987, Archive Helmut Schmidt. This 'overdetermination' has become better known as '*inconsistent quartet*', developed at the same time by Padoa-Schioppa *et al.* (1987).
56 This was Etienne Davignon's impression, who was present at the meeting, interview, 26 July 2001. Unfortunately, Pöhl does not remember the meeting. (Interview, 22 November 2001.)
57 As Marx has said, dominant ideas always express the ideas of the dominant. In terms of our consensus model Chapter 1, ideas become consensual because those who dominate receive high weights of respect.
58 For evidence, see the article by Jean-René Fourtou in *The Ecu for European Business*, quoted in Chapter 4.
59 For more details also see Chapter 4.

60 Giscard recalls that he had to deal with a French establishment dominated by *dirigiste* and *étatist* ideas and an employer's association (CNPF) who expected a regular growth rate of 6 per cent; interview, Valéry Giscard d'Estaing, 14 November 2001.
61 Interview, Helmut Schmidt, 6 July 2001.
62 The snake was the first example. The second was that the Bundesbank prevented the emergence of a symmetrical EMS with the Ecu as its core.
63 See Collignon (1994a: 14) for details.
64 Interview, Valéry Giscard d'Estaing, 14 November 2001.
65 This bias results from the fact that the anchor country with the lowest inflation rate accumulates current account surpluses within the bloc. Only an appreciation towards other floating key currencies (the dollar) can re-establish a fundamental balance. However, the equilibrium in the anchor country automatically creates disequilibria in the periphery, where the combination of a real appreciation within the bloc and a nominal appreciation with the rest of the world create an external deficit that ultimately requires a realignment in exchange rates. For a formal model of bloc floating and its drawbacks see Collignon (2002).
66 Heisenberg emphasizes that Schmidt and Giscard were guided in their negotiations by *their* preferences, and not those representing other actors collectively: 'This point is quite simple, yet it is occasionally ignored by scholars: these executives could and did make the monetary decisions based on their own inclinations, rather than some amalgamation of preferences.' In fact, the amalgamation into the social consensus only happened *after* Schmidt and Giscard had submitted their original plans to their European colleagues in Copenhagen.
67 Interview, Davignon, 26 July 2001.
68 The European Round Table of Industrialists will not play an important role in our assessment of the private sector's engagement in the run up to EMU as there was an explicit agreement among the AMUE and the Round Table that the Association would engage in favour of EMU while the Round Table would work for the accomplishment of the single market. Both institutions stuck to this commitment.
69 See Chapter 3 for details.
70 See Chapter 4 for details.
71 Interview, Cornelis van der Klugt, 27 September 2001.
72 De Maigret had written to Giscard in 1961 when he was a young student at the French elite business school HEC congratulating him on an excellent speech on global strategy that Giscard, then State Secretary for Economics, had given in Chile (forty years later, de Maigret learned that Giscard's speech in 1961 had actually been written by Michel Poniatowski, a close political ally of Giscard and de Maigret's father in law). At the time, de Maigret was President of the French branch of the AIESEC and fascinated by geopolitics. When Giscard founded a small policy think-tank in the early 1960s under the name 'Perspectives et Réalités', de Maigret was the third member of the club with Giscard, Poniatowski, and some other early founders sitting on an empty floor in the new offices in the sixth arrondissement in Paris. A few years later, when de Maigret married Poniatowski's daughter Isabel, Giscard was her marriage witness.
73 Initially, they had thought of creating a foundation but according to French law this would have required a representative of the French government on the Board of the foundation and they decided that an association under the French law of 1901 would give them greater freedom and independence.
74 Interview, van der Klugt, 27 September 2001.
75 Minutes of CMUE meeting on 15 June 1987, Archives Helmut Schmidt.
76 Etienne Davignon, who was not yet chairman of Société Générale de Belgique, did not join the Association at this point but remained active in the Giscard–Schmidt Committee.
77 For a full list of AMUE Board members, see Annexe 6.

78 When he was chief executive of Barclays, Martin Taylor served as a board member of AMUE. The often expressed his personal doubts about the project and after leaving both functions he publicly rejoiced about the second rejection of EMU by the Danish voters in 2001.

3 A common or a single currency?

1 The poll by Gallop and Faits et Opinion was conducted in 1988 to find out what business leaders in the European Community thought about the European Currency. It sampled 1,036 companies with more than 300,000 million Ecu in export or import in seven countries: Belgium (82 cases), Federal Republic of Germany (174), Spain (160), France (171), Italy (182), The Netherlands (80), and the United Kingdom (187).
2 For details, see Chapter 1.
3 Vissol trained as an economist with a PhD on the birth of free-trade and monetary approach to the balance of payment's theories joined the commission in 1980 and the Directorate for Monetary affairs in 1985. He was involved in the reform of the EMS and the preparation of the Maastricht treaty then as head of the Ecu unit in the practical preparation of the EMU. In 1996, he was asked by Commissioner Bonino to prepare the changeover of the consumers to the euro and their information in the Directorate General for Consumers affairs. In 1989 he was encouraged by Pons to create a research centre CEPIME (Centre Ecu et Prospective d'Intégration Monétaire Européenne) and a review De Pecunia, to stimulate the academic debate on EMU. Robert Triffin accepted the presidency of the centre.
4 Another, although embarrassing project at the time was the production of a 10-minute promotional film on the Ecu, co-financed by the Commission, the AMUE and the Ecu Banking Association. The film turned out to be too simplistic and was never really used.
5 For more details on the strategic partnership between the AMUE and the Commission see Chapter 3.
6 Collignon was born in Germany and was trained as an economist in Berlin, Paris, Oxford, and London. While teaching in Tanzania in the late 1970s he wrote a PhD thesis on economic disintegration in East Africa. In the 1980s, he built a London-based business of 400 employees in office cleaning and maintenance. He had learned practical salesmanship in London's High Streets and, although he was a member of the German Social Democratic Party, he considered himself socializined as an entrepreneurial product of the Thatcher years.
7 This so-called portfolio effect is due to the compensating movements of the individual components of the basket.
8 Club Med's Chief Financial Officer pointed out these arguments to Stefan Collignon in 1989.
9 See Chapter 1.
10 Interview, Padoa-Schioppa, 29 August 2001.
11 See minutes of CMUE Meeting on 15 June 1987.
12 Jean François Pons claims that the idea to make Delors Chairman of the later Delors Committee came originally from Giscard and Schmidt. Interview on 27 July 2001.
13 Interview, Karl Otto Pöhl, 22 November 2001.
14 Correspondence by Joachim Bitterlich, 19 November 2001.
15 Interview, Daniel Gros, 26 July 2001.
16 Committee for the Study of Economic and Monetary Union, 1989.
17 Interview K. O. Pöhl, 22 November 2001.
18 Jacques de Larosière, Correspondence, 6 November 2001.
19 Interview, de Larosière, 25 September 2001.
20 Interview, de Larosière, 25 September 2001. See also Dyson and Featherstone (1999; 180–7).

21 Interview, Giscard d'Estaing, 14 November 2001.
22 Interview, Pöhl, 22 November 2001.
23 On 26 March 1998, the day after the Bundesbank had approved the EMI and Commission Report on the convergence criteria. This opened the way for Italy joining the EMU.
24 Discussion with Stefan Collignon.
25 Interview, Günter Grosche, 20 June 2001. See Chapters 4 and 5 for more details.
26 Interview, Pöhl, 22 November 2001.
27 Pöhl claims that he had talked to Margaret Thatcher several times and explained his careful support for EMU but she did not seem to understand or want to listen to what he was saying, interview, 22 November 2001.
28 See Chapter 4.
29 Wim Duisenberg became the first President of the European Central Bank in 1999.
30 Wim Duisenberg, contribution to the Delors Committee 1989, in: Committee for the Study of Economic and Monetary Union (1989: 185–90).
31 Wim Duisenberg, contribution to the Delors Committee, 1989, in: Committee for the Study of Economic and Monetary Union (1989: 185–90).
32 Karl Otto Pöhl, contribution to the Delors Committee, 1989 in: Committee for the study of Economic and Monetary Union (1989: 129–56).
33 Delors Report, in: Committee for the Study of Economic and Monetary Union (1989; paragraph 46). Our emphasis.
34 Press statement of AMUE, London, 3 May 1989.
35 This analysis was confirmed during the early years of EMU (1999–2002) when there were no euro notes and coins yet.
36 A different view is given by Connolly (1995: 105): '*One Market, One Money* was a piece of blatant neo-functionalist propaganda, a set of specious anti-economic arguments and rigged model simulation results intended to give support to the idea – which we saw in Chapter 4 to be totally false – that the Single Market in the Community required a single currency if it was to work properly. The document was long, heavy, deliberately technical, and abstruse in order both to mask its twisted logic and to impress 'opinion-formers' with its 'scientific' authority. It achieved its aims – at least in the short term, which was what mattered politically – with dismaying completeness'.
37 Interview, Jean François Pons, 27 July 2001.
38 Although these costs were rather small in size, they had a significant impact on the macropolitical outcome of the integration process. There is a similarity here with 'small menu cost' models developed by Mankiw and Akerlof. See Mankiw and Romer (1991).
39 The AMUE only addressed the optimum currency area argument in its *Sustainability Report* published in 1998 (see Collignon 1999b, 2002), before the final decision on the member selection for EMU was taken. See Chapter 5.
40 See correspondence in AMUE archives.
41 Giovanni Agnelli, *The European Industry and the Ecu*. Speech at the Ecu Banking Association Meeting, Madrid, 4 March 1988.
42 Minutes of Board Meeting, 20 September 1989.
43 Ecofin, General Affairs Councils, European Commission, Committee of European Central Bank Governors.
44 AMUE, press release, 20 September 1989.
45 Ibid.
46 Congruous connection.
47 Discussion with Stefan Collignon.
48 External contributors were: Eric Svindland from DIW (Berlin), Jacques le Cacheux, Catherine Mathieu, Henri Sterdyniak of OCFE (Paris), Lorenzo Bini-Smaghi from the Banca d'Italia and Age Bakker from the De Nederlandsche Bank.

49 The external Advisory Board consisted of: Prof. Niels Thygesen, University of Copenhagen and a member of the Delors Committee; Dr Norbert Walter, Deutsche Bank; Alain Prate, European Investment Bank in Luxembourg; Christopher Johnson, Lloyds Bank; Richard Freeman, ICI; Anastassios Gagalis, National Bank of Greece; Jean-François Pons, Claude Mingasson, Thierry Vissol, Marc van Heuklen, all from the European Commission Services; Andrew Britton and Prof. David Mayes from the NIESR, Paul Mentré, President of the Crédit National represented the Giscard–Schmidt connection.
50 For a more recent and detailed analysis see Talani (2000).
51 After all, the Bundesbank had first-hand experience of how to prevent subsequent steps to monetary integration as the history of the EMS had shown. See also above, Chapter 2.
52 Connolly (1995: 70) argues that the 'dirty politics of the British ERM entry' (p. 43) 'were destroying Tory radicalism'.
53 In his book *Les Français* written ten years later, Giscard seemed even more disappointed. He considered that an historic opportunity was lost by not having united Europe *before* German unification : 'Faute de décisions appropriées, le système risque d'évoluer vers une Conférence des Etats d'Europe, gérant un large marché, pratiquant une coopération intergouvernementale, mais dotée d'un pouvoir décisionnel faible'. Giscard d'Estaing (2000: 91).
54 Interview, Giscard d'Estaing, 14 November 2001.
55 Chris Taylor, correspondence 24 November 2001.
56 Interview, Chris Taylor, 25 July 2001.
57 Interview, Paul Mentré, 30 August 2001.
58 Most perplexing was an anecdote told by President Jacques Chirac to Giscard in 1996. Only few months before the general elections, and at a time when he was already in serious political difficulties, John Major told Chirac that he was contemplating a return of pound sterling into the ERM, starting simultaneously with EMU in January 1999. Interview, Giscard d'Estaing, 14 November 2001.
59 Kenneth Clarke observed that Thatcher initially was quite pro-European, as was public opinion in the United Kingdom during the 1980s. The creation of the single market contributed to this positive attitude. Apparently, Thatcher only turned anti-European after German unification, especially after the Strasbourg European Council in December 1989 where Kohl had difficulties in accepting the finality of the German Oder–Neisse border. Interview, Kenneth Clarke, 24 October 2000. See also note 45 in Chapter 4.
60 Letter by Butler, AMUE Archieves.
61 Interview, Etienne Davignon, 26 July 2001.

4 The crises and the Phoenix

1 The fact that collective group preferences are always an amalgamation of individual preferences does not exclude the assumption that states are *unitary*, actors acting in international negotiations 'as if' with a single voice. See Moravcsik (1999: 22). For the role of civil servants in the Maastricht negotiations, see Mazzucelli (1997).
2 See Chapter 3.
3 Interview, Elisabeth Guigou, 15 November 2001.
4 The Maastricht Treaty in the end settled that the European Monetary Institute (EMI) should be set up at the start of stage two in order to prepare stage three of EMU.
5 Minutes of Thirteenth Board Meeting in Frankfurt, 6 December 1990.
6 Interview, Belmiro de Azevedo, 17 September 2001.

7 Minutes of the Annual General Meeting and Board meeting in London on 30 May 1991.

8 Cornelis van der Klugt had resigned as chairman of Philips and also as President of the Association.

9 Jean-François Pons of the European Commission and Tommaso Padoa-Schioppa, now Vice Governor of the Banca d'Italia, and Bertrand de Maigret were also present.

10 The meeting was attended by: Davignon, Agnelli, de Azevedo, Mentré, Merkle, Ortoli, Papalexopoulos, Plachetka, de Maigret, Collignon, Ahlborn (Arbed), Ahnefeld (Bosch), Cuervo (Grupo March), Heegard (FLS Industries), von Hülsen (Volkswagen), Johnson (BAT Industries), Kirschen (Fiat), Lomax (BAT Industries), Maleki (Bosch and Volkswagen), de Meyer (Philips), Praet (Société Générale de Belgique), Rodriguez (Grupo March and Confederacion Espanola de Organizaciones Empresariales), Ronner (Philips), de Schaetzen (Agfa-Gevaert), and Mrs Sirel (Crédit National Group).

11 AMUE Board Press Release 30, November 1991.

12 Interview, Etienne Davignon, 26 July 2001.

13 Interview, Hilmar Kopper, 13 December 2001.

14 This was also Joachim Bitterlich's impression. Interview on 17 September 2001.

15 Interview, Umberto Vattani, 30 August 2001. See also Dyson and Featherstone 1999: 518.

16 Interview, Umberto Vattani, 30 August 2001.

17 Interview, Joachim Bitterlich, 17 September 2001.

18 This is at least Elizabeth Guigou's impression. See Favier and Martin-Roland (2000: 103).

19 Interview, Theo Waigel, 18 September 2001.

20 Opinion poll carried out by EOS-Gallup in October 1990 for the AMUE questioning 6,049 people.

21 Data published in: de Villepin (1990).

22 AMUE Newsletter *The Ecu for European Business*, January 1992.

23 In May 2001, Patricia Hewitt became Secretary of State for Trade and Industry.

24 AMUE Newsletter *The Ecu for European Business*, January 1992.

25 AMUE Newsletter *The Ecu for European Business*, January 1992.

26 Interview, Birgit Nielsen, 2 October 2001.

27 Interview, Niels Thygesen, 26 September 2001.

28 AMUE Newsletter *The Ecu for European Business*, January 1992.

29 The CNPF was renamed MEDEF (Mouvement des Entreprises de France) in October 1998.

30 Interview, Périgot, 20 August 2001.

31 Note by de Maigret to Ortoli on 18 January 1990, AMUE archives.

32 In fact, the AMUE had argued the opposite: the currency would only become common if it was single.

33 See for example the article by Georges Jollés, Président de l'union des industries textiles in *Le Figaro*, 20 April 1995.

34 Interview, Francois Périgot, 20 August 2001.

35 Speculations were increasing at the Paris stock exchange, while renowned French economists forecast rising interest. They expected the Banque de France to raise rates in order to prevent a too strong exchange rate devaluation of the Franc which was expected in case of a rejection of the Treaty.

36 Today Aventis.

37 Marie de Saint Cheron later became Director of Communication of Renault, France.

38 As Niels Thygesen points out, this argument played a much stronger role in the French debate that it did before in the referendum in Denmark. Interview, Niels Thygesen, 26 September 2001.

39 AMUE: Traité de Maastricht. Arguments en faveur de l'Union Economique et Monétaire, 27 August 1992, AMUE archives.

40 AMUE: The French vote on 20 September 1992 – a decisive factor for the future of the European Community, AMUE archives.
41 One example among several is de Maigret's successful initiative to convince Gilbert Gantier to question the Minister for Economic and Finance on the slow use of the Ecu in France in July 1993.
42 Note from Fiat to the authors, 28 November 2001.
43 Interview, Günter Grosche, 20 June 2001.
44 Minutes Board Meeting, 6 December 1990. A year later, Malcolm Levitt of Barclays Bank suggested that a working group should examine the practical implementation. This led to a series of studies, which provided crucial evidence and knowledge on the private sector's need in the changeover process.
45 Marsh (1992: 229). Dyson and Featherstone (1999: 367) report that the European Council at Strasbourg in December 1989 was 'a very unpleasant personal experience' for Kohl. 'He was subjected to sharp questioning about Germany policy intentions and made aware of the depths of Mrs Thatcher's distrust of German motives. This experience underlined for Kohl the implications of German isolation if she were to be seen as pursuing a 'go-it-alone' policy. Hence he became determined to reaffirm German ambitions to give a new impulse to European unification'. According to Grant (1994: 133), the dispute developed at dinner over Kohl's refusal to recognize the Order–Neisse line as Germany's Eastern border to Poland because German public opinion 'was not ready'. Delors warned of a serious crisis if no date was set for the start of the IGC. The next day, the summit conclusions stated: 'The German people will gain its unity through free self-determination [...]. This process [...] has to be placed in a context of European integration'. Kenneth Clarke (interview, 24 October 2001) also emphasized that 'Kohl's way of bringing in a new population into the European community without asking' was an essential factor in turning Thatcher into an anti-German and anti-European. Mitterrand probably shared some of her concerns, especially on the border issue, but he kept mainly quiet. Elisabeth Guigou, who was present at most meetings between Kohl and Mitterrand, is formal: 'There were never any negotiations linking EMU to German unification', interview, 15 November 2001.
46 *The Ecu for European Business*, No. 6, November 1990.
47 Minutes of Board meeting in Brussels, 17 March 1991.
48 *The Ecu for European Business*, No. 8, May 1991.
49 The proceedings of the conference were published by the review *De Pecunia* (Special issue, June 1991) and widely distributed.
50 The conference papers were published by Collignon, Pisani-Ferry, and Park, 1999.
51 Board Minutes on 25 March 1991.
52 It was subsequently published in several journals and books. See for example Collignon (1994a).
53 Technically, this was a consequence of the increasing use of intra-marginal interventions in the Exchange Rate Mechanism, which allowed the Bundesbank to pursue its stability-orientated domestic monetary policies. Until the Basle-Nyborg agreement in 1987, intra-marginal interventions by weak central banks had to be done by using own foreign exchange reserves, primarily Deutschmarks. As a consequence, stabilising bilateral exchange rates within the system did not affect the Bundesbank's monetary strategy because peripheral countries would not draw on their credit lines with the Bundesbank.
54 See Chapter 3.
55 With the exception of the technical adjustment of the Italian lira in January 1990, when Italy narrowed the band width from ±6 to ±2.25 per cent.
56 The Finnish markka pegged its exchange rate against the Ecu on 7 June 1991 after the Norwegian krona (22 October 1990) and the Swedish krona (19 May 1991). The Hungarian forint also used an exchange rate peg which consisted of 50 per cent Ecu and 50 per cent US dollar.
57 See Table 8, in Collignon, 1994.

58 Nigel Lawson, the Chancellor of the Exchequer in the United Kingdom, who had resigned over the difficulties of taking the United Kingdom into the exchange rate mechanism, later wrote: 'Sterling joined at a rate which the Bundesbank regarded from the outset as too high and which it felt under no moral obligation to support – a fact that was later to become all too apparent to the financial markets'. (quoted in Johnson, 1994.)
59 However, France had consistently lower inflation rates during this period, due to the the *Franc fort* policy of competitive disinflation. See Chapter 5.
60 See Chapter 5.
61 The exception was Greece.
62 Giscard d'Estaing (2000: 94) regrets that 'no initiative of significant repercussion was taken to put this unification into the larger project of the European Union. [...] Nevertheless, history had opened an extraordinary window of opportunity for a European proposition [...] and [...] there was no French leader ready to make one, each of them secretly preferring Germany to shoulder the burden of its reunification alone'.
63 Domestic demand increased by 5.2 and 3.6 per cent, respectively. See European Economy, No. 58, 1994.
64 In comparison, Marshall-plan transfers to West Germany after the war only amounted to 2 per cent of GDP.
65 Taking the previous black market rate. See Roeper and Weimer (1996: 363).
66 See also Lindlar and Holtfrerich, 1999, on Germany's foreign trade structure.
67 The GDP deflator, which indicates domestic price developments, went up to 4.4 per cent in 1992.
68 Employment in Western Germany increased by 700,000 in 1990 and reached its highest level in history with 28.4 million employed (Roeper and Weimer 1996: 367).
69 In Germany from 5.6 to 8.4, in France from 9.5 to 12.6, in Italy from 8.3 to 11.3, and in Belgium from 6.6 to 10.0 per cent. All figures from European Economy, No. 60, 1995.
70 For a partisan view of the detailed events, see Connolly (1995).
71 However, from today's Euro-area point of view, the Irish devaluation was a mistake that caused a significant price gap and inflation potential for subsequent years.
72 Kenneth Clarke, interview, 24 October 2001.
73 Outside this Community agreement, the Deutsche Bundesbank and De Nederlandsche Bank agreed bilaterally to maintain ± 2.25 per cent narrow band between the DEM and the NLG.
74 The assessment is also shared by Jacques de Larosière who was at the time Governor of the Banque de France. Interview, de Larosière, 25 September 2001.
75 See Chapter 5.
76 Discussion with Collignon on 17 September 1993.
77 Conversation with Collignon, on the occasion of AMUE Board Meeting 25 January 1995 in Paris.
78 This was the subject of a heated debate in Cologne in a meeting organized by the Works Council Chairman and MEP Winfried Kuckelkorn where Collignon was invited as a speaker.
79 Minutes of Sherpa Meeting in The Hague on 8 September 1994.
80 Meeting in Paris with Collignon on 6 February 1992.
81 Interview, Kenneth Clarke, 24 October 2001.
82 As the Ecu-basket contained both weak and strong currencies, a devaluation of some currencies automatically led to a devaluation of the Ecu against the not-devalued currencies.
83 The Board met under the Chairmanship of Mr Davignon and with the participation of Messrs Agnelli, de Azevedo, Eustace, Faber, Leysen, Mentré, Ortoli, Papalexopoulos, Plachetka, Riisager, de Maigret, Collignon, Johnson (BAT Industries), Heegaard (FLS Industries), Kirschen (FIAT), Lomax (BAT Industries), Maleki (Bosch

and Volkswagen), de Meyer (Philips), Mondello (Confindustria), Pena do Amaral (Sonae), Praët (Société Générale de Belgique), Prugnat (Rhone Poulenc), Isaias Rodriguez (CEOE), Ronner (Philips), de Schaetzen (Agfa Gevaert) and Mrs Sirel (Giscard–Schmidt Committee).

84 Minutes of the twenty second Board meeting on 5 November 1993 in Brussels.

85 See Chapter 5.

86 Minutes of the twentieth Board Meeting on 5 March 1993 in Frankfurt.

87 *Le Monde*, 7 September 1993, p. 28.

88 See Chapter 5 for more details.

89 Written with input from Peter Bofinger, a German Professor specialized on monetary policy.

90 See Annexe 5 for names.

91 At the time, Ruggiero was on the Board of Fiat. Later, he became General Secretary of World Trade Organization (WTO) and Italy's Foreign Minister in 2001. He resigned from the Berlusconi government in 2001 over disagreement on European policy.

92 Broadening the anchor meant re-equilibrating intervention obligations during the transition period to stage three by setting up unlimited credit facilities and not sterilizing these interventions between core countries. It would, therefore, have created a temporary symmetry among member states until full EMU started.

93 Collignon (1994: 148).

94 See Chapter 5.

95 Interview, Declan Costello, 26 July 2001.

96 After the arrival of Romano Prodi's Commission in 1999, all Directorate Generals were renamed. The numbering was replaced by self-explicatory names as one attempt to make EU politics more accessible and understandable by the broad public. DG 2 was then renamed DG Ecfin.

97 Interview, Yves-Thilbaut de Silguy, 6 September 2001.

98 Radaelli (1999), outlines the technocratic nature of EU public policy making which includes notably the politics of expertize and the depoliticization of the public sphere. While the involvement of experts was a necessary condition to develop the Green Book, the depoliticization of preparing EMU was a strategy to more beyond the fierce political debates which questioned the whole project.

99 Interview, Declan Costello, 26 July 2001.

100 Interview, Thierry Vissol, 31 July 2001.

101 See Chapter 3. Written comments on the manuscript by Thierry Vissol, June 2002.

102 Soon thereafter, Barclays' Chief Executive Martin Taylor joined the AMUE Board and Levitt became an active Sherpa for the United Kingdom.

103 The report was published in a special issue of De Pecunia, June 1992.

104 Note to the authors on 25 September 2001.

105 Note to the authors on 25 September 2001.

106 von Dewall, 1995. Dewall was co-secretary of the Maas Group and member of the general management council of ING Group.

107 See note 106.

108 Note to the authors on 25 September 2001.

109 Interviews with various present and former Commission officials in July/August 2001.

110 Interview, Yves-Thilbaut de Silguy, 6 September 2001.

111 The Maastricht Treaty set out three *stages* for the introduction of the single currency. The discussions about the transition scenarios made a further distinction into sub-periods called *phases*. Stage two, phase (a) began in 1994 as a preparatory stage. IIb began with the European Council's decision on a starting date for stage three and setting up the ECB. In IIc the Governing Council of the ESBC defined operational rules and procedures for the ECB monetary policy. Stage three – the actual start of EMU – was also divided into three phases. IIIa involved irrevocably fixed exchange rates and

a single monetary policy, but national notes and coins would still be circulating. In IIIb, national currencies were to be withdrawn from circulation and euro coins and notes were to be put into circulation. IIIc is the final stage – the European currency is the only and single currency. See Collignon (1995).

112 The euro was therefore a monetary unit like the *Guinea*, an old British currency unit representing twenty-one old shillings for which no material support existed. China also had this distinction between functional and material money in the form of *renminbi* and *yuan*.

113 André Low, a Commission official publicly acknowledged that it had clarified the issue of speculations in stage three.

114 For a detailed analysis of the risks see the AMUE report prepared for the European Commission by Stefan Collignon: Exchange Rate Stability in the Transition to a Single Currency: Problems and Tentative Solutions, 30 March 1995.

115 Note to the authors on 25 September 2001.

116 For more details on public opinion see Chapter 5.

117 Minutes of the AMUE Sherpa Meeting on 10 January 1995.

118 Minutes of the AMUE Board Meeting on 21 September 1994.

119 A high-ranking Dutch official even went as far as saying that Germany blackmailed on this and most other issues (conversation with Collignon).

120 At an AMUE Board Meeting in Frankfurt on 20 September 1994, Tietmeyer declared: 'The active promotion of the Ecu as a payment medium and currency of denomination recommended by the European Commission, the European Parliament, the AMUE and other bodies in order to prepare the transition to a single currency in my opinion likewise leads on a problematic course. Such measures could divert attention from the real core issue, the convergence problem, and would go beyond the objective of the EU Treaty to facilitate the use of the Ecu (...). Instead of promoting the basket Ecu, it therefore appears to be more convincing to me to tell our citizens clearly that their national currencies will be abolished some time after entry into EMU and that, instead, they will receive European money which meets all the preconditions necessary for being accepted as a strong, reliable currency, even in the Community countries with the best monetary policy performance until then'. After the meeting Hilmar Kopper, Chairman of Deutsche Bank remarked to Giovanni Agnelli, President of Fiat, that Tietmeyer had lectured them like schoolboys.

121 Others were for example the Federation of European Accountants (FEE) or UEAPME, the European Association for small- and medium-sized enterprises.

122 Interview, Declan Costello, 26 July 2001.

123 Some foreign visitors reported to us at the time that a leading CDU politician in the German Bundestag had emphasized 'All major decisions in the Federal Republic, from rearmament, to the emergency laws in 1968 and tactical nuclear missiles in the 1980s had been taken *against* public opinion'.

5 Campaigning for EMU

1 Interview, Christa Randzio-Plath, 7 July 2001.

2 Some historians have detected latent 'nativism' and even fascism behind the Populists' analysis of their social and economic position. See Pollack (1962: 6), Parsons (1973: 31). Yet, populism is distinct from (neo-)fascism in that the latter turns xenophobia into open aggression and follows an eliminatory logic.

3 Kaufman and Stallings distinguish: 'whereas populism signifies the redistribution of income, socialism denotes redistribution of property and wealth'. In our view, which is consistent with their analysis, populism focuses on horizontal distribution marked by relative prices, socialism on vertical distribution between labour and capital. As a consequence, we can distinguish 'left populism' giving greater weight to improving relative wages and 'right populism' focusing on relative profit margins.

4 Our emphasis is on the intellectual coherence of policy approaches with the daily business practices. We do not wish to fall into the trap of mechanical or naturalistic explanations, whereby policy choices are a direct function of economic interests.
5 'One Nation' British Conservatives also shared the post-war welfare consensus, see Turner (2000: 27). Similarly, Hayward (1994) shows that in France, Giscard d'Estaing's UDF was much closer to this European model than the Gaullist movement. See p. 24.
6 Small operators could not get the rebates that large industrialists could extract from railroads. They were also hampered by high tariffs that favoured big business over small producers and retailers. See Tindall and Shi (2000: 766–85).
7 American populism is often seen as a farmers' revolt. However, Parsons (1973: 28) shows that mid-western farmers were really small capitalist businessmen who became highly indebted by investing in machinery and other items associated with farmer–businessmen operating in an expanding commercial market.
8 The study identified 40 industrial sectors out of 120 that were most affected by the removal of non-tariff barriers, covering about half of the industrial value added in the EU. These sectors were classified in four groups according to their level of intra-Community trade and the level of price distortion that indicated the relative degree of protection.
9 In Greece, this development did not take place in the early 1990s, but seems to have started in 1995.
10 GVA is the sum of wages and capital income.
11 Data for Ireland are not available.
12 Taggart (1996) distinguishes between left populism, which he calls 'New Politics' and 'New Populists' mainly extreme right parties. As New Politics concentrates more on issues related with the break-up of the post-war welfare state consensus in the 1980s, we concentrate on New Populists.
13 We will explain the special case of Italy in the section 'Convergence and dissent in Europe'.
14 The most coherent formulation of this strategy was given by the OECD's Job Report in 1994.
15 See, for example, the paper presented by Franco Modigliani and the reply by Collignon at the AMUE Conference in Kronberg, 1995, published in Collignon (1997).
16 See the section 'German dissensus over EMU'.
17 See Chapter 2.
18 The Maastricht convergence criteria for EMU were defined as follows: (a) the annual government deficit must not exceed 3 per cent of GDP; (b) total outstanding government debt must not exceed 60 per cent of GDP or be on a declining path; (c) rate of inflation within 1.5 per cent of the three best performing EU countries; (d) Average nominal long-term interest rate must be within 2 per cent of the average rate in the three countries with the lowest inflation rates (interest rates shall be measured on the basis of long-term government bonds or comparable securities); (e) exchange rate stability, meaning that for at least two years the country concerned has kept within the 'normal' fluctuation margins of the European ERM.
19 The same was true for the five-point plan on 'core Europe', put forward by the German Christian Democrats Wolfgang Schäuble and Karl Lamers, suggesting that 'variable geometry' might give a better chance to complete the process of European unification. This insistence increased the pressure on Italian and other policy makers to accelerate their efforts to reach the convergence criteria.
20 Conversation with Günter Grosche, 20 June 2001.
21 For a discussion of neo-functionalist integration theory see Chapter 1.
22 The European Parliament was involved in 25 per cent of the EU-legislation in 1997: for 10 per cent it had to approve or reject legislation ('co-decision procedure'). See Crombez (2001: 120).
23 Maastricht-Urteil des Bundesverfassungsgerichts vom 12. Oktober 1993 – 2 BvR 2134/92-2 BvR 2159/92.
24 Interview, Gilbert Lichter, 17 July 2001.

25 Many AMUE members had, in addition, their own public speaking engagements. French and German banks, in particular, embarked on a crusade to explain EMU to their clients.
26 Most of these formulations can be found in Jochimsen (1998). Reimut Jochimsen, a professor who served as Bundesbanker for Nordrhein Westphalen, was a respected Social Democrat.
27 One of the few who were always aware of this historic fact was Chancellor Helmut Kohl. He was convinced that people would only start to accept the euro when they had their notes and coins in their pockets. Interview, Joachim Bitterlich, 17 September 2001.
28 Interview, Norbert Wieczorek, 5 July 2001. Norbert Wieczorek became deputy head of the parliamentary group in 2000.
29 This hypothesis was already advanced by Frieden (1991).
30 German academia was also in the main opposed to EMU. While the Deutsches Institut für Wirtschaftsforschung with chief economist Heiner Flassbeck in Berlin and the Institut in Halle led by Reinhard Pöhl were arguing from the start in favour of EMU, the Institut der Deutschen Wirtschaft in Cologne and the Institut für Weltwirtschaft in Kiel were closer to euro-sceptics.
31 Horst Köhler became Managing Director of the IMF in 2000.
32 See Chapter 4.
33 Minutes of AMUE board meeting on 25 September 1995.
34 *Financial Times*, 31 October 1995.
35 Gerhard Schröder became Chancellor of the Federal Republic of Germany in September 1998.
36 The German press discussed the anti-euro populism, see for example *Die Woche*, 15 December 1995.
37 Nölling was President of the Landeszentralbank in Hamburg until his retirement and as such a member of the Bundesbank Council. Hankel was Pöhl's predecessor as Secretary of State in the Finance Ministry and later became President of the Landesbank of Hessen, which nearly collapsed under his leadership.
38 Elections to the regional Parliaments took place in Baden-Württemberg, Rheinland-Pfalz, and Schleswig-Holstein in March 1996.
39 It never became public and was buried for good after the national convention in Mannheim in November 1996, when Oskar Lafontaine took over as new party leader.
40 The last German emperor Wilhelm II had called them '*vaterlandslose Gesellen*' (companions without fatherland). In 1925, it had been the first political party that called for the creation of the 'United States of Europe' as part of its platform.
41 For Schmidt's initiatives for the European Monetary System see Chapter 2. Willy Brandt acknowledged Schmidt's efforts explicitly in his memoirs, Brandt (1989: 458).
42 Heide Simonis in an interview with *Die Woche* on 11 November 1995, p. 8. Later, however, her position on EMU was less decided.
43 A pile of rubble.
44 Press release by the DGB on 6 December 1995.
45 After the EP elections in 1999, she became chairwomen of the Committee for Economic and Monetary Affairs.
46 Randzio-Plath, interview, 7 July 2001.
47 Giscard d'Estaing, interview, 14 November 2001.
48 MP Charles Josselin in a Parliamentary Debate in the Assemblée Nationale on 20 June 1995. Ironically, Josselin's daughter, Daphne, worked as the AMUE rapporteur on the EMS-Report for the European Parliament.
49 http://www.fes.de/fes-publ/eurohandbuch/index.htm. The book was published by the Friedrich-Ebert-Stiftung, a foundation politically close to the Social Democrats and

received significant attention within the party. Interview, Christa Randzio-Plath, 7 July 2001.

50 In 1998, Wieczorek-Zeul became Minister of Economic Co-operation, Peter Struck Parliamentary Party Leader in the Bundestag, Otto Schily Minister of the Interior, and Oskar Lafontaine Finance Minister.

51 As the AMUE felt an increasing need to work in Germany, it recruited new German colleagues. The authors of the first edition of the SPD handbook were Stefan Collignon and Daniela Schwarzer. The second and third editions were authored by Collignon, Schwarzer, and Susanne Mundschenk, who had joined the AMUE as an economist in 1996. Ulrike Guérot, who had been directing the office of the CDU-member of parliament Karl Lamers before she joined the AMUE in Paris, also contributed to the handbook. Lamers once commented on this German version of *cohabitation*; 'The only divide is between pro- and anti-Europeans'.

52 For example, SPD party's Chairman, Oskar Lafontaine, took up this view. On several occasions and on his request, Oskar Lafontaine (Head of the Social Democratic Party from 1995 to April 1999 and Minister of Finance from September 1998 to April 1999) received input on EMU from the AMUE.

53 For an overview of the German debate and analysis of the competitive situation of Germany see, for example, DIHT (1996). For a German–French comparison see Schwarzer and Uterwedde (2000).

54 Helmut Schmidt in *Die Zeit* 8 November 1996. The IFO-Institute later estimated that the exchange-rate effect was two-thirds of the *Standortproblem*.

55 The French central bank only gained political independence in 1994 in anticipation of the EMU-entry criteria spelled out in the TEU.

56 Aeschimann and Riché (1996) give a detailed account of the domestic struggle in France.

57 Interview, Norbert Wieczorek, 5 July 2001.

58 Conclusion from the various interviews with SPD members quoted above.

59 Interview, Helmut Schmidt, 6 July 2001.

60 The Christian Democrats are formed of the nation wide party CDU and its Bavarian sister party CSU.

61 However, for Stoiber things soon became complicated. Bavarian farmers discovered the potential benefits of the single currency as unilateral devaluations of the Italian lira harmed their export activities after the EMS crisis.

62 In discussions with members of the AMUE.

63 Interestingly, this message was also defended in France by the Governor of the *Banque de France*, Jean Claude Trichet.

64 See Chapter 4 for details.

65 See Annexe 3 to this chapter for the discussion of relative prices, and Edwards (1989) for a textbook treatment of exchange rate economics.

66 This was the view given independently by two German officials in interviews.

67 The difficulties the Bundesbank had in adapting to its new less important role also showed in the struggle for a reform of the Bundesbank System in 2000.

68 Interview with an EMI official.

69 Various forms of forced savings prevented citizens from investing capital freely. It was illegal to create a new bank or open a new shop without prior government approval. Even the ability to establish official residency anywhere was inhibited by law.

70 See also Dyson and Featherstone (1999) on French political traditions.

71 For an interesting analysis of the fruitful interaction between Italy and Europe, see Padoa-Schioppa (2001a).

72 The primary surplus is the balance between government revenue and expenditure before making payments for the debt service.

73 See Collignon and Mundschenk (1999) for a detailed analysis.

74 See Chapter 4.
75 Taking manufacturing and construction as our proxy, relative productivity between tradables and non-tradables improved between 1990 and 1994 by 19.5 per cent, while the relative mark-up and relative wages fell, respectively, 6.6 and 5.8 per cent for non-tradables. The relative GVA deteriorated, therefore, by 12.4 per cent.
76 Like Sergio Pininfarina, President of Confindustria, many AMUE members had some sympathy for Berlusconi due to his personal business background and the interest he demonstrated in business concerns. As soon as Berlusconi's critical attitude toward EMU became obvious, the business leaders turned away from him and criticized him publicly.
77 Valéry Giscard d'Estaing, interview, 14 November 2001.
78 The story of Italy's miraculous stabilization of public finances has been described by Spaventa and Chiorazzo (1999, 2000).
79 Interview, Theo Waigel, 18 September 2001.
80 Interview, Francesco Alfonso, Chief of Staff of the Italian President, 30 August 2001, and Theo Waigel, 18 September 2001.
81 On the insistence of Germany, it had been decided that the assessment of the Maastricht criteria would take place on the basis of definite figures for 1997.
82 Interview, Francesco Alfonso, 30 August 2001.
83 Waigel had said that Italy would not be able to join EMU if it did not meet the convergence criteria, which he thought at this time, was unlikely. His statement was leaked to the public by an administrative mistake and was misinterpreted subsequently. Interview, Theo Waigel, 18 September 2001.
84 Karl Lamers observed that he is nowadays received as a hero in Italy, who has made it possible for her to join EMU. Interview, Karl Lamers, 5 July 2001.
85 Eight days earlier, Michael Röskau, Deputy Diretor General in the German Ministery of Finance had tested the idea at a research conference in Stuttgart-Hohenheim, where he was discussing EMU on a panel with mainly Eurosceptic speakers. While they did not fully grasp the dimension of his suggestions, they welcomed the idea to constrain national fiscal policies in EMU to rule out negative spillovers. Interview, Michael Röskau, 3 September 2001.
86 The book was published in German (Collignon, 1996); a shorter English version was also distributed through the AMUE network.
87 Waigel, therefore, also claims the political responsibility or the pact for himself. When President Chirac declared in Dublin that the Stability Pact 'was an invention of German bureaucratss' he requested an excuse which was finally delivered by the governor of the Banque de France, Claude Trichet.
88 Norbert Wieczorek claims that Waigel had anticipated this would happen at the SPD congress in Mannheim, where Oskar Lafontaine unexpectedly became party chairman. Interview, Norbert Wieczorek, 5 July 2001.
89 Gerhard Schröder became Chancellor of the Federal Republic of Germany in September 1998 and was thus Head of Government when EMU started on 1 January 2001. Waigel (interview 18 September 2001) noted that Schröder even sought a formal decision by his state government in 1996/97 to keep the door open for a no-vote on EMU.
90 See Chapter 4 for details.
91 It should be mentioned that historically France's commitment to balanced budgets has been at least as strong as Germany's to price stability.
92 A high-ranking Bundesbank official indicated this view at a semi-public seminar organized by the Bertelsmann Foundation in 1997.
93 Interview, Elisabeth Guigou, 15 November 2001.
94 A list of the members of the group can be found in Annexe 5. Some board members, for example, Spiro Latsis from Greece, also took a special interest in this academic work although they were not members of the study group.

95 Minutes of the Board of Directors, 5 November 1996, Brussels, AMUE archives.
96 For a further development of these ideas, see Collignon (2002).
97 Friedrich Merz was a convinced European, who had served as a member of the European Parliament before joining the Bundestag where he supported the pro-European policies of Helmut Kohl. In 2000, Merz became opposition leader of the parliamentary group of the CDU/CSU in the German Bundestag.
98 Interview, Karl Lamers, 5 July 2001.
99 One piece of evidence was provided in June 1998, after the participation of Italy in EMU was decided. Stefan Collignon was participating in a conference with Umberto Vattani, then Secretary General of the Italian Foreign Ministry. They were taking a water-taxi in Venice on the *Canale Grande*, when Vattani received a phone call on his mobile phone from Joachim Bitterlich, Chancellor Kohl's European Sherpa. When Vattani asked: 'I am here with Stefan Collignon. Do you know him?', Bitterlich's answer was: 'Of course, objectively he and the AMUE helped us enormously to ensure that Italy could join the monetary union'.
100 Letter of 4 December 1996, AMUE archives.
101 Report on the Annual General Meeting, 19 June 1996, London, p. 4, AMUE archives.
102 The AMUE regularly distributed questionnaires to its members, which was a useful source of information about how large companies and banks, whose euro awareness was generally the strongest, were preparing for and analysing the coming transition. In September 1997, the AMUE united 100 euro managers from large companies and banks for an information exchange in Brussels. In February 1998, the AMUE released its first report on the progress made by companies, which was subsequently updated in regular intervals.
103 Report on the Annual General Meeting, 31 March 1998, Paris, p. 2, AMUE archives.
104 The guide was developed by a small working party directed by AMUE Director for Corporate Relations, Guillaume Lepecq, and included a representative of the European Commission and unpaid consultants from Andersen Consulting, which was an AMUE founding member. In other projects, Bossard Consultants, Ernst & Young and Deloitte & Touche provided their expertise.
105 Financially through their membership fees and practically by providing speakers, case studies from their own experience, and purchasing large quantities of guides for their own network and business partners.
106 Report on the Annual General Meeting, 19 June 1996, London, p. 5, AMUE archives.
107 For example, Bertrand de Maigret regularly participated in the French industrial federation's euro group (MEDEF) and in the national euro committee; Stefan Collignon was a member of the German BDI working group and regularly co-operated with the national Aktionsgemeinschaft Euro; David Croughan, Chief Economist of the Irish Business and Employers' Confederation was a member of Irish working groups but, for example, also chaired an AMUE working group on retail issues that prepared the European Commission Round Table on Consumer issues (15 May 1997). Through Board Member Cesare Romiti, then CEO of FIAT , the AMUE contributed to a group on preparations of the Italian public administrations. Not all can be named here but AMUE members, board members, and sherpas were all very active in national preparation groups and linked these debates to the discussions on a European scale they experienced in the AMUE network and in contact with, for example, the European Commission.
108 The results of the conference were subsequently published by the European Commission as part of the Euro Paper Series, see www.europa.eu.int. The conference took place on 5 November 1998 in Brussels.
109 Report on the Annual General Meeting 1 July 1997, Frankfurt, p. 2, AMUE archives.

110 Auchan had learned from a survey it had conducted among its suppliers in 1997 that there was a severe lack of awareness and preparation for EMU. As Auchan feared business failure especially among its small suppliers, it engaged in intensive communication efforts across eleven countries.

111 According to Morina-Patissier, a pastry supplier of Auchan, this initiative helped Morina to assess the technical and strategic implications of the euro, particularly in terms of new euro pricing strategies and the impact on product specifications.

112 Contribution by Philippe Bodem, Opel dealer in Belgium, who participated in activities offered by General Motors.

113 In each member country, further partners participated in organizing the competition. In Germany, these were Deutsche Bank, the German Mechnical Engineering Industries Federation, and the Bundespresseamt. In the Netherlands, the Dutch Business Federation, the Dutch Accountants Federation, and ABN Amro supported the project.

114 According to a study published by the DIHT, 84 per cent of German companies believed in the beginning of 1998 that EMU was likely to start on 1 January 1999, although only 58 per cent favoured this step. In 1997, 65 per cent believed that EMU would start on time, while in 1995 only 24 per cent did so (DIHT 1998).

115 The Minister for the Economy Nikos Chrisodoulakis opened the event with the president of the Greek Industrial Organization Jason Stratos and the Managing Director of E.F.G. Eurobank Nikos Nanopoulos.

116 Minutes of the Board Meeting, 27 February 1998, Brussels, AMUE archives.

117 The AMUE organized these conferences with the European Commission, local partners, and AMUE members, especially the consultancy firm Deloitte & Touche.

118 As a vast variety of organizations had become involved in euro-related issues, we cannot trace in how far the AMUE paper made a difference. One important claim shared by especially retail organizations from throughout the EU was not taken into account: cutting the dual currency period as short as possible.

Epilogue

1 Present day research resembles Mullah Nashrudhin who one night saw his friend looking for the key in the front of the house. After searching for a while, he asked; 'Are you sure you lost it here?', 'No' his friend replied, 'over there in the dark. But I am looking here where the light is!'

2 Collignon (forthcoming) explores the importance of deliberation and democratization for a European Economic Constitution.

Annexe

1 Options are expected future states of the world.

2 Giddens (1993) has called background knowledge 'mutual knowledge', that is, the taken-for-granted knowledge, which actors assume others possess, if they are 'competent' members of society and that is drawn upon to sustain communication in interaction. It is a diffuse stock of knowledge and mostly remains unarticulated.

3 If $p(E|B)$ is high, we may interpret the evidence E as reflecting knowledge implied in the background. If $p(E|B)$ is low, it adds significantly new evidence to the existing body of knowledge. See also Keuzenkamp (2000: 61).

4 In the logically extreme case where the whole background consists only of common knowledge, individual preferences would be identical. This does not imply that their desires would also be identical. It is rather a preference-theoretical formulation of Kant's categorical imperative.

5 Hence, our interpretation of deliberation is a constitutive norm of society, not a regulative norm as in the theory of deliberative democracy, which postulates the principle of reciprocity.
6 A change in preference intensity may actually lead to changes in preference *ranking*, that is, an overwriting of individual by social preferences, but this is not necessarily so.
7 The formation of the weight matrix may itself be subject to Bayesian probability revisions.
8 A change in the weight matrix **W**.
9 deGroot (1974).
10 This is our condition of mutual respect.
11 We may define society as a group that fulfils the connectedness condition.
12 The matrix multiplication converges toward a matrix with every row the same, though the columns may differ. See Lehrer and Wagner (1981: 24).
13 Lehrer and Wagner (1981: 21). Giddens (1993: 15), is therefore correct in pointing out that new evidence seems to 'disappear' when it gets integrated into the background.
14 Lehrer and Wagner (1981: 22).
15 The convergence is to be seen as a model of information aggregation. Hence, it is a synchronic rather than a dynamic model of rationality. Lehrer and Wagner (1981: 26).
16 Sen (1970: 26), our emphasis.
17 Technically, this implies that dissensus is measured by the sample variance at the *t*th round of deliberation.
18 Arguably this is what Helmut Schmidt and Valéry Giscard d'Estaing did when founding the EMS (see Chapters 2 and 4) or Helmut Kohl when he resisted German hostility against the euro.

Bibliography

Adler, E. and Haas, P. M., 1992. Conclusion: epistemic communities, world order, and the creation of a reflective research program. *International Organization*, 46.1 (Special Issue), pp. 367–90.

Aeschimann, É. and Riché, P., 1996. *La guerre de sept ans*. Paris: Calmann-Lévy.

Agnelli, G. and Cabiati, A., 1918. *European Federation or League of Nations?* Torino: Edizioni della Fondazione Giovanni Agnelli.

Amery, J., 1952. The British commonwealth or Western Europe. *British Commonwealth Affairs*, 7.9.

Arrow, K. J., 1963. *Social Choice and Individual Values*, 2nd edn. London: Chapman & Hall.

Artis, M. and Ormerod, P., 1994. Is there an 'EMS effect' in European Labour Markets?, in: Johnson, C. and Collignon, S., eds, *The Monetary Economics of Europe*. London: Pinter.

Aspinwall, R. and Schneider, G., ed., 2001. *The Rules of Integration: The Institutionalist Approach to European Studies*. Manchester: Manchester University Press.

Association for the Monetary Union of Europe, 1992. *How to Prepare Companies for the European Monetary Union*. Special issue: De Pecunia.

Association for the Monetary Union of Europe, 1994. *Preparing the Transition to the Single Currency*. Paris.

Association for the Monetary Union of Europe, Ernst & Young and The National Institute of Economic and Social Research, eds, 1990. *A Strategy for the Euro*. London: Kogan Page Ltd.

Association for the Monetary Union of Europe and The Royal Institute for International Affairs, 1991. European Monetary Union in a Turbulent World Economy. Paper read at *European Monetary Union in a Turbulent World Economy Conference*, London.

Association for the Monetary Union of Europe, ed., 1998. *The Sustainability Report*. Paris. Reprinted in: *Economia Internazionale*. Supplemento al Vol L11.1. February 1999. Genova, Italy.

Austen-Smith, D., 1997. Interest groups: money, information, and influence, in: Meuller, D., ed., *Perspectives on Public Choice: A Handbook*. Cambridge: Cambridge University Press.

Balanyá, B., Doherty, A., Hoedeman, O., Ma'anit, A. and Wesselius, E., 1999. *Europe Inc., Liaisons dangereuses entre institutions et milieux d'affaires européens*. Translated by Gaboriaud, M., Discepolo, T., ed., Marsaille: Agone.

Balme, R., Chabanet, D. and Wright, V., 2002. *L'action collective en Europe*. Presses de Sciences: Paris.

Banking Federation of the European Union, 1995. *Survey on the Introduction of the Single Currency: A First Contribution on the Practical Aspects*. Bruxelles.

Bartolini, S., 2002. National cleavages and European issues: should we 'politicize' the European Union?. Paper presented at the seminar *Acteurs* Politiques. Commissariat au Plan: 21 March.

Basu, K., 2000. *Prelude to Political Economy. A Study of the Social and Political Foundations of Economics.* Oxford: Oxford University Press.

Biorcio, R., 1997. Forza Italia e il centro-destra. Una sconfitta imprevista, in: Diamanti, I. and Lazar, M., eds, *Stanchi di miracoli, Il sistema politico italiano in cerca di normalità.* Milan: Guerini e associati, pp. 195–206.

Blejer, M. I., Frenkel, J. A., Leidermann, L. and Razin, A. in cooperation with Cheney, D. M., eds, 1997. *Optimum Currency Areas, New Analytical and Policy Developments.* Washington DC: International Monetary Fund.

Bofinger, P., Reischle, J. and Schächter, A., 1996. *Geldpolitik; Ziele, Institutionen, Strategien und Instrumente.* Munich: Verlag Franz Vahlen.

Bogdanor, V., 1996. The European Union, the political class, and the people, in: Hayward, J., ed., *Élitism, Populism, and European Politics.* Oxford: Clarendon Press.

Bordo, M. D. and Eichengreen, B., eds, 1993. *A Retrospective on the Bretton Woods System, Lessons for International Monetary Reform.* Chicago: The University of Chicaco Press.

Bouwen, P., 2001. *Corporate lobbying in the European Union: Towards a Theory of Access.* San Domenico: European University Institute, Department of Political and Social Sciences. Working paper No. 2001/5.

Braaten, J., 1987. Rational consensual procedure: argumentation or weighted averaging. *Synthese*, 71, 347–54.

Brandt, W., 1989. *Erinnererungen.* Germany: Propyläen.

Buholzer, René, P., 1998. *Legislatives Lobbying in der Europäischen Union. Ein Konzept für Interessengruppen.* Bern: Paul Haupt.

Checkel, J. T., 1999. Social construction and integration. *Journal of European Public Policy*, 6.4, (special issue) pp. 545–60.

Checkel, J. T., 2001. Why comply? Social learning and European identity change. *International Organisation*, 55.3, Summer.

Chiorazzo, V. and Spaventa, L., 2000. *Astuzia o virtù? Come accadde che l'Italia fu ammessa all' Unione monetaria.* Roma: Donzelli editore.

Cohen, J., 1995. Interpreting the notion of civil society, in: Walzer, M., ed. *Toward Global Civil Society.* Providence, RI: Berghahn Books.

Collignon, S., 1994a. *Europe's Monetary Future.* London: Pinter.

Collignon, S., 1994b. On widening the EMS to Central and Eastern Europe, in: Johnson, C. and Collignon, S., eds, *The Monetary Economics of Europe.* London: Pinter, pp. 102–9.

Collignon, S., 1995. Exchange rate stability in the transition to a single currency: problems and tentative solutions. A study prepared at the request of the European Commission. Paris: Association for the Monetary Union of Europe.

Collignon, S., 1996. Geldwertstabilität für Europa: die Währungsunion auf dem Prüfstand. Gütersloh: Bertelsmann.

Collignon, S., 1997. Unemployment and monetary policy in the single market: a dialogue with Franco Modigliani, in: Collignon, S., ed. *European Monetary Policy.* London: Pinter, pp. 271–89.

Collignon, S., 1999a. Bloc floating and exchange rate volatility: the causes and consequences of currency blocs, in: Collignon, S., and Pisani-Ferry, J. and Park, Y. C., eds, *Exchange Rate Policies in Emerging Asian Countries.* London: Routledge, pp. 285–322.

Collignon, S., 1999b. The Sustainability of EMU. A fresh look on optimum currency area theory, in: Association for the Monetary Union of Europe, ed., *The Sustainability Report.* Reprinted in: *Economia Internazionale.* Supplemento al Vol L11.1. February 1999. Genova, Italy, pp. 101–60.

Collignon, S., 2001. Economic policy coordination in EMU: institutional and political requirements. Program for the Study of Germany and Europe. Working Paper No. 01.5. Paper presented at The Centre for European Studies, Harvard University.
Collignon, S., 2002. *Monetary Stability in Europe*. London: Routledge.
Collignon, S., forthcoming. *Reflections on Europe's Economic Constitution*. London: Federal Trust.
Collignon, S. and Mundschenk, S., 1999. The sustainability of public debt in Europe, in: Association for the Monetary Union of Europe, ed., *The Sustainability Report*. Reprinted in: *Economia Internazionale*. Supplemento al Vol L11.1. February 1999. Genova, Italy, pp. 101–60.
Committee for the Monetary Union of Europe, 1988. *An Action Programme*. Paris.
Committee for the Study of Economic and Monetary Union, 1989. *Report on Economic and Monetary Union in the European Community*. Luxembourg: European Communities.
Committee for the Monetary Union of Europe, 1992. Europe 1992: *An Evaluation*. Paris.
Connolly, B., 1995. *The Rotten Heart of Europe*. London: Faber and Faber.
Cooper, R., 1994. Yes to European monetary unifaction, but no to the Maastricht Treaty, in: Steinherr, A., ed., *30 Years of European Monetary Integration from the Werner Plan to EMU*. London: Longman
Corden, M. W., 1992. European Monetary Union. The Intellectual Pre-History. Paper read at CEPR Conference, December 11–12, La Coruna.
Crafts, N. and Toniolo, G., eds, 1996. *Economic Growth in Europe since 1945*. Cambridge: Cambridge University Press.
Crombez, C., 2001. The Treaty of Amsterdam and the co-decision procedure, in: Schneider, G. and Aspinwall, M., eds, *The Rules of Integration, Institutionalist Approaches to the Study of Europe*. Manchester: Manchester University Press, pp. 101–22.
Cullis, J. and Jones, Ph., 1998. *Public Finance and Public Choice*. Oxford: Oxford University Press.
Dahrendorf, R., 1996. Introduction: Mediocre élites elected by mediocre peoples, in: Hayward, J., ed. *Élitism, Populism, and European Politics*. Oxford: Clarendon Press.
Deakin, N., 2001. *In Search of Civil Society*. Basingstoke, New York: Palgrave.
deGroot, M. H., 1974. Reaching consensus. *Journal of American Statistical Association*, 69.
de Grauwe, P., 1992. *The Economics of Monetary Union*. Oxford: Oxford University Press.
de la Dehesa, G., 2001. *Comprender la globalización*. Madrid: Alianza Editorial.
de Silguy, Yves-Thibault. 1998. *L'Euro*. Paris: Le livre de poche, références.
de Villepin, X., 1990. Rapport d'information, no. 172 sur l'union Economique et Monétaire. Annex au procès-verbal de la sèance du 13 décembre 1990. Paris: Sénat.
Denizet, J., 1989. *Le Dollar*. Paris: Fayard.
Dewall, F. A. von. 1995. The Transfer to the Ecu: from concept to hard currency. Accessed at www.ecu.be on 25 August 2001.
Dominguez, K. M. and Frankel, J. A., 1993. *Does Foreign Exchange Intervention Work?* Washington, DC: Institute for International Economics.
Dornbusch, R. and Edwards, S., 1991. The macroeconomics of populism, in: Dornbusch, R. and Edwards, S., eds, *The Macroeconomics of Populism in Latin America*. Chicago: The University of Chicago Press, pp. 7–14.
Drazen, A., 2000. *Political Economy in Macroeconomics*. Princeton, NJ: Princeton University Press.
Duchêne, F., 1994. *Jean Monnet. The First Statesman of Europe*. New York: W. W. Norton & Company.
Dyson, K. and Featherstone, K., 1999. *The Road to Maastricht. Negotiating Economic and Monetary Union*. Oxford: Oxford University Press.
Dyson, K., ed., 2002. *European States and the Euro: Europeanization, Variation, and Convergence*. Oxford: Oxford University Press.

Edwards, S., 1989. *Real Exchange Rates, Devaluation, and Adjustment. Exchange Rate Policy in Developing Countries*. Cambridge, MA, London: MIT Press.

Eichengreen, B., 1997. *European Monetary Unification; Theory, Pratice, and Analysis*. Cambridge, MA: The MIT Press.

Eriksen, E. O. and Fossum, J. E., eds, 2000. *Democracy in the European Union. Integration Through Deliberation*. London, New York: Routledge.

European Commission, 1990. *European Economy*. Special edition. The impact of the internal worker by industrial sector.

European Commission. 1994a. *Communication: Practical Problems Involved in Introducing the Ecu as the European Union's Single Currency*. De Pecunia – Revue du CEPIME VI. 1, mai.

European Commission, 1994b. *Measures Concerning the Ecu Published in the Official Journal of the European Community*. De Pecunia – Revue du CEPIME VI. 1, mai, pp. 161–4.

European Commission, 1995. *Green Paper on the Practical Arrangements for the Introduction of the Single Currency*.

Fabbrini, S., 2000. *Tra pressioni e veti, Il cambiamento politico in Italia*. Gius: Laterza and Figli.

Fantacone, S., Ginerbri, S. and Padoan, P. C., 1999. Who's afraid of Italy's adjustment? Sustainability of EMU as seen from an undisciplined country, in: Association for the Monetary Union of Europe, ed., *The Sustainability Report*. Reprinted in: *Economia Internazionale*. Supplemento al Vol L11.1. February 1999. Genova, Italy, pp. 173–94.

Favier, P. and Martin-Roland, M., 1999. *La Décennie Mitterrand*. Les Déchirements. 4, 1992–1995. Paris: Éditions du Seuil.

Favier, P. and Martin-Roland, M., eds, 2000. Elisabeth Guigou. *Une femme au coeur de l'Etat*. Paris: Fayard.

Fitoussi, J.-P., 1995. *Le Débat Interdit; Monnaie, Europe, Pauvreté*. Paris: Arléa.

Fitzpatrick, S., 1994. *The Russian Revolution*. Oxford: Oxford University Press.

Flores d'Arcais, P., 1996. *Il populismo Italiano, da Craxi a Berlusconi*. Rome: Donzelli.

Føllesdal, A., 2000. Subsidiarity and democratic deliberation, in: Eriksen, E. O. and Fossum, J. E., eds, *Democracy in the European Union. Integration through Deliberation?* London, New York: Routledge.

Fossum, J. E., 2000. Constitution-making in the European Union, in: Eriksen, E. O. and Fossum, J. E., eds,. *Democracy in the European Union. Integration through Deliberation?* London, New York: Routledge.

Fourtou, J.-R., 1990. *The Ecu for European Business*. Chapter 3.

Freedman, B., forthcoming. *The Moral Consequences of Economic Growth*. New York: Random House (Knop 7).

Freeman, S., 1990. Reason and agreement in social contract views. *Philosophy and Public Affairs*, 19.2, Spring.

French, J. R. P., Jr., 1956. A formal theory of social power. *Psychological Review*, 63.

Frieden, J. A., 1991. Invested interests. The politics of national economic policies in a world of global finance. *International Organization*, 45, 4, Autumn 1.

Funabashi, Y., 1988. *Managing the Dollar: From the Plaza to the Louvre*. Washington, DC: Institute for International Economics.

Gargarella, R., 2000. Demanding public deliberation: the Council of Ministers – some lessons from the Anglo-American history, in: Eriksen, E. O. and Fossum, J. E., eds, 2000. *Democracy in the European Union. Integration through Deliberation?* London, New York: Routledge.

Gauthier, D., 1986. *Morals by Agreement*. Oxford: Oxford University Press.

George, S., 1999. *An Awkward Partner*, 3rd edn. Oxford: Oxford University Press.

Giddens, A., 1993. *New Rules of Sociological Method. A Positive Critique of Interpretative Sociologies*, 2nd edn. Oxford: Polity Press.

Giscard d'Estaing, V., 1988. *Le pouvoir et la vie*: Compagnie 12.

Giscard d'Estaing, V., 1989. *Jean Monnet*. Lausanne: Foundation Jean Monnet pour l'Europe Centre de recherches européenes.

Giscard d'Estaing, V., 2000. *Les Francais, Réflexions sur le destin d'un peuple*. Paris: Plon / Cie12.

Goldstein, J., 1993. *Ideas, Interests and American Trade Policy*. Ithaca, NY: Cornell University Press.

Goldstein, J. and Keohane, R., 1993. Ideas and foreign policy: an analytical framework, in: Goldstein, J. and Keohane, R. O., eds, *Ideas and Foreign Policy: Beliefs, Institutions and Political Change*. Ithaca, NY: Cornell University Press.

Grant, C., 1994. *Delors, Inside the House that Jacques Built*. London: Nicholas Brealey Publishing.

Greve, M. F. and Jørgensen, K. E., 2002. Treaty reform as constitutional politics – a longitudinal view. *Journal of European Public Policy*, 9.1, February.

Gros, D. and Thygesen, N., 1992. *European Monetary Integration. From the European Monetary System to European Monetary Union*. London: Longman.

Guérot, U., 1997. Deutschland, Frankreich und die Währungsunion – über Diskussionen und Metadiskussionen, in: D.-F. Institut, ed., *Frankreich-Jahrbuch*. Opladen: Westdeutscher Verlag, pp. 223–40.

Haas, E. B., 1958. *The Uniting of Europe: Political, Social and Economical Forces, 1950–1957*. London: Stevens.

Haas, P. M., 1992. Introduction, Epistemic communities and international policy coordination. *International Organization*, 46, 1–35.

Habermas, J., 1982. *Zur Logik der Sozialwissenschaften*. Frankfurt: Suhrkamp Verlag.

Habermas, J., 1984. *The Theory of Communicative Action*, Vol. 1. *Reason and the Rationalization of Society*. London: Heinemann Education.

Habermas, J., 1987. *The Theory of Communicative Action*, Vol. 2. *Lifeworld and System : A Critique of Functionalist Reason*. Translated by McCarthy, T. Boston, MA: Beacon; Cambridge: Polity.

Habermas, J., 1992. Further reflections on the public sphere, in: Calhoun, C., ed., *Habermas and the Public Sphere*. Cambridge, MA, London: MIT Press.

Habermas, J., 1996. Some further clarifications on the concept of communicative rationality, in: Cooke, M., ed. 1998. Habermas, J. *On the Pragmatics of Communication*. Cambridge, MA, London: MIT Press.

Habermas, J., 1999. *Die Einbeziehung des Anderen*. Frankfurt: Suhrkamp.

Hall, P. A., 1986. *Governing the Economy: The Politics of State Intervention in Britain and France*. Cambridge: Polity Press.

Hall, P. A., ed., 1989. *The Political Power of Economic Ideas: Keynesianism across Nations*. Princeton, NJ: Princeton University Press.

Hall, P. A., 2001. The evolution of economic policy, in: by Hall, P.A., Hayward, J. and Machin, H., eds, *Developments in French Politics*. Houndmills, England: Macmillan Press Ltd, pp. 172–90.

Hayek, F. A., 1990. *Denationalisation of Money, The Argument Refined*, 3rd edn. London: The Institute of Economic Affairs.

Hayward, J., 1994. Ideological change: the exhaustion of the revolutionary impetus, in: Hall, P.A., Hayward, J. and Machin, H., eds, *Developments in French Politics*. Houndmills, England: Macmillan Press Ltd, pp. 15–32.

Hayward, J., 1996. Conclusion: has European unification by stealth a future?, in: Hayward, J., ed., *Élitism, Populism, and European Politics*. Oxford: Clarendon Press.

Heath, E., 1994. 'When and how to introduce the European currency, in: Steinherr, A., ed., *Thirty Years of European Monetary Integration from the Werner Plan to EMU*. Sponsored by ECU Banking Association with the support of the European Investment Bank. London, New York: Longman, pp. 257–60.

Heisenberg, D., 1997. German Parliament Members' Opinions about European Monetary Union. Working Paper of the Centre for European Policy Studies, Yale, New Haven.

Heisenberg, D., 1999. *The Mark of the Bundesbank, Germany's Role in European Monetary Cooperation.* Boulder, CO: Lynne Rienner Publishers.

Henning, C. R., 1994. *Currencies and Politics in the United States, Germany, and Japan.* Washington, DC: Institute for International Economics.

Hicks, J., 1974. *The Crisis in Keynesian Economics.* Oxford: Basil Blackwell.

Hirschman, A. O., 1970. *Exit, Voice and Loyalty.* Boston, MA: Harvard University Press.

Holmes, S., 1995. *Passion and Constraints.* Chicago, IL: University of Chicago Press.

Howarth, D. J., 2001. *The French Road To European Monetary Union.* Palgrave: London.

International Monetary Fund, 1993. *International Capital Markets: Exchange Rate Management and International Capital Flows.* Washington, DC: International Monetary Fund.

Issing, O., 1996. *Political Union through Common Money?* IEA occasional paper no. 98. London.

James, H., 1996. *International Monetary Cooperation since Bretton Woods.* Washington, DC: International Monetary Fund.

Jochimsen, R., 1998. *Perspektiven der europäischen Wirtschafts- und Währungsunion*, 2nd edn. Baden-Baden: Nomos Verlagsgesellschaft.

Johnson, C., 1994. The UK and the exchange rate mechanism, in: Johnson, C. and Collignon, S., eds, *The Monetary Economics of Europe.* London: Pinter, pp. 84–102.

Jurgensen, P., 1991. *Ecu, Naissance d'une monnaie.* Jean-Claude Lattès.

Kahneman, D. and Tversky, A., 2000. *Choices, Values and Frames.* Cambridge: Cambridge University Press.

Kapstein, E. B., 1992. Between power and purpose: central bankers and the politics of regulatory convergence. *International Organization*, 46.1 (Special Issue) 265–87.

Katz, R. S. and Ignazi, P., eds, 1996. *Italian Politics, the Years of the Tycoon.* Colorado: Westview Press.

Kaufman, R. R. and Stallings, B., 1991. The political economy of Latin American populism, in: Dornbusch, R. and Edwards, S., eds, *The Macroeconomics of Populism in Latin America.* Chicago, IL: The University of Chicago Press.

Keuzenkamp, H. A., 2000. *Probability, Econometrics and Truth.* Cambridge: Cambridge University Press.

Keynes, J. M., 1936. *The General Theory of Employment Interest and Money.* London: Macmillan.

Kissinger, H., 1957. *A World Restored.* London: Phoenix Press.

Kissinger, H., 1994. *Diplomacy.* New York: Touchstone.

Klau, T. and Quatremer, J., 1999. *Ces Hommes qui ont fait L'Euro.* Paris: Plon.

König and Willeke, 1998, in: Frowen, S. and Pringle, R., eds, *Inside the Bundesbank.* New York: St Martin's Press.

Koslowski, R., 1999. EU citizenship: implications for identity and legitimacy, in: Banchoff, T. and Smith, M. P., eds, *Legitimacy and the European Union. The Contested Polity.* London, New York: Routledge.

Krugman, P., 1987. Economic integration in Europe: some conceptual issues, in: Padoa-Schioppa, T. *et al.*, eds, *Efficiency Stability and Equity: A Strategy for the Evolution of the Economic System of the European Community.* Oxford: Oxford University Press.

Lehrer, K., 1990. *Theory of Knowledge.* Boulder, CO, San Fransico, CA: Westview Press.

Lehrer, K., 1997. *Self-trust. A Study of Reason, Knowledge, and Anatomy.* Oxford: Clarendon Press.

Lehrer, K. and Wagner, C., 1981. *Rational Consensus in Science and Society.* Dordrecht, Holland: D. Reidel Publishing Company.

Leonardi, R. and Westman, D. A., 1989. *Italian Christian Democracy. The Politics of Dominance.* New York: St Martin's Press.

Lindlar, L. and Holtfrerich, L., 1999. Germany's export boom at fifty – an enduring success story?, in: Brady *et al.*, eds, *The Postwar Transformation of Germany. Democracy, Prosperity, and Nationhood.* Ann Arbor, MI: The University of Michigan Press.

Lipset, S. H. and Schneider, W., 1983. *The Confidence Gap: Business, Labour and Government in the Public Mind.* New York: Free Press.

Lomax, R., 1991. Commercial applications, in: Johnson, C., ed., *Ecu, the Currency of Europe.* London: Euromoney Books, pp. 138–4.

Ludlow, P., 1982. *The Making of the European Monetary System: A Case Study of the Politics of the European Community.* London: Butterworths.

McNamara, K. R., 1998. *The Currency of Ideas, Monetary Politics in the European Union.* Ithaca, NY, London: Cornell University Press.

Macpherson, C. B., 1962. *The Political Theory of Possessive Individualism.* Oxford: Oxford University Press.

McSmith, A., 1993. *John Smith, Playing The Long Game.* London: Verso.

Mankiw, N. G. and Romer, D., eds, 1991. *New Keynesian Economics, Imperfect Competition and Sticky Prices,* 1. Cambridge, MA: The MIT Press.

Marcussen, M., 2000. *The Social Construction of Economic and Monetary Union, Ideas and Elites.* Aalborg University Press.

Marsh, D., 1992. *The Bundesbank, The Bank that Rules Europe.* London: Heinemann.

Mastropaolo, A., 1997. La 'nuova' classe politica: innovazione o trasformismo, in: Diamanti, I. and Lazar, M., eds, *Stanchi di miracoli, Il sistema politico italiano in cerca di normalità.* Milan: Guerini e associati, pp. 89–107.

Mazey, S. and Richardson, J., 1993. *Lobbying in the European Community.* Oxford, New York: Oxford University Press.

Mazzucelli, C., 1997. *France and Germany at Maastricht, Politics and Negotiations to Create the European Union.* New York: Garland Publishing Inc.

Meier, G., 1996. *Das Ende der D-Mark: Vision oder Wahn? Reportage einer Discussion.* Tübingen: ed. GIE.

Menger, K., 1982. On the origin of money. *Economic Journal,* 2, June.

Modigliani, F., 1997. The shameful rate of unemployment in the EMS: causes and cures, in: Collignon, S., ed., *European Monetary Policy.* London: Pinter, pp. 242–70.

Monnet, J., 1976. *Mémoires.* Paris: Fayard.

Moravcsik, A., 1997. Taking preferences seriously: a liberal theory of international politics. *International Organization,* 51.4, Autumn, 513–53.

Moravcsik, A., 1998. *The Choice for Europe, Social Purpose and State Power From Messina to Maastricht.* London: UCL Press.

Moravcsik, A., 1999. A new statecraftquest? Supranational entrepreneurs and international cooperation. *International Organization,* 53.2, Spring, 267–306.

Müller, J., 1946. Rede bei der CSU-Landesversammlung am 14.15 December 1946 in Eichstätt, in: Müller, J., ed. *Politik für eine neue Zeit.* Munich: Hanns Seidel Stiftung. (O.J.)

Mundell, R., 1961. A theory of optimum currency areas. *American Economic Review,* 51, 657–65.

Niedermayer, O. and Sinnot, R., 1995. *Public Opinion and Internationalized Governance.* New York: Oxford University Press.

North, D. C., 1981. *Structure and Change in Economic History.* New York, London: W.W. Norton & Co.

Ohr, R., 1993. Europäische Währungsunion – ein richtiger Schritt für Europa, in: Bofinger, P., Collignon, S. and Lipp, E.-M., eds, *Währungsunion oder Währungschaos? Was kommt nach der D-Mark.* Wiesbaden: Gabler, pp. 1–13.

Okun, A. M., 1970. *The Political Economy of Prosperity*. Washington, DC: The Brookings Institution.

Organization for Economic Cooperation and Development, 1994. *The OECD Jobs Study, Evidence and Explanations*. Paris.

Padoa-Schioppa, T., 1992. L'europa verso l'unione monetaria. *Economia*, 231. Turrin, Italy: Einaudi Paperbacks.

Padoa-Schioppa, T., 1998. *Corriere della Sera*.

Padoa-Schioppa, T., 2000a. The European union and the nation state, in: *The Hume Lecture 2000*. Edinburgh: The David Hume Institute.

Padoa-Schioppa, T., 2000b. *The Road to Monetary Union in Europe, The Emperor, The Kings and The Genies*. Oxford: Oxford University Press.

Padoa-Schioppa, T., 2001a. *Europa, forza gentile*. Bologna: Società editrice il Mulino.

Padoa-Schioppa, T., 2001b. Italy: resilient and vulnerable, volume I: the European challenge. *Daedalus, Journal of the American Academy of Arts and Sciences*, 130.2, Spring, 44.

Padoa-Schioppa, T. and Saccomanni, F., 1994. Managing a market-led global financial system, in: Kenen, P. B. ed., *Managing the World Economy, Fifty Years After Bretton Woods*. Washington, DC, pp. 235–68.

Padoa-Schioppa, T. *et al.*, 1987. *Efficiency Stability and Equity: A Strategy for the Evolution of the Economic System of the European Community*. Oxford: Oxford University Press.

Parsons, S. B., 1973. *The Populist Context, Rural Versus Urban Power on a Great Plains Frontier, Contributions in America History*. Westport: Greenwood Press Inc.

Pierson, P., 2000. The limits of design: explaining institutional origins and change. *Governance*, 13.4, 475–99.

Pollack, N., 1962. *The Populist Response to Industrial America*. Boston, MA: Massachusetts: Harvard University Press.'

Putnam, R. D., 1988. Diplomacy and domestic politics: the logic of two-level games, *International Organisation*, 42.3, 427–60.

Quaglia, L., 2001a. The domestic political Economy of European monetary integration in Italy. Paper read at EPIC Conference at Corfu.

Quaglia, L., 2001b. The 'Italian Road' from Maastricht. Paper presented at the PSA Conference, 10–12 April.

Radaelli, C. M., 1999. *Technocracy in the European Union*. London: Longman.

Regini, M. and Regalia, I., 1997. Employers, unions and the state: the resurgence of concertation in Italy, in: Bull, M. and Rhodes, M. E., eds, *Crisis and Transition in Italian Politics*. London: Frank Cass

Richards, O. P., 1990. The next stage in an evolutionary approach to monetary union. *British Invisible Exports Council*. London.

Risse, T., 2000. 'Let's argue!': communicative action in world politics. *International Organization*. 54.1, Cambridge, MA: The IO Foundation and MIT, Winter, pp. 1–39.

Risse-Kappen, T., 1996, in: Risse-Kappen, T., ed., *Bringing Transnational Relations Bank in Non-State Actors, Domestic Structures and International Institution*. Cambridge: Cambridge Studies.

Rittberger, V., Schrade, C. and Schwarzer, D., 1999. Transnational civil society actors and the quest for security, in: Alagappa, M. and Inoguchi, T., eds, *International Security Management and the United Nations*. Tokyo, New York, Paris: United Nations University Press, pp. 109–38.

Roeper, H. and Weimer, W., 1996. *Die D-Mark, Eine deutsche Wirtschaftsgeschichte*. Societätsverlag.

Rosanvallon, P., 1992. *Le Sacre du Citoyen. Histoire du Suffrage Universel en France*. Gallimard: Folio.

Sabatier, P., 1993. Policy change over a decade or more, in: Sabatier, P. Jenkins-Smith, H. C., eds, *Policy Change and Learning. An Advocacy Coalition Approach.* Boulder, CO: Westview, pp. 13–39.

Scharpf, F. W., 1999. Selecting cases and testing hypotheses (Review of Andrew Moravcsik. *The Choice for Europe.* Ithaca, NY, Cornell University Press 1998.) in: Wallace, H., Caporaso, J. A., Scharpf, F. W. and Moravscik, A., eds, Review Section Symposium: the choice for Europe: social purpose and state power from Messina to Maastricht. *Journal of European Public Policy*, 6.1, 164–8.

Schlesinger, P. and Kevin, D., 2000. Can the European Union become a sphere of publics?, in: Eriksen, E. O. and Fossum, J. E., eds, *Democracy in the European Union. Integration through Deliberation?* London, New York: Routledge.

Schmidt, H., 1967. *Beiträge.* Stuttgart: Seewald.

Schmidt, H., 1985. *A Grand Strategy for the West* (*The Henry L. Stimson Lectures Yale University*). New Haven, London: Yale University.

Schmidt, H., 1987. *Menschen und Mächte.* Ein Siedler Buch bei Goldmann.

Schmidt, H., 1990. *Die Deutschen und ihre Nachbarn.* Berlin: Siedler.

Schmidt, H., 1996. *Weggefährten. Erinnerungen und Reflexionen.* Berlin: Siedler.

Schmidt, H., 2000. *Europas Selbstbehauptung.* Stuttgart: Deutsche Verlags-Anstalt.

Schneider, G. and Aspinwall, M., eds, 2001. *The Rules of Integration, Institutionalist Approaches to the Study of Europe.* Manchester: Manchester University Press.

Schwarzer, D. and Uterwedde, H., 2000. French and German competitiveness strategies from the perspective of European integration and a global world economy, in: Maclean, M. and Trouille, J.-M., eds, *France, Germany and Britain. Partners in a Changing World.* Houndsmill, New York: Palgrave, pp. 100–24.

Searle, J., 1979. *Expression and Meaning: Studies in the Theory of Speech Acts.* Cambridge: Cambridge University Press.

Searle, J., 1995. *The Construction of Social Reality.* London: Allen Lane.

Searle, J., 1998. *Mind, Language and Society.* New York: Basic Books.

Sen, A., 1970. *Collective Choice and Social Welfare.* Amsterdam, New York, Oxford: North Holland.

Sen, A., 1987. *On Ethics and Economics.* Oxford: Basil Blackwell.

Spaventa, L. and Chiorazzo, V., 1999. The prodigal son or a confidence trickster? How Italy got into EMU, in: Cobham, D. and Zis, G., eds, *From EMS to EMU, 1979 to 1999 and Beyond.* Houndmills, England: Macmillan Press, pp. 129–60.

Stone S. A. and Sandholtz, W., 1998. *European Integration and Supranational Governance.* New York: Oxford University Press.

Strauss-Kahn, D., 2002. *La flamme et la cendre.* Paris: ed Grasset.

Streeck, W., 1993. The rise and decline of neocorporatism, in: Ulman, L., Eichengreen, B. and Dickens, W. T., eds, *Labour and an Integrated Market.* Washington, DC: The Brookings Institution.

Szász, A., 1999. *The Road to European Monetary Union.* Basingstoke: MacMillan Press Ltd.

Taggart, P. A., 1996. *The New Populism and the New Politics: New Protest Parties in Sweden and in a Comparative Perspective.* Basingstoke: Macmillan Press Ltd.

Talani, L., 2000. Who wins and loses in the city of London from the establishment of European monetary union, in: Crouch, C., ed., *After the Euro.* Oxford: Oxford University Press.

Taylor, C., 1997. A common-currency route to EMU: the hard Ecu revisited. *National Institute Discussion Papers.* London.

Thatcher, M., 1993. *The Downing Street Years.* London: Harper Collins Publishers.

Tietmeyer, H., 1993. Europäische Währungsunion und Notenbank als Gestaltungsaufgabe, in: Bofinger, P., Collignon, S. Lipp E.-M., eds, *Währungsunion oder Währungschaos*. Gabler, pp. 34–5.

Tietmeyer, H., 1999. *The Social Market Economy and Monetary Stability*. London: Economica.

Tindall, G. B. and Shi, D. E., 2000. *America*, 5th edn. New York: W.W. Norton and Company.

Turner, J., 2000. *The Tories and Europe (Political Analyses)*, Reprinted in 2001. Manchester: Manchester University Press.

Ungerer, H., 1990. *The European Monetary System: Developments and Perspectives*. Washington, DC: International Monetary Fund.

Uterwedde, H., 1988. *Die Wirtschaftspolitik der Linken in Frankreich. Programme und Praxis, 1974–1986*. Frankfurt am Main: Campus, 320S.

Verdun, A., 1998. *The Role of the Delors Committee in the Creation of EMU: An Epistemic Community?* EUI Working Papers. Florence: European University Institute.

Verdun, A., 2000. *European Responses to Globalization and Financial Market Integration, Preceptions of Economic and Monetary Union in Britain, France and Germany*. Houndmills, England: Macmillan Press Ltd.

Verplaetse, A., 1997. From currency crisis to single currency, in: Temperton, P., ed., *The Euro*. Chichester, New York, Brisbane, Singapore, Toronto: John Wiley & Sons.

Vissol, T., 1994. L'écu dans la phase de transition vers l'UEM. *Revue du marché commun et de l'union européenne*, 380, juillet–aout, 425–33.

Wallace, H. and Wallace, W., eds, 2000. *Policy-Making in the European Union*. Oxford: Oxford University Press.

Weiler, J. H. H., 1997. The reformation of European constitutionalism. *Journal of Common Market Studies*, 35.1, 97–131.

Wolf, D. and Zangl, B., 1996. The European and economic monetary union: two-level games and the formation of institutions. *European Journal of International Relations*, 2.3.

Yee, A. S., 1996. The causal effects of ideas on policies. *International Organization*, 50.1, Winter.

http://www.fes.de/fes-publ/eurohandbuch/index.htm. SPD Handbook on European Monetary Union.

www.europa.eu.int

Name index

Subject index